EDITING

for Clear Communication

EDITING

for Clear Communication

Second Edition

Thom Lieb
Towson University

Boston   Burr Ridge, IL   Dubuque, IA   Madison, WI   New York   San Francisco   St. Louis
Bangkok   Bogotá   Caracas   Kuala Lumpur   Lisbon   London   Madrid   Mexico City
Milan   Montreal   New Delhi   Santiago   Seoul   Singapore   Sydney   Taipei   Toronto

McGraw-Hill Higher Education

A Division of The **McGraw-Hill** *Companies*

1 2 3 4 5 6 7 8 9 0 QPD/QPD 0 9 8 7 6 5 4 3 2 1

ISBN 0-697-35367-2

Editorial director: *Phillip A. Butcher*
Sponsoring editor: *Valerie Raymond*
Editorial assistant: *Jennifer VanHove*
Marketing manager: *Kelly M. May*
Project manager: *Jill Howell*
Production supervisor: *Carol A. Bielski*
Producer, Media technology: *Jessica Bodie*
Coordinator of freelance design: *Mary Kazak*
Cover design: *Paul McNamara*
Interior design: *Karen Lafond*
Typeface: *10/14 Helvetica*
Compositor: **TECHBOOKS**
Printer: *Quebecor World Dubuque Inc.*

Library of Congress Cataloging-in-Publication Data

Lieb, Thom.
    Editing for clear communication / Thom Lieb.—2nd ed.
      p. cm.
    Includes index.
    ISBN 0-697-35367-2 (alk. paper)
    1. Editing   I. Title
PN162.L49 2002
808'.027—dc21

2001034294

www.mhhe.com

*This book is dedicated to
John Keats and Vin LaBarbera,
two teachers who instilled in me
love for the written word and
respect for its limitless power.*

Brief Contents

Contents

CHAPTER 3
Looking for Holes and Other Problems

CHAPTER 6
Establishing an Ethical Foundation   173

CHAPTER 9
Handling Headlines

Preface

For most of the 20th century, the job of editing remained fairly consistent. Editors chose stories, made sure they made sense, fixed grammar, chose photographs, wrote headlines and cutlines, and created dummies to indicate how pages should be laid out.

In the last two decades of the century, though, the job of editing was markedly transformed thanks to new technologies. In addition to their traditional tasks, editors also found themselves being asked to use desktop publishing software to lay out pages, to prepare photos for publication, to create graphics, to prepare stories for the Web — and a host of other new chores.

During that same time, those who teach editing also struggled with new challenges. In addition to trying to figure out how to incorporate all these new tasks into the editing class, college editing professors also found themselves asking how to handle the topics of law, ethics and coaching, all of which were increasing in importance. At many schools, professors faced yet another task: making the editing class that had been conceived of to prepare students for careers as newspaper editors relevant to the majority of their students who planned to work on magazines or newsletters, or in public relations or advertising.

The first edition of this book was my attempt to address these concerns. This second edition takes the next logical steps and in doing so becomes what I believe to be the first editing text that meets the needs of this new century.

This edition departs in four main ways from the previous one.

First, I have made online editing an integral part of the text. Web publishing was in its infancy when the first edition went to press. Rather than just touching on online editing in a chapter as I did in the first edition, I have decided to include an Editing for the Web section in each chapter.

Second, I have consolidated three chapters' worth of material on design and graphics into one chapter. The reason for this is simple. At most colleges now, design has been moved from the basic editing class into an advanced editing or graphics class. The single chapter in this new edition will introduce key concepts of handling type, photographs and infographics and of designing both print and online pages. Editing classes that spend more time on design can use a supplemental text like Tim Harrower's "Newspaper Designer's Handbook." Classes that focus more heavily on Web design can use my new book, "Building Basic News Sites."

Third, I have expanded a few pages of material dealing with coaching into a full chapter. There has been a tremendous amount of interest in this topic since the first edition was published, and it has taken a central place in many editing classes.

Fourth, some exercises have been removed from the book and will be available as Microsoft Word document files on the companion Web site (*www.mhhe.com/lieb*). Doing this allowed me to hold down the size and cost of this volume while at the same time providing exercises that students can do electronically, as well as with pencil and paper.

Beyond those changes, the new edition will retain the focus and features that have made it popular with many students and teachers:

- It takes a broad view of editing, not limiting the focus to newspapers and magazines.

- It provides up-to-date examples to illustrate major principles.

- It includes exercises customized for each chapter (answer keys will be available for instructors).

- It covers not just the macro aspects of editing (libel, headline writing, etc.) but the micro ones as well (grammar, verbosity, etc.).

- It includes pieces written by a wide range of media workers who relate the topics of the chapters to their experience.

This edition is as current as possible as it goes to press. But because of the great rate of change in some areas of editing — particularly online — I plan to include a yearly update with all copies sold in fall 2002 and thereafter. Each yearly update will include:

- New information relevant to topics covered in the text;

- Summaries of stories of great importance to editors, with links to Web sites that offer full accounts; and

- Additional exercises in Word format.

The feedback of countless students, faculty and reviewers has greatly contributed to the success of the first edition of this text. I look forward to your feedback on this new edition. Please feel free to e-mail me at *mail@thomlieb.com.*

Thom Lieb
August 2001

Acknowledgments ●——————————

There's an old saying that nothing good ever was written by a committee, but everyone who has undertaken a major writing project knows that's not true. My experience with this book is testimony to the importance of gathering a good committee. I have talked with innumerable people, asked dozens of others for their comments on the manuscript (including many of my editing students who used this book while it was under development) and been fortunate enough to have several fine professionals write the Editor's Corner pieces for this book.

I am grateful to everyone who has helped me; you'll see many of their names throughout the book. But there are a few people whom I did not have the chance to acknowledge in the book, and a few others who deserve another round of applause.

I have to start with Carl Sessions Stepp of the University of Maryland at College Park, one of the best-known editors and editing instructors in the country. His early and ongoing encouragement helped to inspire me to take this project from the "What if ... " stage to the "Here it is" stage.

Two working editors have provided me with a wide range of support from the moment I formulated the idea to write this book through completion of the second edition. Vince Rinehart, national copy desk chief of The Washington Post, has answered countless queries, helped me track down information and examples, and offered ongoing support in a multitude of ways. Chris Zang, sports copy editor for The Baltimore Sun, has also put up with my repeated requests for help over the last seven years and has written a great Editor's Corner.

One other wonderful source of support for the current edition was Mimi Burkhardt, training editor for the two-year reporter program at The Providence Journal. Mimi provided loads of insight, examples and suggestions for Chapter 8. I simply could not have written it without her help.

Several editors also have gone beyond the call of duty. While some have moved on since contributing to the first edition, I identify them here by their places of employment at the time they helped me. Tony Barbieri of The Baltimore Sun, Mary E. Crowley of Phillips Business Information Inc., Meg Guroff of Baltimore Magazine, Rhonda Holifield of the St. Petersburg (Fla.) Times, Rick Wakely of the Portland (Maine) Press Herald and George Welty of the Carroll County (Md.) Times patiently fielded my requests for in-house critiques, written and graphic examples, and short-notice reviews of the manuscript. Ed Sargent of The Daily Oklahoman, David Guy of the Ottawa Citizen and Kristine Pioch of the Kalamazoo (Mich.) Gazette also provided me with in-house materials and contacts. Maria Stuart, editor of The Livingston County Press in Howell, Mich., kindly double-checked the answer keys in the instructor's manual for the first edition and contributed an Editor's Corner to this edition.

A special thanks has to go to Randy Stano, who, while working as the design director of The Miami Herald, provided lots of the stunning visual examples used in Chapter 10, as well as contacts for other designers. Among his references,

D.J. Stout, art director of Texas Monthly, and Galie Jean-Louis, design director of the Anchorage Daily News, proved to be particularly helpful by providing examples of cutting-edge design.

Two colleagues at Towson University were generous with their time in helping me complete this second edition. Reference librarian Claire Holmes offered many suggestions for updates and additions to the reference sources in Chapter 4. Professor William Horne helped me find updates on several legal issues and questions in Chapter 5.

I also would be remiss not to thank Thomas Cafferty of the law firm of McGimpsey & Cafferty for his critique of Chapter 5.

At McGraw-Hill, my editor Valerie Raymond has proven to be an attentive, flexible and kind person to work with. Editorial assistant Jennifer Van Hove and project manager Jill Howell also have proven themselves to be great partners in this venture. For the first edition, my developmental editor at Brown & Benchmark, Kassi Radomski, was as courteous and supportive an editor as I've ever had the pleasure of working with.

I owe a debt of gratitude to the reviewers who critiqued the manuscript for the second edition: James L. Aucoin, University of South Alabama; Robert Bohle, University of North Florida; Kathryn B. Campbell, Southern Oregon University; Ross R. Collins, North Dakota State University; Judi Cook, Salem State College; Joe D. Hedges, Murray State University; Elizabeth Blanks Hindman, North Dakota State University; Rachele Kanigel, San Francisco State University; Kay Magowan, University of Wisconsin, Milwaukee; Donica Mensing, University of Nevada; Robert Orndorf, University of Kentucky; and Mary Perpich, South Dakota State University.

Also helpful were the reviewers who critiqued the first edition manuscript for Brown & Benchmark: David Sennett, Indiana State University; Gail Chadwick, Jackson State University; Clark Edwards, Duquesne University; DeAnn Evans, University of Utah; John Gibson, University of Maryland; Paul LaRocque, Texas Christian University; David Morrissey, Colorado State University; David Nelson, Southwest Texas State University; and Carl Sessions Stepp, University of Maryland. Their comments were invaluable and helped strengthen this book in more ways than I can count.

Graphic designer Bert Smith of the University of Baltimore deserves a tip of the hat for helping me refine the initial design of this book and for critiquing parts of Chapter 10.

Finally, I have to thank three longtime friends who helped me make my dream of writing this book a reality: Michelle Simpson, Anne Martens and Steve Konick. Without their feedback, support and encouragement, there never would have been a first edition of this book, let alone this second one.

CHAPTER 1

Editing in the Age of Information

Just 20 years ago, most people's daily media diet was limited to a single newspaper, three television networks and a few radio stations. Today, most of us have access to an incredible bounty of choices, thanks in large part to cable and satellite television and the World Wide Web. With the proliferation of cell phones, palm computers and other mobile devices, we can stay plugged in to this flood of information virtually any place, any time.

Despite the increased availability of information, however, we don't have any more time today than our counterparts did in the past. That means most people are looking for the fastest route to the information they need.

For all the buzzwords of this Information Age — broadband, interactivity, community — one important concept is rarely discussed: editing. As Washington Post columnist William Raspberry has written:

> We now have access to information that was beyond our ability to even *desire* — overseas stock market reports, foreign news, speeches, technical reports, even books. In no time at all, it will be possible to get same-day — even same-*hour* — information on military adventures, political crises, ethnic confrontations and natural disasters in countries whose names we hardly know. ... And what we will need then more than ever is someone to play the editor's function: to sort it out, tell us what truly matters, what the trends seem to be.[1]

Editors are also vital in making sure that information is accurate. Consider some recent cases of poorly edited information:

- During summer 2000, the New York Times published a Page One article with the lead: "The North Pole is melting." The article reported that for the first time, "The thick ice that has for ages covered the Arctic Ocean has turned to water." Ten days later, the Times reported that the historic event wasn't quite so historic: It happens every summer.

- Glamour magazine offered five hints for reducing the likelihood of getting yeast infections while pregnant. One hint was to "take 500-mg boric acid tablets (also sold in health food stores) three times a day with meals." If readers had taken that advice, they could have died. The mistake was realized shortly after the magazine hit the stands; many stores immediately pulled it off the shelves.

- A Detroit News article about author Toni Morrison winning the Nobel Prize for Literature was accompanied by a photograph supposedly showing the black writer, then in her 60s. By mistake, the photograph in the first 20,000 copies off the presses pictured a slightly different woman: Madonna.[2]

- An ad for a set of six miniature suits of armor from the Franklin Mint included some historical information on the armor — but as a newspaper column pointed out,[3] much of the "history" was incorrect. For example, the armor from the era of Spartacus, who died in 71 B.C., was dated A.D. 110, nearly two centuries later. The ad copy also noted the Black Prince's triumph during the Tudor period in England — which did not begin until 81 years after his death. It also referred to "The fight to choose a Shogun in old Japan" — but shogunates were inherited, not won in battle.

- A mix-up by The Associated Press — compounded by overeager editors at Reuters — resulted in release of an obituary for entertainer Bob Hope in 1998. Hope, who learned of the obit while eating breakfast, didn't let the report keep him from heading out for a day of golf.

- A "commencement speech" advising graduates to wear sun screen and attributed to Kurt Vonnegut was published on Internet news sites — but turned out to be neither a commencement speech nor the work of the well-known author.

- On election day 1998, ABC news posted complete state-by-state election "returns" on its Web site — before the polls had even opened.[4]

- A special issue of Newsweek focusing on "Your Child" recommended that infants as young as 5 months old be allowed to feed themselves zwieback and carrot chunks — an action that could cause the children to choke. After the mistake was pointed out, Newsweek recalled several hundred thousand copies from newsstands, hospitals and doctors' offices and reprinted and redistributed the issue.[5]

- A huge ad plastered on the sides of Washington, D.C., buses to encourage children to stay in school read "DC Public Schools Wants You!!! Go to Class — It's a Blast!!!"

Obviously, none of this information was very useful — and in two cases could have proven deadly.

Poor editing can alienate an audience in other ways, too, as in this excerpt from a letter sent to a longtime supporter of a major Shakespeare festival:

> Your previous year's contribution of $75.00 was not generous and meaningful. This year we ask that you consider not only renewing your membership but raising it to the next level.

Hundreds of other contributors got similar letters. One unintended word ("not") left some contributors so upset that the letter became the subject of local television news coverage — the wrong kind of publicity for an arts organization trying to create a good public image.

In the worst cases, poor editing allows libelous, unsubstantiated statements to be printed, needlessly destroying a person or company's reputation and costing the source millions of dollars in a libel suit.

To some extent, it's the job of everyone involved in the business of communication to make sure the audience receives accurate information. If you're planning on a career in journalism, new media, advertising or public relations, editing will be part of your job. The ability to communicate accurately and clearly is necessary for every type of media job. Whether you're writing memos to co-workers or letters to the public, reporting information or trying to sell a product, you must get the details right and make sure readers can understand the message. This book is designed to give you the skills and knowledge necessary to meet that challenge.

If you're planning on a career in journalism, new media, advertising or public relations, editing will be part of your job.

Working as an Editor

For some people, the job of sifting, evaluating and verifying information is exciting enough for them to choose a career as an editor. I find this every time I teach my editing course. On the first day, I'll ask my students if any of them are planning to become an editor. They all look at me as though I must have forgotten to take my medication; rarely does anyone raise a hand. Toward the end of the course, though, a surprising thing happens: First one student, then another will pull me aside, well out of earshot of the rest of the class, and admit to considering a job in editing.

As someone who has worked as an editor and taught editing for more than two decades, I don't find that surprising. Actually, there are plenty of other reasons a sane person would consider a career in editing:

- Working as an editor puts you in the middle of things. As an editor, you find out what's happening in the world before virtually anyone else. Being on top of breaking news and choosing how to present it to your audience is an exciting pursuit.

- Editing jobs also offer you the chance to make a difference. Ultimately, editing is all about selection. A job as an editor offers you the chance to showcase information that you believe your audience needs to know, news that may otherwise never be called to their attention.

- Working as an editor is one of the best ways to improve as a writer. When you constantly confront errors of all kinds and need to figure out ways to correct them, you can't help but become a more careful and better writer yourself.

- Few other communication jobs pay as well. Remember the law of supply and demand? Well, there's an ever-growing demand for editors, and few people have the right combination of skills and desire to fill them. As a result, while beginning workers in most media occupations start at salaries in the mid-$20,000 range, a beginning editor can make double that or even more. And editing positions provide the pathway to even higher paying and more prestigious positions at most print and online publications.

The Challenges of Editing

Not everyone is cut out to be an editor, however. It's a demanding occupation that is overwhelming for many people. For starters, it requires you to learn a new way of reading. Most of us have been conditioned to skip over typos, missing letters and other problems when we read. In addition, many people don't critically evaluate everything they read. But working as an editor requires careful attention to every word you read, as well as critical evaluation of the information. A good editor is always on the lookout for holes and contradictions.

Editors also are expected to be experts on a wide range of issues. In addition to reading widely and keeping up on current events, good editors see movies, visit museums, attend the theater and travel.

In addition, editors need to be authorities on English style, grammar and usage. Editors must also be strong writers who can cut an article in half without damaging it; rewrite confusing passages; add punch to dull passages; and whittle complex stories into the few words that will fit in a headline.

Editors also must be fair-minded, able to judge the importance of material regardless of their own prejudices. They must be able to spot ethical and legal problems and take whatever action is necessary to correct them.

More and more, editors also are expected to be fluent in graphic communication so that they can package information for easy reader access. Therefore, editors also need to know how to choose and crop photos, design pages for print and the Web, and select or create information graphics.

Good editors must be self-starters who nimbly move from one task to the next with no prodding. Finally, editors must be willing to make decisions and accept the consequences.

That's a long shopping list. But if you feel you've got all the items on it, you'd do well to consider a job as an editor.

Developing Your Editing Skills

This book is designed to help you master all the editing skills needed to produce clear communication. It approaches editing as a process and takes you through that process just as a working editor goes through it.

The process begins with learning about your readers. You use that knowledge to assign, select and size copy. Copy is then checked for major omissions as well as factual accuracy. You look for legal and ethical problems, as well as issues of sensitivity and taste. Once copy passes all these checkpoints, it can be edited for style, spelling, grammar and punctuation.

The next part of the process is presenting the copy. This phase includes writing headlines, choosing and preparing graphics and photos, and designing pages. Throughout the process, the good editor also strives to bring out the best in every writer. Only when all these steps are completed is the copy ready to be delivered to the reader.

In discussing the process of editing, this book uses a variety of media sources. Examples and exercises throughout the book are drawn from the Internet, magazines, newspapers, newsletters, news releases and advertisements.

Aspiring editors should join the American Copy Editors Society. The organization, established in 1997, has more than 1,000 members from across the country. ACES offers free Web-based courses, discounts on professional seminars, a discussion list, job postings, a list of copy-editing internships and many other resources. The organization's annual conference includes sessions specifically oriented toward students — and plenty of opportunities for job seekers to network. For more information or to join ACES, visit the Web site: *www.copydesk.org.*

By the time you finish the book and complete the practice exercises, you will be on your way to mastering a multitude of skills that will serve you well in any print media career. And you might just wander up to your editing instructor and whisper, "I've been thinking about getting a job as an editor."

Notes

1. William Raspberry, "An Earful for Editors," The Washington Post, 14 April 2000, sec. A, p. 25.

2. "Names and Faces," The Washington Post, 9 October 1993, sec. D, p. 3.

3. Lois Romano, "The Reliable Source," The Washington Post, 4 March 1993, sec. C, p. 3.

4. Adam Clayton Powell III, "In Election-Eve Mistake, ABC News Posts Complete 'Election Returns' on the Web," Freedom Forum Online, 3 November 1998, *www.freedomforum.org/technology/1998/11/3abc.asp.*

5. Liza Featherstone, "Chucking the Checkers," Columbia Journalism Review, July/August 1997, pp. 12–13.

Job Basics

If ever a medium has been an editor's medium, the Web is. Online columnist Ethan Casey explains:

> While electronic media are not constrained by limits on physical space, both Web and e-mail publishing face a constraint just as demanding, if not more so: the limits of readers' patience and attention spans. This makes the Web an editor's medium, on which an editor puts his or her mark by the exercise of sound judgment and good taste.[1]

Online news authority Eric Meyer adds, "The majority of online jobs are in editing or in areas where the skill and mind sets needed are far more similar to those possessed by a typical print copy editor than those possessed by a typical print reporter."

Tom Cekay of the online edition of the Chicago Tribune (*www.chicago.tribune.com*) concurs, and he adds that good editing is good editing no matter the medium: "The traditional role of the editor stays the same. Do readers want to see this? Is it intelligently done? Is it sophisticated reporting?"[2]

But, Cekay adds, online work places additional demands on the editor. Gil Asakawa, who moved from newspapers to Digital City's online guide for Denver (*www.digitalcity.com/denver*), agrees: "My brain is very much into multitasking mode. I need to find some additional RAM chips for my head."[3]

To be a good online editor, you'll need to:

- **Be computer literate:** Know your way around a computer's operating system, folders, etc. (This applies to all editors, but is particularly important for those working with the Web.)

- **Be Web literate:** Understand how to use different search engines to find information on the Web, then be able to evaluate that information.

- **Know New Media theory:** Be familiar with how people use the Web as well as with nonlinear storytelling and interactivity.

- **Be able to work under constant deadline pressure:** Be comfortable handling the nonstop updates and constant deadlines that come with Web work.

- **Be able to work in teams and communicate clearly:** Know how to work well with others and communicate clearly and effectively. The Web environment is much more team-oriented than print media.

- **Know basic production skills:** At a minimum, you should know basic HTML — the actual code, not just how to use a WYSIWYG program like Front Page — and PhotoShop. Familiarity with digital audio and video production, databases and JavaScript wins you bonus points.

Jim Romenesko keeps readers abreast of media news.

- **Be flexible:** Be willing to continue learning. New technologies and new methods of presenting information appear constantly, and the good editor is ready to adapt at a moment's notice. As online news columnist Steve Outing notes, "It's clear that news organizations of the new millennium will be publishing to multiple media: print-delivered, home-printed, the Web, e-mail, PDAs, mobile phones, e-readers (or e-book readers), pagers, Internet radio, and broadcast radio and TV. ... Editors must learn how to craft content packages appropriate to a print edition as well as a PDA edition."[4]

Because of the multimedia nature of their jobs, many editors hired for online publications are called **producers.** The nature of tasks handled by producers varies greatly from one operation to another, depending on staff size, features and other factors. In addition to basic editing and headline writing, producers can be called upon to **repurpose** content from print editions, that is, take material that was printed and repackage it with supplemental material, hypertext links and so on to make it more useful for the Web reader. For example, a travel magazine may run an article about visiting a certain city. An online version of the article could include links to restaurants, shopping, museums, nightlife and galleries, a list of recommended accommodations, and more.

In fact, the new forms of journalism that are developing on the Web depend heavily on editors. For instance, About.com offers a series of pages organized by topics, each hosted by a guide — effectively an editor. Web logs — also know as **blogs** — offer another example of the role of editors in the emerging medium. Blogs are essentially instant messages posted to the Web in which bloggers "comment and link to interesting articles and content that they find on the Web relevant to their chosen topic area, and offer analysis and opinion."[5]

Content Exchange offers daily updates on industry news.

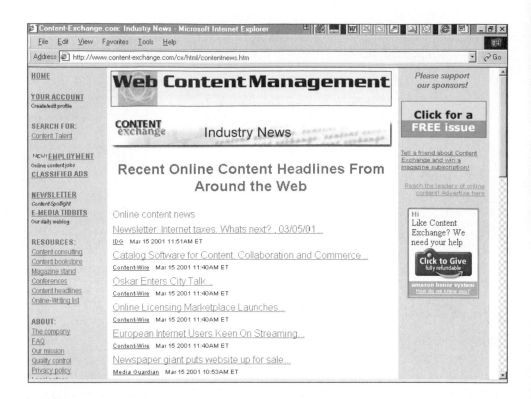

The variety of blogs boggles the imagination, with several focusing specifically on journalism:

- Jim Romenesko's MediaNews (*www.poynter.org/medianews*)

- Online Journalism Review's Spike Report (*ojr.usc.edu/content/spike.cfm*)

- Steve Outing's E-Media Tidbits (*www.content-exchange.com/weblog/ weblog.htm*)

As you can see, there's much more to editing for the Web than editing for print. Fortunately, you can find plenty of help in keeping up with the challenges — on the Web, of course. Among the best resources are Web sites of the Online News Association (*www.onlinenewsassociation.org*), the Poynter Institute for Media Studies (*www.poynter.org*), the Newspaper Association of America's Digital Edge (*www.digitaledge.org*), Ethan Casey's "The Online Editor" column (*www.content-exchange.com/spotlight*) and the Content Exchange's daily roundup of news about online news (*www.content-exchange.com/cx/html/contentnews.html*).

Most online editors find their work extremely rewarding. As Gil Asakawa told Editor & Publisher Interactive, "I love this industry."[6] Chances are good that you will, too.

Notes

1. Ethan Casey, "It's an Editor's Medium, Stupid," Content Exchange, 26 February 2001, *www.content-exchange.com/cx/html/newsletter/2-20/oe2-20.htm*.

2. Christopher Harper, "Doing It All," American Journalism Review, December 1996, pp. 24–29.

3. Steve Outing, "A Newspaper Editor's Transition to New Media," Editor & Publisher Interactive, 18 October 1996, *www.mediainfo.com/ephome/news/newshtm/stop/st101896.htm.*

4. Steve Outing, "Online News Advice for 2001," Editor & Publisher Interactive, 27 December 2000, *www.mediainfo.com/ephome/news/newshtm/stop/st122700.htm.*

5. Steve Outing, "Corante's Mission: 'Professionalize' Web Logs," Content Exchange, 29 January 2001, *www.content-exchange.com/cx/html/newsletter/2-18/wb2-18.htm.*

6. Outing, "A Newspaper Editor's Transition."

Editor's Corner

An Editor Who Writes, a Writer Who Edits

Beth P. Gavaghan, freelance writer and editor

When Thom Lieb, the author of this book, asked me to write a sidebar on the importance of editing, I was both flattered and apprehensive. The last time I submitted anything to Thom in writing (as a college student in one of his writing classes), it came back with a lot of red ink.

However, as much as I cringed at that red ink in college, I realize that I, too, have used it a lot in my career. I have employed editing skills in a wide variety of positions from reporter to public relations practitioner to magazine editor to freelance writer and editor.

As a freelance writer and editor, I want to submit my work in the best possible condition. That means editing and re-editing the copy until I am satisfied that it is as nearly perfect as can be. Companies hire freelancers to save time and better use in-house resources. Having to spend countless hours cleaning up a freelancer's work defeats the purpose.

As the editor of a monthly technical magazine, I edited technical articles written by metallurgical engineers — not professional writers — who often needed help organizing and presenting their work. Before focusing on the nitty gritty of punctuation, I first had to look at the bigger picture: Does this article make sense? Does it say what the author intended it to say? Are there any holes that need to be filled? Does the copy need to be updated?

Besides editing technical papers, I also wrote semitechnical and nontechnical articles for the magazine. Unlike most writers who must write at the sixth-grade level, I had to write for readers who have master's degrees or doctorates. Editing for clear communication was a must. If I didn't catch an error, I knew they would.

I also edited copy from contributors and wrote headlines, cutlines and cover blurbs, as well as laid out the magazine. And, since I was manager of communications, I also oversaw my organization's public relations, marketing, Internet and graphics functions. Having an editor's eye helped in each one of these areas.

Each has the goals of capturing the readers' attention and disseminating information in a concise, effective and attractive manner. From the public relations side, the communication goal also is to motivate people to act (attend a conference, buy a technical book, etc.).

In fact, just about every activity in the communications field shares most of these goals. As a newspaper reporter, I had to edit myself before my copy went to the copy editor. I had to make sure the who, what, when, where and why were present and high in each article. I had to check the spelling of names of companies, people and places. I had to make sure that there were transitions between paragraphs and that tenses matched. And, most of all, I had to make sure the articles were balanced.

I used the same skills when I worked in public relations. I had to have the correct particulars about events and honors. I had to make sense. And I couldn't misspell my company's or clients' names.

Through several years of using editing skills, I've picked up a few tricks that help. One that I find useful is to read copy backward, paragraph by paragraph or sentence by sentence. No, there won't be a message from Satan, but you will be forced to focus on every word. Try it; it works.

Above all else, I've learned that most of the errors in communicating can be solved simply by paying attention. So my advice to all future editors is this: Be careful — and watch out for the red ink.

GRAMMAR SCHOOL

Stylebooks and Dictionaries

The remaining chapters of this book look at editing on the *macro* level. At that level, editors question facts, check organization, look for bias and legal problems, and so on.

Once macro editing is finished, *micro* editing begins. This process involves looking for misspelled words, checking grammar, eliminating redundancies, and doing a great deal of other housecleaning. In order to edit successfully at the micro level, editors must master spelling, grammar and word usage. These areas are the topics of the Grammar School sections that follow each chapter. In this first installment, we begin by taking a look at the editor's bibles: the stylebook and dictionary.

The ad has to go to publication in a half hour, your desk is its last stop and you can't for the life of you remember if "toward" or "towards" is grammatically correct. The only thing you DO know is that if you choose the wrong one, there's a college professor out there who will clip your work from a newspaper or a magazine and hold it up in his class as an example of poor editing.

I know because I took that editing class in college. I was planning on going into advertising, not journalism, so I wasn't entirely sure of its relevance to my future career. But it was required. So, dutifully, I trudged to class at 8 a.m. three days a week for 50 minutes of copyediting, copyediting and, you guessed it, more copyediting.

I left that class with the ability to spot a misplaced comma or a wayward capital letter from miles away. I also left with dog-eared and battered copies of the AP Stylebook and Webster's Dictionary.

The bookstore wouldn't buy them back. And for that, I will be forever grateful. On the way out the door to my first day of work as an advertising copywriter, I grabbed them (mostly so my desk wouldn't be completely empty).

They have proven to be priceless possessions, the final, unbending word for any spelling, punctuation, style or abbreviation question co-workers can throw my way. (You don't think you actually retain all that stuff after the final exam, do you?) Most importantly though, I would hope that, for now, they have kept my work from ending up as the example in someone's college editing class.

Oh, and in case you were wondering, the answer is "toward." (It's on Page 198 in my stylebook.)

Erin Hardesty is a copywriter for Azzam Jordan Advertising.

The AP Stylebook and a Good Dictionary: Don't Leave College Without Them

Erin Hardesty

11

Stylebooks

Many problems in grammar and usage are covered in stylebooks that editors and other media workers use. So it seems only logical to start by taking a look at stylebooks and how to use them.

Stylebooks fall into two general types:

1. Guides to scholarly and technical writing: This category includes the Chicago Manual of Style, the MLA Handbook, the Publication Manual of the American Psychological Association and others. They are used most often for preparing research papers, journal articles and books, and they therefore include extensive rules for using references and bibliographies. But they also are used in the media. For example, a survey of 20 trade and consumer magazines found that five of them use the Chicago Manual of Style.[1]

2. Guides for media work: This category includes The Associated Press Stylebook and Briefing on Media Law, The Washington Post Deskbook on Style, and The New York Times Manual of Style and Usage. These titles usually are used in newspaper, newsletter, magazine and public relations work. The Associated Press Stylebook is the most widely used stylebook in media work. Many publications also use an organizational style sheet, or a supplemental guide to local matters that are not covered in general stylebooks.

Guides to scholarly and technical writing typically are organized by general topics: capitalization, citations, etc. Guides for media work are set up alphabetically, like dictionaries, but the substance of the entries varies greatly, as the following examples from The Associated Press Stylebook show:

- Some entries include only a word or two, to indicate the correct or preferred spelling, or the preferred capitalization:

  insofar as

  IOU, IOUs

- Other entries add information on the use of the word or words:

  infant applicable to children through 12 months old.

- Other entries provide guidance for the use of abbreviations and acronyms:

  Internal Revenue Service IRS is acceptable on second reference. [That means after it appears spelled out once in a story.] Capitalize also Internal Revenue, but lowercase the revenue service.

- Other entries give background information:

  Index of Leading Economic Indicators A composite of 10 economic measurements that was developed to help forecast likely shifts in the U.S. economy as a whole. It is compiled by the Conference Board, a private business-sponsored research group.

As a media worker, you probably won't be expected to memorize a stylebook, but you do need to know rules that you'll use every day, and you need to know how to find the information you need in the least amount of time. Four guidelines can help you use your stylebook efficiently:

1. **Start by learning the basics:** Any stylebook should provide guidance in four essential areas that you'll use almost daily: abbreviations, capitalization, numbers and punctuation. Learn these rules and you'll save many hours on deadline looking them up over and over again.

2. **Don't assume you know the correct style:** Just because you've seen a word handled in a certain way doesn't mean your stylebook says that that's the way to do it. If you don't know what your stylebook says, you need to look it up.

3. **Always start your stylebook search by being as specific as possible:** Chances are that you will find information related to a topic in several places throughout the stylebook. But usually the fastest way to get the answer you need is by looking up the precise word or phrase. For example, if you are not sure whether to capitalize the word "senator," look for an entry under either "capitalization" or "senator." If you can't find your answer there, broaden your search, little by little; try congress, legislative bodies, politics, titles, etc., until you find it.

4. **Read the entire entry:** Many stylebook entries include a rule and exceptions to it — and sometimes exceptions to the exceptions. Nothing is more frustrating than finding the correct entry, reading the first paragraph, following those instructions, then getting chewed out because your case was one of the exceptions covered in the *second* paragraph. Always read an entry in its entirety.

> If you don't know what your stylebook says, you need to look it up.

Spelling

Your stylebook should always be the first place you look when you have spelling questions as well as style questions. The stylebook functions as the Supreme Court: If it lists a spelling as correct, that's the one to use. In most cases, though, your stylebook will be silent on matters of spelling. That's when you need a good dictionary.

Why not just use the spell-checking feature of your word-processing program? In some ways, such technologies make it easier for misspellings to hit print, as the following poem, which has circulated for years in the journalistic community, demonstrates:

A Pome

I have a spelling checker,
It came with my PC;
It plainly marks four my revue
Mistakes I cannot sea.
I've run this pome threw it,
I'm sure your please to no,
It's letter perfect in it's weigh,
My checker tolled me sew.[2]

As this "pome" shows, our language is unbelievably difficult. Part of that difficulty stems from the fact that about 80 percent of all English words are derived from foreign sources, ranging from Arabic to Swedish. The result is a language in which words spelled with the same letters — such as bough, cough, dough, rough and through — sound completely different. And words that sound nearly the same — such as beer and bear, ball and bawl, they're and their — have completely different meanings.

When writers and editors let spelling errors slip through, readers notice. A three-year study by the American Society of Newspaper Editors reported that readers' top complaint was "too many factual errors and grammar or spelling mistakes." Those mistakes undermine reader confidence, undoing a lot of the good work done by writers and editors.[3]

The complexity of English has caused even such masters of the language as Mark Twain to complain about expectations that everyone spell words the same way. "I don't see any use in spelling a word right and never did," he told those gathered at a spelling bee in 1875. "We might as well make all clothes alike and cook all dishes alike. Sameness is tiresome. Variety is pleasing."

If all communications were private ones — keeping diaries, for instance, or writing shopping lists — such anarchy could flourish. But for people writing and editing for the mass media, using the preferred spellings of words is the only way to ensure that they're properly understood by a large audience. Misspellings reflect poorly on those who publish them. Many people would be at least a little hesitant about dining in a restaurant that advertised a $17.95 dinner that included "1/2 giraffe" of wine, or buying a very expensive CD player from a company that quotes a review as saying the player is "Quiet simply the best we've ever heard."

To make sure that prospective employees can get their messages across, many media companies include spelling quizzes in job interviews. So what hope is there for the spelling-impaired? One route would be to memorize the half-million words in the Oxford English Dictionary. A more reasonable approach, though, is to keep a dictionary at hand *and not hesitate to use it*. Unless you are 100 percent sure that you know how to spell a word, look it up. Experience shows that you often will find you didn't know how to spell the word even when you were 100 percent sure. In addition, you always should look up words you haven't seen before. And you should make a quick-reference list — maybe on the inside cover of your dictionary — of words that you always have to look up.

In this age of the Internet, of course there's a Web site that promises fast relief to editors suffering from spelling headaches — or jargon overload. Your Dictionary (*www.yourdictionary.com*) offers basic dictionary and thesaurus functions, but complements them with more than 200 foreign language dictionaries, more than 30 multilingual dictionaries and more than 50 specialty dictionaries, spanning a range from aviation to theater.

A few hints on using the dictionary:

1. If your organization uses a stylebook, always check it *before* consulting the dictionary; the stylebook has the final say. In the case of guarantee and guaranty, for example, The Associated Press Stylebook says to use the latter only in proper names.

> When writers and editors let spelling errors slip through, readers notice.

2.   Use the largest dictionary you can afford. Bigger dictionaries contain (surprise!) more words and are therefore more useful.

3.   Get the same dictionary that others on your staff use. While virtually all dictionaries have "Webster's" in their names, the use of that word is meaningless. Words and even spellings differ among "Webster's" dictionaries. Webster's Third New International Dictionary (G. & C. Merriam Co.) is one common standard. Webster's New World Dictionary is less comprehensive but widely used among media workers.

4.   When two or more spellings are listed for an entry, use the first. If you find two spellings in separate entries,

   a.   and only one is followed by a full definition (e.g., *espresso*) and the other is followed by "same as ... " (e.g., *expresso*), use the spelling accompanied by the full definition.

   b.   and both entries include definitions (e.g., *guarantee* and *guaranty*), you can use either — unless your stylebook says otherwise.

While those rules will help you arrive at the correct spellings eventually, the fewer words you have to look up, the better use you'll make of your editing time — and the better you'll do on a spelling quiz for a job. The following list includes hints that should help you in many spelling predicaments. These spelling rules have been compiled from "Spell It Right!" (Harry Shaw Harper Mass Market Paperbacks, 1994; "Beyond the 'SP' Label" (Patricia J. McAlexander, Ann B. Dobie and Noel Gregg, National Council of Teachers of English, 1992); and "Working With Words: A Handbook for Media Writers and Editors" (Brian S. Brooks, James L. Pinson and Jean Gaddy Wilson, Bedford Books, 1999).

I Before E.   You've heard it a million times, but it's worth hearing again. When you're not sure if a word should be spelled *ie* or *ei:*

•   If the sound is a long *e* sound (e.g., *shriek*), the *i* comes before the *e* unless those letters follow *c*. So it's *fiend, piece* and *retrieve,* but *conceive, deceit* and *receipt.*

•   If the sound is a long *a* sound (e.g., *vein*), *e* comes before *i.*

•   Several words are exceptions to this rule. Among the most often used: *ancient, caffeine, counterfeit, either, Fahrenheit, fiery, foreign, forfeit, height, leisure, neither, protein, seize, weird.*

Plurals.   Add *s* to make a noun into its plural, unless it falls under one of the following exceptions:

•   Nouns that end in *y* preceded by a consonant change the *y* to *i* in forming plurals. *Activity* becomes *activities, fly* becomes *flies,* etc. On the other hand, nouns that end in *y* preceded by a vowel usually add an *s* without changing the final *y* to form a plural. *Attorney* becomes *attorneys, money* becomes *moneys.*

- Nouns that end in a single *f* usually change the *f* to *v* and add *es* (e.g., *shelf/shelves, leaf/leaves, wolf/wolves*). However, some words merely add *s* (*roof, roofs*), so it's best to check.

- Nouns that end in *ch, sh, s, x* and *z* add *es: churches, dishes, bosses, boxes.*

- Nouns that end in *o* preceded by a consonant in some cases take an *s,* in others, an *es: pianos, potatoes.* Always check the dictionary. But nouns that end in *o* preceded by a vowel simply add *s* to form a plural: *radio* becomes *radios.*

- Acronyms and abbreviations also add an *s* to form the plural: *IOUs, VIPs.*

- Many words are irregular. *Woman,* for instance, becomes *women, goose* becomes *geese,* and *fish* remains *fish.* If you're not sure, always check.

Adding Suffixes.   Suffixes are attached to the ends of words: *-ing, -ful, -able, -ible, -ly, -ment, -ness* and others. A few rules will help you make the right connections.

- Suffixes that begin with a consonant typically are added to the root word. Two important exceptions:

  1. Words (other than *public*) that end in *ic* add *al* before adding *ly* (e.g., *tragically, dramatically*).

  2. Words ending in *ue* drop the final *e* when a suffix beginning with a consonant is added (e.g., *argument, truly*).

- If a word ends with a silent *e* (e.g., *hate*), keep the *e* if the suffix begins with a consonant (e.g., *hateful*), but drop it if the suffix begins with a vowel (e.g., *hating*).

- When you add a suffix to a noun that ends in *y* preceded by a consonant, change the *y* to *i* unless the suffix begins with *i* (e.g., *buried, fanciful, happier; trying, dying*).

- Words that can stand without the suffix add *-able* (e.g., *acceptable, agreeable*); words that cannot stand on their own add *-ible* (e.g., *credible, terrible*). While most stand-alone words that end with an *e* drop it before adding *-able* (e.g., *recognizable, desirable*), some keep the *e* (e.g., *traceable*). Your best bet is to check the dictionary.

- Verbs that end in a silent *e* drop the *e* when adding a suffix (e.g., *bore/boring, gaze/gazed* — the *e* comes from the suffix).

- One-syllable verbs that have short vowel sounds and do not end with a silent *e* double the last letter when adding a suffix (e.g., *spin/spinning, cram/crammed*).

Confusing Endings.   Only five common words end in *-eed* (*succeed, proceed, indeed, exceed, deed*); putting together the first letter of each word spells "SPIED." All others end in *-ede* (e.g., *impede, precede*).

Only six common words end in *-ery* (*cemetery, confectionery, distillery, millinery, monastery, stationery*). All others end in *-ary* (e.g., *boundary, dictionary*).

Only four common words end in *-efy* (*liquefy, putrefy, rarefy, stupefy*). All others take *-ify* (e.g., *mollify, solidify*).

Joining Words.   Don't delete letters when joining complete words together, even when the last letter of the first word is the same as the first letter of the second word (e.g., *bookkeeper, roommate, barroom, withhold, misspell*).

Notes

1.   "Style File," Folio:, 1 February 1994, p. 26.

2.   Harriet P. Gross, "The CopyRighter," Press Woman, February 1993, p. 17.

3.   E.R. Shipp, "Taking Our Measure," The Washington Post, 20 December 1998, sec. C. p. 6.

2 Tailoring Your Material

When I was young, I always dreaded receiving presents from one aunt. She'd give me things that I could not possibly use — a shaving kit when I was 9, for example, or clothes that I'm still waiting to grow into.

I'd always manage a polite smile and thank her for the gifts, then take them home and throw them into a corner of my closet. While she had meant well, her gifts were little more than a waste of time and money.

As an editor, you have to do a better job than my aunt did when it comes to choosing items for your audience. In order to do so, you need to:

• Learn about your audience.

• Select material appropriate for your audience.

• Prepare the material for the appropriate medium.

Learning About Your Audience

Only by knowing who it is that you're trying to serve can you do the best job possible in serving them. No matter how well a piece of copy is written and edited, if it is not appropriate for the intended audience, it will not be read. In her former job as ombudsman for The Washington Post, Joann Byrd repeatedly heard readers complaining that the paper often did not give readers what they want and need. "Newspapers blow stories," Byrd wrote. "They miss events or misjudge their importance or decide they don't match the criteria for news."[1]

In light of that criticism, it's not surprising that many people are giving up on newspapers and turning to more specialized magazines, newsletters and Web sites. Those **niche** sources are booming while newspapers are losing readers and folding at a staggering rate (network newscasts, also aimed at general audiences, have lost ground, too). A study by the National Opinion Research Center showed that the percentage of Americans who read a newspaper every day dropped from 73 percent in the late 1960s to 51 percent in the early 1990s, according to Nielsen Media Research.[2]

It's also not surprising that even newspapers are paying more attention to targeting audiences. As an editor at a large daily newspaper told me: "We don't serve a general audience any longer. Today our audience is an elite audience." Newspapers are paying more attention to news selection, and they are also printing customized **zoned editions** for specific geographical areas — generally affluent ones. Even specialized magazines have been looking for ways to come closer to the bull's eye. For example, Child magazine offers age-specific inserts (newborn to 11 months; 1 to 2 years old; 2 to 3 years old; 4 to 12 years old) in copies mailed to subscribers.

Public relations practitioners, too, know the importance of matching messages to audiences — or **publics** — for the most effective communication. A hospital P.R. writer who edits an in-house magazine and a magazine for the community knows that she can't run the same articles in each.

One way of looking at this change is to see it as a change from traditionally **editor-driven** content to **reader-driven** content. Editor-driven content comes from the top down. Media decision makers meet privately and decide what information the audience should receive. The problem with such an approach was clearly stated by Bob McGruder of The Detroit Free Press:

> In a given news meeting, there may be 10 different editors sitting around, all very smart, each with a different idea of what the reader wants. All around the country, declining newspaper circulation suggests that a whole bunch of us may not be right.[3]

Reader-driven content comes from the bottom up. Editors start by learning as much as they can about their audience, then select material based on audience needs and wishes. "A great editor listens deeply to those inside and outside the newsroom to understand the public and personal issues that genuinely concern people," Sebby Wilson Jacobson of the Rochester Democrat and Chronicle observes.[4]

That does not absolve editors from all responsibility to their readers, though. Editors who merely pander to readers breach their responsibility to the public. A balance must be struck. For example, general-interest newspapers carry more celebrity and "people" news now than in the past. However, they continue to carry news about the government, foreign affairs and plenty of other weighty topics.

Editors use a variety of methods to learn about their audiences, as well as to identify their publications' strengths and weaknesses:

Surveys.   Mail, phone and online surveys often are used to learn about the audience **demographics:** age, gender, occupation, income and other vital statistics. Virtually every media outlet collects such data. The data is used primarily as a tool to show advertisers that the publication can deliver readers who are receptive to ad messages, but it also gives editors insight into the audience.[5] Public relations practitioners also use surveys to find out about their audiences. For example, a person who does public relations for a theater often will include a survey inside programs to gather suggestions for future productions.

Some surveys also try to determine audience **psychographics:** information on a reader's self-concept, behavior, thoughts and personal activities. The annual

Study of Media and Markets conducted by the Simmons Market Research Bureau is one study that looks at these variables. This national survey, which includes more than 23,000 adults (other Simmons studies cover children from 6 to 14 and from 12 to 19), asks readers to describe a day in their lives as well as major personal experiences in the preceding and upcoming years.

Even more useful from an editorial standpoint are surveys that solicit direct feedback on the contents of a specific issue of a publication. Some publications ask readers to rate major columns and articles. Other publications go a step further by asking a small group of readers to volunteer to serve on a reader panel. Several panels are set up, each rating a small number of articles for usefulness, clarity, length and other points.[6]

Some newsletter and magazine editors go even further, making telephone calls to readers. Not only does this let the editors ask about reader needs and wants, but it also is a great way to get article ideas.

Focus Groups.   Like surveys, focus groups are used primarily in connection with advertising but also have utility for editorial work. Focus groups of five to 12 people can be used in the planning stages of a new publication or Web site, or at the time of a makeover. Focus groups also can be asked to evaluate competing publications,[7] with comments used to revise the target publication.

Print media editors use two variations of the focus group. The first is a sort of town meeting, in which members of the community are invited to meet with one or more editors to discuss their concerns with the paper's coverage. The second variation is allowing one or more community members to sit in on editorial board meetings. The citizens' opinions are given careful consideration in selecting the news for the day. Steve Crosby recruited editorial board volunteers while he was executive editor of the Lafayette, Ind., Journal and Courier, and he was glad to have them. As he has written:

> ... honestly, we don't know enough to do the job alone. Editors tend to have many of the same interests and talk with many of the same people. Readers have added a rich diversity of ideas and experiences to our discussions. We talk about issues that didn't occur to us before. And we look at them from perspectives we were unaware of previously.[8]

Some newsletters and magazines also rely on readers to help shape editorial policy. Perhaps the best known example is Seventeen magazine's annual competition for its teen advisory board.

Print and Web-based publications also increasingly are using the Internet for reader feedback. Many publications offer readers direct e-mail connections to writers and editors; some offer electronic forums in which readers sound off.

Anne M. Russell, former editor in chief of Folio: magazine and an early adopter of online feedback, praised the use of such feedback:

> Editing a magazine is a power trip. As someone who runs a magazine, you get to make — metaphorically, at least — life and death decisions. ... But [online feedback] threatens the absolute power editors wield within their industries. And that's good because we all know the consequences of absolute power: absolute corruption — or, more accurately, editorial

Some publications ask readers to rate major columns and articles.

arrogance. The bond built by objectivity and fairness is thoroughly destroyed by editors who begin to believe that their own concerns and opinions are more significant than those of their readers.[9]

Ombudsmen. Another way that some newspapers learn about their audiences is through ombudsmen. A few dozen papers employ ombudsmen, whose duties typically include taking calls from and meeting with the public. (The executive editors of many newsletters perform the same functions.) Assigning a person to these tasks can be a great help in determining the needs and desires of typically neglected segments of the audience. When their desires are related to the editorial staff, content can be changed to bring nonreaders into the fold.

Socializing. OK, here's the fun part of editing. In order to keep an ear to the ground, many editors spend time at conventions and meetings where members of their audiences congregate. Editors and reporters for newsletters, trade magazines and specialized Web sites use trade conferences to learn what issues are on the minds of those attending the events.

There are other ways to take the pulse of readers, too. I worked for one editor who bar-hopped to keep in touch with what our audience was talking about. When he advocated giving good play to an article, he did so from his knowledge of its importance to our audience. A good listener can determine not only what the audience is talking about, but also what it's likely to be talking about several months later — an important ability for magazine editors and others who have to plan months ahead. (Of course, there is a potential problem with doing this kind of research: Not all readers hang out in bars, so many prospective readers might be missed.)

One of the most ambitious programs for trying to learn what an audience wants was undertaken by The Olympian, a Washington-state newspaper owned by the Gannett Co. In the first two years of Gannett's News 2000 program, which required papers in the chain to find out what their readers want and then deliver it, The Olympian:

- provided readers with forms on which they were asked to indicate their preferences for news coverage;

- held nine forums in which readers were given the chance to meet with editors;

- organized reader panels to solicit views of the paper from people in the community; and

- had reporters distribute hundreds of surveys at public places to find out how readers ranked community news.

Using the feedback, The Olympian made major changes, including revisions of its design and of its beat system. While some reporters protested the restrictions on their freedom to write about whatever they wanted to, Editorial Page Editor Mike Oakland told Columbia Journalism Review that the changes made the paper much more responsive to the community. Readers seemed to agree: The Olympian steadily gained readers during a period in which other papers across the country were losing circulation or treading water.[10]

A good listener can determine not only what the audience is talking about, but also what it's likely to be talking about several months later.

Civic Journalism

Something that good editors have long known — the public matters — became the basis of a major movement in journalism during the 1990s.

Doing business under the names Civic Journalism or Public Journalism, the movement was based on the observation that most citizens were disconnected from public life. Not only did that bode poorly for government — which depends on citizen participation — but it also was bad news for the news media: Citizens who don't participate in public life have little use for news.[11]

In hopes of preserving the republic — and their own organizations — many journalists stepped up efforts to lessen reliance on official sources and "to rediscover the total community, listen to the total community, cover the total community and advocate for the total community."[12]

Civic Journalism requires journalists to ask people what matters to them, and to value those opinions. Some critics of the movement are put off by the active involvement of the media in community issues. But Hodding Carter III, a former print journalist and more recently president of the Knight Foundation, notes that "civic journalism's chief attraction is that it offers a chance for journalists to reclaim their central place in the community — and in the process to help people refashion healthier communities for themselves."[13]

Using the Knowledge

As the example of The Olympian proves, knowledge is power — power to adapt and power to survive in a competitive market. But that is true only when the knowledge is *used*. Unfortunately, in many cases editorial employees are given little of the information gathered about their audiences, and therefore they are forced to guess what readers should receive. So it's crucial that editors ask for access to any existing audience information.

Next, editors must use that information to develop or refine a **mission statement**. A mission statement sets out an overall shared vision for the organization, publication or editorial department. Communication consultant John Brady noted: "A mission statement acts as a prism, powerfully focusing the efforts of the staff in the right direction. Without it, effort is diffused and weakened — and the [publication] suffers the consequences."[14]

At a minimum, a mission statement for the editorial department of a publication should cover:

- the purpose or focus of the publication (Why are you doing what you're doing?);
- the audience for whom the publication is intended (magazines sometimes prepare this separately and call it a positioning statement); and
- what makes the publication different from its competition.

In addition, a mission statement might include:

- what issues are covered in the publication; and
- what sources and organizations are covered.[15]

A sample mission statement appears on Page 26.

Time Inc.

Sports Illustrated
Sports Illustrated Building
135 West 50th Street
New York, NY 10020-1393

EDITORIAL MISSION STATEMENT   212-522-1212

SPORTS ILLUSTRATED, which made its debut in August of 1954, employs enterprising reporting, lively writing, vivid photography and robust design to cover sports and relate it to the world at large. It considers sports to be worthy of attention, and seeks to inform, excite and provoke by covering the subject with authority, vigor and immediacy.

Because sports is by definition meant to be playful, SPORTS ILLUSTRATED also seeks to entertain. However, SI casts a harsh eye on those who would subvert sports. From an editorial perspective, the magazine's loyalty is not to any athlete, team, or league, but rather to the sports they play or oversee.

The vast majority of SI's 21 million readers are subscribers -- SI's circulation rate base is 3,150,000 and its subscriber-to-newsstand ratio is 97%-3%. The ratio of men-to-women who read the magazine is 77%-23%.

SPORTS ILLUSTRATED has an uncommonly strong bond with its readers. Many of them started reading SI in their teens and continue to do so into middle age. Interestingly, many of them are not sports junkies; in fact some could not even be considered fans. However, they comprise a diverse audience unified in its appreciation of good writing and good photography -- and in an awareness that sports is an elemental and universal part of life worth watching and understanding.

An Olympic Sponsor since 1980, SPORTS ILLUSTRATED has successfully expanded its franchise by creating such extensions as SPORTS ILLUSTRATED FOR KIDS, SPORTS ILLUSTRATED FOR WOMEN, CNN/SPORTS ILLUSTRATED (the 24-hour sports-news network), CNN/SI.com, SI-branded calendars, books, videos, special collector's issues and custom publishing ventures.

Mission statements for publications often also include an **editorial grid** that strives to balance content in each issue as well as over time. Such balance, write J. William Click and Russell N. Baird, requires variety, breadth of coverage, consistency and purpose. "Good editors," they add, "cover a broad range of topics of interest to readers, from recurring themes and routine material to new ideas and developments."[16] An editorial grid can be set up by types of articles (news, features, columns, etc.) or by subject area (for example, in a women's magazine, articles on people, fashions, health and so on).

In some cases, the mission statement includes a list of objectives to be accomplished; in other cases, objectives are developed from the mission statement. In either case, every action an editor takes should advance the mission.

Put all these pieces together and the result is a good mission statement — and a good chance of succeeding. What Mark Beach has written about newsletters is just as applicable to other media: "Newsletters that best accomplish their goals have both audience and content highly targeted."[17]

The job of defining a publication's identity is an ongoing one. A.C. Spectorsky, the editorial director who took Playboy magazine from a circulation of under 1 million to more than 6.5 million, had this to say on the process of evolution:

> A successful magazine must be a process, not an artifact. It must constantly evolve, not just keep pace, to retain leadership. The history of publishing is strewn with the remains of embalmed publications that knew they had a good thing going, and kept it going the same way while the world went by.[18]

"The goal," communication consultant John Brady adds, "is to stay fresh and interesting and to stay in business."[19]

> Every action an editor takes should advance the mission.

Assigning and Selecting Material

Once you've determined what you're doing and whom you're doing it for, you can move on to the next step: deciding what information best accomplishes that goal. This step includes *assigning* and *selecting* material.

Editors typically assign and select material through an instinctual process. Newcomers don't possess those instincts, though, so they need to consider several factors to determine what material to use — and what to avoid.

A good starting point is the basic news values. The news values help editors rank-order stories, choose which points to emphasize, and determine the placement of stories throughout a publication. A typical news story will have several of the following news values.

Effect.   The primary measure of the value of any information is its effect on the audience. If you are editing a magazine for wine connoisseurs, and pending tax legislation would double the cost of wine, the effect of that information is obviously important to your readers. This is a **direct** effect. Effect can also be **indirect** or **potential.** An example of information with an indirect effect is a newspaper carrying an article on severe weather 1,000 miles away. While your audience won't be directly affected by it, some of them will have friends and relatives in the stormy area and will be indirectly affected. If the weather is damaging food crops that are sold in your area, the information also can have a potential effect: Those items will be hard to find or will cost more a few months from now.

Some of the most important news has little direct effect on you or people you know, at least initially. Much foreign news is like that. Chances are that the fall of the Berlin Wall and the collapse of communism in the former Soviet Union didn't affect you directly at first. Over time, however, those events have had important repercussions throughout the world.

Prominence.   Great effects are often connected with well-known people: The leader of a country declares war; the head of a company announces 2,000 layoffs. Sometimes the acts of well-known people are considered newsworthy even when those acts don't seem to have much of an effect. The information is significant because of a potential effect. A bout with pneumonia could lead to the death of a president, for example.

In other cases, the actions of well-known people are considered newsworthy solely because people like to hear what celebrities are up to. The Pamela Anderson-Tommy Lee saga is but one example of many. The popularity of magazines like People and of newspaper "People in the News" columns attests to this point. The information in those pages might not be important, but it *is* popular.

Unusualness.   It is impossible for any publication to cover more than a small fraction of all relevant events. So in most cases, routine events receive little play or are ignored while those out of the ordinary are deemed more important. However, there is a downside to this value: Sometimes the most important story is found in the day-to-day happenings. The riots that broke out in Los Angeles after the first trial of police who beat motorist Rodney King might have been avoided had the news media paid attention to routine complaints of police abuse in the black community. Instead, the media waited for an unusual event — the video-taped beating of King — before acting.

Currency.   News is one of the oldest examples of recycling. Topics that are popular today will disappear, then reappear years from now. This cycle is fueled largely by the focus on unusual events: When something dramatic happens, it attracts attention to similar events and underlying conditions. For example, a national study reports that the percentage of high school graduates who are functionally illiterate is at record levels. That astounding finding will lead writers and editors to ask why, and it also will make them more alert to related stories. Those stories then have currency: a direct tie to stories already in the news.

Conflict.   In a sense, any journalistic endeavor is an exercise in storytelling. And most interesting stories have some sort of conflict: people battling nature, other people, themselves, disease, the system — you name it. A profile of a person born into a wealthy family and given the family's huge corporation to run is not very interesting; a profile of a person who was born into poverty and created a successful business is much more interesting because that person had to overcome great odds.

A caution on conflict: Because conflict can make a story more appealing, writers and editors tend to play up minor conflicts, sometimes at the expense of the

---

Some of the most important news has little direct effect on you or people you know, at least initially.

truth of a story. If 10,000 people harmoniously attend a convention but two of them get into a fistfight, that fistfight shouldn't dominate the story — or even the lead.

Timeliness.   Timeliness refers to how recently an event happened. All else being equal, an event that is more timely is more newsworthy than a similar event. So if you publish a newsletter on the first of each month, and you have room to publish a short piece on one of two similar events that occurred during the past month, you should choose the more recent one.

Events do not have to have happened in the immediate past, as long as there is some timeliness to them. The release of a 30-year-old report just declassified by the government or the discovery of the tomb of a ruler who died 2,000 years ago both have timeliness.

Proximity.   Proximity refers to nearness and can take two forms. First is **geographical** proximity: If all factors are equal in two events, the one that has occurred nearest to your audience is more newsworthy. For newspaper editors in particular, this is an essential news value. While well-written stories about unfamiliar people in distant places can be fascinating, most readers are far more interested in people and events in their own communities. In fact, aside from a few national newspapers (such as USA Today and The Wall Street Journal), the emphasis on local news is largely what sets a newspaper — or an online news site — apart from its competition.

The second type of proximity is **affinity:** People are interested in other people who share characteristics with them (religion, nationality, race, etc.). Note that neither timeliness nor proximity alone make information newsworthy. They are merely additional considerations to help you weed out competing candidates for publication.

Human Interest.   Stories that have strong emotional content are said to have human interest. Some make the reader feel good; others bring tears to readers' eyes. Upbeat human-interest stories are used to lighten a heavy news section by giving the reader a short break. Similar stories also often are used to end television news broadcasts.

Visual Appeal.   You've probably seen a television newscast lead with a story on a small plane crash thousands of miles from where you live; possibly a handful of not-well-known people were killed in the crash. Not much of a story — so why was it the lead? Such stories often are picked because someone has managed to videotape the crash, so the stories have strong visual appeal. Newspapers, too, give prominent play to such stories, almost solely because of the accompanying visual materials.

Agenda Setting.   The same stories often are repeated throughout various media because certain media set the agenda for other media. Stories reported in one of the **prestige media** are considered musts by less-powerful media so that they don't miss "a big one." Generally, the prestige media are considered to include The New York Times, The Washington Post, The Wall Street Journal, The Los Angeles Times, Time, Newsweek, U.S. News and World Report, ABC, CBS, CNN and NBC news. In addition, some "insider" newsletters (such as Communications

Stories reported in one of the **prestige media** are considered musts by less-powerful media so that they don't miss "a big one."

Daily, which brings industry executives the latest news every morning) also play a strong agenda-setting role.

These media not only set the agenda for each other, they also set the agenda for other broadcast outlets and publications, partly through their news services. The Associated Press also does a great deal of agenda setting through its daily **budget** (a list of the biggest anticipated news stories). Even the lowly tabloids can set the agenda for other media, as The National Enquirer did twice in the first two months of 2001: first with the news that Jesse Jackson had fathered a child with a staff member, then with news that Hillary Rodham Clinton's brother received $200,000 to help arrange a pardon by departing President Bill Clinton.

While the role of certain media in setting the agenda for other media is undeniable, the good editor will always consider any story in light of the needs of his or her specific audience. While journalists care greatly about what's on the front page of The New York Times, most readers do not. They prefer to get the news that has the most relevance to and impact on their lives.

News Is Relative.   One other factor needs to be added: the importance of information in relation to other available information. A piece of information that generally might be considered highly newsworthy may not even be printed or broadcast when more important information comes along. For example, on the day David Koresh's headquarters burned in Waco, Texas, the story led newscasts and newspapers all over the country. But it didn't make Page One on some newspapers in South Dakota, because on the same day the governor of that state was killed in a plane crash.

Applying the News Values

Let's analyze the news values in one of the biggest stories of recent years. In June 2000, computer software giant Microsoft was found to have engaged in illegal practices and was ordered to split into two divisions. The story led newscasts, topped the front pages of newspapers and was the lead feature in countless magazines and online news sites. Why was it such a big story?

Effect.   This story has tremendous effects over a wide range of issues and people.

- **The company and its employees:** Financial loss, job cuts and many other major actions were among the potential effects of the decision.

- **Wall Street:** The ruling came just after technology stocks had lost a great deal of value, and a change in the value of Microsoft stock price could affect the market and countless investors.

- **Microsoft customers:** The overwhelming majority of computer users rely on Microsoft's Windows operating system, Internet Explorer Web browser and Office suites. The ruling would require the company to separate its application and operating system divisions.

- **Microsoft's competitors:** Because the decision was based on Microsoft's practices that tended to drive competitors out of business, the ruling had a major potential effect on old and new competitors. It also had potential effect on competitors that were engaging in the same types of behaviors as Microsoft had.

- **Computer manufacturers:** During the years preceding the ruling, Microsoft had forced computer makers who wanted to use its products to follow its wishes on the use and prominence of Netscape Navigator and other products. The ruling unshackled manufacturers from following those rules.

Prominence.   Microsoft Chairman Bill Gates is known worldwide as one of the shrewdest business people alive — and the richest (at the time of the breakup, his worth had dropped from nearly $100 billion to what one news story called "a meager $60 billion"). Because of his wealth, he was the man many people loved to hate.

Unusualness.   The Microsoft ruling was the biggest antitrust decision since the 1984 breakup of AT&T (which was by consent decree, not court order).

Currency.   By the time of the ruling, the Microsoft case had been in the news for a full decade. The story began in 1990 with the Federal Trade Commission opening an investigation of the company's software marketing practices. The story also gained currency from other news, such as the slow rise of the Linux operating system, seen by many as the first real competitor to Windows.

Timeliness.   When initially reported, the story was very timely, with the judge's decision having just been announced. Throughout the preceding stages, timeliness was also a factor, with new developments and disclosures announced regularly.

Proximity.   In some parts of the country, the story also had great proximity: Washington state, home of Microsoft; Washington, D.C., where the trial occurred; and the Silicon Valley area of California, home to many companies that routinely deal with Microsoft.

Conflict.   The Microsoft story was rife with conflict. The company had had run-ins with competitors and software makers and aggressively took on the U.S. Department of Justice during the trial. In addition, many computer users viewed Microsoft unfavorably for releasing buggy, bloated software.

Obviously, this was a big story (and, in fact, one likely to be continuing even as you read this). Just as obviously, the way the story was played depended in large part on publication and audience. A business magazine would most likely focus on the antitrust aspects of the story; a computer magazine would concentrate on the consequences for computer users.

Another Tool for Selection

Another useful tool for selecting material for publication is psychologist Abraham Maslow's **hierarchy of human needs.** This hierarchy often is used in creating advertising copy, but it is also appropriate as a measure of the importance of other copy, especially feature articles. Maslow's five levels of needs are:

1. **Physical:** The need for food, air, water, rest and the ability to reproduce as a species. These are the most fundamental needs; until these needs are filled, people do not think much about higher levels. News articles dealing with pollution would address these needs, as would feature articles about safe food handling.

2. **Safety:** The need to protect ourselves from threats. News stories about crime address this need, as do features on self-protection, sunscreens and security systems.

3. **Social needs:** The need to relate to or help others, to escape, to have fun. Such needs are the focus of articles on places to go and things to do, as well as articles on making friends and finding mates.

4. **Self-esteem:** The desire to believe that people are worthwhile and valuable. Features on volunteers within a company or community, news coverage of local organizations, and even wedding announcements fall into this category.

5. **Self-actualization:** The desire to develop one's potential to the maximum, to be the best one can. This is the highest level in Maslow's hierarchy and is reflected in articles on self-improvement.[20]

Good editors realize that no list of factors can ever be complete. They keep in touch with the world around them and watch for shifts in what might be considered newsworthy. Before the feminist movement surged in the 1960s and 1970s, few newspaper editors regarded child care, birth control and other "women's issues" as newsworthy. Today it is hard to find an issue of any newspaper that doesn't have some coverage of such issues.

Using Outside Information

Most copy is written especially for a publication, either by staff members or freelance writers. But many publications also rely heavily on news releases and wire service copy. Because these materials come from outside sources, an editor must give them special treatment.

Always Verify the Contents.   Every part of a news release should be verified, from the spelling of names to the accuracy of major points. News releases always should be considered as promotional materials; the editor's job is to verify what is being promoted.

Verifying wire service copy is now easier than ever thanks to the Web. While in the past many wire service accounts were the sole source of information from a distant place, it's now easy to compare those accounts with Web news sites. Discrepancies should be investigated. When comparisons reveal holes in the original article, editors can combine accounts from different sources. Such surgery requires a delicate touch and careful attention to making sure that the information in the accounts does not conflict.

Make the Copy Fit Your Audience.   Readers don't want "generic" news; they want information relevant to them. So information from wire service accounts and news releases often is customized for an audience in one of two ways:

- **Localize it:** National news often can be made more relevant to readers by supplementing the information with local material. The local material either can be used as a separate **sidebar,** which accompanies the main article, or can be combined with the wire information in a single story. One example: A wire service sends newspapers an article about a federal study of crime trends. Writers at a

News releases always should be considered as promotional materials; the editor's job is to verify what is being promoted.

specific newspaper gather information on local crime trends and add it to the article. In such cases, the wire service still should be credited for its work.

- **Use it as the basis of a new article:** Sometimes a piece of copy is of little use on its own, but it suggests another article. For example, a national health center sends out a release about a new research program for victims of a rare disease. While that news might not be interesting to your audience, a story about a local person involved in the research project might be.

Article ideas also can be found in articles published in similar media. For instance, the editor of a city magazine will read city magazines from all over the country and find ideas that can be done locally. An article on the best local day trips in a Detroit magazine may inspire an editor in Seattle to assign a similar piece about day trips in the Pacific Northwest.

Preparing the Material for the Appropriate Medium

The final step in an editor's tailoring is the same as a tailor's final step: getting a precise fit. Look through any publication — newspaper, magazine, newsletter, Web site — and you'll notice that some items are given plenty of space while others get only a paragraph or two. How does an editor know how much space to give to an item?

While the news values and Maslow's hierarchy provide some help in making these decisions, editing is far more of an art than a science. But editors who know their readers and know what information is most important to those readers can estimate how much readers will want to know about a given topic. Two guidelines:

News.   In handling news, it may be helpful to think of the following four categories developed by Stephen Meyer while he was the editorial director of Progressive Business Publications:

- **Interesting:** Information that readers may look at if they have the time. This is the least compelling type of information and merits little or no coverage.

- **Important:** The next step up the ladder. Readers are more likely to find the time to read such material, so it should get at least modest coverage.

- **Actionable:** Information that readers can use to accomplish goals. Such news is often referred to as "News You Can Use" (a phrase that U.S. News & World Report has gone so far as to have registered as a trademark). Stories that are actionable should receive substantial coverage.

- **Essential:** The highest level. Readers cannot afford to miss this information, so it should receive the greatest amount of coverage and the most prominent play.[21]

For newsletters, the "3–30–3" rule offers guidance on article length. Developed by Howard Penn Hudson, author of "Publishing Newsletters" (Scribner's, 1988), the rule says that readers should have to spend no more than three seconds on a headline, 30 seconds on an article or three minutes on an entire newsletter to get its essentials.

Features.   Because feature articles are by definition more interesting than important, determining the best size is trickier than doing so for news articles. The best starting point is to assess how many of your readers are likely to be interested in the topic. The more widespread the interest in the topic, the more space the article should be given. A magazine for cat owners might devote a large amount of space to an article on choosing the best cat food — all cats eat — but a much smaller amount of space to an article on a rare cat disease.

Of course, the length of a piece is partly determined by the medium in which it is going to be presented. Generally speaking, magazines run the longest articles, followed by newspapers, Web sites and then newsletters. Material prepared for delivery to wireless devices is even shorter.

The style of presentation also varies greatly from medium to medium:

- Newsmagazines are published only weekly. Therefore, articles tend to have delayed leads and take a feature approach. The long pieces are regularly broken up by subheads.

- Newspaper articles still rely on direct leads and largely follow the inverted pyramid model.

- Newsletter articles typically run no more than a few paragraphs.

- Web site reports vary in length considerably, but because text is harder to read on a screen than on paper, the reports tend to be short. Longer articles should be broken into chunks, each with its own subhead.

- Wireless device users typically don't want to read much at all — the small display on a cell phone or Palm Pilot is far from ideal for reading — so a headline and story summary generally suffices.

Making Major Cuts

Whenever possible, editors should provide writers with specific guidelines on length. Unfortunately, final determinations about size often are made only late in the process of editing, after the copy has been received. Unanticipated space limitations often require copy to be cut substantially. As a writer, I've seen copy that I've written trimmed by 25 percent or more; as an editor, I've had to combine 12 news articles — each at least 8 column inches long — into one 12-inch article. That's a cut of almost 90 percent.

Trimming even 10 percent from copy can be tough work when writers have done their jobs. The following tips should help make that work a little easier:

1. Separate what readers *need* to know from what readers might *like* to know. Stephen Meyer's classifications offer a good way to begin this process: Maintain the essential information while eliminating the merely interesting. In an article in Writer's Digest, author John M. Wilson offers additional hints for trimming. He suggests cutting material if "it slows the article down without adding information; it repeats a point; it's short on specifics and concrete details; [or] it isn't relevant to what's immediately around it or to [the] article's angle or theme."[22]

2. Strive to maintain the writer's style. Most writers work hard organizing material and carefully choosing smooth transitions, colorful phrases and precise descriptions. Careless editing can obliterate all that effort. An editor should try to make trims undetectable to the writer by tightening wordy phrases and cutting non-essential information. Such a gentle approach is especially critical in editing feature articles, which often depend on the writer's style for much of their effect.

3. Always reread the entire piece after your cutting. In cutting copy, editors unintentionally can create holes or scramble the meaning of the piece. Many editors have cut information from the beginning of a piece of copy but failed to either clarify or remove later references to it. Only by reading the final trimmed version of the copy can editors be sure that they've done more good than harm.

Let's look at a few examples of trimming. We'll start with a short piece submitted for the annual "Best of Baltimore" edition of Baltimore magazine. The writer's assignment was to find a great local politician and explain what he or she is "best" at. As former Editor Meg Guroff explains: "The writer is a terrific reporter and very plugged into local politics, so his work automatically has the knowing air we affect. But sometimes his writing is a little wonkier than our usual breezy style, so we correct for that." In addition, the piece was longer than companion entries in the "People" category of "Best of Baltimore." So Guroff went to work. Here's the original piece:

Other than to prepare, consider, and vote on legislation, the 19 members of the City Council have a decidedly vague job description. Sure, they try to steer city services to their constituents, and they may take to the bully pulpit on various issues on occasion. But if you stack those duties up, there's still plenty of time to spare. First District member Lois Garey (D) stands out as a legislator who uses her extra time conscientiously by attempting to stay abreast of what's up in city government. She's there at weekly Board of Estimates meetings, trying to keep tabs on how the city's spending money. She goes to weekly liquor board hearings to see which places, in her bar-heavy district, are causing problems. She pops in regularly for meetings of other public bodies, just to make sure she knows what they're up to. In short, she takes her oversight responsibilities to heart. Too bad more of her colleagues aren't like her on that score. (164 words)

And the edited piece, as it appeared in the magazine:

The Baltimore City Council has a vague job description. Sure, its members write and pass laws. But there's no clock to punch, and it *is* a part-time gig. Except for a few dogged members, most don't make time to watch city government in action. Among those who do, First District member Lois Garey (D) stands out. She is there at weekly Board of Estimates meetings. She goes to weekly liquor board hearings to see which places, in her bar-heavy district, are causing problems. She pops in regularly for meetings of other public bodies, just to make sure she knows what they're up to. In short, she earns her keep. (109 words)

In other cases, trimming requires much more effort. For the same issue, Guroff had to trim 200 words out of a 700-word essay because the photos to be used with the piece turned out to be vertical rather than horizontal, as originally planned — thereby changing the entire page layout.

Only by reading the final trimmed version of the copy can editors be sure that they've done more good than harm.

Here's the original:

Keep the faith. Yes, your first turn out of Mount Airy yields a mundane landscape of liquor store, food store, karate school, and tanning salon. But stick with Ridgeville Boulevard, up a little hill, across the old B&O tracks and around a bend for your first dramatic vista: the immense concrete plateau of Interstate 70.

Soon enough, you'll arrive at an intersection with Bill Moxley Road, where a sideways glance at the street sign confirms that you really are on "Old National Pike," as the National Road is known along this stretch. Here is where Conestoga wagons rolled in the early 19th century, carrying pioneers bound for the godforsaken wilderness of the West (which at that point meant Ohio). Here is where the skinny wheels of so many horseless carriages rolled, signalling a new age in America's long love affair with mobility. And here, on the interstate built in the old Road's shadow, is where a constant blur of traffic rumbles, carrying commuters to and from the increasingly suburbanized counties of Howard, Carroll, and Frederick.

Here, in other words, runs American history, stretching from dawn of the nation to dawn of this day. The entirety of the Road's story is detailed in the dense and fascinating two-volume anthology *The National Road,* edited by University of Kentucky geographer Karl Raitz and published in 1996 by the Johns Hopkins University Press. Therein, we learn of its ever-shifting and always-evocative role in American commerce, technology, culture, and more.

The National Road dates to 1806, when Thomas Jefferson approved a plan to build an overland route to the Mississippi River. It took more than four decades to finish building the first federally funded highway, from its starting point near what's now Baltimore's Inner Harbor to Vandalia, Illinois. In Maryland, its route travels through Southwest Baltimore along Lombard Street and Frederick Avenue, and then along Maryland 144 and U.S. 40 through Catonsville and Ellicott City and Lisbon and New Market and Frederick and Cumberland and Frostburg before crossing into Pennsylvania just beyond Keysers Ridge.

The Road's story is shaped just like the hills it traverses, an up-and-down, boom-and-bust affair. By the time of its completion in 1850, it was already obsolete; by then, travelers preferred riding by train. In the early 1900s, the automobile's arrival spurred a reconstruction and a revival that lasted until the interstate highway system arrived in the years after World War II.

Now comes another century and another Road revival, this time as a tourist attraction for history buffs and blue-highway devotees. Happily, the Road isn't all strip malls and interstate vistas. Driving its length in Maryland, you'll find idyllic Main Streets, expansive state parks, odd little museums, costumed interpreters, scenic overlooks, historic inns, cheap souvenirs, pricey gifts — the whole modern-day tourist shebang.

Just a few miles from Bill Moxley Road, Old National Pike becomes Main Street and enters New Market, which Raitz calls "the consummate 19th-century Road town." Here, more than a dozen antiques shops occupy meticulously restored former inns and taverns and homes along the Road, as do a handful of B&Bs and restaurants.

But part of what makes a National Road trip so fascinating is what was *not* restored: what may exist only in rumor and memory. Beyond New Market, you'll make a couple of turns and then find yourself on a four-lane highway headed for Frederick across a bridge over the Monocacy River. According to Raitz's book, the crumbling foundations of the Old Jug Bridge lie somewhere below.

Perhaps you'll have more luck than I did in finding these ruins. I couldn't spot them while driving over the bridge. Nor could I find them after parking on the shoulder and walking back up as too-close-for-comfort trucks whizzed past. I wandered along side roads, too, descending into residential neighborhoods filled with signs issuing dire warnings against trespassing.

Judging from those signs, I wasn't the first outsider to look for the old bridge. And, presumably, you won't be the last. But whether you find the bridge or not, hunting for such a vestige seems a natural way to bookend a trip on the National Road. It reminds you that in some places, history gets all gussied up. In others, it gets paved over and buried. And in still others, it's down there somewhere, daring you to find it.

The same piece, 200 words lighter:

Keep the faith. Yes, your first turn out of Mount Airy yields a mundane landscape of liquor store, food store, karate school, and tanning salon. But stick with Ridgeville Boulevard for your first dramatic vista: the immense concrete plateau of Interstate 70.

Soon enough, you'll arrive at Bill Moxley Road, where the street sign confirms that you really are on "Old National Pike," as the National Road is known along this stretch. Here is where Conestoga wagons rolled in the early 19th century, carrying pioneers bound for the godforsaken wilderness of the West (which at that point meant Ohio). Here is where the skinny wheels of horseless carriages rolled. And here, on the interstate built in the Road's shadow, is where a constant blur of traffic rumbles, carrying commuters to and from Howard, Carroll, and Frederick counties.

Here, in other words, runs American history, stretching from dawn of the nation to dawn of this day. The Road's story is detailed in the two-volume anthology *The National Road,* edited by Karl Raitz. Therein, we learn of the road's ever-shifting and ever-evocative role in American commerce, technology, culture, and more.

The National Road dates to 1806, when Thomas Jefferson approved a plan to build an overland route to the Mississippi River, from what's now Baltimore's Inner Harbor to Vandalia, Illinois. Its path travels along Maryland 144 and U.S. 40 through Catonsville and Lisbon and Frederick and Frostburg before entering Pennsylvania.

The Road's story is shaped like the hills it traverses, an up-and-down, boom-and-bust affair. By the time of its completion in 1850, it was obsolete; travelers preferred the train. In the early 1900s, the car's arrival spurred a revival that lasted until the interstate system was built mid-century.

Now comes another century and another Road revival, this time as a tourist attraction. Happily, the Road isn't all strip malls and interstate vistas. Driving its length in Maryland, you'll find idyllic Main Streets, expansive state parks, odd museums, costumed interpreters, historic inns, cheap souvenirs — the whole tourist shebang.

Just a few miles from Bill Moxley Road, Old National Pike becomes Main Street and enters New Market. Here, more than a dozen antiques shops occupy meticulously restored former inns, taverns, and homes, as do a handful of B&Bs and restaurants.

But part of what makes a National Road trip so fascinating is what was *not* restored: what may exist only in rumor and memory. Beyond New Market, you'll find yourself on a four-lane highway across a bridge over the Monocacy River. According to Raitz's book, the foundations of the Old Jug Bridge lie somewhere below. Perhaps you'll have more success than I did in finding these ruins. I parked and wandered along side roads, descending into neighborhoods filled with no-trespassing signs, but no luck.

Judging from those signs, I wasn't the first outsider to look for the old bridge. And, presumably, you won't be the last. But whether you find the bridge or not, hunting for it seems a natural way to end a trip on the National Road. It reminds you that, in some places, history gets all gussied up. In others, it gets paved over and buried. And in still others, it's down there somewhere, daring you to find it.

Guroff explains her cuts:

It's just the usual rigor of cutting things that aren't necessary: book author's affiliation and publisher; the fact that you have to look sideways to see a road sign, etc. Some was strict condensation, e.g., "in the years after World War II" became "mid-century," which is much less evocative but also much shorter.

Looking back, it seems like a lot of what I cut was what gave a sort of rambling character to the essay that mimicked a ramble on the road — the corners and hills and litany of towns. A shame, but we didn't have time for a ramble!

Editors who tailor material to their readers will rarely disappoint them. Tailored publications will be eagerly awaited and read in their entirety — never just tossed aside like unwanted gifts.

Notes

1. Joann Byrd, "14 Hot Complaints," The Washington Post, 5 September 1993, sec. C, p. 6.
2. David Shaw, "Trust in Media Is on Decline," The Los Angeles Times, 31 March 1993, sec. A, p. 18.
3. David Shaw, "Media Set Agenda But Often Misjudge Public's Interests," The Los Angeles Times, 26 October 1992, sec. A, p. 16.
4. APME Reporting Writing and Editing Committee, "Line Editors Speak Out" (Associated Press Managing Editors, 1997), p. 22.
5. "Using Research to Support Media Decisions," SRDA Report, no. 2 (4 February 1990): p. 1.
6. J. William Click and Russell N. Baird, "Magazine Editing and Production" (Dubuque, Iowa: Wm. C. Brown Publishers, 1990), pp. 118–119.
7. Click and Baird, "Magazine," p. 121.
8. Steve Crosby, "Wanted: Editorial Board Volunteers," The Journal and Courier, 13 June 1993, sec. A, p. 10.

9. Anne M. Russell, "Power to the People," Folio:, 15 June 1994, p. 7.

10. Doug Underwood, "The Very Model of the Reader-Driven Newsroom?" Columbia Journalism Review, Nov./Dec. 1993, pp. 42–44.

11. "Civic Journalism: Six Case Studies," The Pew Center for Civic Journalism, *www.pewcenter.org/doingcj/pubs/cases/intro.html.*

12. Hodding Carter III, "Is Civic Journalism an Answer?" American Society of Newspaper Editors, December 1998, *www.asne.org/kiosk/editor/98.dec/carter1.htm.* (Excerpted from a speech delivered to the Public Journalism Conference, University of South Carolina, Columbia, S.C., October 1998).

13. Carter, "Is Civic Journalism an Answer?"

14. John Brady, "The Search for Mission Control," Folio:, 1 November 1993, p. 42.

15. Mary Crowley, Business Publishers Inc., internal memo, May 1993.

16. Click and Baird, "Magazine," pp. 62–63.

17. Mark Beach, "Editing Your Newsletter: How to Produce an Effective Publication Using Traditional Tools and Computers" (Portland, Ore.: Coast to Coast Books, 1988), p. 8.

18. A.C. Spectorsky, "13 Steps to Editing a Successful Magazine," Folio:, 1972.

19. Brady, 15 November 1993.

20. A.H. Maslow, "Toward a Psychology of Being" (New York: Van Nostrand Reinhold, 1968).

21. Meyer and Guay, "Writing Market-Driven Editorial."

22. John M. Wilson, "Pick Up the Pace!" Writer's Digest, November 1993, pp. 45–47.

Exercises

1. Pick a magazine you know well and write a mission statement for it. In your mission statement, be sure to include *the purpose or focus* of the publication; *the audience* for whom the publication is intended; and *what makes the publication different* from its competition.

2. Below is the text of a news release from a local company.

   a. Write a lead for each of the following three publications:

      Town Crier (daily newspaper) Business section: Reaches a majority of the business leaders in the area.

      Future Daze (monthly magazine): Readers come from a wide background and share an interest in advances in technology as well as in other futuristic trends. Many are fans of science fiction.

      Crime Prevention Monthly (biweekly newsletter): Subscribers are in top law-enforcement positions across the country and are key decision makers about new techniques and equipment.

   b. In which of the three publications would you run the shortest article based on this information? The longest?

For Immediate Release

Hometown Robotics Introduces Remote Mobile Investigator

Contact: Lil Krane
589-3213

Hometown Robotics today began production of the model RMI-1 Remote Mobile Investigator, company chairman Frank Barker announced.

"With the release of the RMI-1, Hometown Robotics moves law enforcement into the 21st Century," Barker said.

The RMI-1 is a remote-controlled robot designed to be used by police to investigate situations that are too dangerous for officers to investigate. The RMI-1 can climb stairs and has a mobile arm that can open doors and move materials that weigh up to 300 pounds. The RMI-1 also is equipped with high-intensity lights and a video camera, which transmits a picture to its remote operator.

Barker said the RMI-1 is the only device of its kind produced in the world. "The Remote Mobile Investigator will set the standard for a whole new way of doing police work," he said.

Base price of the RMI-1 is $100,000. Options include a shotgun and an X-ray machine, and the unit can be customized for SWAT operations.

3. Take a recent issue of a newspaper or magazine and categorize the articles in it according to the various tools discussed in this chapter: the news values, Maslow's hierarchy and Meyer's scale of importance.

4. Using the news values discussed in this chapter, rank these stories. They will be used in a general-circulation local newspaper that is the primary print source of news for its readers.

    Sun: St. Petersburg, Fla., is back in the record books, having just passed 800 sunny days in a row. The city also held the previous record for the most days when the sun shined.

    Interest: After the Federal Reserve raised interest rates earlier this week, local mortgage lenders followed suit and raised their rates to the highest levels in five years. Economists say the higher rates could hurt the economy if they result in fewer home purchases.

    Governor: Speaking at a luncheon on the other side of the state yesterday, the governor suffered a heart attack. He remains in critical condition today.

    Plane: A Boeing 757 had to abort its takeoff from the local airport yesterday after having engine trouble. Passengers were transferred to another plane that took off two hours later. The incident is the fourth instance of engine trouble in 757s across the country during the past two months.

    Crash: A truck overturned on the main route into town at 1 p.m. yesterday. Traffic was halted for an hour until it could be removed. The driver suffered minor injuries.

    Checks: A former member of the local City Council was arrested and charged with passing bad checks. Sam Sardellis served on the council during the early 1990s but lost his bid for reelection in 1994.

    Dance: A Russian dance troupe canceled its eagerly awaited U.S. tour after members received threats that they would be killed if they came to the United States.

    Power: About 3,000 local residents lost electricity after construction equipment cut a line yesterday. Power was restored after four hours.

    Quake: An earthquake in Japan has left at least 700 people dead and extensive damage to property.

    ATM Scam: A local ring of thieves has been posing as bank employees at automated teller machines. They tell customers they are there to demonstrate new features of the machines, then manage to get the customers' card numbers and PINs. At least five people have found their accounts emptied, and police warn that the thieves are still at work.

EDITING FOR THE WEB

Targeting Your Audience and Content

Tailoring your content is even more important on the Web than in print. A reader may well skip an irrelevant article in a magazine, newsletter or newspaper, but chances are that he or she will continue reading the publication. Not so on the Web: With a seemingly infinite number of choices, a reader jumps quickly to another site.

Author Mai-Lan Tomsen uses the phrase "killer content" to identify what Web site editors need to offer their audiences. Tomsen defines killer content as content so compelling that it hooks readers and keeps them coming back to the site.[1] As columnist Steve Outing notes:

> Compelling, original content that can be found nowhere else is what it's all about, then, if you want to attract loyalty among your online users. If you run a sports news site, you've got to have content — original columnists, exclusive athlete interviews, stats that no one else has, etc. — that makes people want to visit your site over and over again.[2]

Unfortunately, many publishers have created Web sites not because they've determined that their audience wants one, but just to stake a claim in cyber-space. More than one editor has been ordered to "Put the paper online." With newspapers losing readers and many online news sites facing tough times, it makes little sense to offer the same content in a harder-to-get package — especially when thousands of other competitors are doing exactly the same thing. Instead, newspaper publishers and other would-be Web publishers need to define a particular audience they want to reach, then design the site to reach that audience.

Of course, in order to do that, Web site editors need to know who their audiences are. As mentioned earlier, many Web sites use online surveys to identify their audiences. Some sites require readers to provide this information during an initial registration process. In addition, many sites place "cookies" on users' computers to learn what other sites their audience members are visiting. Arizona Central (*www.azcentral.com*) goes even further, encouraging its readers to "Help plan the future of Arizona's Home Page" by joining an advisory panel. Members are asked to review new features and participate in focus groups.

It's important that a Web team assess its site's strengths and resources when designing online content. When Publisher Jake Oliver began thinking about the online edition of the Afro-American newspapers, he had more than a hundred years of coverage of the black community at his disposal. So one of his first decisions was to create an online Black History Museum (*www.afroam.org/history/history.html*). The section offers features on the first black combat pilots in America; Jackie Robinson, the first black baseball player in the major leagues; black advertising from the 1920s and 1930s; reports from Afro correspondents

The Afro-American's Black
History Museum offers a rich
repository.

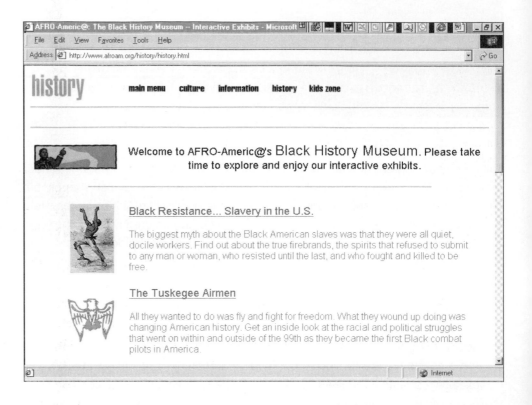

following black troops during World War II; and others that continue to draw lots of visitors to the site.

Another good example: Arizona Central offers visitors a searchable directory of more than 250 golf courses in the state; a guide to dining in the Phoenix area; customizable television listings; and much more.

Just as their print counterparts do, Web editors should use the information they gather on their audiences and strengths to draw up a mission statement. Because the Internet changes so rapidly, creating a mission statement for a Web site is more of a challenge. But a good mission statement with clearly defined goals lets a Web team assess the success of its site.

For instance, the online edition of the Tampa (Fla.) Tribune (*www.tampatrib.com*) includes five objectives in its mission statement:

- Extend the brand of the Tampa Tribune.
- Guard the Tribune's classified franchise.
- Solidify the Tribune's position as the leading information provider in this market.
- Strengthen the Tribune's role in forging connections in our community.
- Build a Web operation that produces profit for the company.[3]

The Web makes it easy to see what features are popular with readers and which are not. Visitor statistics provide definitive and immediate feedback. In June 2000, Salon magazine (*www.salon.com*) dropped several sections — and laid off the writers who had contributed to them — based on the low number of hits they had been receiving.[4]

Writing, Structure and Beyond

Editors typically have to do a fair amount of preparation to make articles work well on the Web. A long block of text that might be fine in a printed publication is a recipe for eyestrain — and loss of audience — online. Because reading on a screen is harder than reading on paper, editors should either intersperse informative subheads liberally throughout longer pieces or — even better — physically break long stories into shorter self-contained segments.

Reworking information will become even more crucial in the next few years, as more people access information with cell phones, e-book readers, small screens in cars and planes and a host of other nontraditional devices. Publishing consultant Vin Crosbie sees a need for three types of content to serve this wide variety of devices:

- Headlines and blurbs, for devices with tiny screens, like wireless Internet phones.

- Articles, for devices with screens big enough to comfortably read full stories, such as palm computers and phone/PDA combos, or tiny screens on airline seats.

- Publications, for devices like desktop and laptop computers, and wireless tablets that can present a publication in its full presentation format and content.[5]

Whenever possible, Web content should have a distinctive voice. While the style of journalism that's come to be known as "objective" still finds a home in print, Web visitors expect writers to have distinct voices. Compare some of the writing in the online edition of the Philadelphia Daily News (*www.dailynews.philly.com*) with what you find in most print newspapers. Follow that example, and don't edit the life out of Web writers' work — help them find their own voices to add life to their writing.

Editors also should look to add opportunities for reader interaction. In part that means providing ready access to writers. The old model worked like this: A writer spent days, weeks or months researching, wrote an article, it was published, and that was that. Maybe a letter to the editor would show up in print a few weeks later. The Web doesn't work that way. Readers expect to have immediate means to respond to what they read, to take part in a discussion that lives long after the story is published. Giving readers the chance to do that is a great way to build community.

Creating a community should be one of the key goals of an online editor. A good Web site is not as much of a thing or a publication as it is a place. In her account of starting the online version of the Washington Post, Mindy McAdams notes that journalists without much experience online tend "to think in terms of stories, news value, public service, and things that are good to read." But those with more online experience think more about other aspects, especially connections and communication among people.[6]

That's a profound change, and one that many online editors who worked for old media are finding hard to adapt to. But if there is one key to keeping visitors stopping by a site, this is it. And keeping visitors stopping by is vital to the health of any online publication. Unlike the old media (newspapers, television, radio), the Web does not deliver its content to the audience; the audience must come looking

WashingtonPost.com's Live Online has won awards for interactivity.

for content. And bringing a steady audience back to a site is the one sure way to build advertising revenue needed to make the site viable.

Creating community isn't a simple matter of adding a chat feature to a Web site. Community flourishes only on sites that understand what the word means: a place for likeminded people to meet and talk. Attempts at creating community are many and varied:

- Plastic (*www.plastic.com*) lets readers join in on discussions of the issues of the day.

- Discovery Channel Online (*www.discovery.com*) invites viewers to join expeditions — like the channel's underwater research trip to the Galapagos — via e-mail, and features viewers' own adventures.

- Many WashingtonPost.com writers hold live online discussions each week.

- Motorcycle Online (*www.motorcycle.com*) lets readers add their opinions to reviews.

Dan Froomkin, metro editor of WashingtonPost.com, suggests adding several other features to online news sites to increase the sense of community. Among them:

- Obituaries

- Birth announcements

- Traffic reports

- Health inspection databases

- School report cards

- Neighborhood profiles
- Local voices, local views
- Home sales, tax rates and mortgage rates[7]

Another way online editors can enhance the value of their sites is by offering links to related material. These may offer the reader a chance to learn more about a topic or to take follow-up action on the subject of an article. For example, an article about a shortage of volunteers for charitable organizations would be nicely complemented by a link to VolunteerMatch (*www.vounteermatch.org*), a Web site that helps "individuals nationwide find volunteer opportunities posted by local non-profit and public sector organizations."

In some cases, editors also are called upon to create or find multimedia enhancements for an article. The Web differs most markedly from other media in that it allows for the use of virtually any type of content: text, graphics, audio, video and animation. While complicated animations and video productions usually require experts to produce, editors often turn out graphics, charts, simple animations, and audio and video clips or at least conceptualize these elements and provide guidance for the specialists.

An editor who can sift through all these options and present the most appropriate content for an audience will be quite a successful tailor.

Notes

1. Mai-Lan Tomsen, "Killer Content: Strategies for Web Content and E-Commerce" (Reading, Mass.: Addison-Wesley, 2000).

2. Steve Outing, "It Takes Killer Content to Generate Killer Revenue," Editor & Publisher Interactive, 28 June 2000, *www.editorandpublisher.com/ephome/news/newshtm/stop/st062800.htm*.

3. Steve Outing, "Your Mission, If You Choose to Write It ... ," Editor & Publisher Interactive, 8 June 1998, *www.editorandpublisher.com/ephome/news/newshtm/stop/st060898.htm*.

4. Howard Kurtz, "The Reader's Choice," The Washington Post, 24 June 2000, sec. A, p. 23.

5. Steve Outing, "So Many News Devices, So Little Time," Editor & Publisher Interactive, 19 July 2000, *www.editorandpublisher.com/ephome/news/newshtm/stop/st071900.htm*.

6. Mindy McAdams, "Inventing an Online Newspaper," 5 October 1995, *www.sentex.net/~mmcadams/invent.html*.

7. Mark DeCotis, "Online Editors: Many Hats," Poynter.org, 27 November 2000, *www.poynter.org/centerpiece/112700.htm*.

Editor's Corner

Meredith Curtis, former assistant editor, *Congress Daily*

Are You Talking to Me? Making Content Fit Your Audience

Until recently, I worked for one the driest publications on earth. It's a daily newsletter that covers activity in Congress, and when I started there, right out of a college English program, I had a sinking feeling they had hired the wrong person. The lines of text seemed to drone on and on. I would try to read an issue and just couldn't get into the stories. The words would fade from my field of vision like when a TV screen blinks out. Although the publication certainly has its audience, when I started there I just wasn't it. In time, however, I came to appreciate and even enjoy the stories.

Unlike editors, readers don't have the luxury of time and they're not paid to read, so they shouldn't have to work to maintain interest in what you write. It is vital to know your readers and keep them in mind when selecting content and deciding how to present it.

News organizations do not simply guess what their readers need and want to know. They often use focus groups, polling and surveys to fine-tune what and how information should be presented. The readers of Congress Daily are members of Congress, their staff, lobbyists and government officials, and it's easy to figure out what they want from the publication. They use Congress Daily to follow legislation and the political maneuvering surrounding legislation so they can decide the best plan of action to meet their goals. (Sometimes their goal is to keep anything from being done, but that's another matter.) Even though what Congress Daily readers want is fairly obvious, editors still send out surveys to gauge the popularity of the columns and the quality of the coverage. Such feedback helps the editors determine what issues get priority and how information is tailored.

The kind of language used in stories is determined by the audience — an element not usually noticed unless it is crafted poorly. The readers of Congress Daily want to quickly scan content for information useful to them, so we use language that is clear and direct. Flowery words and elaborate sentence structure are taboo. For instance, we always use the word "physician" instead of "doctor" in stories about health care. Many of our readers have Ph.D.s and, technically, are doctors, but I'm sure most of them couldn't give you CPR to save their own lives. One time, another editor and I let slip a feature-ish lead that compared a hearing by the Senate Banking Committee to Alice in Wonderland. We were called into the Box — the editor-in-chief's office — for a little chat about that one.

It is crucial to know your audience's biases and general orientations. In an ideal world, good journalism is without bias. Unfortunately, editors sometimes pander to their audiences in order to boost readership, sacrificing critical coverage to keep people happy. There are always two or more sides to every story. But presenting a side that has a valid point but which is anathema to a segment of your readership can be a problem for editors.

Congress Daily is in a unique position, however. One of the reasons it is so boring to read is that its editors are vigilant about avoiding any hint of bias. Congress Daily readers vary from Christian Coalition true believers to Greenpeace advocates, and are of nearly every political stripe. So, it's easy for us to get into trouble. For instance, Congress Daily editors often use the phrase "so-called" when referring to legislation by a common catch phrase. A Congress Daily editor once used the expression referring to a bill concerning a particular abortion procedure, calling it the "so-called partial birth abortion bill." The next day we heard from an anti-abortion rights activist who was sure the expression was meant to be dismissive of the effort to ban the procedure.

No audience is completely homogeneous and even editors who feel they have a solid understanding of their readership are often surprised. Although Congress Daily is serious and dry, each issue ends with a funny "Final Word." Of course, everyone loves a joke, but we were really surprised at the response we received when one Final Word made a pun on a song by the Grateful Dead. The song's title comes from the refrain, "Driving that train, high on cocaine, Casey Jones you better watch your speed." But we identified it as "Driving that Train" rather than the true title, "Casey Jones." More of our stuffed shirt audience called to complain about that song title than for any other reason I can remember. Go figure. I suppose the lesson is that there is always something else to learn about your audience.

Verbosity and Clarity

A news release from the FDA carried this important notice:

The FDA's Radiofrequency Micronucleus Working Group holds a meeting to discuss the types of studies needed to further investigate and refine prior reports of micronucleus formation caused by radiofrequency exposure.

Washington Post writer Gene Weingarten recounted his efforts to decipher the passage in a hilarious column. After a number of experts — including the editor of the Merriam-Webster Unabridged Dictionary — were unable to decode the passage, Weingarten ultimately ended up attending the meeting to figure it out. Afterward, he still didn't know what it meant.[1]

While such constructions are good for a chuckle, they also point out a serious problem. Far too often, writers use jargon or verbosity to do the job, wasting valuable time and space and confusing the reader. In this Grammar School, we look at common problems of verbosity and lack of clarity.

Using Too Many Words

Examples of writers using more words than are necessary are common. For example, a news release announced that a speech would be held "at the Friday morning Democratic breakfast from 7:30 to 9 a.m. Friday."

Let's see now: The writer has told us *twice* what day the speech will be given and has told us *three times* that it will be given in the morning (by using the words *morning, breakfast* and *a.m.*). While such dedication to making sure that the reader gets the message seems to deserve recognition, chances are this revision would have worked just as well: "at the Democratic breakfast from 7:30 to 9 Friday." The revision uses 25 percent fewer words than the original. Consistently cutting such verbosity leaves more room for needed information.

Another example manages not only to repeat information in two subsequent paragraphs but also to dish up a stylistic inconsistency in the process. The first sentence reads in part:

GUM (pronounced "goom," it is an acronym for the Russian words meaning state department store) is attempting a makeover.

Second sentence:

When GUM — the Russian acronym for "State Department Store" — was built, "it was the biggest trade building in the world," Samonov said.

One explanation of what GUM means would be enough, presuming that the writer could determine whether "state department store" should be capitalized and put in quotations.

Excess words often hide in tighter spots where they can escape all but the most careful scrutiny. Redundant phrases are one typical example. For instance, look at this sentence:

After the Triple-A farm club totally dominated the season, team owners announced plans to build a new stadium.

At first glance, that looks fine. But the sentence contains three redundancies. Here it is again, without them:

After the Triple-A club dominated the season, team owners announced plans to build a stadium.

The difference is three words. That might not seem like much, but it's about a 20 percent reduction.

Other examples crop up all over the place. Some common ones:

ATM machine (the M stands for machine)

burst open

complete stop

continue on

Easter Sunday

HIV virus (the V stands for virus)

hot-water heater

Jewish rabbi

new discovery

newborn baby

personal opinion

PIN number (the N stands for number)

pizza pie

preheat

tuna fish

Dozens of other entries also merit careful attention. "Working with Words: A Handbook for Media Writers and Editors" contains an excellent list of many of them.

Nominalizations also pose problems. A nominalization is turning a verb or an adjective into a noun:

She tendered her resignation May 16.

can easily be rewritten as

She resigned May 16.

and

The police conducted an investigation into the matter.

The police investigated the matter.

Other words to watch for are adjectives and adverbs that add nothing to a sentence. They include *little* (as in "a little warm"), *pretty* ("pretty cold"), *rather, very, few, some, a lot* and *really.* These are the words Strunk and White in "The Elements of Style" call "the leeches that infest the pond of prose, sucking the blood of words."[2]

Using Long Words and Phrases

Another type of verbosity occurs when long words are sent to do the work of their shorter relatives. For example,

The meeting commenced at 10 a.m.

can just as easily be changed to

The meeting began at 10 a.m.

In another example, a newsletter ran this sentence:

Our analysis produced a finding that indicates that the engineers have a tendency to be too heavily dependent upon results that are not applicable to the whole group.

Readers undoubtedly would have had fewer problems with this revision:

We found that the engineers depend too heavily on results that don't apply to the whole group.

Two little words that can add up to a lot of verbosity are *do* and *be.* For example:

Women do like cars that have a reputation for reliability.

In the next section, we will be explaining four approaches to correcting the problem.

In the first sentence, *do* can be cut; in the second, *be* and the *-ing* from *explaining* can be cut. Those cuts may not seem to make much of a difference, but multiply them 10 or 20 times and they sure *do.*

Some words contain shorter words hidden within them. For example, *encourage* can be shortened to *urge* and *precipitate* to *rain.* Can you find the "kangaroo words" in *myself, regulate, illuminated, deliberate* and *destruction?* (The answers: *me, rule, lit, debate* and *ruin.*)

Clarity

Wordiness is only half of the problem in making copy easy to read. As the FDA example that started this section demonstrates, no matter how many words you cut from some copy, it still is going to make no sense to most readers.

That kind of murky prose seems to breed best in government and corporate documents, oozing onto paper like a mutant strain of virus. Unfortunately, examples often are found in the print media, too, as this sentence from a newsletter shows:

One concern expressed in many comments submitted on the Part 503 rule was that source identification and control were going to be thorny issues, because in some cases the extent to which molybdenum is added to a product is even proprietary information.

That 42-word sentence came in the middle of a four-sentence paragraph. The average sentence length in the paragraph was more than 35 words.

Such writing hinders clear communication. Even much simpler writing poses a problem for many readers. A national survey conducted in 1992 found that the majority of adults cannot comprehend or use information of the sort routinely found in the print media. For example, fewer than 4 percent of those surveyed could interpret the phrase "recently won mandate" in a magazine article about the selection of a judge.[3]

Editing Tips

Editors have few options when confronted with the worst cases of unclear writing. Trying to make the words make sense, editors may not end up with the intended meaning — making matters worse. The only hope is to go back to the writers and diplomatically ask that unclear passages be rewritten so that "even an editor" can understand them.

Moderately fuzzy writing often can be aided by good editing, though. The following suggestions can help.

Keep Subjects Close to Verbs.   One of the most common causes of confusion is leaving a gap between the subject and the verb in a sentence. Some writers seem engaged in a competition to see how many words they can cram in between subject and verb, as this newspaper lead shows:

Developers of a 1,445-acre office park proposed for the Brandy Station Battlefield near Culpeper, Va. — where the Civil War's largest cavalry battle was fought — have filed for bankruptcy, placing the controversial development in doubt but offering hope that Civil War buffs may be able to preserve part of the site.

It's easy enough to find the subject — the first word, *Developers* — but then it's a 24-word stretch to the verb, *have filed*. In the interim, other nouns and verb forms flash by the reader — *park, Battlefield, Culpeper, Va., battle, proposed, was fought* — causing potential confusion about what the subject and verb are. At a minimum, an editor should ease that confusion by simplifying the sentence:

> Trying to make the words make sense, editors may not end up with the intended meaning — making matters worse.

A Virginia developer's bankruptcy filing places in doubt the controversial develop-ment of an office park on the site of the largest cavalry battle in the Civil War.

Use Short Sentences.   The battlefield lead also illustrates another common obstacle to clear communication: sentence overload. The original lead is 51 words long. Lengthy sentences often indicate that writers have not worked hard enough to determine the most important part of the messages. With their profusion of phrases and clutter of clauses, long sentences typically leave the reader wonder-ing what the point is. Editors should try to break long sentences into more easily digestible nuggets, preferably each containing one idea.

Try breaking up this sentence that ran in a feature article:

While his interest in mechanics goes back to when he was a boy fixing up old cars, in Houston where he grew up, and then continued through his years in the oil patch and while operating a machine shop in Houston before the oil bust, it wasn't until about five years ago that he became interested in antique engines, and that was quite by accident.

Ready with your revision? Here's one way it could be handled:

His interest in mechanics began as a boy fixing up old cars in Houston. It contin-ued through his years in the oil patch and while operating a machine shop in Houston before the oil bust. Only about five years ago, however, did he become interested in antique engines — by accident.

Not only is this revision easier to follow than the original, it also is almost 20 per-cent shorter: 50 words versus 65.

Use Common Words.   Writers often tend to use the jargon and specialized language of their companies or their sources. For example, catalog copy describes a pad used in bicycle shorts as being "a solid viscoelastic polymer." It's doubtful that many nonscientists would know what that means. If a word or phrase doesn't make sense to an editor, it won't make sense to the reader, either. It's the editor — not the writer — who will get the blame. (Of course, in this case it's likely that the advertising agency copy editor consciously chose the phrase to avoid admit-ting that the pad was simply *plastic*.)

If you're forced to use specialized language or concepts that likely will be diffi-cult for the average reader to understand, take the time to translate or explain. Even The Wall Street Journal, which has a better-educated audience than most publica-tions, defines terms like "gross national product" each time they appear in print.

Use Concrete Rather Than Abstract Words and Ideas.   Two reporters covering the earthquake that shook San Francisco during Game 5 of the 1989 World Series filed these accounts of the same sensation:

1. The first sign of trouble was some slight shaking.

2. ... just moments ago [Candlestick Park] was shaking as if the entire stadium were on a wagon being wheeled over cobblestone.

Not only is the second passage more vivid, but it also sounds as if "slight shaking" doesn't convey the right idea. While it uses more words than the first passage, every word carries its weight.

Use Precise Rather Than Relative Language.   A student in a feature writing class turned in a profile article that described his subject as "a short man." The professor teaching the feature writing class told the student that "short" was not a good word to use because it is too subjective. The student nodded attentively and went off to revise his paper. When he handed it back, the subject was described as "a tall man."

If you're 5 feet tall, you might consider a 5-foot-6-inch person tall. If you're 7 feet tall, however, that person is surely short. Similar problems occur with references to age (Is 25 young? 30? 40?); wealth (Just how much does someone have to make to be considered middle class?); and general measurement (How many is several?). As with other problems, imprecise language requires editors to consult with writers. Good guesses won't do.

Avoid Clichés Like the Plague.   One often-seen example of vague writing is the cliché. A cliché is an expression that started life as a sparkling way of making a point. Over time, though, clichés are used so often that they become threadbare and meaningless: as smooth as silk, as dark as night, as big as all outdoors, ad nauseam.

Also watch for clobbered clichés and mixed metaphors. A story said that members of a city council "were wrestling with a hornet's nest." That doesn't sound very intelligent. A sports story described a victory as "a tuneup for the meat grinder of Howard University's schedule." Readers could only wonder how often other universities have their meat grinders tuned up.

Like general words, clichés should be replaced with specifics, and the writers are the best people to make such changes.

> Over time, clichés are used so often that they become threadbare and meaningless.

Watch for Writing That Can Be Read More Than One Way.   In a classic episode of "Saturday Night Live," workers in a nuclear power plant encounter a potential meltdown. They're given this advice: "You can't put too much water in the core of the reactor." One worker takes that to mean that they need to be careful not to put an excessive amount of water in the core; the other understands it to mean that no amount of water is too much. Ultimately, the confusion leads to a meltdown.

While the point of a piece of writing may be obvious to the writer, it often can mean something completely different to the reader. Editors have to scrutinize every piece of copy to determine if it can be read more than one way — and, if it can, to rewrite it.

Here's an example from an article about a natural foods store:

A typical supermarket will carry about 8,000 products from nationally known brands, while Fresh Fields has between 200 and 300 products.

Is that 200 to 300 total products, or 200 to 300 products from nationally known brands? Readers only can guess because the editor didn't ask the writer to clarify the sentence.

Avoid *It Is/There Are* Constructions.   Sentences that begin with *it is* or *there are* are passive and need lots of words to make a point. In most cases, those opening words can be cut and a few other edits made to add vigor to a sentence. Take this example:

There are frequent occasions when students visit the campus health clinic to pursue answers to questions regarding sexually transmitted diseases.

And the rewrite:

Students frequently visit the campus health center for information about sexually transmitted diseases.

Can't My Computer Handle This?

If computers can guide the space shuttle, can't they fix your grammatical problems? For several years, word-processing programs have included grammar checks that promise to do just that. But as Paula LaRocque recounted in a column in Quill, that promise has not quite been fulfilled.

LaRocque commended her grammar checker for picking up long sequences of noun modifiers and for pointing out *that/which* problems. But overall, she noted, "grammar checkers can be downright hazardous."

For example, when LaRocque asked her software to check the sentence "How much of the following sentence do you understand?" the program suggested she change *do* to *does.* In another case, it recommended she change the word *lightning* to *lightening* in the phrase "lightning war." Perhaps most amusingly — and annoyingly — the program in some cases suggested changes that it later flagged as incorrect. As LaRocque concluded, "Electronic intelligence can process information like a house afire, but it still can't *think*."[4]

Notes

1.   Gene Weingarten, "Danger! Neoplasms!" The Washington Post Magazine, 10 Sept. 2000, pp. 5, 8.
2.   William Strunk Jr. and E.B. White, "The Elements of Style" (New York: Macmillan, 1972), p. 65.
3.   U.S. Department of Education, National Center for Education Statistics, "National Adult Literacy Survey," as reported in The Washington Post, 9 Sept. 1993, sec. A, p. 15.
4.   Paula LaRocque, "Does Your Computer Really Know Grammar? You Be the Judge," Quill, June 1999, p. 52.

Exercise

Correct all spelling, punctuation and style errors in the following article. Also edit to improve clarity and eliminate verbosity.

Okay, you've graduated from college and you have your foot in the door of your first job interview. Are you nervous? You realize that the previous year represented both the worst job market for new graduates in the last two decades and a 56 % drop from the number of college graduates hired five years ago, according to a North Western University study. Are you nervous yet? After coming to the same realization that college graduates across the country have — that it won't be easy to get the first job right out of school — how cna you better yourself to ace that interview and get that dream job.

"You should do your homework," says Alice Feeney, director of Ryan State University's Career Placement center. "Don't walk into an interview wihtout knowledge of the company your seeking employment with." Entering an interview with solid knowledge makes you come across as intelligent and perceptive, and a person who will fit in well with others in the company.

Likewise, Feeney advises arriving at the interview with a few questions of your own. If you don't ask questions of your own, you run the risk of being percieved by the interviewer or interviewers as a person who is uninterested.

At all costs, Feeney says, resist the temptation to talk about salary figures. You're in a much better position to dicuss this matter after the firm has made you a job offer. To state your desire for a particular job salary may result in your being judged by your price tag and not your credentials, so avoid questions regarding salary all together.

Try to remain positive in the face of an interviewers'loaded questions, Feeney adds. Whenever possible talk about opporutnities and successes rather than talking about limitations and failures. Admit only to weaknesses and mistakes that are trivial and inconsequential.

In addition, Feeney says, it's important to refrain from speaking critically of your former teachers, employers, and institutions of learning. To do so only reflects upon you as a trouble maker. Look for positive things and accentuate them.

It's important to be careful with how you close an interview, Feeney suggests. Almost as important as the first impression you make is the way you leave an interview. be cautious to end the interview on a positive note, not a negative one. Don't drag a finished interview on for several more minutes after it is over, but be sure to thank the interviewer for his or her time and effort and express your gradiitude for the opporutnity.

After the interview, there's still one critical step. "Failing to follow-up an interview with a personal note is the one oversight that can cost you a job," according to Feeney. So the next day put a follow-up thank you note in the mail. Include in it your interest in the job once again, recap the strengths you offer and how they apply to the new infomration you learned about the comany, and request to meet again at their convenience.

Then you can sit back and relax — and, with luck, wait for the phone to ring.

Looking for Holes and Other Problems

In mid-2000, at the height of the controversy over use of Napster music file-sharing software, digital rights management company Reciprocal issued a news release. The release began:

> In a revealing landmark study released today by Reciprocal™, Inc., the global leader in digital rights management (DRM) transaction services, online file sharing was deemed the likely cause for a steady two-year decline of college market album sales.
>
> The study, conducted by VNU Entertainment Marketing Solutions, a sister company of SoundScan, concluded that while overall retail sales steadily increased between January 1997 and March 2000, album sales in more than 9,000 SoundScan reporting retail stores within a 5-mile radius of more than 3,000 colleges declined by 4% over the last two years. Stores near the 67 schools that had banned Napster by late February showed a greater sales decline of 7% over the past two years.

The release was quoted in many news reports that cited the figures as proof that college students were illegally downloading music from the Internet rather than buying compact discs.

There was just one problem with that story — all right, maybe four or five problems:

- During that same time period, large retailers such as Wal-Mart had begun selling popular CDs at prices far lower than most music stores charged. At least some cost-conscious students probably switched to the larger stores.

- Web sites such as Amazon.com and CDNow.com had also gained immense popularity with college students during that period, offering low prices, wide selections and regular promotions.

- With CD prices on the rise, many students had begun buying used CDs instead of new ones.

- The price of computer CD burners had dropped to less than $200 and blank CDs were being virtually given away, a combination that led at least a few students to make copies of their friends' discs.

- One last little point: Napster became available only in May 1999, and most college students had not heard of it until around the time the study results were released.[1]

In short, the release — and the news reports based on it — didn't prove anything.

Readers don't have to look far to find many other examples of copy that leaves out important information or doesn't make sense. While the copy may have been carefully selected for its target audience, it suffers from one or more problems that should have been corrected by an editor before the copy was printed.

This chapter and the next one deal with these big editing problems. To avoid them, editors read copy as detached observers, asking questions that an intelligent but uninformed reader would ask. When editors notice problems in content, they have to find solutions or return the copy to the writer, time permitting.

The following list includes the most common major errors that an editor is likely to encounter. The list is, unfortunately, by no means exhaustive.

Buried Leads.   Writers often bury the most interesting or important aspect deep in the bowels of the copy. Here's an example from an article on the annual Marine Corps Marathon in Washington, D.C.:

Yesterday, for the 17th consecutive year, hundreds of Marines and thousands of untested and unknown marathon runners circled Washington's monuments in search of nothing more than personal glory.

That lead is so dull that I can't imagine even the writer being interested in it. In the following paragraphs, however, she relates that the race was dramatic, with a professional runner from the Mexican Navy winning the traditionally amateur event, and his three team members all placing in the top 11. In addition, there is a nice twist in Navy runners winning the Marine Marathon. In writing the headline, the editor wisely focused on this information:

Mexican Navy Runners Sail in Marine Marathon

When readers reached the lead, they had to wonder whether the headline belonged on the story it accompanied. For the sake of cohesiveness — and to help attract readers — the editor should have rewritten the lead or asked the writer to do so.

Leads can mislead in several ways. The most common lead problem is "underselling."

Misleading Leads.   Leads can mislead in several ways. The most common lead problem is "underselling." For example, the lead on an article dealing with occupational safety read:

Illiteracy and lack of training in the proper use of pesticides have contributed to worker poisoning in developing countries, researchers said last week at the National Council for International Health Conference in Washington, D.C.

Aside from being wordy, the lead doesn't seem bad. But four sentences later, the story notes that "more than 50 percent [of agricultural workers] have been or will be poisoned at least once in their lifetimes." That's a staggering figure — much more dramatic than the vague "worker poisoning" mentioned in the lead. A more compelling lead would read:

One of every two agricultural workers in developing countries is poisoned because of illiteracy or lack of training in the proper use of pesticides, researchers said last week at the National Council for International Health Conference in Washington, D.C.

In another case, on the day before the 2000 Tour de France bicycle race ended, a major newspaper ran an article with this lead:

One day from the finish line, Lance Armstrong stands poised to win his second consecutive Tour de France and join Greg LeMond as the only American to triumph more than once.

While the lead was true, it also understated the accomplishment of both riders: No other American had ever won the grueling race even once.

In contrast to underselling, other leads promise more than they can deliver. In these leads, writers blow details and events out of proportion. For example, the lead of a newsletter article read:

Most states are beginning to take a pro-active role in developing effective programs to help pregnant women with alcohol and drug problems, the National Governors' Association says.

Most editors would agree that "most" is a vague phrase. But it seems reasonable to expect that "most states" would include at least 26 of the 50 states in the United States. Unfortunately, that's not what the writer was thinking, as the article continued:

NGA's new report ... examines the experiences of 10 states with innovative programs to help substance-abusing women and their children.

Even if all 10 of the states surveyed were developing such programs, that's not "most states."

A third problem occurs when leads don't indicate the scope of an article. For example, the lead of an article on hospital patient relations said that patient satisfaction surveys and other means of comparing quality and costs would be necessary in any universal health plan. Two pages later, the article switched to an in-depth discussion of efforts to control the quality of food service and housekeeping vendors — a related topic, to be sure, but one the reader hadn't been prepared to expect. The lead should have included both ideas.

Mismatches.   This term refers to a variety of problems in which parts of an article are not treated similarly. One example is mixing numbers and percentages, as in this passage:

There are an estimated 2 million to 3 million lesbians in the United States — far fewer than the approximately 5 percent of the population represented by gay men.

For a reader to make sense of the comparison, the reader must (a) know the male population of the United States and (b) be able to figure what 5 percent of that figure is. That's a lot of work, and most readers simply can't or won't do it.

Lack of Balance.   In a section on "Fairness," The Washington Post Deskbook on Style notes: "No story is fair if it omits facts of major importance or significance. Fairness includes completeness." In other words, a good article must be *balanced.* That's a good standard for all media work, not only in news work, but also in public relations writing, where balanced copy is preferred over one-sided copy that readers may easily dismiss.

Unfortunately, a great deal of copy does not live up to this standard. The most common problem is providing the reader with only a limited perspective. That is not surprising in dealing with advertising copy. The objective of such copy is, after all, to cast one's company, products or services in the most favorable light. So no one is surprised when, for example, advertising copy for an alkaline battery notes that "No other battery outlasts it" — but fails to mention the fact that all alkaline batteries have the *same* life span.

Such omissions are far more troublesome when they occur in a news report, particularly when the report includes only one side of a story. *Every* story has multiple sides to it, and editors always should verify that each side has been given the opportunity to be heard. If a person or organization is accused of wrongdoing, that person or organization deserves the right to reply to the accusation. If an advocate of a cause discusses the issue in a news article, opponents of that cause should also have the opportunity to discuss the issue.

A few words of warning: First, many stories have more than two sides, but few editors consider all of them. Writers often frame questions as "this-or-that" oppositions; for instance, "Should drugs be legalized or should users be given stiff prison sentences?" Giving advocates from both positions a chance to be heard does not provide true balance, however, because many people might give higher priority to education and other preventive measures. Without their input, the story cannot be balanced.

Second, in order to be fair, a writer must make an effort to give all sides the opportunity to be heard. If a writer spends virtually all available time listening to advocates of an action but makes only a futile last-minute effort to get in touch with opponents, the story will not be balanced. In most cases, it is better to delay publication than to publish unbalanced material.

Third, the requirement to be balanced is not the same as requiring equal time or space for all sides; such false balance can greatly distort the truth. I found this problem often while I was researching news coverage of the feminist movement. For example, hundreds of feminists would gather for a harmonious meeting;

across the street, a few opponents would gather to protest loudly. In a misguided effort to "balance" the story, the writer gave both sides the same amount of coverage, which led readers to think they were equally strong. Worse yet, the protesters often were featured in the lead of the story because of the tendency of many news writers to play up conflict.

Fourth, in some cases outspoken critics on one side of an issue have no credentials, and readers who are not experts in the field won't know that unless they are told. In the 1990s, for example, environmentalists and others were pushing to eliminate manufactured sources of chlorine because of its harmful effects on the ozone layer. Opponents of the ban got plenty of air time and print space for their argument that such efforts were misguided because volcanic eruptions and other natural phenomena pumped far more chlorine into the stratosphere — an argument that had no scientific basis.[2]

Source Bias.   Everyone who provides information has a reason for doing so, and that reason typically has to do with the source's own interest, rather than the public's interest. In an article in The New Republic, Katherine Dunn wrote:

> ... people have always been willing to lie as well as to die for what they believe in. ... But that doesn't mean we have to swallow what they're feeding us. The press can refuse to print what they tell us unless it's verified. Ask real questions — Where did that number come from? Who did this study? How was that information collected? What kind of credibility does that report deserve? Who says so? And who disagrees? And why?[3]

Checking source bias requires digging by writers or editors, but it's digging that must be done. When it isn't, the result is an incomplete picture for the reader.

Source bias presents a special problem for any publication that publishes articles by freelance writers. Some outside writers have no qualms about concealing their ties to a cause, business or organization that may make them biased. For example, an article citing a report on cancer risks noted that the public shouldn't be concerned with the "minor cancer risks" of nuclear power. Readers were not told that one of the report's three authors had worked as a consultant for the public relations arm of the nuclear power industry.[4] In another case, a former U.S. trade representative wrote an opinion piece promoting the North American Free Trade Agreement. He did not let the publication know that his firm was receiving $25,000 to represent a group of Mexican businesses that would benefit from the agreement — nor did the editors bother to check for such conflicts.[5]

Identifying source affiliations can be tough for editors. At the very least, an editor always should ask writers if they have any associations that could be perceived as conflicts.

Unanswered Questions.   Not all omissions undermine the honesty of a piece of copy; sometimes, an omission simply leaves a reader with unanswered questions. For example, the lead of a newsletter article reported that a tornado was "the third disaster of the year" at a center for juvenile offenders. Nowhere in the story were the other two disasters mentioned. In another case, a three-page, full-color ad offering a free videotape left out one vital piece of information: how to get the

Everyone who provides information has a reason for doing so, and that reason typically has to do with the source's own interest, rather than the public's interest.

Anonymous Sources

It only makes sense that for readers to judge the credibility of sources, they must know who the sources are. Unfortunately, it's not uncommon to come across a passage like the following:

Sources said the president is likely to change his position in light of the new information. One administration official said that it had made the president "go back to square one and reconsider." But a senior adviser disagreed with that assessment.

"It's not just the credibility of one story, or one quote," former Washington Post Ombudsman Joann Byrd wrote in a memo to staffers. She continued:

When the paper appears to be casual in granting confidentiality, it allows readers to wonder what standards are applied in this controversial practice, and it spreads the expectation among sources and potential sources that they can speak from behind a veil only because they want to.

To avoid anonymity overload, some publications have specific policies on the use of unnamed sources. The following guidelines are based on a policy developed for The Cincinnati Enquirer.

1. Writers should make legitimate efforts to get all sources on the record. Only when those efforts have been exhausted will the use of anonymous sources be permitted.

2. Writers should independently verify the identities of all sources and, if requested, disclose them to the editor or the publication's attorney.

3. Using misleading information about the identity of a source is prohibited. Examples include using the word "sources" when there is only one source, and allowing a source to lie on the record while providing contrary information for anonymous attribution.

4. Information from an anonymous source should be verified independently unless an individual is the only person with certain information or the source's integrity is unassailable.

5. Anonymous sources should be quoted only when the information they provide is factual and important to an article. They should not be quoted on matters of opinion.

6. Readers should be told why the identity of a source is being withheld, and they should be given enough information about the source to establish the source's authority to speak on the subject.

Editors also need to keep in mind that there's a big difference between including an anonymous source in an article and building an article around anonymous sources. Rarely will an article based entirely on anonymous sources pass muster with most editors *or* readers.

video. A line from yet another article leaves the reader wondering whether there could even be an answer to the obvious question it poses: "Half of all pregnancies in the United States result from unprotected sex or contraceptive failure." How else could someone get pregnant?

Another common problem is assuming that "everybody knows" all the background and details of topics under discussion. Former Washington Post Ombudsman Joann Byrd listed this as a "hot complaint" from readers. They protest, she wrote, that

> Journalists often write stories as if the communications stopped with their editors. Never mind that readers haven't been in on the background and may not be able to intuit that this installment never meant to cover more than a sliver of the larger subject.[6]

While news articles always should lead with the latest information, those articles also should include background for readers who haven't been following the story daily.

Good editors remember that no matter what the publication — from the most general newspaper to the most specialized newsletter — there are always new readers who don't know everything yet. A weekly community newspaper distributed in my neighborhood nearly always includes a Page One article about local "covenant regulations." Never do the articles explain what covenant regulations are, so new members of the community can only be puzzled by the articles rather than informed by them. (A daily newspaper owned by the same publisher ran this quote about covenants: "In general, people do not know what covenants are all about." How surprising!)

In some cases, the information that would answer readers' questions is included in the copy — but it is buried. For instance, the lead of a newspaper article focused on a vote to increase the state sales tax in Michigan by 50 percent. Because the article was published hundreds of miles away, most readers undoubtedly wondered: What is the current sales tax in Michigan? The answer was in the article, but readers had to wade through more than a foot of copy before finding out what the old rate was and what the new rate would be. It should be obvious that the tax rate is a crucial piece of information in this story, especially since state sales taxes span a wide range — from 0 to more than 8 percent. A good editor would have pulled the tax rate to the top of the article.

Failing to Show Relevance.   An even better editor would have taken the tax rate in the previous article and computed how much the change would cost the average Michigan resident. Doing that would accomplish one of the most important tasks that an editor can do: Tell readers why they should care. To accomplish this goal, some editors insist that news articles have **implication leads** — that is, leads that tell the readers what the copy means to them.

For example, the lead of an article in a publication for physicians noted that physician office labs and testing facilities would be required to start conducting proficiency tests in three months. Later in the article, physicians were warned that they should start planning for the testing well before the deadline, or they could face problems. *That's* the news that belongs in the lead. Arriving at that lead takes more work, but doing that work makes the difference between copy that's merely interesting and copy that's essential.

When the lead of an article does not include information that directly affects the reader, it should be followed by a **nut graf,** a sentence or paragraph that tells the reader why an article is being run. For example, a sports story reached editors at The Baltimore Sun with this lead:

The uncertainties of arbitration have influenced the Orioles to not offer contracts for the next season to relief pitchers Gregg Olson and Todd Frohwirth.

The editors decided that they had better add perspective on what those moves meant and added this nut graf:

By not tendering contracts by the midnight deadline last night, the Orioles allowed the players to become free agents. But the Orioles can continue to negotiate with both and appear determined to re-sign Olson.

Some newspaper editors believe that letting readers know how the news affects them and what they can do about it is vital to a paper's survival. Davis Merritt Jr., former executive editor of the Wichita Eagle, discussed his paper's adoption of this philosophy in a published interview:

> You don't just dump bad news on the reader; you talk about why it's there ... and what can be done about it. ... It's an attempt to engage people in deciding about their own future — and for newspapers to be seen as a vehicle that empowers them to do something, that facilitates doing something.[7]

Including Irrelevant Information. The Washington Post Deskbook on Style also notes: "No story is fair if it includes essentially irrelevant information at the expense of significant facts." To a large degree, this matter is an ethical one, with editors needing to determine when it is proper to include certain information and when it might not be. Irrelevant information often comes in the form of unrelated information about events in a person's past. For instance, a newspaper article about a consulting pathologist's report on the death of David Koresh in Waco, Texas, included a reference to an unrelated legal matter the pathologist had just settled after 10 years of litigation. The reference could have been construed to cast doubt on the pathologist's competence. In a letter to the editor, the pathologist wondered why that reference was included — and included a long list of credentials that were far more relevant to his competence.

Including Contradictory Information. The headline of an article read "Quintet makes stop on long road." But the article referred to "the Eric Mintel Quartet." Such inconsistencies are not uncommon — but are highly confusing to readers.

Cause and Effect Problems. Writers sometimes mistake correlation — events happening at the same time — for causation — one event that causes

---

Some newspaper editors believe that letting readers know how the news affects them and what they can do about it is vital to a paper's survival.

another. So, for instance, if a car crashes during a heavy rainstorm, a reporter might assume that the storm caused the crash. Editors must watch for such assumptions and remove them if they are not supported by facts.

Inappropriate cause and effect is often easy to spot. For example, an article quoted a college professor talking about a new faculty handbook:

He said the handbook is "anti-faculty" because it states that professors must hold office hours and turn in students' grades on time.

An alert editor would question why the professor would label such traditional requirements "anti-faculty." In fact, the professor had done nothing of the sort. What he told the reporter was that he considered the handbook, which required professors to hold office hours and turn in grades on time, to be disrespectful *because* professors at the school already did those things. That's why the professor called the handbook "anti-faculty." As you can see, the reporter's interpretation was far different from the professor's message.

Writers also sometimes seem to forget the rules that govern cause and effect. Consider, for instance, this copy from an advertisement for a credit card:

Only Chevy Chase gives you a fixed rate of 11.9% APR for one year. Plus our new CashRewards program pays you 1% cash back on your purchases, so you may never have to pay another annual fee.

Or, stated more simply:

Because *the APR is 11.9%,* and *you get a 1% rebate,* therefore *you may never have to pay another annual fee.*

That doesn't make sense. Elsewhere in the ad, it is stated that the annual fee is waived with minimum usage; it has nothing to do with the APR or the rebate. So the writer should have used an "and" rather than "so" in the copy:

Only Chevy Chase gives you a fixed rate of 11.9% APR for one year. Plus our new CashRewards program pays you 1% cash back on your purchases, and you may never have to pay another annual fee.

Lack of "the Big Picture."   Perhaps the most serious criticism that can be levied against news reports of all types is that they too often focus on individual events and provide little **context.** For instance, when a series of people are murdered in a specific area, readers often are given only individual reports on the killings. It would be far more useful to readers to have the events placed in context so the reasons for the murders can be understood — and steps taken to end the killings. Editors always should ask why events have happened, and when they detect trends, they should ask writers for additional material or separate articles to provide context.

For example, an article reported on deficiencies in record-keeping at a particular hospital, but the article did not mention that 90 percent of all hospitals had the

Writers also sometimes seem to forget the rules that govern cause and effect.

same problems. The editor should have asked the writer how the hospital compared with others and forced the writer to provide that needed perspective.

Confusing Time Sequences.   A news story about the trial of a man accused of killing a police officer included this paragraph:

Walker [the suspect] made it to the District line when Fleming [the officer] bumped a curb ... spun off the road and slammed into a tree. Other Prince George's officers who had joined the chase abandoned it to help Fleming. Fleming, 36, was an 18-year member of the force and the father of two small children. His widow, Patti Fleming, wept and clutched a photograph of her husband as the prosecutor replayed a tape of Fleming's radio transmissions to a police dispatcher before the fatal crash.

The first two sentences are easy enough to follow, as they present the events in straight chronological order. Then the third sentence delivers background information, and the fourth moves to the present-day trial. Minor editing makes the material much easier to follow:

Walker [the suspect] made it to the District line when Fleming [the officer] bumped a curb ... spun off the road and slammed into a tree. Other Prince George's officers who had joined the chase abandoned it to help Fleming.

Fleming, 36, was an 18-year member of the force and the father of two small children. During the trial yesterday, his widow, Patti Fleming, wept and clutched a photograph of her husband as the prosecutor replayed a tape of Fleming's radio transmissions to a police dispatcher before the fatal crash.

Incorrect Interpretation.   One morning while I was working as an editor, I was stopped by this lead:

There's good news for consumers. The state Milk Marketing Board has approved a plan to increase the price of milk by 2 cents a gallon.

That didn't quite make sense to me, so I consulted the writer. After 10 minutes, he agreed that it didn't make sense to him, either, so he came up with a lead that properly noted that an increase in the price of milk was *not* good news for consumers.

The same problem surfaced in an article about the rate of homicides among people who own guns. The article was based on a study that investigated a set of homicides to determine what proportion of them occurred in homes of gun owners. The study found that *homicides are three times as likely to be committed by people who own guns than by people who do not.* The story that appeared in most news media distorted that finding and stated that *people who keep guns in their home are three times as likely to be victims of homicide as are people who do not own guns.* That's a big difference.

Such misinterpretations are often the result of a fundamental problem: Writers tend not to be great mathematicians, but many of the most important stories being written are based on numbers. Editors need to find out which of the writers they work with are weak with numbers and carefully scrutinize their work.

One common problem that editors encounter is misuse of averages. In his book "Statistical Deception at Work," John Mauro writes that averages can be "devastatingly misleading" and can conceal more than they reveal. An editor should always ask how an average was derived and what the motivation is of the person or organization supplying the average.[8] Even when an average seems straightforward, it may not be easy to determine which of three averages it represents: the **mode** (the most frequent value), the **median** (the value in the middle when values are listed from lowest to highest) or the **mean** (the traditional average: all values added, then divided by the number of values).

Here's an example of how an average can distort the truth. Assume five of your neighbors have purchased cars for these prices: $12,000, $12,000, $25,000, $40,000 and $60,000. The mode is $12,000; the median is $25,000; the mean is $29,800. If you want people to think you live in a poor neighborhood, you'll tell them the mode; if you want to impress them, you'll tell them the mean.

Generalizations.   A radio commercial inadvertently raises another concern for editors. The commercial begins, "They say a fool and his money are soon parted. They say time heals all wounds." After a few more sentences beginning, "They say ... " the announcer demands, "Who are *they* anyway? Why should we listen to them?"

That's a good question for editors to ask in a number of different situations. Several problems with generalizations are identified in "Working with Words." Three of them are particularly important to check:

- Whenever you encounter a remark that supposedly applies to all members of a large group, check it out. "Women are poor drivers," "Blacks are natural athletes," "Japanese-American children are the smartest students" — all of these generalizations have been made at one time or another. Your job as an editor is to verify whether they're accurate.

- Whenever you see a reference to a group that is not clearly identified, check into it. General statements such as "Experts say ... " and "Studies show ... " need to be made specific.

- Whenever you encounter a rule — "People should do this," "No one should ever do that" — you need to check it out, too. What's the basis for that rule? Why is it a rule? What happens if someone breaks the rule?

In short, you should greet all generalizations with skepticism. As one classic rule of journalism advises, "If your mother tells you she loves you, check it out."

Poor Organization.   This is one of the most deadly problems, as well as one of the most difficult to correct. As editors read through copy, they need to make sure that ideas are fully developed before new ideas are introduced and that ideas are introduced in a logical order.

Obviously no set of formulas will cover every piece of writing; writing is at least as much art as science. At a minimum, editors should ask these questions in checking for organization:

1. **Is all related information in the same place?** Generally, readers are better able to grasp information when they are given all related material at

one time. The more complex the article, the more important such organization is. For example, many of the best trend articles are organized in three main blocks: a description of the trend (present state), an explanation of the trend (past) and an evaluation of the trend (future).[9]

Articles that present two opinions on an issue can be organized in two basic ways. The first is to present all of one side first, then all of the other, making sure the lead indicates that the article will cover both sides. The second approach is to organize the article by points raised, with both sides of one point given before moving on to the next. This approach is better for readers who don't want to finish the article, and it's essential if the story is subject to being cut from the bottom.

2. Does the copy flow smoothly from point to point? The inverted pyramid style used for much newspaper writing doesn't require much attention to transitions. The writer lets the facts trickle through until they're all presented, and paragraphs are not necessarily tied to the ones surrounding them. For all other types of media writing, though, transitions are essential to help take the reader from one point to another — they're the road signs the reader follows. Transitions can be as long as a sentence, or as short as a word; whatever their length, they can be a tremendous asset to readers trying to find their way through copy.

Transitional Words and Phrases

Consecutive paragraphs can relate to each other in many ways. The information in the second paragraph can support, oppose, neutralize or draw conclusions from the first paragraph. In some cases, the information in the second paragraph is compared to that in the first paragraph or is related to it by time or causation. The following list offers several common transitional words and phrases that can help clue the reader in to those connections. These all-purpose transitions can help pull material together when time is limited.

Supporting transitions

In addition

Not only . . . but also

Besides

For example

For instance

Furthermore

Neutralizing transitions

Still

Regardless of

In spite of

Nevertheless

Unfortunately

Opposing transitions

In contrast

Contrary to

On the other hand

Although

But

Yet

Conversely

Concluding transitions

Therefore

Consequently

Temporal transitions

Earlier

Then

Previously

Later

Until

No sooner

Formerly

Previously

Causal transitions

As a result

Because of that

Miscellaneous.   Some problems defy categorization. Take this line, for instance:

Former Gov. Ellis Arnall, 85, who brought sweeping changes to Georgia's colleges and abolished prison chain gangs during four years in office in the 1940s, died Sunday after suffering the first of several strokes.

If he died after the *first* stroke, when did he have the others?

An article on rebuilding a school contained this line:

The reconstruction of the entrance should reduce heavy and sometimes damaging west winds that hit the building.

Obviously, the reconstruction cannot *reduce winds,* but rather *their effect* on the building. The article didn't explain how that would be done.[10]

Sometimes, holes arise from graphic elements. A Page One newspaper article on the rates charged for garbage pickup included a mug shot of a person identified as "Russell." No one by that name was mentioned in the copy on that page. Inquiring minds finally found out who Russell was when they turned to the jump on Page 12.

An ad for a videocassette recorder featured a half-inch-wide photograph of the VCR and noted that the VCR was shown "actual size."

Filling Holes

Editors can detect
holes more easily
than they can fix
them because a hole
means that something
is missing.

Editors can detect holes more easily than they can fix them because a hole means that something is missing. In most cases the editor needs to send the copy back to the writer to supply that information, but sometimes the writer is unavailable. The editor then might be able to plug the gap by talking with one of the writer's sources. If neither the writer nor the source can supply the missing information, the best course of action is to hold the material until it can be fixed. Holding a confusing article isn't always an easy task for the editor, but it's one that readers will appreciate.

The Trouble With Polls

Editors need to be especially careful in handling stories based on polls and surveys. By their nature, polls never can be more than a close approximation of reality: They are generalizations based on only a sample of the population. Further, devious pollsters can produce any results they want. For those reasons, it's important that the public be given enough information to judge whether reported results are valid. Writers and editors always should ask the following questions when handling an article based on poll results; any pertinent missing information should be added.

Who sponsored the survey? If the poll is sponsored by an organization with a specific constituency or ideology, chances are good the organization did everything it could to produce the results that it wanted.

Was the sample representative? The only useful surveys are those that include a randomly selected sample of the population under study (e.g., all U.S. residents, all doctors, all women). If the sample is not representative, it is impossible to generalize the results. If the sample *is* representative, it is possible to generalize the results only to the population under study. For example, the results of a survey of college students can be generalized only to all college students, *not* to all adults.

Even when samples are carefully selected, refusals to participate and other factors can make the results useless. John Mauro, author of "Statistical Deception at Work,"[11] writes that unless at least 70 percent of the sample has responded, the results are not valid.

Surveys that ask readers to respond by phone or fax or via the Internet tend to be representative only of those with extreme views. For example, when a newspaper asked its readers to call in with their views on local bus service, about 60 percent of the callers rated the service as bad, poor or terrible. The article was topped with a headline reading, "Transpo riders unhappy with service, survey says," and it was accompanied by a large box featuring negative comments from riders. Readers who stuck with the article until the 12th paragraph, however, learned that a professional survey conducted by the bus company had found that the majority of riders were satisfied with the service.

The worst surveys are based on interviews with people on the street. As Mauro points out, even if locations are scientifically selected, it is impossible to draw a random sample of *people.* So the results of such surveys cannot be generalized. Mauro notes, "Persons on the street represent only themselves."[12]

What is the margin of error? The larger the sample, the lower the margin of error — that is, the more likely it is that the sample represents the entire population. It is not uncommon to find surveys that have a margin of error of 5 percentage points or more. That means that the results from the entire population could vary by as much as 5 points from the sample results. This problem was widespread during the 2000 presidential campaign. Throughout the months leading up to the election, news media routinely ran stories showing George W. Bush projected to win the popular vote by around 1 percentage point. Because the surveys those articles were based on had a margin of error of 3 points, the projection was meaningless — borne out by the fact that Bush **lost** the popular vote on election day.

Are the questions biased? When possible, anyone writing an article based on poll results should take a look at the questions used in the survey. According to Robert Berkman, author of "Find It Fast,"[13] several factors pose problems:

a. Loaded language — The use of words with positive connotations can produce greatly different responses than the use of words with negative connotations. Berkman notes that far more people are likely to say they favor increased spending "to help the poor" than they are to say they favor increased spending "for welfare."

b. Requests for memories and recollections — People do not do well at remembering past actions.

c. Complex questions — People will try to answer questions even when they do not understand them. For instance:

Do you favor a national single-payer system of health insurance, or would you prefer to see Congress enact one of the other plans under consideration?

A person needs a fair amount of knowledge about the subject to even understand that question.

continued

If a question can be taken more than one way, it will be. Therefore, any answers it produces are invalid.

d. Vague questions — If a question can be taken more than one way, it will be. Therefore, any answers it produces are invalid. Example:

Have you been affected by a crime within the last six months?

If you went to a local convenience store and found it closed for an hour while workers replaced glass that had been broken by vandals, you were affected by a crime. If you were robbed and beaten at gunpoint, then buried alive, you also were affected by a crime. There's a big difference between the two. Some people can be affected by a crime merely by reading about it — the article can make them take action to protect themselves, help others, and so forth.

e. Sensitive questions — People are not always forthcoming when asked about socially unacceptable behaviors, especially if the survey is being done in person.

If time permits, Berkman suggests calling the organization and asking the director or head researcher these questions about the findings:

• How do you know?

• Is the data preliminary or final?

• Do others in your field concur with your findings?

• What is the information based on?

• Who funded your work?

• Who disagrees with you and why?

• How sure are you?

• Are other explanations possible?

• Who else in the field has seen your work?

• What was your methodology?

• What are your study's weak points?[14]

Critics found several of these problems in the "Sex in America" study in 1994. The study, which was widely reported in the media, announced that most Americans have sex only about once a week, are faithful to their spouses and don't do anything kinky. Not reported were the facts that the survey excluded millions of Americans, including those living in college dormitories; that pre-interview notices implicitly encouraged interviewees to refrain from talking about "harmful" sexual practices; and that more than 20 percent of the "confidential" face-to-face interviews took place in front of spouses and children. Excluding those interviews on top of another 20 percent of prospective subjects who refused to be interviewed gives a response rate of under 60 percent — which makes the results invalid.[15]

Notes

1. Michael Learmonth, "Finally, Some Numbers on Napster," The Industry Standard, 5 June 2000, p. 55.

2. Gary Taubes, "The Ozone Backlash," Science, 260 (11 June 1993): pp. 1580–1583.

3. Katherine Dunn, "Fibbers," The New Republic, 21 June 1993, p. 19.

4. "Radioactivist," EXTRA! Update, October 1993, p. 2.

5. Sandra Pollen, "Identifying a Financial Interest," letter to The Washington Post, 11 Nov. 1993. The original article, "Only One Way to Go on NAFTA," by Robert S. Strauss, appeared in the Post on 19 Oct. 1993, sec. A, p. 23.

6. Joann Byrd, "14 Hot Complaints," The Washington Post, 5 Sept. 1993, sec. C, p. 7.

7. David Shaw, "Some Papers Seek Readers' Guidance in Shaping Coverage," The Los Angeles Times, 1 April 1993, sec. A, p. 18.

8. John Mauro, "Statistical Deception at Work" (Hillsdale, N.J.: L. Erlbaum Associates, 1992), pp. 4–10.

9. J.T.W. Hubbard, "Magazine Editing for Professionals" (Syracuse, N.Y.: Syracuse University Press, 1989), pp. 72–78.

10. Carl Hartman, "Be Kind to Your Readers and Viewers," Quill, April 1990, p. 29.

11. Mauro, "Statistical Deception," p. 87.

12. Mauro, "Statistical Deception," pp. 92–93.

13. Robert Berkman, "Find It Fast" (New York: Harper and Row, 1990).

14. Robert Berkman, "But Is It the *Whole* Truth?" Writer's Digest, September 1993, p. 43.

15. Mike Males, "Sex Survey's 'Warm Oatmeal' Sold as Solid Social Science," EXTRA!, January/February 1995, pp. 24–26.

Exercise

Rewrite the following article to correct holes in it. Also correct any errors in style and spelling.

When people think about the annual Swim Across Lake Anne (SALA), they usually think of the fun of it: charging through the warm water on a prefect summer day as clouds scud past in the sky above.

"I can't thing of a better way to spend a day," said Clarissa Lambert at the start of the race, with the temperature in the low 80s. "I just get in the water and start smilling."

But this year, the event proved more frnatic than fun. In both the man's and womens events, the winner beat out the the second-place swimmers by less than a minute. On the men's side, Jack Elliott edged out Crhis Kastoff by 15 seconds, finishing the 4.4-mile course in 1:33.22. Among women, Candy Balfour took first place in 140:58, defeating Allison Zinz by 27 seconds.

Race officials had prepared for a repeat of the rough waters that plaqued the event last year, causing 470 of the 507 entrants to withdaw from the race. More than 100 canoes were ready to pick up those having difficulties, but smooth water and high temperatures in the 70s made them all but unecessary. Only 12 of the 505 swimmers who entered failed to make it to the finnish line.

The only fatality of the event occured shortly after the race started. Michael Fritchey, 65, of Glen Allen died of a heart attack. His death was the first killing in the ten years that the event has run.

The event is a fund-raiser for the state Heart Assocaition. More than $10,000 was raised from entry fees and sponsorships. The funds will be used to aid in the battle against heart disease.

Using the Web to Provide Additional Information

As the Web has exploded as a medium for communicators to present information, it's also exploded as a resource for communicators to find information. By 2000, nearly three-quarters of journalists surveyed said that they went online daily, and their most popular activity online was conducting research.[1]

For editors, that often means looking for links to additional sources of information related to news and feature articles. These additional sources of information can help readers learn more about a topic or take action on an issue. By offering such links, editors can save readers countless hours of research.

In many cases, the best links are obvious. If an article refers to a new study, a link to the study lets readers check it out for themselves. An article about a major speech might similarly link to a transcript of the entire speech.

One good example of editors researching and preparing online packages is Word.com's account of the events leading up to the murder conviction of Mumia Abu-Jamal, a man sentenced to death for a crime many say he did not commit (*www.word.com/machine/Mumia/Docs/home.html*). The package includes the complete defense motion for his release, an image map of the scene of the crime, biographies of all witnesses and a chronology of events.

Links to multimedia also can enhance a text article. Many online news sites have teamed up with broadcast organizations for just this reason, allowing their audiences to listen to an interview, watch an on-the-spot news report or view an animation showing how an accident occurred.

Start With a Question

Sometimes it's not so obvious, though, what items would enhance the audience's experience. That's when your editing skills come into play. Any time you edit content for distribution on the Web, you should take time to ask yourself "What else would a reader want to know?" Even the most thoroughly researched article will not contain all relevant information. The trick is to anticipate the kinds of information readers would be interested in. Doing so requires you to look at the material with a fresh perspective and assume you know nothing about the topic.

For instance, an article might focus on a shelter for battered women. A reader might finish reading it and wonder:

- Are there other shelters like this in the area?
- Are there similar shelters for battered men?
- How can I help these shelters (volunteering, donations, etc.)?

Readers can try to find answers to such questions on their own. But you can make the piece much more useful by offering links to additional Web sites that provide the

HotBot lets Web searchers look for pages containing specific media types.

answers. The next step is a little harder: You actually have to find those sites. Fortunately, several search engines are available to assist you. Three steps will get you started:

1. Identify simple and specific terms for your search. The more specific, the better the chances you have of finding what you want. If you want to learn about cats, use that word as your first search term.

2. Consider alternate words, phrases and spelling. If your initial terms don't produce the results you want, think of other terms that might. For instance, **feline** might bring results that **cats** didn't.

3. Try multiple search engines and techniques. Different search engines operate differently from one another. In addition, each engine covers only a small fraction of all existing Web sites. A phrase that yields no results on one engine could yield a bounty on another.

4. If you're looking for multimedia, you might want to start your search with HotBot (*www.hotbot.lycos.com*). Using that search engine, you can specify that you only want to find sites that contain images, sound files or video clips.

In the next chapter, we'll look at specific search engines and strategies for using them to get the best results.

Note

1. Steven Ross and Don Middleberg, "Sixth Annual Middleberg/Ross Media in Cyberspace Study," 2000, *www.middleberg.com.*

(*Some of the material in this section has been adapted from "Building Basic News Sites," copyright 2001, Thom Lieb.*)

Editor's Corner

Cross-checking

When I was studying textbooks rather than contributing to them, I had a journalism professor who insisted that newspaper editors check every name "at least five times" before it goes in print.

Well, 24 years of newspaper experience have come and gone and I can assure you that we don't have time to check every name twice, let alone five times. But the professor's theory of the need for checking — or in this case cross-checking — is indeed alive and well.

Nowhere is this gatekeeper more necessary than in the statistically saturated world of sports, my area of employment at The Baltimore Sun. This is particularly important when dealing with numerous elements relating to the same topic, as we have during the Orioles' baseball season or the Ravens' football season.

Because the Orioles play nearly every day over a six-month stretch, let me use them to illustrate.

In one issue, we'll have an Orioles game story, an Orioles notebook, sometimes a column and/or sidebar, Orioles tonight box, Orioles averages, sometimes a chart or two, American League standings, AL leaders and AL schedule, among other things.

With luck, by the first edition at 11:30 p.m., but definitely by the time we close the fourth and final edition at 3 a.m., all those elements, plus several others, need to agree. For instance, "Orioles tonight" on our cover each day lists the opponent, time and place of the game, TV and radio coverage, and starting pitchers with their records and earned run averages.

Simple thing, right? It takes only an inch or two of copy. But it takes a lot of cross-checking. The time of the game has to agree with that in the American League schedule. Radio and TV information has to be cross-checked with our "Sports on TV" and "Sports on Radio" that day on Page 2. The pitching records and ERAs should agree with the pitching chart that runs with the AL schedule, and those of the Orioles starter with the Orioles averages.

Had enough? We've only done an inch or two of the section.

If in the game story we have Cal Ripken going 3-for-4 to raise his batting average to .270, that should agree with the box score that runs with the jump of the story and the Orioles averages, plus any other stories that mention his performance. If Boston's Nomar Garciaparra goes 2-for-5 to lift his average to .334, that should agree with the box score and the American League leaders. That goes for all other stats, too. If Pat Hentgen throws 6 2/3 innings in the game story, the box score better not say he pitched 6 1/3 or you have a change to make. If the story says he was making his 10th start and Orioles averages say he has 12, a question should arise.

**Chris Zang,
sports copy editor,**
The Baltimore Sun

That's why I keep a log on each Orioles starting pitcher. When Scott Erickson goes out on the mound and our writer says five walks were his most of the season, I can quickly check, see that he had six at Texas on May 21 and make the necessary change.

And this is just with one story. What if the columnist says Hentgen pitched 6 2/3 innings, the sidebar says 6 and the game story says 6 1/3? We need to check the box score, the final authority, and make the stories agree. A scoring summary runs with the box score, and that should also agree with all details elsewhere, that the game-winning home run came with one out in the seventh inning on a 3-1 pitch, etc.

Kidding? I wish I were. It's our job to make sure we are consistent throughout the section, a difficult task at best. Sending similar stories to the same copy editor usually helps with this. And time can be tight. Games can end at 11:10 when our setting deadline is 11:20, and headlines, cutlines and a sensible story are my first concern. But a high priority is printing out the box score and scoring summary, which I place next to my pitching chart and Orioles' day-by-day review, and start cross-checking and updating. Stories written before the game ends, such as notebooks, need to have averages, RBIs, records and other stats updated.

Quotes are another thing we watch. If we have the same quote in more than one story, first we determine which story needs the quote more. If, as happens occasionally, we decide it's germane to both stories, we make sure the quote is identical. The player or manager said it only once in the locker room, so, again, let's be consistent.

The last stop on this abbreviated cross-checking tour is headlines. Sometimes, especially back when the Orioles were good, we would have as many as four Orioles-related headlines on the cover. In Monday papers during the football season we run into this with the Ravens. In this case, we try to avoid the same words. In the good old days, the Orioles had a pitcher by the name of Mike Mussina. If Mussina was used in the main head, "Moose" might be used in the head on a sidebar. Or if he was only part of the story, perhaps the main head would focus on the offense, or lack of it, and let him be the sidebar head, with the word "Orioles" not in every head either. Don't think of headlines, or cutlines for that matter, as individual things. Think of the page — and the section — as a whole.

And yes, professor, we do regular checking, too. Before he was an ESPN commentator, Harold Reynolds was a second baseman who spent some time with the Orioles. Years back, a story that mentioned he was a "veteran player" failed to include his age, sending me to his bio in the Orioles media guide (also at my side). That said he was 29, which didn't sound right to me (you need common sense in the editing game, too) so I checked the roster in the media guide. That said he was 33. That sounded right, but was it? The Baseball Encyclopedia, another source, said it was. So his age, and the proper one at that, was plugged into the story, and somewhere my old journalism professor was smiling.

Phrases, Clauses and Sentences

One of the most common grammatical problems is misunderstanding what makes a complete sentence. The best way to avoid this problem is by understanding the differences between **phrases, clauses** and **sentences.**

A phrase is a group of words that includes neither a subject nor a verb. Because it lacks these elements, a phrase never can be considered a full sentence. Phrases can be either **prepositional** or **verbal.** Prepositional phrases include a preposition, such as *to, in, from, over* or *for,* and an object of the preposition. Some examples:

PREPOSITION	OBJECT
for	her sake
from	the first step
over	the buildings
in	seven years

Verbal phrases include a form of a verb but function as a noun or an adjective. In the first example below, an infinitive (the *to* form of verb) phrase acts as a noun, as the object of *hoped:*

They hoped to reach the target by March.

In the next example, a gerund phrase (the *-ing* form of verb) acts as an adjective modifying *he:*

Eating two eggs a second, he won the championship.

The same phrase could be used as a noun, as it is in the next sentence:

Eating two eggs a second proved to be the best strategy for winning the championship.

A phrase used by itself is not a sentence — it's a **sentence fragment,** such as in this example from a promotional packet for a theater company:

Winning the Tony Award and the Outer Critics Circle Award.

Clause Confusion

A clause differs from a phrase in that it contains a subject and a verb (although in some cases, the subject *you* is understood: *Go,* for example, is a clause). If that group of words can stand alone, it is called an **independent clause.** When used on its own, such a clause is a complete sentence:

SUBJECT	VERB
Discounts	*are available.*
The cabinet	*resigned.*

When a clause cannot stand on its own, it is called a **dependent clause.** It can be used as a noun, an adjective or an adverb, and it must be used with an independent clause. The dependent clause in the next sentence functions as an adjective, modifying *bicycle:*

She commutes to work on a bicycle **that she bought for $5 at a Goodwill store.**

The dependent clause below functions as an adverb, modifying *commutes* and answering the question "why?":

She commutes to work on a bicycle **because she says it keeps her fit and helps the environment.**

The dependent clause in the next example functions as a noun, serving as the direct object of the verb *produces:*

He produces **what many call pornographic works.**

   Sentences contain various combinations of dependent and independent clauses.

- A sentence that contains only an independent clause is known as a **simple** sentence:

  Turnout at the gala reception is expected to top 1,000.

- A sentence with at least two independent clauses is known as a **compound** sentence:

  The new models showed up on dealers' lots last weekend, and thousands of people turned out to see them.

- A sentence with one independent and at least one dependent clause is known as a **complex** sentence:

  The troops were told that the attack would take place before midnight.

- A sentence with at least two independent clauses and at least one dependent clause is known as a **compound-complex** sentence:

  Mr. Williams bought the tickets, and Mrs. Williams packed their bags before an hour had passed.

Writers often misuse clauses. The following are typical clause problems and suggestions for editing to correct the problems.

- A dependent clause used as a full sentence is a **sentence fragment:**

Before the general public is admitted.

A dependent clause can be combined with an independent clause to form a complex sentence:

Those holding membership cards can enter the store at 8 a.m., before the general public is admitted.

Fragments can be used effectively, if writers realize they are using fragments. For example:

It was a perfect spring day. Light winds blowing. Sun kissing your cheeks. Birds singing everywhere.

But it's often evident that writers do not realize they are using fragments, such as in the following example:

Costing hundreds of dollars less than the competition. This new product beats all of them, feature for feature.

- Two independent clauses connected with no punctuation create a **fused sentence:**

The lecture is scheduled for 7 tonight a reception follows.

- Two independent clauses joined with a comma create a **comma-splice sentence:**

The players easily won the game, they move on to the championships.

In either case, you have three possible solutions:

1. Use a semicolon between the independent clauses:

    The lecture is scheduled for 7 tonight; a reception follows.

2. Separate the clauses into two sentences:

    The players easily won the game. They move on to the championships.

3. Add a conjunction:

    The players easily won the game, and they move on to the championships.

- Several independent clauses containing unrelated items are combined into a **run-on sentence:**

Residents of the community complained about the leash law, and they decided to call a public meeting, and they looked into using a private contractor to haul away their garbage.

That's quite an eyeful, and few readers will be able to grasp all three aspects of the sentence in one pass. The best way to handle a run-on sentence is by cutting it up into bite-size chunks:

Residents of the community complained about the leash law, and they decided to call a public meeting. They also looked into using a private contractor to haul away their garbage.

Some Restrictions

Phrases and clauses can be either **restrictive** or **nonrestrictive.** Punctuation and word choice are different between the two variations. Failing to distinguish between restrictive and nonrestrictive material can confuse or mislead a reader.

Restrictive — or limiting — material is necessary to distinguish a particular item from others in its class, such as in the following sentence:

The actor who played Steve Douglas' son on the TV show "My Three Sons" won the Nobel Prize in literature yesterday.

The reader doesn't know which of the three sons was so honored (and an editor won't, either, without checking). So the proper name should be inserted after the word *son* — but in this case you do not place commas around it:

The actor who played Steve Douglas' son Chip on the TV show "My Three Sons" won the Nobel Prize in literature yesterday.

The name is not set off in commas, because it is necessary to understand the reference. It *restricts* the reference to one person.

A name following a title is restrictive when the title is not preceded by *the:*

Team general manager Marvin Slagle would not comment.

If you cut the name, you end up just short of a sentence:

Team general manager would not comment.

So the name is restrictive and is not set off by commas.

> Failing to distinguish between restrictive and nonrestrictive material can confuse or mislead a reader.

When an entire phrase is restrictive, it should be preceded by the word *that:*

The speedboat that was seized in the latest raid was found to have 50 pounds of cocaine hidden in it.

There are several speedboats under discussion; the restrictive phrase *that was seized in the latest raid* distinguishes this speedboat from the others.

Material is nonrestrictive — or nonlimiting — when there is only one item in a class, such as in the following sentence:

President George W. Bush's wife, Laura, visited her hometown.

The name of Bush's wife is nonrestrictive because he has only one wife. Even without including her name, readers would still know the reference is to her. The commas around *Laura* indicate that the word can be removed with no loss of meaning.

A name following a title is nonrestrictive if the title is preceded by *the:*

The team's general manager, Marvin Slaglc, would not comment.

The name could be cut and the sentence would still make sense:

The team's general manager would not comment.

So in this case the name is nonrestrictive and is set off by commas.

Nonrestrictive phrases also are set off by commas. In addition, they should be preceded by *which:*

The speedboat, which was seized in the latest raid, was found to have 50 pounds of cocaine hidden in it.

There is only one speedboat under discussion; the phrase "which was seized in the latest raid" adds information about the boat but is not necessary to understand which speedboat is being discussed. The material can be cut with no loss in meaning.

For either restrictive or nonrestrictive information, always use *who* or *whom* when referring to people:

The man who founded the company died last year.

The skiers, whom rescue squads had assumed were dead, walked into park headquarters the next morning.

Material is nonrestrictive — or nonlimiting — when there is only one item in a class.

4

Checking Facts

Retraction

In the April 1998 cover story of The Washington Monthly, a number of statements were made concerning a Florida-based company that owns the greyhound track in Hudson, Wisconsin, and the Hecht family, including Florence Hecht, the late Isadore Hecht, and sons-in-law Fred Havenick and Neil Amdur. We did not have proof for the following:

- *That the Hecht family has been "linked to organized crime."*
- *That the "local corporate identities" of the companies involved in the Hudson dog track were "intentionally confusing."*
- *That the patriarch of the family, the late Isadore Hecht, was a "friend and business associate of the late gangster Meyer Lansky."*
- *That Neal Amdur "has a stake in a Florida company with mob ties."*
- *That Fred Havenick only became involved with the dog track and casino applications in 1995.*
- *That the three Wisconsin Chippewa Indian tribes are acting as a "front" for the Hecht family in the Hudson casino venture.*
- *That the Hudson casino contract is "a throwback to the bad old days of Indian gaming."*
- *That the Hudson dog track companies are "shady."*

In preparing this story, reporters and editors of The Washington Monthly did not attempt to contact the Hecht family, the companies or tribes involved in the proposed Hudson casino venture, or any of their representatives. We apologize for any embarrassment we may have caused members of the Hecht family and the companies with which they are involved.

— The Washington Monthly, July/August 1998.

***

The mushroom identified as an edible bolete in this picture that ran on Page H3 of the Food section Wednesday is actually an amanita, which can be poisonous. It is most easily identified by a small ring midway down the stem.

— The Los Angeles Times

***

CORRECTION

We regret to say that we did not have the information about John Ehrlich, 28, correct. He is not an instructor, but just a fellow. Dr. Wolf is not the head of the botany department. There is no botany department; it's in biology. It's not Durham University, but Duke University in Durham, North Carolina.

— The Cornell (N.Y.) Countryman

***

Information is the essence of mass communication. Whether that information concerns a presidential assassination attempt, the introduction of a new product, a corporate promotion, or any of countless other topics, it is essential that the information is accurate. As the examples above and in Chapter 1 show, inaccurate information can cause embarrassment, insult, physical injury, loss of credibility or loss of money in libel suits.

Van Gordon Sauter, the former president of CBS News who went on to become president of Fox News, told an interviewer in early 1993 that the news media are "no longer as trustworthy as we used to be; we're no longer as credible as we used to be." He added, "There is a repository of trust and goodwill, but it's very much on loan, and I think some people are really beginning to doubt the value of that loan."[1]

Since then, the public's trust for the media has fallen even further. A record proportion of the public no longer trusts the media, and one leading reason is because the media so often get the facts wrong.

To help address that problem, beginning in early 2000 USA Today started mailing "accuracy surveys" to people quoted or mentioned in articles to verify that facts, numbers and quotes were correct, that the articles were fair, and that the paper resolved any problems that had been brought to the attention of its editors.[2]

Later that year, The New York Times joined in the effort to make it easier for readers to report problems with articles. After noticing that the Times was averaging more than six corrections a day, Executive Editor Joseph Lelyveld announced an initiative to "publish a daily announcement on Page 2 inviting readers to phone or write us about not just errors and corrections but their larger concerns as well."[3]

In a perfect world, writers would always double-check every detail of their copy, and editors could assume that all the facts are fine. But tight deadlines and carelessness can cause writers to overlook errors. In addition, errors can occur when writers are unfamiliar with the material they're writing about. In such cases, the writer doesn't think to question a fact because there doesn't seem to be a reason to do so. For example, if a person assigned to write an article about nuclear power knows nothing about the topic, there is nothing to tip the writer off to inaccuracies.

Factual errors are rare in magazines and books because their relatively long production schedules allow more time to check information. Many magazines employ fact checkers who carefully read all manuscripts and verify every fact they find in them. The multiple-review process used by some book publishers, and with much public relations and advertising copy, also helps weed out inaccuracies before publication. Even then, however, errors inevitably creep in.

People who work in media that are published daily or weekly typically don't have the time for such thorough fact checking; the long corrections columns in many daily newspapers attest to this. Still, lack of time is no excuse for editors to do a poor job. As this chapter will show, with a little effort editors can catch most factual errors most of the time. Doing so is a two-part process: first, determining when to question facts; second, knowing where to go to get answers to those questions.

When to Question the Facts

One of the best editors I've ever worked with was a former high school history teacher. He knew detail after detail about the history of the city in which we worked. Consequently, he was able to spot errors in copy that no one else would catch. A story would state, for example, that a bridge was built in 1957; he knew the actual date was 1947.

Not every editor shares this background, but there is an important point here for every editor: Good editors are storehouses of information. An important part of being a good editor is having an insatiable appetite for information. Newcomers to a company or a city must devour information on that company or city. Only by doing so can they catch many factual errors.

Of course, even with a steady diet of reading materials and a full social life, you'll never know everything there is to know. And chances are good that you won't have the time to check every fact you come across. That's OK; no one will expect you to. But you will be expected to always check the following.

Names

Virtually every piece of copy that is written involves people. People like to read about people, especially themselves. But as much as people like to read about people, they *hate* to see names misspelled — especially their own. As the editor of a small-town newspaper in Ohio told a group of other editors:

> Beyond the constant detractors, those who have an axe to grind with the paper for political or like reasons, our biggest barrier to credibility is probably a basic one: mistakes. While these errors rarely involve key facts or elements of a story, little things like a wrong first name or misspelling are problems we need to correct. This is especially true given the small size of our paper and its closeness to the community.[4]

> With a little effort editors can catch most factual errors most of the time.

If lack of time prevents you from checking every name, at least check names in the following situations:

Names of People Involved in Undesirable Circumstances. Whenever the copy concerns the firing of an employee, the arrest of a crime suspect or any other defamatory information, you must verify that the name is correct. Carelessly letting the wrong name slip through in such a story not only can ruin an innocent person's life but also can bring financial ruin upon your organization — deservedly so.

Unusual Spellings and Foreign Names. When pressed for time, you can probably skip simple names with common spellings: Mary Smith, for instance, is probably spelled correctly. There is no guarantee of that, but the odds are better that that name is spelled correctly than is Merrie Smyth. I worked with one editor, though, who would let an oddly spelled name slip by but would jump up to challenge a conventionally spelled one. He assumed that the oddly spelled name must have been double-checked by the writer, whereas the conventionally spelled name could have just been the writer's assumption. Needless to say, he missed many errors — and because he was always running around checking correctly spelled names, he didn't get much copy edited.

Foreign names present special problems for an obvious reason — unfamiliar spellings — and one not-so-obvious one: While it's customary to refer to John Doe simply as "Doe" after first reference, that practice doesn't work with names from other countries. Spanish and Portuguese names, for example, don't follow this practice. As The Associated Press Stylebook points out: "The family names of both the father and the mother are considered part of a person's full name. In everyday use, customs vary widely with individuals and countries." Spanish and Portuguese names typically include a person's given name, the father's family name, and the mother's family name (for example, Jose Lopez Portillo). Depending on circumstances, the proper second reference could be either Lopez (standard) or Lopez Portillo (if the person is well-known by the multiple last name) — or, if he uses a "y" (meaning "and") between Lopez and Portillo, the correct second reference would be Lopez y Portillo. On the other hand, some residents of Portugal and Brazil use only the mother's family name on second reference, and others prefer to be referred to by both mother's and father's names. You'd be foolish to assume you know how to handle such names without checking.

You also have to be careful with foreign names that contain "particles" such as *de* and *von*. According to The Associated Press Stylebook, these are typically lowercased except when used as the first word of a sentence.

Attentive editors also will notice when the spelling of a foreign name in a piece of copy differs from the spelling of the name in other publications. Discrepancies with external sources don't mean that a spelling is wrong; it may be that the spelling in your copy is the preferred spelling in your organization, while the alternative spelling is preferred by another organization. For names of famous people, you can resolve disputes quickly by consulting the stylebook or other references that your organization uses.

An editor should check not only foreign names, but also other foreign words. The following are some of the most commonly used foreign words and phrases:

Common Foreign Words

au contraire	quid pro quo
bon appétit	raison d'êtat
coup de grâce	respondez s'il vous plait
coup d'état	savoir faire
déjà vu	semper fidelis
enfant terrible	tempus fugit
et tu, Brute?	tête-à-tête
je ne sais quoi	tout le monde
laissez-faire	über alles
magnum opus	veni, vidi, vici
nom de plume	vis-à-vis
pièce de résistance	vox populi
plus ça change, plus c'est la même chose	zeitgeist

Names That Are Spelled More Than One Way.   Check the spelling of a name every time it appears in a piece of copy. If you find a discrepancy, you need to verify which spelling is correct — or whether both might be wrong. Don't assume that the way the name appears most often is the correct spelling; you have no better than a 50 percent chance of being right. In editing, 50 percent is *not* a passing grade.

Gender-Bender Names.   A few years back, acquaintances of mine were interviewed for a story by a large metropolitan daily newspaper. We were surprised to see that one of them, whose first name was Terry, had undergone a sex change during the publication process: A male, Terry was referred to in the article as "she." Because the writer had spoken to Terry in person, there are two possible explanations for that change: Either the reporter was not perceptive of subtle personal traits such as gender, or a careless editor made the change. My vote is for the second possibility.

That was also the explanation for another error in the same publication in which a lawyer named Jamie changed from a *she* to a *he* within the same article. To keep yourself from making such an embarrassing mistake — for you and for the subject — always double-check the sex of a person whose name is shared by males and females. And make sure you get the spelling right while you're at it: Frances for her, Francis for him, for example. In cases involving nicknames such as Tommy/Tommi, Gene/Jean, Chris/Kris, Mary/Merry and the like, either you or the writer should ask the person for the correct spelling.

Don't assume that the way the name appears most often is the correct spelling; you have no better than a 50 percent chance of being right.

Names with Other Tip-Offs.   I couldn't help but notice the coincidence one day while editing a newspaper article in which the last name of the subject of the story was also the name of the street on which he lived. The writer assured me that as odd as the situation seemed, he had double-checked it, and he swore the information was correct. But after the first edition came out, the writer sent me a new version of the article — with a different street name.

Referring to a different article, another writer assured me that the unusual spelling of the subject's name was correct: Belloccq. Again, after the first edition, the writer admitted what I had suspected: The "cq" at the end of the name was shorthand for "checked"; the name Belloc had indeed been checked, but the "cq" was not supposed to be published as part of the name.

The moral is simple: If names don't seem to make sense, someone has probably fallen asleep at the wheel. If you're not satisfied that the writer is correct and you have enough time, double-check the name in a directory or call the person whose name is in doubt.

Places

I grew up in Pittsburgh, Pa.; I've never been to Pittsburg, Kan. I doubt many people have, but I often see that second spelling in stories about my hometown. Similarly, Milwaukee is in Wisconsin; Milwaukie is in Oregon. Whenever two cities share the same name but are spelled differently, verify that you have the correct one.

And make sure you put the city in the correct state. While it would be hard to imagine someone mistakenly placing the home of the Steelers and the Penguins in Kansas, it's a lot easier to imagine someone mistakenly placing Kansas City in Kansas. Yes, there *is* a Kansas City in Kansas, but the better-known Kansas City is in Missouri.

Just as names of foreign people pose problems, so do names of foreign countries, and never more so than with the restructuring of Eastern Europe. Even stable countries with familiar names can prove problematic, however. For example, while many people use Britain as a synonym for England, the two words are not interchangeable. Great Britain includes England, Scotland and Wales, and is itself part of the United Kingdom (as is Northern Ireland).

Getting the names of places correct is just a start; editors also have to make sure that the facts about the places are correct. The editor who approved an article describing Angola as "small" was not a careful editor. The country is, in fact, the fifth-largest country in Africa and one of the largest in the world. (To be most helpful to readers, the editor should have compared the country's size to the United States.)

Finally, editors need to make sure that foreign people are correctly matched with their countries. While he was president of Poland, Lech Walesa was once identified as the president of the Czech Republic.

Corporate and Organization Names

Most people give little thought to the large number of corporate and organization names they see and use every day. But editors have to give a great deal of thought to those names. Editors need to be careful on two fronts: spelling and use of trademarks.

1. Spelling: If you had a Big Mac attack, where would you head: McDonalds, McDonald's, McDonalds', MacDonalds, MacDonald's or MacDonalds'? If you wanted to wash it down with a Slurpee, would you head to Seven-Eleven, 7-11, Seven-11 or 7-Eleven? Is the school in New Orleans called Loyola University or Loyola College? How about the university in Baltimore: Is it John Hopkin, John Hopkins or Johns Hopkins? Is that famous Seattle-based department store Nordstrom, Nordstroms or Nordstrom's? Are they Macintosh computers or Mcintosh? Would you take a train trip on Amtrack, AMTRACK, Amtrak or AMTRAK? While Americans pride themselves on having many choices, there is only one correct choice in each of these examples — and it's the editor's job, with the help of reference works, to pick that one.

2. Trademarks: Manufacturers of popular products invest a great deal of time and money in protecting their greatest assets: their trademarks. If a trademark falls into general use, the company can lose it. That's happened with corn flakes, escalator, aspirin, trampoline, nylon, yo-yo and many other former trademarks.

Unless the use of a trademark is essential, the trademark should be replaced with a generic term. For instance, use soda, cola or soft drink instead of Coke. When the use of a trademark name is essential:

- Make sure it is capitalized.
- Make sure it is used as an adjective and accompanied by the descriptive (generic) term on first reference: "He grabbed his Dustbuster portable vacuum."
- Don't use plural forms. "Kleenexes," for example, is incorrect; "Kleenex tissues" is correct.

Commonly Misused Trademarks

Trademarks	Generic equivalents
Ace	elastic bandages
Alka-Seltzer	antacid analgesic tablets
Anacin	analgesic
Baggies	plastic bags
Band-Aid	adhesive bandages
Ben-Gay	analgesic preparation
Breathalyzer	alcoholic content measuring apparatus
Brillo	scouring pads
Cat Chow	cat food
Chap Stik	lip balm

continued

Clorox	bleach
Crisco	shortening
Day-Glo	fluorescent materials
Dog Chow	dog food
Dumpster	trash containers
Dustbuster	portable vacuums
Equal	sweetener
FedEx	overnight and international delivery services
Fiberglas	glass fibers
Fig Newtons	fig bars
Flair	pens
Formica	laminated plastic
Freon	refrigerant
Frigidaire	refrigerator
Gore-Tex	waterproof fabric
Handi-Wipes	towelettes
Hi-Liter	highlighting markers
Hot Wheels	toy cars and accessories
Hula Hoops	plastic hoops
Instamatic	cameras
Jacuzzi	whirlpool baths
Jeep	four-wheel-drive vehicles
Jell-O	gelatin
Jockey	clothing, underwear
Jujyfruits	candy
Keds	athletic footwear
Kitty Litter	cat box filler
Kleenex	facial tissues
Kool-Aid	soft drink mix
Kotex	sanitary napkins
Laundromat	coin-operated laundry (A Laundromat is a coin-operated laundry that uses products of White-Westinghouse Appliance Co.)
Lava	lamps
Lego	building blocks
Levi's	jeans

Lifecycle	stationery cycle
Life Savers	roll candy
Lite	light beer by Miller
Little League	baseball sports services
Loafer	shoes
Lycra	stretch fiber
Lysol	disinfectant
M & M's	candy
Magic Marker	felt-tip pen
Mailgram	message services
Masonite	fiber boards
Mercurochrome	antiseptic
Minute	instant rice
Mr. Coffee	coffee maker
Muzak	background music systems
Nautilus	weight-lifting equipment
Nicad	batteries
Nike	athletic footwear and clothing
No Doz	drowsiness-relief tablets
Novocain	local anesthetic
NutraSweet	sweetener
Oreo	cookies
Pampers	disposable diapers
Pepto-Bismol	upset-stomach remedy
Perrier	sparkling water
Ping-Pong	table tennis equipment
Plexiglas	acrylic plastic
Polaroid	instant camera
Popsicles	flavored ice on a stick
Porta-John	portable toilet
Post-It	notepads, self-stick notes
Q-Tips	swabs (usually not cotton)
Raisinets	chocolate-covered raisins
Realtor	real estate agent (A Realtor is a member of the National Association of Realtors.)

continued

Roach Motel	insect traps
Rollerblades	in-line skates
Rolodex	card files
Sanka	decaffeinated coffee
Saran Wrap	plastic film
Scotch	cellophane tape
Sno-Kone	flavored ices
Spackle	surfacing compound
Spic and Span	cleaner
Stairmaster	exercise equipment
Styrofoam	plastic foam (Styrofoam is blue and is used only in building materials — not in food and beverage containers.)
Sucrets	sore-throat lozenges
Super Glue	adhesive
Tampax	tampons
Teflon	nonstick coating
Toll House	chocolate morsels (Cookies made with other brands are known as chocolate chip cookies, not Toll House cookies.)
Tupperware	plastic housewares
TV Guide magazine	television listings, program guide
Vaseline	petroleum jelly
Velcro	hook and loop fasteners
Velveeta	processed cheese
Vise-Grip	hand tools, clamps
Weed Eater	lawn trimmer
Weight Watchers	weight-loss programs and products
Wiffle	plastic balls and bats
Wite-Out	correction fluid
Xerox	photocopiers, photocopies
Ziploc	storage bags

To check others not on this list, call the International Trademark Association's Trademark Hotline at (212) 768-9886, from 2 to 5 p.m. weekdays or e-mail *tmhotline@inta.org*.

Assertions of Fact

On an otherwise unremarkable news day, the lead of one story that arrived at the copy desk caught my attention: "The world will end tomorrow," it read. I resisted my first inclination to leave work right then and make the best of the rest of the day. Instead I read on to the second paragraph, which said something like, "At least that's the opinion of Joe Blow, who spends his days walking around the city with a sign warning that the end is near."

OK, I'll grant that not too many people will take the lead literally. Even so, it still misrepresents the truth. Most readers don't like to be toyed with like that. Unless copy is clearly satirical, it should not make unwarranted claims. A good rule of thumb is that to maintain credibility, all information should be attributed (also called **sourcing** information) unless (1) the information is common knowledge or (2) any observer can verify the information, such as the fact that a building burned down.

Editors also should check attribution carefully for every quote (direct and paraphrased) in copy that has more than one source. It's not unheard of to find people quoted as saying something that only their opponents would say. For example, a person supporting a pay raise for teachers ends up saying, "Teachers don't even deserve what they're paid now." If it doesn't make sense for a source to have said something that has been attributed to him or her, chances are good he or she *didn't* say it.

It's also important to verify that what a writer cites as a famous quotation *is* the famous quotation. More than half of the time, the famous line is flawed. It may not seem that there's anything wrong with "Music soothes the savage beast" or "The proof is in the pudding," but a check with the references will reveal otherwise. The correct quotes are "Music has charms to soothe a savage breast" and "The proof of the pudding is in the eating" (which makes much more sense, too).

> Unless copy is clearly satirical, it should not make unwarranted claims.

Dates/Chronology/Ages

Always double-check dates in copy. Sometimes, there is no internal clue that a date is wrong. An article on dueling, for instance, reported that two Naval Academy midshipmen were killed in duels in 1822 and 1835 — but the academy was founded in 1845. In another article, a writer described a new dance as "the hottest dance craze since the Twist in the 1950s." While the song was first recorded in 1959, the dance swept the nation in the *1960s.*

Editors have less excuse for missing errors in date and chronology that any careful reader could easily spot. For example, the lead of an October 1982 news article read, "Just 10 years ago this summer two of the cities hardest hit by Tropical Storm Agnes were Wilkes-Barre and, across the line in New York state, Corning." Four paragraphs later, the story turned to a chronology of events since the flood, noting, "When the Susquehanna River overflowed its banks on June 23, 1982, it did over $1 million worth of damage in Wilkes-Barre and the rest of Luzerne County." The correct year was, of course, *1972.*

In addition, editors always should double-check ages against other information in copy. If a release on the promotion of a 53-year-old person notes that she received her bachelor's degree in 1958, either that person was precocious or the writer was careless.

Numbers

Writing an article for a special "Spending" issue of The New York Times Magazine, Amy Barrett reported on Ivana Trump's amazing bra frenzy. Barrett reported that Trump told her:

> I go to [Bloomingdale's] for two hours and I buy 2,000 of the black [bras], 2,000 of the beige, 2,000 of the white. Then I ship them around between the homes and the boat, and that's [the] end of it for maybe half a year, when I have to do it all over again.

In actuality, Trump had said she bought two *dozen* of each color every six months. Barrett had apparently misunderstood because of Trump's Czech accent. Had Barrett done her math, she would have realized that Trump would have had to wear about 33 brassieres a day — and then throw away each one after one wearing — for Barrett's numbers to make sense.[5]

To repeat an important point made in Chapter 3: Many writers are poor with numbers. Even articles that do not suffer from the problem of misinterpretation often include other math errors. An inexpensive calculator can go a long way in correcting math errors, and some mistakes don't require even a calculator. One article reported that 400 employees were to be laid off at a local factory in addition to the 1,200 already laid off, for a grand total of 1,500 layoffs. In another instance, a survey of the "top 10 things most likely to make people blush" listed *14* items. Another article broke down 332 city employees as follows:

White	217
Black	115
Asian	2
Hispanic	1

But those figures add up to 335, not 332.

An article explaining how insurance works included this paragraph:

The underlying idea of insurance is that it spreads risk. It is reasonably predictable, for instance, that every year, one home in a community of 100 houses worth $200,000 each will be destroyed by fire. But there's no way to know which it will be. If everyone kicks in $200 annually, there's a pool of money to compensate the one unlucky homeowner.

Talk about unlucky: First your home burns down, then you end up $180,000 short of the cost of rebuilding! (If you didn't catch it, 100 times $200 is only $20,000.)

Calculators are essential for checking percentages. An article in The Wall Street Journal reported on a computer that uses between one and four processors:

System performance starts at 25 million instructions per second [MIPS] with one processor and increases by 25% each time a new processor is added for a total of 106 MIPS, according to AT&T.

Get the calculator:

Starting system speed	25 MIPS
Second processor adds 25 percent	31.25 MIPS
Third processor adds 25 percent	39.06 MIPS
Fourth processor adds 25 percent	48.82 MIPS

Something's obviously wrong here — 48.82 is a long way from 106. In fact, even if each supplemental processor increased the speed of the base processor by 100 percent rather than 25 percent, the total would be 100 MIPS, not 106. This one should have been sent back to the writer or the source.

While the math in the preceding example might seem frightening, it is easy to derive percentages to check the figures in copy.

To Determine the Percentage Change When the Amount of Increase or Decrease Is Given.   Divide the amount of the increase or decrease by the original figure. For example, if a story says that a 2,000-square-foot expansion increased the size of a 30,000-square-foot building by 15 percent, divide 2,000 by 30,000:

$$\frac{2{,}000}{30{,}000} = 0.0666$$

Move the decimal point two places to the right, and you get just under 7 percent, *not* 15 percent.

To Determine the Percentage Change When the Amount of Increase Is Not Given.   Subtract the original figure from the new figure, then divide the result by the original figure. For example, if copy says the number of members in an organization increased 10 percent from 4,000 to 4,400,

1. subtract 4,000 from 4,400 to determine the amount of increase (in this case, 400);

2. divide 400 by 4,000. The answer is 10 percent, so the copy is correct.

To Determine the Percentage Change When the Amount of Decrease Is Not Given.   Subtract the new figure from the original figure, then divide the result by the original figure. For example, if copy says the number of members in an organization decreased 10 percent from 4,000 to 3,600,

1. subtract 3,600 from 4,000 to determine the amount of increase (in this case, 400);

2. divide 400 by 4,000. The answer is 10 percent, so the copy is correct.

Even when percentages are correct, they can distort the truth. For instance, a report on drug use among junior high school students noted a 20 percent increase in use of LSD during one year. That increase seems startling, especially for sixth-graders through eighth-graders. But the figures it is based on tell a different story: Usage rose from 1.5 percent to 1.8 percent during the period. The percentage increase cited *is* correct — but it's also misleading.

Another percentage problem occurs when a comparison is implied but not explained. For instance, an ad or a news release promoting a product that has "30 percent fewer calories" has not answered the basic question: fewer than *what?*

Editors also should check ratios. Ratios compare two numbers and allow readers to easily assess similar situations. For instance, if one local high school has 1,200 students and 60 teachers and another has 1,800 students and 70 teachers, which offers the better student–teacher ratio? To find out, simply divide 1,200 by 60 (which yields 20 to 1, or 20:1), then 1,800 by 70 (which yields 25.7 to 1 or, rounding up, 26:1). Even though the first school has fewer teachers, it has a substantially better student–teacher ratio.

Editors also should check that numerical information in body copy matches information in headlines, cutlines, graphs and charts.

In addition to being skeptical of numbers used in articles, editors also should check that numerical information in body copy matches information in headlines, cutlines, graphs and charts. For example, a profile of a college basketball player noted that he needed 432 points to become the all-time leading scorer at his school; the cutline under his picture on the opposite page said he needed 455 points. Another article said seven baseball players were ejected after a brawl in the middle of a game; the headline raised the number to eight.

Finally, it's important to check not only figures but also the accompanying words. For example, an article reported that the recommended daily allowance for folic acid is 400 milligrams. But anyone who took that amount would actually be getting *1,000 times* the recommended amount of 400 micrograms. The writer had confused milligrams, each one-thousandth of a gram, with micrograms, each one-millionth of a gram.

Rankings

Any time a ranking is included in copy, and especially when the ranking is an absolute such as the worst, the first or the most, editors should confirm the ranking.

But editors don't always do their job. For one example, many media accounts referred to Hurricane Andrew, which left great destruction in its wake in 1992, as "the worst natural disaster" in the nation's history. But at least in terms of deaths, it was *far* from the worst disaster ever: While more than 30 people died as a result of Andrew, 500 people were killed in a hurricane and flooding in Galveston, Texas, in 1900.[6]

And remember the passage mentioned earlier about "the biggest dance craze since the Twist?" That's almost impossible to prove, especially with disco and other major dances appearing in the intervening years. It would be far safer to describe the new dance as "one of the most popular dances in years."

Incorrect ranking information in advertising copy can lead to legal action. For example, a Microsoft advertisement billed its word-processing program, Word, as the world's most popular word-processing program. The claim was based on sales during the previous year. WordPerfect Corp. sued Microsoft, saying that WordPerfect deserved the title because many more copies of its program had been sold in *all* previous years.[7]

Translations

Some writers are too eager to make translations of foreign phrases. Unfortunately, even when translations are literally correct, they may be factually wrong. Case in point: The title of the well-known French satirical publication Le Canard Enchainé was translated by a writer to its literal equivalent, "Duck in Chains." That translation doesn't seem to make sense, and an observer pointed out why: In the context of a publication, "canard" would translate not as "duck" but as "rag," and "enchainé" not as "in chains" but as "censored" or "gagged." It's a far cry from a "Duck in Chains" to "The Censored Rag."

Titles

"County commissioner" might sound like "city councilor," but they're worlds apart. So are lecturer and professor emeritus, copy editor and editor in chief, and box office manager and theater manager. To let a wrong title slip through is often to deprive someone of an honor he or she has worked hard to achieve.

Facts That Aren't

Many years ago, I was ready to sign a lease for a second-floor apartment when I noticed a clause prohibiting waterbeds. Because I had recently purchased a waterbed, I asked the landlord about the clause. He told me he didn't allow waterbeds because they tended to crash through floors. Everybody knew that, he said.

The only problem was, it wasn't true. I researched the matter and found that there had never been a documented case of a waterbed crashing through a floor. I told the landlord, he let me move in, and the waterbed quietly stayed in its place.

The myth of the wayward waterbed is only one of many "facts" that people assume are true but aren't. Some "facts" seem so indisputable that writers and editors don't think to check them. Many big stories that the news media have jumped on in recent years have turned out not to be true. For example, during the 1980s the media reported that a million and a half children were missing, with as many as 50,000 being abducted every year by strangers. Those figures, made available by a group seeking to publicize its efforts at finding missing children, were treated as facts by the media. The story was big news for years — until The Denver Post investigated the figures and found that they were vastly overinflated. (The Post won a Pulitzer Prize for doing what any decent news organization should have done: checked the facts.)[8]

In addition to that type of nonfactual fact, there are what have become known as "urban legends": the story about the young man who picked up a woman in a bar for a night of wild sex, then woke in the morning to find the woman gone and

"Welcome to the world of AIDS" scrawled in lipstick on the bathroom mirror; the story about the child who tried to dry his wet poodle in a microwave — and blew up the pup in the process. These and many other urban legends have been printed and reprinted, something that would not have happened had alert editors asked, "Where's the proof?" (For a great collection of stories like these that have gotten past editors and into print, check out "Too Good to Be True: The Colossal Book of Urban Legends" by Jan Harold Brunvand, or check out *www. urbanlegends.about.com.*)

When Good Editors Go Bad

If there's anything worse than an editor missing a factual error in an article, it's an editor making a factual error. Writer Paul Raffaele learned that firsthand.

Raffaele was surprised when he read the lead on an article he had written for Reader's Digest. As the article appeared in print, it has Raffaele reflect on a plane trip over the Australian countryside:

> Beside me, a sunburnt English migrant smiles as he peers out the window at his adopted town. "It's about as far away from anywhere as you can get," he says.

What struck Raffaele as odd was that that migrant hadn't been on the plane with him — or in his article. As a subsequent issue of Brill's Content reported, "editors have made up facts and quotes, and even added characters, in at least three Reader's Digest stories, one of which ran in the U.S. edition — all despite the objections of the writers."

Eric Schrier, editor of Reader's Digest, told Brill's Content that the "sunburnt English migrant" had actually been sitting on a plane next to the editor who handled Raffaele's article — "not clean journalistic practice," Schrier admitted.[9]

Where to Check

The resources available to editors for fact-checking vary greatly. A small publication or public relations agency may have a handful of reference works; a large daily newspaper may have a reference section that rivals many libraries. Even a modest collection of resources will answer many of the questions editors are likely to have. The volumes listed in the following section can serve as the cornerstone of a good general reference library. Every editor should be familiar with these works. The list is based on conversations with editors and librarians, as well as on suggestions from researchers.[10] In most cases, Web sites offer all or some of the information available from the print editions, sometimes for a fee.

General

Encyclopedia: A good encyclopedia like the Encyclopaedia Britannica (Online at *www.britannica.com*) or the Encyclopedia Americana provides entries on a wide range of topics. While the entries don't supply in-depth information, they do provide quick access to general facts.

World Almanac and Book of Facts: This unassuming volume is packed with useful information spanning a wide range of topics. **State almanacs** offer similar collections of information specific to individual states.

Statistical Abstract of the United States: Whether you want to know the number of refrigerators in the United States or the cost of health care, you can track down an answer in this publication, published by the U.S. Bureau of the Census. The statistics are compiled from a variety of government agencies. (Online at *www.cache.census.gov/statab/www*).

County and City Extra: Annual Metro, City and County Data Book: The Census Bureau publishes this work, which presents a variety of information on states, counties, cities and places in the United States, including health, households, vital statistics and crime statistics.

New York Public Library Book of Chronologies: This source offers an easy way to verify time sequences and make sure historical events occurred when a writer says they did.

Encyclopedia of Associations: This listing of thousands of groups concerned with virtually every imaginable topic is useful primarily as a means of finding a person to answer a question. I turned to this reference when I was trying to satisfy my landlord that my waterbed wouldn't crash through his floor. A call to the Waterbed Manufacturers Association got my proof.

Facts on File: Published weekly, Facts on File summarizes newspaper articles on major news events. Indexes let you quickly find major stories that have occurred since 1940. (Online at *www.factsonfile.com*)

Guinness Books of Records: From sporting events to eating events to sales records and many other topics, these books provide the authoritative word on the biggest, the longest and the strongest.

Biography

Biography and Genealogy Master Index: This is a good first stop in tracking down information on a person. The index includes hundreds of thousands of listings of biographical sketches in a variety of current and retrospective biographical sources.

Who's Who: The Who's Who library includes Who's Who in America, Who's Who of American Women, Who's Who in the World, Who's Who in American Politics, Who's Who Among African Americans and a number of other titles. All provide short biographies of notable people, but the usefulness of the Who's Who volumes is limited because the entries are written by the subjects, and not all those who are asked to write entries do so. (Online at *www.whoswho.com*)

Current Biography: An annual collection of biographical articles compiled from a variety of sources, Current Biography offers a more objective look at its

subjects. Each volume contains an index for the current decade; separate cumu-
lative indexes let you find articles published between 1940 and 2000. (Online at
www.hwwilson.com/Databases/biobank.htm)

African American Almanac: Covers the history of black America.

Geography

Rand McNally Atlases: These collections of large maps are updated yearly
to provide the latest information on our changing world.

American Places Dictionary: A four-volume guide to 45,000 populated
places, natural features and other places in the United States.

Columbia Gazetteer of the World: This three-volume set of geographical
places and features covers a wide scope of information including the political
world, the physical world and places of interest.

County and City Extra: Annual Metro, City and County Data Book: The
Census Bureau publishes this work, which presents a variety of information on
states, counties, cities and places in the United States, including health, households, vital statistics and crime statistics.

Quotations

Bartlett's Familiar Quotations (Online at *www.bartleby.com/index.html*) **and
The Oxford Dictionary of Quotations:**   Both allow editors to verify famous
quotes quickly — and to find out when quotes aren't really quotes.

Government and Politics

United States Government Manual: This reference is a good place to start
for information on the executive, legislative and judicial branches of government.
Some individual states have similar manuals.

Almanac of American Politics: This book offers information on state senators, representatives and governors, as well as information on state elections and
voter characteristics.

Congressional Directory: This biennial publication lists congressional committees and includes biographical information on members of Congress and key
aides.

Congressional Quarterly: For the history and background of legislative
action, this is your best source.

Congressional Quarterly's Washington Information Directory: This
volume organizes information into broad areas, such as health, science, energy

and so forth. It provides information on all departments and agencies of the federal government, as well as on congressional committees and private nonprofit organizations.

Congressional Quarterly Almanac: Each volume is devoted to one session of Congress; organization is by broad topics.

Government Assistance Almanac: This guide covers all federal financial and other domestic programs.

Europa World Yearbook: This comprehensive annual includes summaries of all countries and their demographics, industries, and government and economics. It also includes a directory of government, tourism and important organizations.

World Fact Book: This is a reference book prepared by the CIA of countries and general statistics.

Dictionaries

Webster's Third New International: This unabridged dictionary is a standard in many newsrooms.

Acronyms, Initialisms and Abbreviations Dictionary: This three-part dictionary includes acronyms — from the United States, Britain, Canada and other countries — that are encountered in magazines and daily newspapers; it's also available on CD-ROM.

The Oxford Dictionary of Slang: Arranged by category, with each citation giving the origin and meaning of the word. The book includes an alphabetical index and a table of contents of categories.

Periodical Indexes

Expanded Academic Index: Covering more than 400 magazines, journals and newspapers, this index lets editors quickly find articles dating back to 1977. It's available online, as well as on CD-ROM and microform. **Reader's Guide to Periodical Literature** and other printed titles index earlier articles.

National Newspaper Index: This guide to the content of the Christian Science Monitor, The Los Angeles Times, The New York Times, The Wall Street Journal and The Washington Post is available online and on microform. Full text is available for a fee.

Local Newspaper Indexes: Many newspapers offer indexes, and more are becoming available in electronic formats that allow keyword searches.

CAUTION: Be careful in using periodicals to verify facts — think about all the corrections in newspapers. You need more than one source to confirm a fact. Also, it's always best to use primary sources if possible. If a newspaper or magazine article quotes a government study, you should track down a copy of the study itself if time permits.

Local Sources

Telephone Books: A quick means of verifying names and addresses, local phone books also offer a way to check the correct spellings of business names. But they are not flawless; phone book listings should be used with caution. (Online equivalents at *people.yahoo.com* and *www.bigyellow.com*).

Stewart Criss-Cross Directories: Newspaper reporters often use these directories, which are set up by street address followed by the name of the person or business at that address. The directories offer a good alternative method of making sure names and addresses are correct. CD-ROMs that include all phone numbers in the United States offer a powerful new way to get such information. (Online equivalent at *www.anywho.com/telq.html*)

Street Maps: World atlases don't help much when editors are dealing with a city or town, but local street maps will let them pinpoint where Main and State streets intersect — or if they actually run parallel. (Online equivalent at *www.mapquest.com* or *www.mapblast.com*)

Trade Directories

Editor and Publisher International Yearbook: Primarily useful for its listings of newspapers around the world, this reference also includes information on the newspaper industry.

Newsletters in Print: A guide to thousands of newsletters and other specialized publications, this work can lead to unexpected gold mines of information. Unfortunately, few of the publications listed are readily available to the general public.

Gale Directory of Publications and Broadcast Media: This massive, multivolume set provides information on media outlets ranging from campus radio stations to the largest publications.

Ulrich's International Periodicals Directory: As the name implies, Ulrich's lists thousands of publications from around the world.

Books in Print: Lists all currently available books. (Online equivalent at *www.amazon.com*)

Working Press of the Nation: A five-volume set of directories that list newspaper and allied services, magazine and editorial, TV and radio, feature writing and photography, and internal publications.

One of the most obvious ways to help ensure that an article is accurate and thorough is to run it by the sources who contributed to it. That's what Christoper H. Schmitt of the San Jose Mercury News did while working on two articles about the Nasdaq. Schmitt felt the review made his stories better, but he found out such pre-publication review can be extremely controversial. Schmitt's decision led to a staff meeting that produced sharply varying opinions, Executive Editor Jerry Ceppos said. Ceppos sided with Schmitt, noting:

> I just think in a story that deals with such arcane and difficult economic issues, it makes perfect sense. In this case, there was no way that reading back pieces [of the article] would have worked.[11]

Like Ceppos, most editors agree to let a source verify or clarify quotes or look over sections of the article in which the source figures. In addition, many editors won't balk at letting an economist, scientist or other expert not involved in a story check an article to make sure the writer has not made a mistake in handling highly technical information.

The most radical policy permits sources to look over an entire article before it is published. Writing in Quill magazine, Steve Weinberg notes that doing that is not much different from submitting an article to magazine fact checkers, who routinely contact sources in reviewing copy. In addition to helping ensure that information is correct, Weinberg writes, pre-publication review also can remind sources of other information they hadn't mentioned before or lead sources who had held back information to be more forthcoming. Further, Weinberg writes, the review is a "great tool for building solid relations with sources." He continues:

> Next time I go to those sources, their doors will be wide open. Furthermore, the sources will tell other potential sources about my desire for accuracy, so that additional doors will open.[12]

Some editors will not agree to such a policy. Letting a source review a complete draft, they say, is an invitation for the source to insist that unfavorable facts are deleted. As communication consultant John Brady writes in his "10 Commandments of Editorial Integrity":

> Check back with a source for an accuracy review of quotes obtained during an interview, if you promised to do so, but never give a subject the right of final review and approval of a manuscript. Your job is to play fair with a subject, not to be a rewrite department in the ego division.[13]

If a source is allowed to review a complete manuscript, the review should come at the initiative of the writer and editor, *not* at the initiative of the source.[14] When a writer is pressed by a source to provide final review privilege, the writer should say either that time will not permit it or that such a decision must be approved by the editor.

Pre-publication Review

When in Doubt, Leave It Out

Sometimes, despite your best efforts, you cannot confirm a fact. Fortunately, there's an easy solution if the information is not essential to the article: Just pull it out. Dee Lyon, a librarian at The Baltimore Sun, recalled an instance when a reporter was checking on the name of a horse entered in the Preakness. The reporter had been told that the horse was named after a character in an opera. Lyon checked a dictionary, reference books on music and several other sources, but she could not come up with a definitive answer to whether the name really was that of an opera character. The reporter didn't refer to that "fact" in writing the article, and the article didn't suffer for the omission. The moral: When in doubt, leave it out.

When All Else Fails: Running Corrections

Many editors believe that a correction should be displayed as prominently as the original article.

When errors make it into print, editors should correct them as quickly as possible. Many editors believe that a correction should be displayed as prominently as the original article; at a minimum, corrections should be easy for the reader to find. Although admitting mistakes makes readers aware that a publication is not perfect, it is only by running thorough and timely corrections that editors can expect to keep the trust of those readers. And, if the errors defamed a person or company, running a correction can go a long way toward limiting a publication's liability. Chapter 5 will deal with that topic in more detail.

Notes

1. David Shaw, "Poll Delivers Bad News to the Media," The Los Angeles Times, 31 March 1993, sec. A, p. 16.

2. Howard Kurtz, "The First to Blink? It Wasn't the Camera," The Washington Post, 24 April 2000, sec. C, p. 1

3. David Carr, "New York Times, in Hyper-Self-Criticism Mode, Invites the Public to Tell It Just What It Has Gotten Wrong," Inside Media, 17 October 2000, *www.inside.com*.

4. Kevin Coffey, remarks to the American Press Institute seminar for News Editors and Copy Desk Chiefs, August 1993.

5. Neal Travis, "Bra-zen Times Errs on Ivana," NYPost.com, 18 October 2000, *www.nypost.com*.

6. Ernest F. Imhoff, "Hyperbole Reaches New Heights," The Baltimore Sun, 21 February 1993, sec. G, p. 3.

7. Reported in Business Digest, The Washington Post, 16 October 1993, sec. C, p. 1.

8. Valerie Basheda, "Separating Fact from Fad," Presstime, December 1992, pp. 13–15.

9. Howard Kurtz, "Critical to a Fault, Journal Targets Gore," The Washington Post, 11 September 2000, sec. C, p. 14.

10. One particularly valuable source is William L. Rivers, "Finding Facts" (Englewood Cliffs, N.J.: Prentice-Hall, 1975).

11. Carol Gusensburg, "Show Time in San Jose," American Journalism Review, October 1998, p. 9.

12. Steve Weinberg, "So What's Wrong with Pre-publication Review?" Quill, May 1990, pp. 26–28.

13. John Brady, "The Erosion of Editorial Integrity," Folio:, 1 August 1993, p. 38.

14. In a survey of magazine executives conducted by Folio: magazine, only about a third of the editors responding said they would be very likely or somewhat likely to deny a source's request to read an article before it is published. See Tony Silber, "A Big Silence Out There," Folio:, 15 February 1994, pp. 49–50.

EDITING FOR THE WEB

Using the Internet for Fact Checking

Editing for print and editing for the Web converge in using the Internet for fact-checking and research. The Internet offers a splendid tool for tracking down and verifying information. Even Web sites that aspire to nothing more than moving product can be tremendous resources. As Nancy McKeon of The Washington Post has written about her research use of Amazon.com:

> I don't go to Amazon just to buy books. As an editor, I go to the site to do things quickly that I used to do more laboriously in the library or on the phone — check titles, spell authors' names, find new books on a subject.[1]

Whether you use shopping sites or more conventional resources, the Internet is a great tool for any editor. But using that tool effectively means understanding how it works and how to evaluate information you find.

Once you understand those things, the Internet can make your life immensely easier. For instance, in writing the second edition of this text, I found myself with countless facts that I needed to verify were still accurate. A person identified as the managing editor of a newspaper in the original edition may well have left that post; a newsletter might well have ceased publication. The Web allowed me to check such facts either by finding the relevant information on publications' online sites or by tracking down the e-mail address of someone at the publication who could answer my questions. In addition, I was also able to get ready access to several years of back issues of industry publications to update information throughout the book. I'd estimate that using the Internet to check facts saved me hundreds of hours of driving to libraries, making long-distance phone calls and writing letters.

Unearthing Information

If you're just beginning to use the Internet for research, you'll likely find it worthwhile to read "Super Searchers in the News" (Information Today Inc., 2001), written by Paula Hane and edited by Reva Basch. If you want or need to dive right in, though, the following tips should get you started.

Whenever possible, your best bet is to go directly to the source. If you want to verify the amount the Postal Service is planning to increase the price of mailing a 1-ounce letter, start by visiting *www.usps.com*. To double-check details on a proposed corporate merger, stop by the companies' Web sites (usually just the companies' names, preceded by *www.* and followed by *.com*). To check a quote in a presidential address, swing by *www.whitehouse.gov* (**not** *www.whitehouse.net,* which is a satire site, or *www.whitehouse.com,* which will whisk you to a porn site).

Several information sources can offer a quick route to answers to questions concerning the federal government. FirstGov (*www.firstgov.gov*) searches 20,000

U.S. government Web sites and 27 million pages of data. FedStats (*www .fedstats.gov*) offers direct access to the latest data from more than 70 U.S. government agencies. Two other good sources of government information are UncleSam (*www.google.com/unclesam*) and GovSearch (*usgovsearch.northernlight.com/ publibaccess*).

If you need to find an expert, try Profnet (*www.profnet.com/profsearchguide .html*), which links to experts at universities, research organizations, government agencies and corporations around the globe. You often can turn up experts in online discussion groups, too. To find a group that focuses on a topic of interest to you, try the archives at *groups.google.com* or *www.topica.com.*

Three other resources can help answer common questions. The Internet Public Library (*www.ipl.org*), compiled by researchers at the University of Michigan, provides an index of links to Web sites in a range of disciplines. The Librarian's Index to the Internet (*www.lii.org*), sponsored by the Library of California, offers a similar index. LibrarySpot (*www.libraryspot.com*) allows users to search for information in two ways: through links to the Web sites of public libraries and other information warehouses, or through a "You asked for it" archive of answers to common questions.

If you want to make sure that a story that seems too good to be true is, indeed, true, you might want to head to the Urban Legends Reference Page (*www. snopes.com*).

If you can't find your answer at one of those destinations, you may want to try a **scout site** or **specialized search index.** The former is a type of site that attempts to gather the best information on a given topic. To keep tabs on new scout sites, visit the Scout Report (*www.scout.cs.wisc.edu*), a weekly publication offering a selection of new and newly discovered Internet resources of interest to researchers and educators. Mailing lists are available by subscription.

Specialized search indexes offer lists of Internet resources on a specific topic. For example, FindLaw (*www.findlaw.com*) offers links to legal information, while The Medline Fool (*www.medportal.com*) offers one-stop access to the National Library of Medicine's databases.

When no ready source of information leaps out at you, you'll need to use one or more search engines. Search engines generally fall into three types:

1. **General search engines:** These are created by computer programs that use "spiders" or "bots" to find new sites. These engines offer a large quantity of pages accessible by keyword. The most popular general search engines include:

Altavista (*www.altavista.com*)

Excite (*www.excite.com*)

Google (*www.google.com*)

GoTo (*www.goto.com*)

Hotbot (*hotbot.lycos.com*)

Infoseek/Go Network (*www.infoseek.com*)

Lycos (*www.lycos.com*)

Northern Light (*www.northernlight.com*)

WebCrawler (*www.webcrawler.com*)

Because each search engine covers only a limited number of Web sites, it's a good idea to use more than one.

2. Subject directories: Subject directories are created by humans, rather than computer programs. The indexers organize information into general categories. Such engines include:

About (*www.about.com*)

DMOZ (*www.dmoz.com*)

Looksmart (*www.looksmart.com*)

WWW Virtual Library (*www.vlib.org*)

Yahoo (*www.yahoo.com*)

Some subject directories, such as Listen.com (*www.listen.com*) and the Internet Movie Database (*www.imdb.com*) focus on a specific topic — in this case, music and movies.

3. Meta-search engines: These engines search a number of other search engines at the same time. They include:

Dogpile (*www.dogpile.com*)

Metacrawler (*www.metacrawler.com*)

Ask Jeeves (*www.askjeeves.com*)

To keep abreast of the latest search engines — and to find tips for getting the most out of them — check Search Engine Watch (*www.searchenginewatch .com*).

In addition to the search engines, you might try some of the online equivalents of the reference works discussed earlier in this chapter. Beyond those already mentioned, you might find the following useful:

Biography.com (*www.biography.com*)

Encyclopedia.com (*www.encyclopedia.com*)

Information Please (dictionary, encyclopedia and almanac) (*www.infoplease.com*)

If you have more time, you might be able to get an answer to your question by tracking down an expert. If you know an expert's name, online equivalents of white and yellow pages can help you find a phone number or address. Online sources include:

Bigfoot (*www.bigfoot.com*)

BigYellow (*www.bigyellow.com*)

InfoSpace (*www.infospace.com*)

Switchboard (*www.switchboard.com*)

Yahoo People Search (*people.yahoo.com*)

Yahoo Yellow Pages (*yp.yahoo.com*)

Advanced Strategies

Different search engines provide different ways to home in on the information you want. It's worthwhile to take the time to read the "how-to-use" information for any engine you're considering. Search engines offer a variety of advanced techniques to limit the items they return. Note, however, that meta-search engines do not support these advanced features.

- **Phrases:** A specific phrase generally delivers better results than a single word. For example, a search for "AIDS prevention" will return fewer and more useful results than just searching for AIDS. Most search engines require you to put quote marks around a phrase.

- **Case sensitivity:** Beginning a search term with a capital letter will tell some engines to look only for instances of the term that are capitalized. For instance, if you want information on Specialized Bicycles, make sure you capitalize both words so the engine looks for the trade name and not just the words *specialized* and *bicycles*.

- **Required and prohibited terms:** To require that one of your terms be included in all documents resulting from your search, place the + symbol in front of it. To eliminate a term, place a – symbol in front of it. For example, to find information on women's shelters, you might try

    +women +shelter –fallout

- **Wildcards:** Entering a wildcard character (usually the * symbol) at the end of a word will substitute for a combination of letters. So searching for theat* will return theater, theatre and theatrical.

- **Boolean terms:** The Boolean operators AND or NOT function the same way as do the + and – symbols. But the ability to mix and match those terms with another operator, OR, and to group terms in parentheses makes Boolean searching more powerful. For example, to search for information on feline distemper, you could try this:

    (cat OR feline) AND distemper NOT canine

Looking for News

Several search sites regularly index content from news Web sites, offering a great way to find recent coverage of a topic. The only problem with such sites is that most news sites move content to a pay-per-view archive section after a week or two, so unless you're looking for coverage of a fresh story, you may end up getting mostly Web addresses that no longer work. Among the news search sites:

- Excite's NewsTracker (*nt.excite.com*) searches more than 300 online newspapers and magazines and also can be used as a clipping service to gather articles on specific topics.

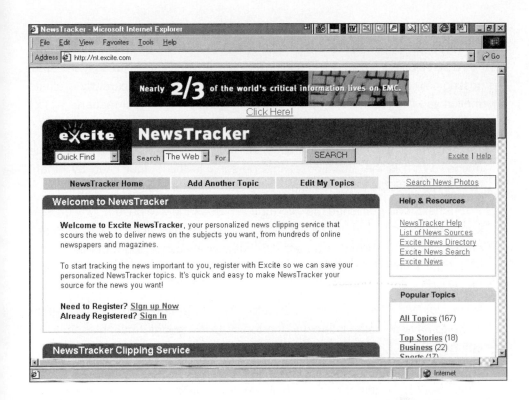

Excite's NewsTracker offers personalized clipping service.

- Wired Digital's NewsBot (*www.newsbot.com*) indexes about two dozen news sites, updating hourly.

- TotalNews (*www.totalnews.com*) offers a search engine and directory of news sites.

- WiseWire (*www.wisewire.com*) covers a wide range of Web sites including news sites.

- Yahoo's search engine (*dailynews.yahoo.com*) offers access to a week's worth of news from several news sites, and also can e-mail you alerts when it finds a news article that matches an area of interest you've specified.[2]

- Net2One (*www.net2one.com*) offers searches of news sources as well as personalized press reviews and e-mail alerts when keywords appear in the news.

- The Poynter Institute's Nelson search engine (accessible from the Poynter home page: *www.poynter.org*) lets users search a wide range of news Web sites using a variety of criteria (geographical location, beats, etc.).

- HeadlineSpot (*www.headlinespot.com*) offers searches of wires, newspapers, and radio and TV Web sites by subject, location or media type.

- OnlineNewspapers (*www.onlinenewspapers.com*) claims to index 10,000 online newspapers from around the world.

If you'd like to see how news organizations around the world are covering a topic, you can find the Web sites of countless news outlets by visiting either News and Newspapers Online (*library.uncg.edu/news*) or NewsLink (*ajr.newslink.org*). And you can find links to a wide range of Internet sources for journalists at the Special Libraries Association News Division (*www.ibiblio.org/slanews*).

Evaluating Information

You must carefully evaluate information you find on the Web before you pass a link along to your readers.

As the White House example earlier should indicate, anyone can buy a domain name, get hosting service and place content online. Therefore, you must carefully evaluate information you find on the Web before you pass a link along to your readers.

To evaluate information on the Web, you'll need to question several aspects:

- **Author:** Who wrote the material? Are this person's credentials available online? What is the affiliation of this person? Is the author cited by others whom you trust? Is this site linked to by other credible sites?

- **Publisher:** Who published the information? Does the site have a *.gov* or *.edu* address to lend it authority? If so, is this Web page part of an official Web site or just part of an individual's personal Internet account? You can learn more about the owner of a site by searching for the domain name at Whois.net (*www.whois.net*).

- **Purpose:** Does the site seem to exist to inform or persuade? Does the author seem to have a vested interest in the topic? Does the information seem to be balanced?

- **Coverage:** Does the information appear to be a thorough examination of the topic area? Does the site offer a bibliography or links to other sources?

- **Currency:** When was the information placed online? Has it been updated since then?

A few popular sources of online information also can prove useful for verifying facts, but they also pose risks. Online newspapers and magazines are the first source, and they are full of potential problems. First, it's impossible to know how much care went into an article. An article written on deadline may have been thrown together haphazardly. Second, corrections and follow-ups are not always attached to articles. Elizabeth Haworth, a former researcher for Newsday, illustrated this pitfall in an interview with American Journalism Review:

> At least once a year at Newsday we'd get a call from someone asking how many Marines died [in 1983] in the bunker in Lebanon. If you go into a database to get the official number after the attack, you're missing all the residual deaths over the next two years.[3]

A third problem with using periodicals is that online holdings are limited: Few online sources date back beyond the 1980s.

Two other sources of great promise are **discussion lists** and **news groups.** E-mail discussion lists are generally the more trustworthy of the two, because subscribers tend to know one another. On the other hand, many of those posting to newsgroups — a large number of which are searchable through *groups.google. com* — are anonymous. While some of the people gathered in these spots can provide valuable information quickly, not all online sources can be trusted. "A lot of this information is anonymous," says Carl Hausman, president of the Center for Media in the Public Interest. "Some of this stuff is crazy. You have no idea where it came from. If I read it in The New York Times, I know it's reputable. At least they have something at stake."[4]

When Web Editors Do Good

Virtually since the birth of online news sites, they have been criticized for a lack of rigor in reporting and editing. But one site showed that online news editors can outperform their print counterparts when it broke one of the most embarrassing media stories in recent years.

The story started in May 1998, after The New Republic printed an article, written by Associate Editor Stephen Glass, about a 15-year-old master computer hacker. The article recounted how Ian Restil, the hacker, broke into the databases of a major software firm, then demanded money, porn magazines and a sports car from the company. Glass's article further reported that hackers like Restil were hiring agents to broker lucrative deals.

After reading the article, Adam Penenberg, an editor at the online Forbes Digital Tool, was shocked that he had been scooped on a story in an area of his expertise. After digging, Penenberg concluded that the information in the article was made up. He then set out to determine whether Glass had been the victim of a hoax — or the perpetrator. In the process of investigating, Penenberg and Charles Lane, editor of the New Republic, determined that Glass had fabricated the story and characters. In addition, he had used his brother's cell phone number as the contact for the supposed hacked company, had concocted a fake corporate Web site for the company, and had set up fake voice and e-mail accounts for his sources.[5]

After Penenberg's exposé on Forbes Digital Tool, editors at the New Republic and other major print magazines Glass had written for conducted further investigations and found likely or proven fabrications in more than two dozen articles. In every case, Glass's false notes and explanations had gotten his articles past the editors.

Not surprisingly, Glass was fired from the New Republic and the demand for his work dried up elsewhere — all thanks to a hard-working online editor.[6] "I feel strongly that we've been dissed by traditional media so often," Penenberg said at the time. "Maybe this whole incident will show that we deserve some respect."[7]

Other resources abound on the Internet, many of them requiring a little sleuthing. One good guide for editors is "The Online Journalist" by Randy Reddick and Elliot King. And, of course, you can find guides online. One of the best is "A Journalist's Guide to the Internet" (*www.stlouisspj.org/surf/surf.html*), developed by the Society of Professional Journalists, St. Louis Professional Chapter.

Notes

1.   Nancy McKeon, "If I Can't Click, It Will Be … a Real Drag," The Washington Post, 9 July 2000, sec. B, p. 1.

2.   Steve Outing, "News-Only Search Sites Proliferate," Editor & Publisher Interactive, 8 October 1997, *www.mediainfo.com*.

3.   Christopher J. Feola, "The Nexis Nightmare," American Journalism Review, July/August 1994, p. 41.

4. Kurt Kleiner, "Side Trips to Cybersites," Columbia Journalism Review, March/April 1994, p. 43.

5. Adam L. Penenberg, "Faked Out," Forbes Digital Tool, 1 June 1998, *www.forbes.com.*

6. Rick McGinnis, "A Tissue of Lies: The Stephen J. Glass Index," 16 July 1999, *www.interlog.com/~rmcginn/Glassindex.htm.*

7. Pete Danko, "Print Media in Glass Houses," Wired News, 13 May 1998, *www.wired.com/news/print/0,1294,12279,00.html.*

(*Some of the material in this section has been adapted from "Building Basic News Sites," copyright 2000, Thom Lieb.*)

Editor's Corner

Liza Featherstone, journalist and editor based in New York City

Just the Facts

I worked as a professional fact-checker from 1992 to 1998. Don't feel bad if you don't know what a fact-checker does: Most editors and writers don't know, either. But I'll be glad to tell you.

Fact-checkers work mostly at magazines, where they independently verify every contestable fact they see in print. Fact-checkers provide yet another set of eyes to make sure that what ends up in print is correct, relieving editors of some of the burden. That's important because writers aren't always careful to make sure their facts are straight. Sometimes they just make up a "fact" — or leave a blank space for the fact-checker to fill.

The first step in fact-checking is going through an article and identifying everything that a reader could contest or contradict, anything that could be considered a fact. Some things are easy to check. Is the Caspian Sea really a sea, for instance, or is it a very large lake? Check a geographical dictionary.

Not every fact is as easy to check. If a fact cannot be verified quickly in a reference book, a fact-checker needs to do more work. If the sources of the information are identified, a phone call is in order. For example, checking a profile, I would call the subject himself.

Usually, though, verifying facts is more complicated than that. For example, in checking an article, I came across a sentence that said there were almost no documented cases of lesbians who have AIDS. So I called the Lesbian Health Project, and they gave me completely different information: Approximately 8,000 cases had been documented. That's not a little different from "almost none," it's wildly different. So I called another source, the Centers for Disease Control. They agreed with the article: Almost no cases of lesbians with AIDS have been documented. So I had to start questioning how these groups were defining terms. I asked how CDC defined a lesbian, and they said that a lesbian is any woman who has not had sex with a man since 1978. To me, that seemed to exclude many women. I made another call to the Lesbian Health Project and got more information on their figures, which were the ones I finally used. And so it goes in most cases: back and forth between sources, evaluating their information and agendas.

One of the most important things in fact-checking is checking a fact in its context. Sometimes a writer will include facts that seem fine on their own but completely contradict other information in the article. So a fact-checker has to ask when the information was gathered, who gathered it and so on, until she can determine which "fact" is the correct one.

A fact-checker also has to think about how her work will affect the editor. For example, when she finds an error, it might require cutting a complete paragraph. The editor might already be laying out the page at that point, so the fact-checker may need to find a way to change the information in the paragraph to make it usable.

People who have never worked as fact-checkers don't realize how complicated it is. Writers believe there shouldn't be any holes for me to deal with. Editors think what fact-checkers do is easy. I've often heard editors say: "I can't believe you're not done with that article yet. It was only a page long!" It doesn't make life any easier that sources don't know what fact-checkers do, either. Often they have already talked to a reporter, and they are confused about why they're being called again by the same publication.

Despite this lack of recognition, fact-checkers realize that what they do is important. They help prevent libel suits. They help our publications avoid embarrassment. And most importantly, they help fulfill a publication's unwritten contract with its readers that it tries to bring them the most accurate story possible. Even when you can't be proved wrong, or no one will care, you want to give readers something they can trust. Checking a story on tabloid television in Brazil, I called people in Brazil to ask them if they've ever watched the show. I sought out a second opinion on the translation of a Sanskrit proverb. This aspect of fact-checking isn't motivated solely by fear of corrections boxes or summonses. It is simply dedication to readers, and that, after all, is a big part of what got most of us into this business.

Of course, fact-checkers don't have a monopoly on this kind of dedication. Editors, too, show the same kind of commitment every time they carefully check the facts in the copy they're editing.

Misplaced Modifiers

The following sentence was part of a feature article in a sports publication:

The Ultra-Glide in-line skate is designed for the novice skater with three buckles.

That passage illustrates one of the most common writing problems: misplaced modifiers. Because readers expect phrases and clauses to modify the nearest word, the final phrase (*with three buckles*) seems to modify the noun *skater*.

Such mistakes are often called **dangling modifiers** or just **danglers,** and fixing them is simple. Just put the phrase or clause next to the word it modifies:

Designed for the novice skater, the Ultra-Glide in-line skate has three buckles.

Like the first example, many danglers are so obviously wrong that they are good for a chuckle. But danglers sometimes can cause confusion, as in this pair of sentences from a news article:

A man was shot in the parking lot of the Kentucky Fried Chicken at 3310 Reisterstown Road last night. Minutes later, after staggering into the restaurant to seek help, the assailant followed him in and shot the victim again, city police said.

Contrary to what the sentence says, it wasn't the *assailant* who staggered into the restaurant to seek help, but the *victim*. The confusion could be clarified with a little work:

Minutes later, the victim staggered into the restaurant to seek help. The assailant followed him in and shot the victim again, city police said.

Many danglers are **participial phrases.** A participial phrase is a phrase that begins with a **participle** — a verb form ending most commonly in *-ing,* but also occurring with endings of *-ed, -t* or *-en.* Some examples:

Lighting the oven, he inadvertently blew up the kitchen.

Haunted by the memory of a fatal crash the year before, the bicyclists decided to cancel their annual trip to the Eastern Shore.

Hurt by his rejection, Shantelle decided to re-evaluate her priorities.

Bitten by the cobra, the herpetologist struggled to call for help.

In all of these cases, the participial phrase directly precedes the word it modifies. But writers don't always check the placement:

Hanging from the tree, Charlie Brown abandoned his efforts to retrieve the kite.

Obviously, it isn't Charlie Brown who's hanging from the tree, but his *kite.* To eliminate the dangler, we could try this:

Charlie Brown abandoned his efforts to retrieve the kite, which was hanging from the tree.

What appears to be a participial phrase is sometimes a **nominative absolute** (a noun or pronoun followed by a participial phrase). Because a nominative absolute modifies the entire sentence, it does not have to be placed as carefully:

The workers having finally finished, we settled in for a quiet dinner.

Of course, you can't stick a nominative absolute just anywhere; the sentence must be comprehensible. You would not, for instance, rewrite the last sentence like this:

We settled, the workers having finally finished, in for a quiet dinner.

Exercise

Correct all spelling and style errors in the following article. Also correct any comma splices, fragments, incorrect clauses and misplaced modifiers.

A pregnant employ — not her companies owner — is resposible for making decisions effecting her safety and that of her child, a federal district court ruled recently. Therefore, the court explained, the fact taht the employers owner, who discharged the pregnant employee, acted on his perception of her best interests is irreverent.

Michelle Faillers was hired to work at Beau Shane. A horse stable in Matthews, Virginia. Becoming pregnant, her employer's owner, Walter Alford expressed his concern about her safety and the safety of her unborn child. As well as his own potential libalilty if she continued to work while pregnant.

Failler explained that she had worked around horses all her life, including durung her first pregnancy, and that she did not feel that she was in danger. She also told Alford that she intended to work until her doctor told her to stop.

Saying he was worried about her safety and his liability, Failler was dismissed in her third month of pregnancy. Alford said her condition gave him no choice but to terminate her.

Faillers filed a claim with the United States Equal Employment Opportunity Commision aleging pregnancy discrimination. EEOC evnetually brought suit on her behalf.

Reaching the Federal District Court, the court found that Failler had proven by a preponderance of evidence that her employer had discharged her because of the pregnancy. She was awared $23,000 in back pay and prejudgment interest.

Legal Issues

As editors check copy, they also keep their eyes open for potential legal problems. That work can be the most important work editors do. A single word or phrase can cause great harm to a person or a business and — if the harm is caused by carelessness — can cost thousands or even millions of dollars in a lawsuit.

Editors need to watch for several potential problems, which are sometimes intertwined. The major problem areas are *libel, invasion of privacy, copyright infringement* and *trademark infringement.*

Libel

Libel is the most common legal problem editors face, and it also is the most potentially catastrophic: Verdicts of more than $10 million are not uncommon. Unfortunately, libel can be difficult to detect. Libel laws vary from state to state, and courts sometimes rule differently on similar issues — or even on the same case. It is not unheard of for the verdict in a libel case to be reversed upon appeal, then reversed again at the next level.

With that in mind, it should be apparent that no discussion of libel can promise to answer every question. But editors need to know at least the basics about the greatest problem they may face. And they need to seek advice immediately from lawyers when they are not 100 percent certain on questions pertaining to libel.

Historically, slander applied to spoken defamation and libel applied to printed defamation. Libel was regarded as worse than slander because words in print are more permanent than spoken words. But the invention of broadcast media changed that assumption: Defamation occurring in a movie or a radio or television broadcast that reaches millions of people has to be considered at least as harmful as defamation on a printed page — or a Web page — that reaches a much smaller audience. So today defamation made in the broadcast media is considered to be libel.

Libel vs. Slander

The Price of Libel

People who bring libel suits against the media generally are looking for big money. In early 1994, for instance, Nation of Islam leader Louis Farrakhan sued the New York Post for $4.4 *billion.* His suit stemmed from a quote the paper ran in which Betty Shabazz accused Farrakhan of playing a role in the murder of her husband, Malcolm X.

Most plaintiffs content themselves with mere millions. The average libel award in the 1990s was $5,354,154.[1] In 1997, a jury awarded $223 million in a libel suit against Dow Jones and Co., publisher of the Wall Street Journal. (That verdict was later reduced to $23 million, and finally thrown out on the grounds that the plaintiff had won its initial victory through misconduct.)[2] Even when the media win, they can lose: Penthouse magazine spent more than a million dollars defending itself against a $26.5 million libel suit filed in the 1980s.[3]

What Is Libel?

Much of what is considered news reflects negatively on a person, an organization or an institution. Crimes, scandals, lies: No one charged with any of these feels good about seeing the charges in print. But media work isn't about making wrongdoers feel good; it's about giving the public information that they need. When that information legitimately includes material that reflects poorly on someone, editors have little to fear from publishing it (although in our litigious society, people sometimes will sue anyway). But when a publication or organization *unfairly* accuses a person, an organization or an institution of a less-than-noble activity, the accuser is open to a libel suit.

When a publication or organization *unfairly* accuses a person, an organization or an institution of a less-than-noble activity, the accuser is open to a libel suit.

In order for libel to occur, three conditions must be met. First, a defamatory statement must be made. Second, a person must be identified. Third, the material must be published. Let's look at each of those conditions in depth.

A Statement Must Be Made That Defames Someone.   Libeling a person means injuring his or her reputation or harming his or her ability to make money. A libelous comment causes people to think less of a person or causes an employer to fire the person or deny him or her a promotion. Corporations also can be libeled; libelous remarks can cause people to think less of the corporation or refuse to buy its products.

In addition, several states allow **disparagement** suits to be filed when products are defamed. The first widely reported disparagement case occurred when several thousand apple growers sued CBS after the network's "60 Minutes" program reported that the pesticide Alar used on apples posed a health risk to children. The growers claimed to have lost up to $100 million because of the report.[4] In 1998, Oprah Winfrey found herself on trial in another disparagement case after she hosted a guest who said that an epidemic of "mad cow disease" was likely. Oprah responded by noting, "It has stopped me cold from eating another hamburger." A group of Texas cattlemen sued her to recover $12 million in lost sales.[5] In both cases, the suits were thrown out, but disparagement claims still carry the potential to chill critical reporting.

Libelous statements typically do one of the following:

- **Accuse a person of a crime.**   Accusing a person of any crime that the person has not been officially charged with or convicted of is libelous.

- **Accuse a person of incompetence or dishonesty.**   Unproven charges that a person is unfit to hold a job or has lied also are libelous.

- **Charge a person with association with a generally disreputable group.** While it may not be illegal to be a Hell's Angel or a neo-Nazi, membership in such groups will not enhance a person's status in most other people's eyes. Again, if the charge is not justified, it is libelous.

- **Charge a person with a repugnant disease or mental illness.**   Spreading false rumors that a person has AIDS or other sexually transmitted diseases or suffers from mental illness also can lead to a libel suit.

- **Charge a person with anti-Semitism or other religious, racial or ethnic intolerance.**   Charges of intolerance can reflect negatively on a person, both in business and professional dealings.

- **Charge a person or business with financial insolvency.**   Especially for a business, reports of financial difficulties can cause loss of customers, investors and so on.

The Material Must Defame an Identifiable Person or Organization.   Let's say you pick up a news magazine and come across an article headlined "College students' use of illegal drugs on the rise." The article reports that more college students are using LSD, Ecstasy and other drugs. Although you're a college student,

---

Per Quod vs. Per Se

For any type of libel, it is just as bad to make a defamatory implication (known as **libel per quod**) as to make a direct charge (**libel per se**):

Bob Smith has embezzled more than $50,000 from his employer, First National Trust. (libel per se)

Bob Smith started work as a $10-an-hour teller at First National Trust just two months ago. It was his first job out of college. Last week, he paid cash for a new $54,000 Mercedes-Benz. This week, his employer realized that $55,000 had been embezzled. (libel per quod)

In one notable case of libel per quod, the tabloid National Examiner was sued after reporting that "Kato" Kaelin was suspected of a crime during O.J. Simpson's criminal trial. While Kaelin was indeed suspected of committing perjury while on the stand, the National Examiner's front page headline gave a different impression: "Cops Think Kato Did It." Kaelin sued for libel and received an undisclosed settlement.[6]

you of course would never indulge in such behavior, and you believe that this article will make other people think less of you.

Have you been libeled?

The answer is: only if the article directly or indirectly cites *you* as a drug user. Otherwise, it would be impossible for you to show that the article caused you personal harm. In short, a person or organization has to be identifiable in order to be libeled.

While that example may sound straightforward, determining whether a person is identifiable often isn't easy. Obviously, giving a person's name identifies him or her. So does giving enough details about a person that others would recognize him or her without a name — for example, "the president of the local branch of First National Bank" or "a 6-foot-tall blonde who stars in action movies."

A person also can prove identification if he or she is part of a group, but not a group as large as "college students." For example, an accusation against a local city council also is an accusation against the individual members of the council because they are few in number and clearly identifiable. Charges against other groups of as many as 100 people — church groups, social organizations, sports teams — also have been held as identifying individual members. Even a defamation of a group larger than that can cause trouble. If an article in a local publication notes that "all acupuncturists are quacks," and only two or three acupuncturists work in the publication's circulation area, they might prevail in a libel suit. As in most editing matters, when in doubt it's best to play it safe.

Works of fiction also can lead to libel suits. Slightly disguising a person's identity and calling a piece of writing fiction doesn't rule out identification. If the person whom the fictional character is based on can be identified, he or she may successfully sue for libel if the fictional character is depicted as engaging in defamatory actions. This provision primarily affects editors of books and magazines that print fiction; the same rule applies to movies and television shows.

The only people who can't be libeled are dead people. Libel is regarded as an offense against a person. If a person is dead, there are no grounds for a lawsuit unless the material also defames others who are alive. If a person brings a libel suit and then dies, however, the picture is different: Some states declare the case closed at that point, but others will allow it to proceed.

The Material Must Be Published.   This requirement sounds simple enough, but there is more to it than meets the eye. Three aspects of the requirement deserve special attention:

•   Publication does not refer only to material printed or broadcast in the mass media. Material appearing in magazines, newspapers and newsletters and on Web sites is obviously published. But for the purposes of libel, so is material appearing in unpublished drafts of articles, memoranda and letters, or in any other form. In an often-cited case, the Alton (Ill.) Telegraph was successfully sued for $1.4 million after two reporters sent a memo to a U.S. Justice Department investigator. The memo, in which the reporters said they suspected a local builder was connected to organized crime, was passed on to bank regulators, who in turn forced a savings and loan association to cut off credit to the builder. No story ever was published.

- In these days of electronic data, material does not even need to appear on a piece of paper to be published. Electronic mail and electronic drafts of an article that never saw print would count as publication.

- Publication can involve as few as three people — but never just two. At a minimum, libel requires one person to write something about a second person and show the material to a third person. When dealing with the media, the third person would have to be someone outside the newsroom — an editor reviewing and then spiking a reporter's libelous article would not count. Neither has publication taken place if one person writes something about another person and gives the material *only* to that person. If the recipient shows the defamatory material to other people, the recipient cannot sue the sender for libel.

> At a minimum, libel requires one person to write something about a second person and show the material to a third person.

- Any part of a publication can be libelous. Rarely do major articles prove to be libelous; most publishers routinely have their lawyers review articles dealing with sensitive information. A major investigative piece that reveals criminal activity will receive a thorough evaluation before publication. Therefore, libel wars typically are fought on much smaller battlefields: the defamatory sentence in an otherwise positive piece of copy; the accusatory headline that depends on the accompanying story for clarification; the hastily written photo cutline. In addition, libel can be created by the juxtaposition of elements that are fine on their own. For example, a newspaper article reported that a former drug addict was among those attending an anti-drug rally. The headline read (not very sensitively), "Former dope head joins Midland rally to boot drugs out." Under the headline was a picture — unfortunately, not of the former addict, but of a woman who sang at the rally. From all appearances, she was the "former dope head."

In short, the potential for libel is greatest when editors least expect it, so good editors must keep a constant vigil. One example of editors not being vigilant enough sticks in my mind. At a college where I once taught, the student newspaper ran an article about a student photographer who was stringing for The Associated Press. The story and headline were in no way defamatory. The article was accompanied by one of the photos the student had sold to AP; the photo, too, was fine. But in writing the cutline for the photo, an editor asked the photographer to identify the man in the photo. The photographer gave the editor the man's name and said the man was known for conning women whose husbands had just died. The man would call the women and tell them that their husbands had ordered expensive Bibles before their deaths, and the Bibles were now ready for delivery. That's what the editor wrote. But when a copy of the paper got into the hands of the man in the photo, he called the paper to inform them that he never had been charged with any such scam, let alone convicted of it. The newspaper settled the case by paying the man several thousand dollars — almost the full annual operating budget of the paper — to keep him from filing a libel suit.

Libel suits also have resulted from letters to the editor, editorials, cartoons, advertisements, headlines — you name it. In fact, the most important case in U.S. libel law — U.S. v. Sullivan — arose from an advertisement. So editors have to regard *everything* they handle as potentially libelous.

Defenses Against Libel

Throughout this discussion, libel has been referred to as an unfair or unjustified defamation. In some instances, of course, defamation is justified — or at least can be made without the threat of losing a libel suit. The three primary defenses are provable truth, privilege and fair comment. Let's look at them, as well as at a minor defense, consent.

Provable Truth.   The best defense against libel is provable truth. That sounds simple enough, but like much of libel law, it's more complicated than it seems.

First, it's not enough for a writer to say that a defamatory charge is true; the writer needs to be able to produce materials that *prove* the charge is true. A writer who calls someone a murderer should have a record of that person's conviction on charges of murder. Rumors will not do.

Second, merely being able to prove that someone made a charge is not the same as proving that the charge is true. A writer may have thorough documentation that the owner of Joe's Garage said that the owner of Gus' House of Gaskets is doing unnecessary repairs on customers' cars, but that does not prove the truth of the charge. In short: Attributing a charge does *not* prove the charge is true. Generally, an editor can count on provable truth *only* when an article cites documents that substantiate a charge.

Qualified Privilege.   In a democracy, the public must know what's going on in government in order to act responsibly. The media have the job of providing that information. But hearings, meetings, reports and other governmental activities that produce such information often include charges that defame people — charges that a writer either may not have the time to verify or may know are not true. Barbara Dill, a former member of the legal staff of The New York Times, writes in "The Journalist's Handbook on Libel and Privacy":

> Official charges against a person are often lodged well before any proof of their validity is publicly available. Public reports of investigations may draw conclusions that are not otherwise substantiated or formalized with legal proofs. Private citizens' litigation against one another may go on for years before there is any resolution. And inflamed opponents' debates over public projects and problems can extend over a series of public meetings before coming to a head.[7]

Fortunately, qualified privilege gives writers the right to report charges made in many proceedings and reports.

Qualified privilege covers activities at all levels of government, including the following:

- police actions (arrests and charges)
- meetings of legislative bodies and their committees
- petitions, complaints and other items received by legislative bodies
- hearings and trials (but not ones that are closed to the public)
- court opinions

- grand jury indictments

- actions of government officials on official matters

Editors should not assume privilege is in effect until an official action has been taken. For example, privilege might not apply when teachers draw up a complaint for state legislators, but it would when the legislators receive the complaint. And it might not apply when police pick up a person for questioning, but it would when they charge him or her. Some major media organizations learned this lesson the hard way when they named Richard Jewell as a suspect in a bombing at Centennial Olympic Park in Atlanta in 1996 — even though he had not been charged with any crimes. Jewell, who was later cleared of all connection with the bombing, sued CNN, NBC and the Atlanta Journal-Constitution for libel.[8]

While privilege applies to what's said in official contexts, it does not necessarily apply to what officials say informally. A statement on crime made by a mayor would be privileged, but the remarks of an aide to the mayor at a luncheon might *not* be privileged. A police officer's comments about how an arrest was made are probably privileged, but the officer's suspicions about the suspect's connections to other crimes are almost certainly *not* privileged.

In "Major Principles of Media Law," Wayne Overbeck suggests a good rule of thumb: "In general, the less official the occasion and the lower the status of the person making the statement, the less likely it is to be privileged."[9]

In some states, privilege extends to meetings of nongovernmental groups that are open to the public and deal with matters of widespread public interest. If a church holds a meeting to discuss ways to reduce gun deaths in the community, reports on that meeting could be privileged. Only an attorney familiar with media law can determine what is and isn't privileged in any given state.

Even when coverage of a meeting is privileged, a writer must be careful to stick to matters of public concern. For example, if during a school board meeting one parent defames another in a matter unrelated to the public issues, chances are good that a report of the defamation will not be privileged — and that if an editor allows it to be published, the publication will be sued for libel.

Privilege is contingent on the writer providing **fair and accurate** coverage. As Barbara Dill writes:

> Only an attorney familiar with media law can determine what is and isn't privileged in any given state.

Who Gets Sued

When a person is quoted in print as making a defamatory statement, the injured party more likely will sue the publication than the individual who made the statement. The reason for that is simple: The publication is likely to have much more money than the individual who made the remark.

A libel suit brought against a publication typically names every writer and editor who has had contact with the offending material, as well as the organization or publication itself. But a freelance writer who has sold a defamatory article to a publication may end up battling the suit alone, with the publication getting off the hook because the material was written by an outsider.

A fair report places charges and accusations in context and gives a balanced rendition of both sides of the issue if both sides are represented in the record or proceeding that forms the basis for the report. When reporting on a record or proceeding in which only one side of a dispute is presented, the journalist should place the information in context for the readers by summarizing the official opposing positions or at least referring to the existence of an opposing position.[10]

In addition, fairness requires writers to clearly identify their sources of information. If writers use defamatory material that ordinarily would be privileged but fail to identify the sources of the material, they may lose the protection of privilege.

Finally, fairness requires that writers make every attempt to locate the latest records. An article that reports defamatory charges in a lawsuit will not be privileged if the suit was dismissed before publication. Such a lack of follow-up cost the Pittsburgh Post-Gazette nearly $3 million. The paper published a story reporting an allegation that an attorney had prepared a fraudulent will to help his lover. The allegation had been made in a sworn pretrial statement. But the Post-Gazette did not publish the article until after the court had ruled that the will was not fraudulent.[11]

While it is not essential for privilege, editors always should double-check the court names in any article based on court action, whether it's defamatory or not. Failure to check might not cause a publication to lose a libel suit, but it will lower reader credibility. One good source of court information is the Blue Book.

Editors should insist that writers counting on the privilege defense have seen the records or attended the events on which their accounts are based. Libelous statements based on second-hand accounts — even accounts from police and other officials — may not be privileged if those statements are not found in the original proceeding or record. And it is essential that writers *understand* what the record says. That's not always easy when working with legal documents; often, the best bet is to have a lawyer help untangle them.

Fair Comment and Criticism.   The third major defense is fair comment and criticism, which permits criticism of those who put themselves in the public eye. Included are actors, dancers, artists, writers, politicians, athletes and journalists, among many others. In addition, fair comment covers otherwise private people who have thrust themselves into the middle of a public controversy. Fair comment also covers criticism of restaurants, movies, books, plays, television shows, and products and services offered for public sale.

Fair comment covers even the harshest criticisms, as long as the criticism is fair and does not include false allegations of fact.

To be fair, the criticism has to be based upon facts rather than based on hatred, revenge or other evil motive. A reviewer who tears apart a play because the acting was poor, the script was confusing and the sound was inaudible may be covered by fair comment. A reviewer who blasts a play solely because it stars someone he or she dislikes, however, will not be covered.

The distinction between criticism and factual allegation can be difficult to make. It is OK to write that the filet mignon served in a restaurant is dry and tough;

The distinction between criticism and factual allegation can be difficult to make.

it's not OK to write that the meat "should have been labeled filly mignon, because it surely didn't come from a cow." The second sentence makes a factual allegation: The meat was horse meat. Unless it can be proved, the comment is libelous.

Labeling a piece of writing "opinion" does not protect it if it contains false allegations of fact. The U.S. Supreme Court confirmed that in a 1990 ruling that let a high school wrestling coach sue a sports columnist who accused the coach of lying under oath.[12]

People who are public figures (see Page 142) must prove that a defamatory comment was made with **actual malice.** Actual malice is defined as follows:

a. The writer and/or editors knew the charge was false but published it anyway; or

b. The writer and/or editors had obvious reason to check the charge, but acted with **reckless disregard** in publishing it. Reckless disregard, an important concept in libel law, was defined this way in a classic court case:

Reckless conduct is not measured by whether a reasonably prudent man would have published, or would have investigated before publishing. There must be sufficient evidence to permit the conclusion that the defendant in fact entertained serious doubts as to the truth of its publication. Publishing with such doubts shows reckless disregard for truth or falsity and demonstrates actual malice.[13]

An example will help clarify what is and what isn't actual malice. In researching a profile of a prominent person, a writer talks to the subject's sister, who is close to the subject. The sister reveals that although the subject doesn't like to talk about it, he had a few rough years during his teens; at one point, he spent time in a juvenile detention center for auto theft. On deadline, the writer uses that information in the profile, without checking with the subject. If the information turns out to be inaccurate, the writer probably will *not* be found to have acted with reckless disregard. There was no compelling reason to verify the information. Instead, the writer will be guilty of **simple negligence.**

But suppose the information about the subject's run-in with the law comes from an anonymous phone call, and suppose further that the writer has a month until deadline. Publishing the charge without checking further will almost certainly result in a finding that the writer acted with reckless disregard.

One other aspect of fair comment is worth noting. Cartoons, jokes, and satirical articles and columns aimed at public figures generally enjoy extra protection. Courts have held that readers know not to take such items seriously, so those types of materials are not considered as harmful as straight news and feature articles. In addition, such materials usually target public figures, who are fair game for criticism. Finally, humorous materials often have political content, which helps justify their special treatment.

Consent.   A final means of escaping liability for libel is by getting the consent of the person being defamed. A person who voluntarily consents to the publication of such material cannot bring a libel suit when it is published.

Private vs. Public Figures

In libel actions, people may be classified in one of three ways. Those classifications are critical to how the media fare in defending defamatory publications.

1. **Private figures:** People who have done nothing to thrust themselves into the public eye are considered private figures. For private figures to win libel suits in most states, they merely need to show that the publication of false defamation resulted from simple negligence. Several states, however, require private figures to prove **gross negligence** — that is, the publication ignored the obvious need to verify a claim.

2. **Limited public figures:** Otherwise private citizens who take active roles in public controversies or events are regarded as limited, or **vortex,** public figures. For example, a person who organizes or leads a campaign or acts as a spokesperson for a group or movement likely will be ruled a limited public figure. In order for limited public figures to win libel suits based on defamation that applies to their public roles, they have to prove actual malice. If the defamation applies to another aspect of their lives, however, they are regarded as private figures and need to prove only negligence.

3. **Pervasive public figures:** Entertainers, sports figures, authors, major corporate executives and other well-known personalities are sometimes considered pervasive public figures. Think of celebrities who openly discuss their families, their marriages and divorces, and you can see people who hold nothing off limits to the media. Such people are regarded as public figures for all purposes, and they always must prove actual malice to win a libel suit.

Obviously, that doesn't happen often. More typically, consent is used as a defense against privacy suits, which are discussed later in this chapter. For example, a photographer who shoots people in a private place will ask them to sign a release form giving their consent to publish the photo. Once they sign, they relinquish their right to sue unless the photo is used in a way that suggests something unsavory was occurring that really wasn't.

Looking for Libel

Several strategies can help editors catch libelous material before it's too late:

- **Check every word that could possibly be construed as a defamatory statement of fact.** A reporter picked up a police officer's claim that his wife and children "deserted" him after he was severely injured by a bomb that he was attempting to dismantle. Although both the reporter and subject used the word as a synonym for "left," a state Supreme Court ultimately upheld a jury's view that saying the subject's wife had deserted him indicated that she had abandoned him while he was extremely vulnerable.[14]

Admit it: You've read the articles — or at least looked at the headlines — about the movie star who gave birth to an alien, the singer who has had affairs with Michael Jackson *and* Elizabeth Taylor, the nun who runs a chapter of the Hell's Angels. Such stories are the staples of the tabloid press. Occasionally, Roseanne, Cher or another celebrity may take on the tabs, but usually the papers get away with printing whatever they like. How can that be?

Well, by now you know at least part of the answer: Public figures have a much harder time winning a libel case than do private figures. For example, Christie Brinkley sued the National Enquirer after a series of articles described her as having delusions, paranoia and an irrational fear of cows — not to mention having had a nervous breakdown and having spent $30,000 on clothes in a single day. A New York judge threw out Brinkley's $42 million lawsuit, noting that although the stories were "truly obnoxious," they did not subject her to "hatred, contempt or aversion."[15]

But there's more to it than that. First is the time it takes to wage a libel suit. Few celebrities with active careers can afford to take months or even years to battle the tabs. Second is the fact that, as they say in Hollywood, "The only thing worse than bad publicity is *no* publicity." In fact, sometimes the stories in the tabs are planted by celebrities' agents to keep the celebrities' names in the public mind.

How Do the Tabloids Get Away with It?

- **Look for evidence of "the other side."** In the same case, the state Supreme Court ruled that the reporter's failure to investigate the charge constituted reckless disregard. As Chapter 3 suggested, any time a charge is published, attempts should be made to obtain a reply. If doing so means delaying publication of an article, then delay it. Rushing to print without obtaining a reply can be construed as reckless disregard.

- **Separate name from illegal actions in crime reports.** Until a person is formally charged with a crime, it is safest to not report the person's name. As the Richard Jewell case indicates, printing a name before a person is charged can be a costly mistake. Further, as Washington Post Metropolitan Editor Bob Barnes notes, "Once we name someone as a suspect, it's going to be hard for anyone to take that back." Another Post editor, Scott Vance, concurs: "If the police are not willing to go out on a limb, then we need to think carefully whether we do — as a matter of fairness."[16]

  Even after a person has been charged with a crime, writers and editors must make a clear distinction between the perpetrators and those charged with the crime, as the following example shows:

  A local man has been charged with the Friday robbery of a liquor store in which $300 in miniature bottles of liquor — but no money — was taken.

  Bernard Shaw Jr. was arrested Monday at his home at 112 Merritt Parkway. He was charged with the robbery of Quicker Liquors in the East Valley Shopping Center.

According to police reports, a man entered the shop just before it was to close at 9 p.m. Friday. He walked directly to the clerk and pulled out a gun. He then opened a canvas sack and demanded that the clerk fill it with miniature bottles.

The clerk loaded about 100 bottles into the sack; then the man told him to lie on the floor. After the gunman left, the clerk got back onto his feet and wrote down the man's license number as he drove away.

Police matched the license to Shaw, but they could not locate him over the weekend. A patrol officer noticed Shaw's car parked in front of his home Monday morning and made the arrest. The bottles were not recovered.

Notice how the suspect's name is not mentioned in the paragraphs that describe the robbery. That's because at this point, no one can prove the suspect was involved in that robbery.

- **Clearly identify the source of privileged information.** Whenever privileged information is used in an article, the source should be cited in the lead and, if possible, the headline.

- **Clearly indicate when material is intended as opinion.** Barbara Dill has compiled a list of several "indicators" that courts consider as signals that statements are intended to be opinion, not fact. Among the indicators:

1. A subjective evaluation is accompanied by the facts on which it is based. A writer should provide evidence to back an opinion. If a column says a candidate is not a good choice for governor, it should include reasons that support the evaluation.

2. When a writer is merely speculating, the material is phrased so that the reader knows that. Words such as "In my opinion" or "I suspect" are a tip-off. But the words following these phrases must contain opinion, not fact.

3. The statement does not charge anyone with an illegal or dishonest act.

4. The statement cannot be proved or disproved. Saying that a politician "hasn't supported his party's basic goals" is open to dispute, but cannot be proved or disproved. Unfortunately, determining whether a statement can be proved can be tricky. In 1994, the U.S. Court of Appeals in Washington, D.C., reinstated a libel suit based on a book review. The reviewer had called the book, based on investigative journalism, "sloppy." While one of the three judges reviewing the case argued that "sloppiness" is not verifiable, his two colleagues disagreed. One of them noted, "Although 'sloppy' in a vacuum may be difficult to quantify, the term has obvious, measurable aspects when applied to the field of investigative journalism."[17] Three months later, however, the judges took the rare step of reversing themselves. One of the judges noted that their verdict could be upheld only if "no reasonable person" could find the criticism supported in the book.[18]

5. The statement is not based on undisclosed facts that would be libelous if false. This was the problem with the use of the word "deserted" in the case cited earlier. The court ruled that the word suggested an undisclosed fact — that the wife left her husband in the lurch. That "fact" was false — and defamatory.

6.   The statement is so exaggerated that it is clearly opinion rather than fact.

*   **Be careful in choosing photos to accompany articles.** Editors should not use pictures of a person to illustrate a story about a defamatory topic (drug use, venereal disease, etc.) unless the person in the photo has been proved to be a member of the group discussed in the article. Also, editors should scrutinize anecdotes about people used in such articles. Unless the people themselves are the source of information, the material should not be used.

*   **Look at every element of a package individually.** As the student newspaper example cited earlier should have made clear, it's not enough that an overall package — article, headline, photograph, cutline and other elements — is not defamatory. Editors have to examine each element on its own. If any libelous material is found, it must be corrected or removed.

How Helpful Is "Allegedly"?

A common misconception is that it's OK for writers to make just about any defamatory claim they care to as long as the claim is preceded by "allegedly." That idea is simply wrong — and dangerous. Correctly used, "allegedly" means that someone has made an accusation without proof. While it can be used in detailing official charges against a person ("Dubai allegedly entered the store through an air duct, according to the police report"), it is qualified privilege and *not* the use of the word "allegedly" that provides protection from a libel suit. If no official charge has been made, using "allegedly" will not provide protection. On the contrary, it may be an invitation to sue.

Further, the words **alleged** and **allegedly** work only in certain ways. A person cannot be an alleged anything; only an action can be alleged. So it's wrong to write:

The alleged vandals entered the building at 9 a.m.

This revision is OK, though:

The vandals allegedly entered the building at 9 a.m.

And by all means, avoid using *alleged* with statements of fact. Here's a line I heard in a broadcast news story:

He was convicted of setting the fire in which four people allegedly died.

One would hope that investigators could determine whether those four people were really dead.

- **Make sure charges don't go beyond what is privileged.** Another article in a student newspaper reported correctly that two women had been charged with the murder of two foreign-born college students. But the headline read, "Women murder two college students." The women had not yet been convicted, so the publication was privileged only to write, "Women charged with murder of two students." The student editors caught the mistake just before the paper was to be distributed. Several thousand copies of the newspaper went to a shredder instead, and a potential suit was averted.

The Role of Retractions

Many libel suits could be avoided if only the libelous material were retracted as soon as it became known. In fact, the steps that editors take after receiving a complaint may be more important than what was published. Washingtonian magazine, for example, averted a libel suit brought by talk-show host Larry King by publishing a correction — even though the original article insinuated that King had a sexually transmitted disease, alleged that he was paying a former wife only a third of her alimony and made several other charges that could not be supported.[19]

Some tips on dealing with complaints:

Investigate the Complaint. It's not good policy to automatically run a retraction every time the phone rings, nor is it good policy to stand blindly behind what was published. Editors need to determine whether the material is libelous.

Print Retractions Quickly. If the material is libelous, a retraction should be printed as soon as possible. Doing so helps calm the person who was libeled — and can help save the publisher lots of time and money. Case in point: In 1996 a German magazine printed a quote attributed to actor Tom Cruise indicating that he could not become a father because he is sterile. Cruise denied having said that, and he asked for $60 million. The magazine gave him a retraction, and he dropped the suit.[20]

Retractions should be conspicuous and frank, to dispel any notion that the publication acted with reckless disregard for the truth. Several states have retraction statutes that specify how retractions are to be handled. Some states require corrections to be made "in a timely manner." Following the guidelines in such a statute can limit substantially the award in a libel suit.

Don't Republish Libel. If the material was libelous, editors should make sure it isn't reprinted in the retraction.

Privacy

While libel law exists to protect people's reputations, privacy law exists to protect their tranquility. In the simplest terms, privacy law protects people's right to be left alone. Even if the published facts about people are correct, they may be able to sue if their privacy has been invaded. The two aspects of most concern to editors in the area of privacy are publication of information that places a person in a false light and disclosure of embarrassing private facts about a person.

False Light

People can sue for being portrayed in a false light whenever the facts of an article make them out to be worse off than they really are — or even better off than they really are (although, not surprisingly, few people sue over errors that make them look better). The material does not have to be defamatory. While people occasionally sue for both libel and false light, some courts have held that if the material is defamatory, libel is the only appropriate charge. To complicate matters, some states require false-light complaints to be handled through libel suits.

What kinds of things could make a person look worse than he or she is without being defamatory? Well, for one thing, an incorrect claim that a person is living in poverty. It's not illegal to be poor, nor is it defamatory in any way, but it does make the person look worse off than he or she is.

Two kinds of problems that can lead to false-light actions are of concern to editors:

Adding Made-up Details to or Omitting Information From an Otherwise Accurate Story.　Detecting made-up information can be extremely difficult. In the 1980s, Washington Post reporter Janet Cooke made up an entire article about an 8-year-old drug addict. The article made it through the paper's editors and won a Pulitzer Prize before it was exposed as a hoax. (Once the deception was revealed, Cooke lost the Pulitzer and her job — and the Post lost at least some of its credibility.)

The difficulty of detecting fabrication does not excuse editors from trying, however. Editors always should be alert to details that don't seem genuine or don't fit the rest of the article. If they suspect information is false — or too good to be true — they should ask to see writers' notes. Similarly, editors also have to be alert for omissions that can lead readers to see a character in a false light.

The Use of a Photograph That Creates an Offensive Portrayal of a Person.　This is the more common basis for false-light lawsuits. In most cases, a publication uses a photograph that is fine on its own but puts a person in a false light when used with an accompanying article or cutline. In one classic case, a photograph of a married couple sitting together affectionately was used to illustrate an article on the dangers of love at first sight. The article in Ladies Home Journal said such love was based on "instantaneous powerful sex attraction — the wrong kind of love." The couple won their suit.[21]

Public Disclosure of Private Facts

The second problem area in privacy concerns a dispute between an individual's right to privacy and the public's right to know. An editor must decide whether private information is newsworthy enough to outweigh the subject's right to privacy.

For a person to win a suit over disclosure of private facts, the first step is to show that the facts were indeed private. If an article reports information from a public government record or information that the person has made no attempt to hide from others, or if a photograph shows a person in a public setting (even if the photographer did not get the person's permission to take the photograph), the information will not be considered private. But if the information is not widely

Merely printing private
information is no
grounds for a lawsuit.

known — or if it comes from a government record that is private, such as the proceedings of a child abuse case — it would be considered private.

Of course, merely printing private information is no grounds for a lawsuit. Even
if no one knows it, a publication cannot be sued for mentioning in a profile that a
person collects matchbook covers. For a suit to succeed, the material must be
highly offensive to the average person and *not of legitimate public concern.* These
are hard points to prove. Only the most vulgar material — information used
solely out of morbid curiosity — is likely to pass the first test. And because "public concern" is such a broad concept, almost any material can pass that test, as well.

Even in cases in which past charges about a person are reprinted, publications are in little danger of losing a suit for revealing private facts. Columns and
articles that take a historical look at events — even unflattering or tragic ones —
are sheltered from successful suits.

That doesn't mean editors can work on snooze control. In articles that recount
the past as well as any others that are based on private facts, it's important to examine the intention of the writers. If the only reason that such material is used seems
to be to embarrass the subject, then the subject probably would prevail in a lawsuit.

Editors also should look carefully at the status of the subject of any article that
reveals private facts. As in libel cases, it's important to determine whether the subject is a private or public figure. Publications have more latitude with public figures
in privacy cases, just as in libel cases.

One final aspect of publishing private facts is among the most controversial
issues writers and editors have faced in recent years: publication of the names of
rape victims, sexually abused children, juvenile offenders and clients of prosti-
tutes. Generally, courts have held that the media have the right to publish these
names if they are contained in the public record. Given that right, the question for
editors becomes one of ethics: Is publishing such material the right thing to do?
These and other ethical questions are dealt with in Chapter 6.

Other Privacy Issues

In addition to false light and private facts, two other areas of privacy can pose
problems for publications. Neither of them typically involves editors directly, however, so we'll take just a brief look at them.

First is **intrusion.** Problems arise when reporters and photographers enter
private places without permission. Editors should be especially careful in approv-
ing the use of photos that were not taken within camera range of a public place.
Unless a photographer has received subjects' consent, such photos may violate
the subjects' privacy.

The second area is **misappropriation.** Misappropriation involves using a person's name or image, without permission, for commercial purposes. This is usually
more of a concern for advertising staffers than for those on the editorial side, but
editors can become entangled. In a case in 2000, for example, twin brothers from
California sued gay youth publication XY Magazine for running photos taken of
them when they were 16. The brothers — who are not gay — had posed for photos to be used in personal modeling portfolios. When the photos turned up in connection with a feature headlined "Young and Gay," they sued for misappropriation,
libel and infliction of emotional distress.[22]

Editors also can face potential problems with misappropriation when they use names or images for promotional purposes. As long as such use does not imply an endorsement, however, it is not considered misappropriation.

Copyright

One of the most perilous areas emerging for editors is copyright law. All materials that have been published are copyrighted, even some that seem to be in the public domain. In 1993, for example, the estate of Martin Luther King Jr. sued the publisher of USA Today for the unauthorized publication of the text of King's "I Have a Dream" speech. While the text could have been used freely immediately after the speech was given in 1963, King's estate said that unauthorized use of the text 30 years later was an infringement of King's copyright.[23] The suit was settled out of court in 1994. No details of the settlement were released.

Publications can use limited amounts of copyrighted material, however, under the fair use provision of the Copyright Act. Four factors are weighed in determining whether a use is fair:

- Whether the use is for commercial purposes or nonprofit educational purposes.

- Whether a work is fiction or nonfiction, and whether it has been published already.

- The proportion of a work reproduced.

- The effect of reproducing the material on the market or value of the original work.

Notice that having a copyright holder's permission to reproduce material is *not* a consideration.

Based on those factors, lawyers Howard Zaharoff and Brenda Cotter offered some hints in Folio: magazine:

- Use as little of a copyrighted work as is necessary for your purposes.

- Don't reproduce the juiciest parts of a work (i.e., the parts that could most reduce the original work's commercial appeal).

- Don't base an article or story on a copyrighted work.

- Be careful in reproducing fictional or unpublished works. While unpublished works may not be copyrighted, the author has first rights to commercial gain from the material.

- Don't use any form of promotion emphasizing that material you're publishing contains excerpts from a copyrighted work.[24]

While those guidelines apply to graphics as well as words, the ease with which photos can be digitally manipulated raises a related copyright concern. For example, an art director who wants to create a composite photograph needs to get permission from the owners of each of the original works, as does the designer who plans to use elements of a single copyrighted work in a new design. Failing to get permission — and pay any requested fees — can lead to lawsuits.[25]

Trademarks

As Chapter 4 pointed out, editors need to make sure that trademarks are used properly. Both words and phrases can be trademarked; for example, both American Express and "Don't leave home without it" are trademarked. Generally, editors don't have to worry about lawsuits if they misuse trademarks, but they might receive scolding letters from the trademark owners.

One such letter received by The Wall Street Journal was so good that the paper printed it in the Letters to the Editor section. The letter came after the newspaper published an article about a hotel that allows pets to stay with their owners in eight special rooms. One line from the article read, "Maids turn down the blankets on small cushioned beds and leave a milk bone for a guest dog or a toy for a cat." Nabisco, the maker of MILK-BONE dog biscuits, had this to say in its letter to the paper:

Nabisco has a small bone to pick with WSJ. In your recent May 29th issue, you ran an article titled, "With a Great Dane in the Elevator," in which Judith Valente wrote that Chicago's Ambassador East Hotel "leaves a milk bone for a guest dog."

You are in the doghouse, WSJ, for improper use of our registered trademark MILK-BONE. The MILK-BONE trademark identifies Nabisco's brand of dog biscuits and, as such, should be used (a) as an adjective, modifying the generic noun dog biscuit, and (b) in a typestyle different from that of the surrounding text to distinguish it from an ordinary dictionary word (e.g., "MILK-BONE dog biscuit").

This is not pettifoggery. Failure to follow this grammatical trademark dogma has contributed, in extreme cases, to the genericism of what were once valuable proprietary designations (such as corn flakes and shredded wheat) — which explains why misuses of trademarks are often doggedly hounded by their owners.

We are confident that WSJ did not make this biting error on "pawpose." But we do ask that you tug on the leash of your copy editor and curb the generic use of trademarks, or risk being further chewed out.

That letter made its point in style, undoubtedly leaving the editor who approved the copy chastised but smiling. But the consequences for those who try to profit by using a trademark can be far more serious. In a 1993 case, for example, Quaker Oats, the owner of the Gatorade sports drink company, was ordered to pay a small Vermont company $26.5 million for using the firm's trademarked "Thirst Aid" slogan without authorization in promoting Gatorade.[26]

Notes

1. Sandra S. Baron, "The Media and Libel: Old Concerns Renewed," Columbia Journalism Review, September/October 2000, pp. 55–56.
2. "Record Libel Verdict Cut by $200 Million," The Washington Post, 24 May 1997, sec. A, p. 10.
3. Wayne Overbeck, "Major Principles of Media Law" (Fort Worth, Texas: Harcourt Brace, 1994), p. 90.

4. Grady Auvil et al. v. CBS "60 Minutes"' et al., reported in The Wall Street Journal, 23 June 1992, sec. B, p. 8.

5. Sue Anne Pressley, "Testing a New Brand of Libel Law," The Washington Post, 17 January 1998, sec. A, p. 1.

6. "'Kato' Kaelin Settles Libel Suit," Free! The Freedom Forum Online, 11 October 1999, *www.freedomforum.org.*

7. Barbara Dill, "The Journalist's Handbook on Libel and Privacy" (New York: The Free Press, 1986), p. 79.

8. "Olympic Bomb Case Far from Settled on 3rd Anniversary," CNN.com, 27 July 1999, *www.cnn.com/US/9907/27/olympic.bombing.01/index.html.*

9. Overbeck, "Major Principles," p. 105.

10. Dill, "Journalist's Handbook," p. 81–82.

11. DiSalle v. P.G. Publishing Co., cited in Overbeck, "Major Principles," p. 106.

12. Milkovich v. Lorain Journal Co., 497 U.S. 1 (1990).

13. St. Amant v. Thompson, 390 U.S. 727, 731 (1968).

14. Burns v. McGraw-Hill Broadcasting Co., 659 P.2d 135 (1983), cited in Dill, "Journalist's Handbook," p. 131–132.

15. Howard Kurtz, "Hubbell Tapes: A Select Few Have Heard It All Before," The Washington Post, 11 May 1998, sec. D, p. 1.

16. E.R. Shipp, "The Shifflett Case," The Washington Post, 16 July 2000, sec. B, p. 6.

17. David Streitfeld, "Libel Suit on Book Review Reinstated," The Washington Post, 19 February 1994, sec. G, pp. 1, 2.

18. Joan Biskupic, "In Libel Suit U-Turn, Judge Admits Starting in the Wrong Direction," The Washington Post, 5 May 1994, sec. A, p. 20.

19. Howard Kurtz, "To Larry, With Apologies," The Washington Post, 15 July 1994, sec. B, p. 1.

20. "Mag Retracts Story; Cruise Drops Suit," USA Today, 14 August 1996, sec. D, p. 2.

21. Gill v. Hearst Corporation, 40 Cal.2d 224 (1953), cited in Overbeck, "Major Principles," p. 162.

22. Clark Mason, "Twins Sue Over Gay Magazine Shot," Santa Rosa Press Democrat, 26 November 2000, *www.pressdemo.com.*

23. "King Estate Sues Paper Over 'Dream' Speech," The Washington Post, 10 December 1993, sec. B, p. 13.

24. Jean Marie Angelo, "Altered States," Folio:, 15 February 1994, pp. 60, 62.

25. Howard Zaharoff and Brenda Carter, "Navigating the 'Fair Use' Privilege," Folio:, 15 May 1994, pp. 45–46.

26. Business Digest item, The Washington Post, 9 June 1993, sec. F, p. 2.

Exercises: Libel

Edit the following news article. Each time you see defamatory material, underline it and put a number next to it. On the back of this page, list the type of defamation; the defense (if any) for the defamation; and the action that should be taken. Take any required action in editing your story so the final result is free of libel.

An 18-year old local youth was arrestted after his car struck and killed a Smithstown girl who walking home from a football game.

Patrick J. Bove, of 4869 Lucerne Street, was charged early today with drunkeng driveing, involuntary man slaughter, and homocide by vehicle.

The killer faces a hearing Friday. A breathalyzer test showed that the ahlcohol levl in Bove's blood was twice the leagel limit, police reports show.

The victim, Amy Turner of170 Renfer Street, was struck while walking along the birm of S. Washington street about 10 p.m. last night. She died at 12:30 p.m. thls morning in St. Josephs Hospital.

Police said May and several friends, all nineth graders at Smithstown high, had left the game ahd were walking to a friends home for a pajama party when the car ploughed into the group.

A friend of Bove, who asked not to be identified, said Bove "has a drinking problem."

#	TYPE	DEFENSE	ACTION

Edit the following news article. Each time you see defamatory material, underline it and put a number next to it. On the back of this page, list the type of defamation; the defense (if any) for the defamation; and the action that should be taken. Take any required action in editing your story so the final result is free of libel.

Hugo Carducci a booking agent for gogo girls, was speared a prioson term yesterday because a Federal Judge did not want to "burden" tax payers with the cost of caring for a man with a heart conditon.

Carducci, 44 who has had heart problems since 1992 collapsed after a Federal Jury convinced him of selling 9 oz. of cocane last October. Hus attorney said Carduci did not have a heart attak.

US District judge Gerald Weber sentenced the First Avenue resident man to 5 year's probation and find him three thousand dollars, payable with in thrity days.

Weber said he should have imposed a jail sentence on Carduci because "his friends and clients are on the firnges of the law, if not criminals, plain and simple, hes a pimp.

H, David Rothman Carducis lawyer protested Weber's descritpion, saying there was no evidence introduuced at the trial to support the caracturization. But, the judge interupted and said: "We know what all if them do in addition to dancing."

Rothman changed the subject and asked for probation because of Carduccis heart condition. Also, he said, "the prime requisite for probation is whether hes likely to do the deed again?"

"This man is very likely to, because he's stupid and he has the predispistion to do it again, Weber replied.

Weber told Carucci he would go to jail if he violated probation. Weber also suggested Carducci find another occupation saying: "Mr Carduccis verious ills are to some extant of his own makeing."

#	TYPE	DEFENSE	ACTION

Media Law in Cyberspace

If the law concerning traditional media is at times confusing, it can be a nightmare when it comes to online media. In a medium that is still being formed, it's not surprising that laws governing it can conflict with one another and change rapidly. Fortunately, laws governing online media generally mirror those that govern print and broadcast media. Nevertheless, it's important to understand where the differences occur.

The rules of libel, for example, are in many ways identical for online and traditional media. But several areas merit a close look.

Who's a Publisher?

The first area concerns the question of who or what constitutes a journalist or publisher. That's a simple question to answer in traditional media: if you publish a newspaper, you're a publisher; if you report for a television network, you're a journalist. But the World Wide Web allows anyone to function as both publisher and journalist, with no training or special knowledge required. On its face, that's not a big deal: No matter the medium, any person or company that libels another person is responsible, even if that person or company is neither a journalist nor a publisher. (For example, a former doctor at Emory School of Medicine won a $675,000 libel verdict from the former chair of the school's urology department over a defamatory message posted anonymously to a Yahoo! message board.[1])

The problem when it comes to online libel, however, is determining how far the blame stretches. So far, court rulings have indicated that it stops with the source of the material, and does not extend to an online service that publishes that material. In one classic case, *Cubby v. Compuserve Inc.,* the court ruled that Compuserve was not responsible for libelous material posted on its service because it "has no more editorial control over such a publication than does a public library, book store, or newsstand, and it would be no more feasible for Compuserve to examine every publication it carries for potentially defamatory statements than it would for any other distributor to do so."[2]

Similarly, America Online was let off the hook in two major cases. The first stemmed from a posting offering "naughty" souvenir T-shirts from the Oklahoma City bombing in 1995 (the person to whom the posting was falsely attributed received angry phone calls and death threats). In the second case, a court dismissed White House adviser Sidney Blumenthal's suit against America Online after gossip writer Matt Drudge made defamatory statements about Blumenthal in a column hosted by AOL.[3] The latter case was particularly interesting, because AOL paid Drudge a salary at that time and promoted his work — just as a traditional publisher would. In its defense, AOL said it automatically put his work onto the site with no editing, so in that sense it acted more as a distributor of the news.[4]

Another matter making life more difficult for online editors is the global reach of the Internet. As Denise Caruso notes in Columbia Journalism Review, "The global nature of the Internet creates potentially knotty questions about accountability and liability." For example, while U.S. libel law may permit publication of a critical piece of writing, that same piece may be libelous in England. Laws governing copyright and free speech also differ widely from one country to another. These differences are most problematic for media businesses that have assets in overseas countries; in a libel suit or other matter, those assets can be attached.[5]

The Web does make one thing easier: running retractions. But there's still a catch. On one hand, the Web allows almost instantaneous corrections and retractions, which can help defuse libel suits. But the question then arises about what to do with the original libelous articles. Some publications leave the original online, which risks further circulating the libel (the article may be found, for instance, by a search engine). Others correct the article with no notice made of the change — which strikes many as right out of "1984" and at least a bit dishonest. Perhaps the most honest way to handle a correction is to change the original and add a notice that a change was made after original publication. It's a delicate area, and one Internet site, Slipup.com, exists solely to highlight online news organizations' correction policies — and those cases in which they mess up.[6]

Content Issues

Undoubtedly, the most contentious issue affecting the Web is censorship. The federal government and state governments have passed a variety of laws designed to protect minors from pornography. The action began with the 1996 passage of the Communications Decency Act, which immediately became the target of a lawsuit filed by the Citizens Internet Empowerment Coalition, a group that included the Society of Professional Journalists, the Newspaper Association of America and the Association of American Publishers Inc. The U.S. Supreme Court ruled the law unconstitutional in June 1997 because it was overly broad and would have violated freedom of the press. In mid-2001, the Supreme Court agreed to consider the legality of the Child Online Protection Act, a sequel to the Communications Decency Act.[7]

In another attempt to control the availability of sexually oriented and violent content, the Clinton administration pushed for voluntary rating of content on the Internet. While some news publishers supported the rating plan, major online news organizations — including the Associated Press, MSNBC, CNN Interactive, The New York Times, Time Inc., ABC News, Reuters New Media, Business Week, the Houston Chronicle, the Magazine Publishers Association of America and the Newspaper Association of America — announced their opposition.[8]

Even in the area of hate sites, few attempts have succeeded to control content on the Web. In 1999, a federal judge banned antiabortion activists who ran a Web site called "The Nuremberg Files" from publishing "wanted posters" and personal information about physicians who performed abortions. The operators of the site had been sued by a group of physicians who called it a "hit list." Two years

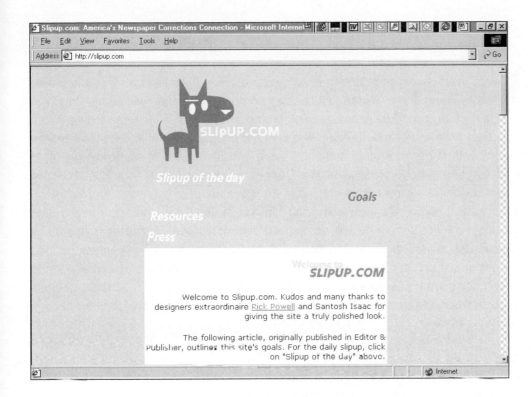

True to its name,
Slipup.com keeps tabs
on media missteps.

later, however, a federal appeals court declared that the site's content was protected free speech and ruled that the site could not be banned or its owners sued for damages.[9] The only success was the decision of a Web hosting company to shut down DateRape.org, which had claimed to help men "get laid" by offering them information on how to drug and rape women.[10]

Copyright

Online editors face two problems in the area of copyright: using material they find and keeping their material from being pirated.

Using Material

Online publishers gained a powerful ally in December 1998, when the Digital Millennium Copyright Act was signed into law. The act was designed to ensure that all forms of artistic creation get full copyright protection online. As a result, the rules for using others' work are generally the same online as in print. In other words, you should presume that all content you find on the Web is copyrighted and make sure you get permission before using it. You should seek permission for content even when it appears to be in a format that you wouldn't think is copyrightable, such as e-mails and posts to online discussion lists; it's not yours just because you find it.

When seeking permission, it pays to be careful about your source. Make sure that the person or organization granting permission is actually qualified to do so. This is particularly tricky in the online world. In some cases the copyright belongs to the creator of the work rather than the owner of the site. In other cases different people may own different rights to the same work (North American rights vs. international, for example).[11]

In most cases, you don't have to get permission if all you want to do is create a link to another site.

In most cases, you don't have to get permission if all you want to do is create a link to another site. As the last chapter noted, editors often will search the Web for links that complement articles. For example, an article on a lunar eclipse might include links to several sites dealing with astronomy. Such links offer readers an easy way to get more information. Generally, adding links to an article (or other Web page) is perfectly fine. As The Copyright Website notes, "A link is a URL, a fact not unlike a street address, and is therefore not copyrightable."[12]

Nevertheless, it's always a good idea to request permission to use a link. Doing so is not just courteous, it's also a matter of finances: Some site owners pay their hosting services based on how many people visit their sites. A link embedded in a popular article on a major Web site could lead to thousands of visitors — and high bills for the site owners.

In three cases, it's mandatory to get permission for using links:

- If the context of the link could be taken as defamatory. You're open to a libel suit if you don't have permission.

- If you want to use not just an individual link but a list of links. The Copyright Website notes that an original list of links "may be copyrightable under a compilation copyright."[13]

- If you not only want to link to a site but want to create a composite page containing text or graphics from it. For example, if I want to include a picture of Mickey Mouse on a Web page, I might link to one at the Disney Web site. Some Web producers have used this technique to grab page backgrounds, sound files, animations and other materials. The Copyright Website argues against such use, noting that "By stripping an element of its context, you also strip many of the copyright privileges that may have been attached."[14]

Keeping Your Material Safe

Before the Digital Millennium Copyright Act was passed, blatant theft was common on the Web. One of the earliest examples was the use of framing technology to make a publication's content appear as if it were provided by another source. For instance, TotalNews.com originally displayed content from several online news sites in a frame on its own site. In the process, TotalNews was able to obscure the original advertising and overlay its own ads — in effect generating revenue from others' work. After being sued by The Washington Post, Dow Jones, Time Warner, Reuters and Times Mirror, TotalNews agreed to send visitors directly to those sites rather than displaying their content in a frame on the TotalNews site.[15] Every now and then, another upstart site tries the same trick, but most publishers have now figured out how to include JavaScript coding on their pages that prevents them from being viewed in a frame.

Before adding such "frame-busting" code or doing anything else, though, online publishers should make sure their sites contain copyright notices. While not technically necessary to provide copyright protection, a copyright notice serves to spell out specifics regarding use of your content.[16]

Photographers and artists can build copyright protection into their work by adding a "digital watermark" to their creations. The watermarks are created with popular image editing programs, such as Adobe PhotoShop. They cannot be seen by the naked eye, but Web spider programs that search the Web for illegal copies can track them down.[17]

Working with Outsiders

A final major area of concern regarding copyright is compensation for authors whose work initially appears in print but then is distributed electronically. As more newspapers and magazines distribute content online, free-lance writers have begun seeking compensation for such secondary distribution of their work. In June 2001, the U.S. Supreme Court ruled that publishers must secure free-lance writers' permission to include their work in digital databases.[18] To be safe, editors at publications that distribute materials electronically need to spell out clearly to writers how their work will be distributed and what compensation they will receive. Editors need to be careful not to misrepresent their publications' policies to writers.

Notes

1. "Doctor Wins Internet Libel Case," USA Today, 11 December 2000, *www.usatoday.com/life/cyber/tech/cti894.htm*.

2. Cubby v. Compuserve Inc., 776 F. Supp. 135 (S.D.N.Y. 1991), cited in "New Technology and the First Amendment" (Greencastle, Ind.: Society of Professional Journalists, 1994), p. 5.

3. Joan Biskupic, "In Shaping of Internet Law, First Amendment Is Winning," The Washington Post, 12 Sept. 1999, sec. A, p. 2.

4. Bill Miller, "AOL Off the Hook in Drudge Case," The Washington Post, 23 April 1998, sec. B, p. 1.

5. Denise Caruso, "The Law and the Internet: Beware," Columbia Journalism Review, May/June 1998, pp. 57–79. See also Frank Houston, "The Media and the Net: Global Precedents," Columbia Journalism Review, September/October 2000, pp. 56–57.

6. Matt Welch, "The Corrector: Slipup.com," Online Journalism Review, 4 March 1999, *ojr.usc.edu/content/story.cfm?id=174*.

7. Charles Lane, "Court to Review Online Porn Law," The Washington Post, 22 May 2001, sec. A, p. 2.

8. David E. Kalish, "Online News Providers Resist Ratings," The Washington Post, 29 August 1997, sec. K, p. 3.

9. Renee Sanchez, "Antiabortion Web Site Handed a Win," The Washington Post, 29 March 2001, sec. A, p. 1.

10. Lakshmi Chaudhry, "Date-Rape Site Taken Down," Wired News, 14 March 2000, *www.wired.com/news/politics/0,1283,34941,00.html*.

11. For a good in-depth discussion of seeking permission for online work, see Amy Gahran, "The Least That Online Publishers Should Know About Copyright," Contentious, 12 July 1999, *www.content-exchange.com/cx/html/newsletter/1-7/vt1-7.htm*.

12. The Copyright Website, *www.benedict.com*.

13. The Copyright Website.

14. The Copyright Website.

15. Dan Mitchell, "TotalNews Settles with Media Giants over Links," Wired News, 5 June 1997, *www.wired.com/news/business/0,1367,4286,00.html.*

16. For more information on effective copyright notices, see Thom Lieb, "Copyright and Wrongs: Putting Visitors on Notice," Journal of Electronic Publishing, March 1999, *www.press.umich.edu/jep/04-03/lieb0403.html.*

17. Jennifer Chu, "Web Design Firm Puts 'Teeth' Into Copyright," Electronic Publishing, November 1997, p. 48.

18. Christopher Stern, "Freelancers Win Fight Over Reuse of Works," The Washington Post, 26 June 2001, sec. E, p. 1.

Editor's Corner

Paul Warren, executive vice president, executive publisher and senior editor, Communications Daily

The Other Side of the Law

Can you copy this page? Maybe. Maybe not.

The copyright laws of this country are somewhat complex, but as an editor in the trade press, I've found that time and again I have to try to answer these types of questions when they apply to my company's newsletters.

Each day we put out a dozen or more pages about news at the Federal Communications Commission, Congress and thousands of companies in the telephone, television and electronic communications business. And each day, somebody, somewhere, is making a copy of our publication, either through photocopying or electronically. They are depriving us of the money we get through additional subscriptions. See, a newsletter almost by definition exists without any income other than subscriptions. There is no advertising, as in newspapers and magazines. Those publications are far less concerned about someone copying their materials because the bulk of their income comes from advertisers.

So when we hear, through an offhand remark or the report of a disgruntled employee, that someone all too frequently is slapping Communications Daily on a Xerox machine or resending it via e-mail, I have to put on my Protector of the Copyright hat.

What usually follows is a conversation or two with the people with the itchy photocopier fingers and an attempt to get the company to compensate my company for what was taken. Sometimes they turn me over to their lawyers, and sometimes I turn them over to ours. It's all a negotiation, but for a small newsletter company like mine, it's vital to our future that we receive compensation for what was ours and imperative that we make it known that copying is verboten. We tend to be unrelenting on this issue and even have gone so far as to file suit. We won an important case against the U.S. Telephone Association, a Washington, D.C., trade association, which had contended that it had the right to make up to 26 copies per day of our newsletter. U.S. District Court Judge Harold Penn in Washington, D.C., ruled they had violated our copyright, and the trade association had to pay some $240,000 for its mistake.

While all this seems a long way from editing, it should be noted that without copyright there would be a lot fewer editing jobs around. In fact, when the framers of the Constitution finished that document, they included provisions for protection of copyright, recognizing that authors were far less likely to create if they knew someone could just pick up their material and sell it as his or her own.

Editors today frequently become well-versed in other laws, particularly libel, but copyright — even for larger publishing concerns and television and radio — is becoming of increasing importance and will continue to do so.

Punctuation

Some aspects of punctuation are simple enough: Put a period at the end of a sentence that makes a statement; put a question mark at the end of a sentence that asks a question. But beyond that safe terrain is murky territory populated by commas, semicolons, dashes and other hobgoblins.

If you're absolutely clueless when it comes to punctuation, you need to get a basic grammar book — quickly. But if you're just rusty, the following review should help you get a better handle on common punctuation problems.

Commas

These tiny punctuation marks have sent chills down the spines of writers and editors for generations. Commas can be tricky to use; in fact, some questions of use are so fuzzy that reasonable people will disagree on whether a comma is needed. Still, in most cases, the use of commas is straightforward:

Commas can be tricky to use; in fact, some questions of use are so fuzzy that reasonable people will disagree on whether a comma is needed.

- **Commas are used to separate items in a series.** This one is tricky only because stylebooks differ on whether a comma is needed before the last item in a simple series. The Associated Press Stylebook says no comma is needed: "The flag is red, white and blue." But other stylebooks insist on an additional comma before "blue." Stylebooks generally agree, however, that a comma is necessary if any item in a series contains the word "and," as in this example: *The menu offers sausages, ham and cabbage, and pork roast.*

- **Commas are used between equal adjectives.** Use a comma between two adjectives when it could be replaced by the word "and." For example, "the new, blue car" gets a comma, but "the worn leather jacket" doesn't.

- **Commas separate independent clauses joined by coordinating conjunctions.** Coordinating conjunctions are *and, but, for, nor, or, yet* and *while*. When two independent clauses are connected with one of these words, a comma is used between the clauses. Example: *She decided to apply for the loan, but she was sure she would be turned down.*

- **Commas set off nonrestrictive phrases and clauses.** See Chapter 3 for more on this.

- **Commas set off long introductory phrases and dependent clauses.** While a short phrase at the start of a sentence does not need to be set off with a comma, a long phrase does. The first example below does not need a comma; the second does:

At midnight the auction will begin.

After three weeks of using the product, consumers reported that it provided more benefits than they had expected.

For the sake of consistency, some publications and organizations require a comma after any introductory material, even a single word. So it's important to check company policy.

- **Commas set off age and address from a person's name.** In a sort of short-hand, media writers often will follow a person's name with an age or address, separating the elements only with a comma:

Patrick McNamara, 42, was promoted to administrative assistant.

Jennifer Katz, 1411 Monroe St., was charged with the crime.

- **Commas help clarify otherwise confusing material.** When material could otherwise be misread, separate words with a comma. An example:

What the problem is, is certain to become clear now.

- **Commas separate attribution from quotations.** A comma is used to set off attribution when a complete sentence of direct quotation follows:

He said, "I promise to turn the company around."

No comma is used if the quote is not a complete sentence:

He said he would "turn the company around."

A comma is used before attribution that follows a complete sentence of either direct or indirect quotation:

"I promise to turn the company around," he said.

Under his direction the company will turn around, he said.

- **Commas are used around states and dates.** When a city is followed by a state, use commas around the state:

Flight schedules at the airport in Missoula, Mont., also are going to change.

When the year follows a month and day, use commas around the year:

The company was founded on May 16, 1968, and did not turn a profit until 1979.

- **Commas are used in numbers over 999.** From 1,000 up, include a comma — unless the number is a year (e.g., 1999) or a trade name that does not include a comma (e.g., Petrol 2000).

- **Commas *are not used* to separate the subject from the verb in a sentence.** Somewhere along the line many writers pick up the bad habit of putting a comma between the subject and the verb. This seems to happen most often when the subject is more than one word long, as in this example:

Hundreds of people wearing Halloween costumes, lined up outside the store three hours before it opened.

If you dissect the sentence, it is easy to see that the subject is "hundreds" and the verb is "lined." So there is no reason for a comma between them.

- **Commas *are not used* to separate two verbs that are ruled by the same subject or two objects ruled by one verb.** These examples are incorrect:

  My boss drew up plans for reorganization, and left on a long vacation.

  The mayor praised the high-schoolers, and the members of the PTA.

Quotation Marks

Generally, there is no need to use quote marks around quotes of fewer than four words or around ordinary words.

- **Quotation marks are used around a speaker's exact words.** Quotation marks serve as a guarantee that a speaker's words are correct. If there are no quotation marks, an editor must not add them.

- **Quotation marks are not needed on short quotes.** Generally, there is no need to use quote marks around quotes of fewer than four words or around ordinary words. The only exception to this rule is that quotes are used around a word or short phrase that is being introduced to the reader. Over time, as the word or phrase becomes familiar, the quotes are dropped.

- **There must be a reason for using quotation marks.** An ad said that a restaurant offered "fresh" swordfish salad. What do the quotes mean? They imply it *isn't* fresh.

- **The style of quotation marks alternates for quotes within quotes.** Ordinarily, a quotation is surrounded by double quote marks. When the quotation contains another direct quotation (or other quoted material — the Associated Press Stylebook calls for quotes around book titles, for example), the inner set of quotes uses single marks:

  "I just called to say, 'I love you,'" she said.

Notice that when both quotes end together, three quote marks are used.

- **Periods and commas always remain inside quotation marks.** Other marks of punctuation go inside quotes only when the marks belong with the material inside quotes, rather than to the sentence as a whole:

  "Can we get more facts and less advocacy?" she demanded.

(Notice that the question mark replaces the comma in this case.)

Have you read "Earth in the Balance"?

- ***Don't use*** **quotation marks at the end of a paragraph when the quote continues beyond that point.** When a paragraph ends with a complete quoted sentence and the next paragraph begins with a continuation of the quote, no quote marks are needed at the end of the first paragraph.

  Chou said, "We like the president's proposal, but we'll have to see what it looks like when Congress gets through with it.

  "One thing we've learned over the years is that what you see initially is rarely what you get."

Colons

- **Colons are used to introduce a list.** Example:

  Everywhere were articles of their lives: slippers, purses, money, a remote control for a videocassette recorder.

- **Colons are used to expand on an idea or make it more specific with another phrase or clause.** Example:

  On that hot day, we all wanted the same thing: a triple-scoop ice cream cone.

  When the material that follows the colon is a complete sentence, the first word after the colon is capitalized:

  The illness has spread like a rodent-borne disease: New cases have cropped up sporadically over a large area, not in the tight clusters you would expect if people were infecting people.

- **Colons are used to introduce a direct quotation of more than one complete sentence.** Example:

  Instead the judge says: "You better get a prescription. I want you back here in two weeks. And you better stop the cocaine."

Semicolons

- **Semicolons are used to separate independent clauses.** Example:

  As investments, they'll never do better than the market they follow; in fact, they'll fall a little behind after deducting fund-management fees.

- **Semicolons are used to separate the parts of a complex series.** When a series contains internal punctuation, using commas to separate the elements may cause confusion. Semicolons are used in such cases:

  Survivors include his wife, the former Ann Wiggins; a son, Robert Jr., of Cambridge; and two daughters, Christine Wheeler of New Orleans, and Mary Kohler of Portland, Maine.

A comma can suffice in simpler sentences:

The panelists were Charles Davis, the former dean, and Amanda Lewis, acting vice president.

Exclamation Marks

- **Avoid them.** If a writer wants to excite a reader, the *writing* has to be exciting. Adding an exclamation mark won't do the job.

Hyphens

- **Hyphens join words that form a compound adjective.** When two words form a single concept that modifies a noun directly following them, the modifiers are joined with a hyphen:

She worked at the company part time for three years.

She held a part-time job at the company for three years.

The following two sentences show the importance of using hyphens correctly:

While waiting for our shrimp to arrive, we saw a man eating shark.

The highlight of our visit to the aquarium was seeing the man-eating shark.

But hyphens *are not used* when the first word in a compound modifier ends in *-ly:*

They spent all night talking about the hotly debated issue.

- **Hyphens don't substitute for the word *to*.** Most stylebooks require you to use the word to in usages such as this:

She plans to retire in four to five years.

Dashes

- **A dash signals an abrupt change or an emphatic pause.** A dash — signified on a typewriter or computer keyboard by typing two hyphens — substitutes for a comma when the following words are dramatic or unexpected:

Endometriosis was once nicknamed the "career women's disease" — but an increasing number of teen-agers are being diagnosed.

If a sentence already contains several commas, a dash makes a good change of pace.

- **A dash can be used to replace commas in a complicated sentence.** Particularly if a sentence already contains several commas, a dash makes a good change of pace. This use has gained wide acceptance in media writing during recent years. Example:

The disease — which health authorities are calling Unexplained Adult Respiratory Distress Syndrome, or UARDS — starts with such minor symptoms as coughing, fever, muscle aches and pinkeye.

In many cases, a sentence using dashes in this manner could benefit from being broken into two sentences:

Health authorities are calling the disease Unexplained Adult Respiratory Distress Syndrome, or UARDS. It starts with such minor symptoms as coughing, fever, muscle aches and pinkeye.

Apostrophes

- **Use an apostrophe to show possession.** Most words are made possessive by adding an apostrophe and an *s: The Army's might; Lorraine's dog.* But some words that end in *s* or *c* sounds take only an apostrophe. Always check a stylebook for such words.

- **Use an apostrophe for contractions.** An apostrophe takes the place of a missing letter in a contraction. So *it is* becomes *it's* and *they are* becomes *they're.*

- *Do not* **use an apostrophe to create a plural.** You keep up with the *Joneses,* not the *Jones'.* He owns three *Fords,* not *Ford's.*

Exercise

Correct all spelling, punctuation and style errors in the following article. Also correct any comma splices, fragments, incorrect clauses and misplaced modifiers.

Roughly 60 percent of college students, in a new survey, admitted they had stolen an item of ten dollars or less at least once in their life; in some cases from their college roomates, says a criminal justice profesor at the University of Nebraska/Omaha.

The survey by Nebraska prof. Chris Eskridge also showed that 20 % of the students had stolen an item worth 10 dollars or less more than once, another 20 percent had stolen an item valued at $10-50 on at least one occasion. About 1 in ten had stolen an item worth $50 or more at least once.

The results were based on surveys, of 2669 students at three midwest Universities.

Many of the thefts occured in the workplace Eskridge said, but a sizeable number happened on or near a college campus. For example, 12.8 percent of the students admitting steeling something from a room mate at least once, 3.5 percent said they had stolen from their roommate more than once.

The study also showed that 65 percent had stolen something from a hotel at least once, while 48 per cent had taken something frmo their work place!

Male students were much more likely than females to commit one or more thefts. 60 percent of men and 40 percent of women admited they had stolen an item on one occsion, of that group, 70 percent of men and 30 percent of women said they had commited more than one theft. Among those who have never stolen 53 percent were women and 47 percent were men.

Establishing an Ethical Foundation

A writer for your newspaper has proposed an article that sounds interesting. She has found that it's common practice for suburban middle-class teen-agers to hold parties at which they take hallucinogenic drugs. She has managed to get invited to one of the parties so she can write about it, as long as she doesn't identify the teens there. She says the article is needed to alert parents as to what's happening in their homes, but some editors are worried that it's improper for the writer to be at a party where the teens are getting high. Do you give her the go-ahead?

Like all ethical decisions, this one won't be easy. In fact, ethical choices are among the toughest decisions editors have to make.

Acting ethically involves making the distinction between what you legally have the right to do and what is *the right thing to do.* Making poor ethical choices usually won't land you in court, but doing so can damage your credibility and your relationship with your audience.

Unfortunately, editors typically have little time to think about ethical problems until they arise. Most of their time is spent dealing with the more immediate problems involved in getting their publications out. As a result, ethical decisions often are made on deadline, and they rarely reflect careful consideration.

While several associations and individual publications have developed codes of ethics for journalists, those codes usually provide general guidelines rather than clear answers to ethical problems. Further, those codes are not enforced — as are codes of ethics for doctors and lawyers — because many believe that enforcing codes of ethics would undermine the freedom on which journalism is based in the United States. That lack of enforcement leads many journalists to ignore ethics codes. While many news organizations *do* enforce their own in-house ethics codes, those codes typically address only a limited number of problems.

Lacking a good source of ready answers, editors should take the time to identify potential ethical problems and consider how to deal with them before they develop. Then, when problems arise, they can be resolved with well-thought-out solutions that should produce the best possible results.

In this chapter, we'll look at the types of ethical situations editors are most likely to encounter; then we'll consider the questions that editors must be prepared

> Editors should take the time to identify potential ethical problems and consider how to deal with them before they develop.

to answer in dealing with such problems. While the material presented here can help you in most situations you will encounter as an editor, it is not intended as a substitute for further study and ongoing reflection on ethics; consider it merely a starting point in a lifelong learning process.

Ethical Problems for Editors

One of the difficulties confronting editors is that ethical problems span a wide range of issues. Among them:

Bias.   The Society of Professional Journalists' Code of Ethics (Figure 6.1) begins with a section titled "Seek Truth and Report It." Chapters 3 and 4 have already stressed the importance of ensuring the truth. There is an additional component to telling the truth: making sure material is free of opinion or bias. As the SPJ code puts it: "Distinguish between advocacy and news reporting. Analysis and commentary should be labeled and not misrepresent fact or context."

Bias can take many forms. Among them:

- Inclusion of loaded words like *only, admits* (instead of *says*) or *guerrillas* (rather than *terrorists*).

- Inclusion of irrelevant information. An article about a school superintendent leaving a hearing on sexual abuse in schools he oversees noted that the man smiled as he "got into his silver Mercedes-Benz." Who knows what he was smiling about — and of what importance is it that he drives a Mercedes-Benz?

- Blatant editorial comments. An article about a protest at a law school ended with a comment by the writer that was unrelated to the focus of the article: that the school taught "'law and economics' legal theory, which places more emphasis on cost-benefit analyses than on the concepts of fairness and justice."

- Failure to cover issues or events. This is perhaps the worst kind of bias, because it is often the most difficult to detect. If you don't already know about an issue, you can't know that coverage is being suppressed.

Writers and editors at many publications serving specialized audiences — particularly trade magazines and newsletters — act as advocates for their audiences. In doing so, their work seemingly conflicts with traditional bans on avoiding bias. In order to best serve their readers, these journalists typically evaluate the news and pass judgment on whether it is good or bad for their readers. That type of "bias" is critical to the success of these publications. Readers might already know what happened; what they lack is knowing how it will affect them.

As a result, news reports in specialized publications differ markedly from news in general-interest newspapers and other mass media sources. For example, a writer for a newsletter covering literacy programs would cover funding news by reporting whether the funding is higher or lower than in previous years and what the implications of that change are for people involved in literacy programs. A report on the same topic in The New York Times would more likely focus on the politics of the funding decision.

SOCIETY OF PROFESSIONAL JOURNALISTS®

Code of Ethics

Preamble

Members of the Society of Professional Journalists believe that public enlightenment is the forerunner of justice and the foundation of democracy. The duty of the journalist is to further those ends by seeking truth and providing a fair and comprehensive account of events and issues. Conscientious journalists from all media and specialties strive to serve the public with thoroughness and honesty. Professional integrity is the cornerstone of a journalist's credibility.

Members of the Society share a dedication to ethical behavior and adopt this code to declare the Society's principles and standards of practice.

Seek Truth and Report It

Journalists should be honest, fair and courageous in gathering, reporting and interpreting information.

Journalists should:

▶ Test the accuracy of information from all sources and exercise care to avoid inadvertent error. Deliberate distortion is never permissible.

▶ Diligently seek out subjects of news stories to give them the opportunity to respond to allegations of wrongdoing.

▶ Identify sources whenever feasible. The public is entitled to as much information as possible on sources' reliability.

▶ Always question sources' motives before promising anonymity. Clarify conditions attached to any promise made in exchange for information. Keep promises.

▶ Make certain that headlines, news teases and promotional material, photos, video, audio, graphics, sound bites and quotations do not misrepresent. They should not oversimplify or highlight incidents out of context.

▶ Never distort the content of news photos or video. Image enhancement for technical clarity is always permissible. Label montages and photo illustrations.

▶ Avoid misleading re-enactments or staged news events. If re-enactment is necessary to tell a story, label it.

▶ Avoid undercover or other surreptitious methods of gathering information except when traditional open methods will not yield information vital to the public. Use of such methods should be explained as part of the story.

▶ Never plagiarize.

▶ Tell the story of the diversity and magnitude of the human experience boldly, even when it is unpopular to do so.

▶ Examine their own cultural values and avoid imposing those values on others.

▶ Avoid stereotyping by race, gender, age, religion, ethnicity, geography, sexual orientation, disability, physical appearance or social status.

▶ Support the open exchange of views, even views they find repugnant.

▶ Give voice to the voiceless; official and unofficial sources of information can be equally valid.

▶ Distinguish between advocacy and news reporting. Analysis and commentary should be labeled and not misrepresent fact or context.

▶ Distinguish news from advertising and shun hybrids that blur the lines between the two.

▶ Recognize a special obligation to ensure that the public's business is conducted in the open and that government records are open to inspection.

Minimize Harm

Ethical journalists treat sources, subjects and colleagues as human beings deserving of respect.

Journalists should:

▶ Show compassion for those who may be affected adversely by news coverage. Use special sensitivity when dealing with children and inexperienced sources or subjects.

▶ Be sensitive when seeking or using interviews or photographs of those affected by tragedy or grief.

▶ Recognize that gathering and reporting information may cause harm or discomfort. Pursuit of the news is not a license for arrogance.

▶ Recognize that private people have a greater right to control information about themselves than do public officials and others who seek power, influence or attention. Only an overriding public need can justify intrusion into anyone's privacy.

▶ Show good taste. Avoid pandering to lurid curiosity.

▶ Be cautious about identifying juvenile suspects or victims of sex crimes.

▶ Be judicious about naming criminal suspects before the formal filing of charges.

▶ Balance a criminal suspect's fair trial rights with the public's right to be informed.

Act Independently

Journalists should be free of obligation to any interest other than the public's right to know.

Journalists should:

▶ Avoid conflicts of interest, real or perceived.

▶ Remain free of associations and activities that may compromise integrity or damage credibility.

▶ Refuse gifts, favors, fees, free travel and special treatment, and shun secondary employment, political involvement, public office and service in community organizations if they compromise journalistic integrity.

▶ Disclose unavoidable conflicts.

▶ Be vigilant and courageous about holding those with power accountable.

▶ Deny favored treatment to advertisers and special interests and resist their pressure to influence news coverage.

▶ Be wary of sources offering information for favors or money; avoid bidding for news.

Be Accountable

Journalists are accountable to their readers, listeners, viewers and each other.

Journalists should:

▶ Clarify and explain news coverage and invite dialogue with the public over journalistic conduct.

▶ Encourage the public to voice grievances against the news media.

▶ Admit mistakes and correct them promptly.

▶ Expose unethical practices of journalists and the news media.

▶ Abide by the same high standards to which they hold others.

Sigma Delta Chi's first Code of Ethics was borrowed from the American Society of Newspaper Editors in 1926. In 1973, Sigma Delta Chi wrote its own code, which was revised in 1984 and 1987. The present version of the Society of Professional Journalists' Code of Ethics was adopted in September 1996.

Figure 6.1
One of the best-known ethics codes is that of the Society of Professional Journalists.

In addition, writers and editors for specialized publications often have a strong "voice" that contrasts with traditional journalistic writing. This voice may include the use of the words *we* and *us,* which are forbidden in "objective" reporting but which help build a sense of community with the specialized publication's audience. So while a typical news story might report, "The Pentagon revealed today that ... " a specialized publication might report, "We learned today that ... "

Editorials and feature articles in general-interest publications also may seem to violate the ban on bias because they take specific viewpoints. As long as those viewpoints are supported by the facts — and no major conflicting facts are suppressed — there is nothing wrong with this type of writing. An editorial that *didn't* have a strong point of view would not serve much purpose, and a feature article without a clear point of view likely would be a meandering mess.

Invasion of Privacy.   Even when it is legal to publish private information about a person, it is not always ethical. The SPJ code could not be clearer on this point: "Only an overriding public need can justify intrusion into anyone's privacy." Writers and editors often face a conflict, however, between the respect for privacy and the primary ethical obligation of journalism: informing the public by reporting the truth as fully as possible. When a media outlet decides that the public's need to know outweighs an individual's right to privacy, the outlet often finds that the public is infuriated rather than grateful.

Privacy issues generally fall into one of three areas:

- Revealing private details about a person's life, as the media were widely criticized for doing in reporting that former tennis star Arthur Ashe was dying of AIDS.

- Revealing the identities of crime victims. While the most sensitive question is whether names of victims of sex crimes should be used, victims of all types of crimes are complaining that they do not want their names published in the media.

- Using photographs of dead bodies or of relatives and co-workers at the scene of a tragedy.

Plagiarism.   Every student learns the importance of attributing information used in term papers and other projects. In the world of the mass media, however, writers have historically "borrowed" ideas and facts from books and articles without giving credit. When was the last time you saw a footnote on a magazine or newspaper feature article? This practice raises ethical questions, especially when a writer uses verbatim the work of another without crediting the original writer.

A model statement of plagiarism, based on The Philadelphia Inquirer's policy, offers these guidelines:

All material used in the construction of a story or a column should be clearly attributed to the proper sources, including newspapers, columnists, or press releases. In addition to direct quotations, all paraphrased material, analyses, interpretations, or literary devices, such as distinctive descriptive phrases, should be attributed.

Using another person's words, phrases or ideas without attribution is plagiarism, an offense which may be cause for dismissal.[1]

By those standards, many media writers plagiarize regularly. For instance, as Chapter 2 pointed out, borrowing article ideas from other publications is common practice because when a publication prints an article on a topic, it validates the topic's newsworthiness.

"I have no problem with stealing an idea," Michael E. Waller, vice president and editor of The Hartford (Conn.) Courant, has said. "Hey, if we couldn't do that this industry would go bust; we'd not be able to operate. After all, it's a form of flattery to copy a successful idea, or to improve on same."[2] It's long been common practice for newspaper and newsletter reporters to rewrite others' work for their own publications, sometimes without giving attribution.

Traditionally, writers have not been reprimanded unless they have used other writers' words verbatim or paraphrased them closely — and even then, writers often were not held accountable for plagiarism. But things are changing. For example, a Philadelphia Inquirer reporter resigned after being accused of using, almost word for word and without attribution, material that had earlier been published in an article in The Chicago Tribune.[3] In another case, a 22-year veteran of The Fort Worth Star-Telegram was fired after she wrote a column that relied on the content and style of an article published in The Washington Post. Within a six-month period, another writer at the same paper resigned after being charged with plagiarism, and a third writer was suspended for the same violation.[4]

Those incidents and a spate of other highly publicized plagiarism cases in recent years have led many publications to adopt new policies on plagiarism or tighten existing policies. As publications look more seriously at plagiarism, editors are expected to question any potential cases they encounter.

Advertising Pressures.   Virtually none of the print media could exist without advertising support. Unfortunately, that support often carries a high cost. The Center for the Study of Commercialism has published a report citing many examples of advertisers interfering with editorial content, either by warning publications not to print certain material or by withdrawing advertising support after material was published.[5] A study of newspaper editors found that 90 percent of those surveyed had been pressured by advertisers to change or withhold copy.[6] After a publication has felt the sting of losing the revenue of one advertiser, it is likely to be more cautious in the future — and it possibly will give lower priority to making sure readers are fully informed.

Source Relationships.   All media depend on sources to get information for articles. The sources realize their importance and often demand special treatment in return. A public person may demand anonymity in supplying information that could destroy a rival's career; police may ask news media to withhold information about a crime or may ask reporters and editors to become involved in undercover operations. These and other similar cases raise great ethical concerns.

In some media, other potential source conflicts are built into the job. For example, the sources and the readership of many specialized newsletters and trade magazines tend to be one and the same. Consequently, these publications may not report critically about some topics with which their readers are involved.

Deception in Gathering Information.   In their zeal to provide the whole truth, some writers abandon truthfulness themselves. Just as television journalists have generated controversy over the use of hidden cameras, so too have print journalists often waded into murky ethical waters in obtaining information. Using false identities, obtaining secret materials, eavesdropping and other practices raise serious questions for editors to consider.

Being Party to Criminal Behavior.   While the use of deception to gather information usually does not break the law, writers sometimes believe the best way to get at the truth of a matter is by placing themselves in a situation where illegal activity is taking place. For a magazine article on violent gangs, for example, a writer might spend time riding with gang members, observing their criminal behavior along the way.

Manipulation of Photographs.   Photographs can be manipulated when they are taken or when they are processed. In taking a photo, a photographer can frame a shot out of context; by using the right lens and distance, for instance, a photographer can make a small crowd look like a mob. A photographer also can stage a photo. One photographer for USA Today caused an uproar when he gave a ride to young black men to pick up guns to hold in a front-page photograph that accompanied a story about fears of gang violence in Los Angeles. The men, who were unaware of the way in which their photo was to be used, were in fact former gang members who advocated an end to violence.[7]

Manipulation can also take place during processing, when elements in a photograph can be removed, replaced or altered. Until recently, most doctored photographs could be detected easily. In this digital age, however, such changes can be imperceptible. While no one would object to touching up a scratch, how about removing a Coke can (as the St. Louis Post-Dispatch did)? Adding a black student's face to a photo of a crowd showing only white students (as the University of Wisconsin-Madison did on an application packet)? Moving the great pyramids closer together to make them fit on a magazine cover (as National Geographic did)? Showing President Bill Clinton and Cuban leader Fidel Castro shaking hands at a U.N. summit — an act that took place out of sight of photographers (as The New York Daily News did)?

The controversy over digital manipulation reached a peak when Time magazine published a digitally enhanced mug shot of O.J. Simpson, the ex-football star charged with killing his ex-wife and her friend. Time's cover shot was darker than the original (which appeared on the cover of Newsweek the same week), making Simpson look more sinister. Initially editors at the magazine defended the decision to run the shot, pointing out that a line inside the magazine noted that it was a "photo illustration." But after readers complained that the picture was "an insult to photojournalism," "grossly irresponsible" and "just plain stupid," the magazine's managing editor offered a page-long apology in the next issue. "I have looked at thousands of covers over the years and chosen hundreds," Managing Editor James R. Gaines wrote. "I have never been so wrong about how one would be received."[8]

Digital manipulation of photos threatens to undermine journalistic credibility more than any other questionable practice. Just as readers expect the words they read to be accurate, so too do they expect that what they see in a news photograph is an accurate depiction of reality. When readers find out that news photos have been altered, they may well come to doubt everything in a publication.

Many organizations and groups have taken a clear stand on the issue of photo manipulation. For example, The Associated Press Managing Editors' Code of Ethics offers this guideline on photo manipulation: "The newspaper should guard against inaccuracies, carelessness, bias or distortion through emphasis, omission or technological manipulation."[9]

Use of Offensive Material.   Editors also need to act as gatekeepers in making sure that materials do not needlessly offend audience members. One problem area is material that fails to acknowledge certain audience members or is insensitive to them. A second problem area is material that includes graphic description or portrayal of violent or sexually oriented nature. These two topics are covered in more detail in Chapter 7.

Questions to Guide Ethical Decision Making

Just as good reporting depends on writers asking the right questions, so too does good ethical decision making depend on editors asking the right questions. The questions that follow are designed to help you gather all the information necessary to make ethical decisions that you can publicly defend. The questions are drawn largely from a model developed by University of Oregon Professor Thomas H. Bivins.[10] His model is a consolidation of the work of many people who have written about media ethics over the years. As you run through the questions, you'll see how they could be answered in one case.

For our case study, let's return to the situation posed at the start of this chapter. Your reporter argues that most suburban parents think that their children are safe from drugs — that drug use is something that happens in bad areas of the city, not where they live. She insists that parents need to know that their children are at risk. The best way to show them this, she says, is to report from a party. She has been invited to a party under the condition that she not name anyone in attendance or provide clues that would identify the location.

What Is the Ethical Issue?   The first step toward good ethical decision making is isolating the ethical issue. The issue typically will be one of those listed earlier; before you're ready to proceed, you should be able to state the issue in a sentence or two.

The ethical issue is whether it's proper to allow a reporter to attend a party at which teen-agers will be taking illegal drugs.

What Are the Relevant Facts?   It's impossible to make a good decision unless you take the time to sort out all the facts that bear on the ethical issue. What facts make this issue a problem? What is happening inside the publication's offices and outside that has a direct bearing on the issue? What could happen as a result of your decision? Might a certain decision cost you an advertiser or readers? Might it cost you your job?

The relevant facts are:

a.   Readers look to your newspaper to let them know what is happening in their community. The article alerts them to a practice that could have harmful effects on their children.

b.   Drug issues have fallen off the radar screen of many media outlets, and therefore are not a high priority for many parents.

Who Will Be Affected by Your Decision, and in What Ways Are You Obligated to Each of Them?   Your decision may affect a wide range of stakeholders, from individuals to other media professionals. As you consider the stakeholders, ask yourself what you owe them: loyalty, fairness, respect, compassion, profits, stability, efficiency, quality and so on. You'll notice that your obligations to one stakeholder often conflict with your obligations to another.

The stakeholders in this case are:

a.   The readers — If your primary goal is to inform your audience, then you owe your readership loyalty in letting them know about important matters.

b.   Those attending the party — The teen-agers have made an offer to your reporter under the condition that she tell their story without identifying them.

c.   The parents of the teens — They need to know that their children are breaking the law and using drugs that could be potentially harmful.

d.   The author of the article — You owe the writer respect for his or her sense of newsworthiness.

e.   Law enforcement authorities — Their mission is to prevent criminal behavior in the community.

In any given case, you should be able to find at least three ways of dealing with the issue.

What Are Your Options?   In any given case, you should be able to find at least three ways of dealing with the issue.

It often seems as though there may be only two options in resolving an ethical issue. For example, in this case, the obvious options are:

Option 1: Let the reporter attend the party and report on it.

Option 2: Do not let her attend the party. No story will be written.

But there are other options, as well:

Option 3: Have the reporter write an article on the topic without attending the party.

Option 4: Alert the parents of the teens to the upcoming party.

Option 5: Let the reporter attend the party and report on it, revealing the names of those in attendance.

Option 6: Alert the police to the party and write an article after they have arrested the teens.

Which Options Would Be Favored by Each Affected Party? Which Could Cause Harm to Any of Those to Whom You Are Responsible?   Once you know your options, you need to consider which would be favored by each stakeholder and which might harm them.

> *Option 1:* The reporter and at least most of the teens would prefer this option. It will also alert the police and parents as to what is happening in their community.

> *Option 2:* Some teens might prefer this option, as they might not trust the reporter and do not desire to have their families find out about the party. Parents and police would not prefer this option, as it would prevent them from finding out about the activities.

> *Option 3:* Some parents would prefer this option, especially if the article were published before the party so they could monitor their children's activities. Some of the teens also would likely prefer it, as there is less chance they can be identified. Police will be informed of the activity.

> *Option 4:* Many parents would prefer this option, but the teens obviously would not. The reporter would not likely favor it, as it would require her to break a promise.

> *Option 5:* Many parents would prefer this option, but the teens obviously would not. The reporter would not likely favor it, as it would require her to break a promise.

> *Option 6:* The police might favor this option, but it could lead to arrests that would not make teens or parents happy. Again, the reporter would have to break a promise.

Do Legal, Professional or Organizational Rules or Principles Automatically Invalidate Any of Your Options?   If you follow any outside or in-house codes of ethics, you may find that they prohibit you from choosing certain options. Other options may require that you break the law, so those options also would be excluded.

The SPJ code mandates that "Journalists should be honest, fair and courageous in gathering, reporting and interpreting information." It adds that journalists should "Show compassion for those who may be affected adversely by news coverage [and] ... use special sensitivity when dealing with children and inexperienced sources or subjects." Further, it notes that journalists should "Recognize that gathering and reporting information may cause harm or discomfort" and warns, "Pursuit of the news is not a license for arrogance."

Recognizing those obligations, we would need to exclude options 4, 5 and 6.

Which Principles Support and Reject Which Options?   The most important part of the decision-making process is grounding the decision in principles. As an editor you have two possible approaches, using professional principles or ethical theories. We'll use professional principles to consider our case; the use of ethical theories is covered later.

Professional principles come from within the profession of journalism, and include many familiar guidelines:

- Inform the public.

- Tell the truth.

- Do not cause avoidable harm.

- Keep promises.

- Act justly.

- Respect people's privacy.

- Don't sensationalize.

- Remain independent.

- Serve the public interest.

Let's examine the options in our test case:

Option 1: Let the reporter attend the party and report on it — This option would seem to be supported by all the principles listed. Some observers might suggest that reporting on the party, however, is a form of sensationalism.

Option 2: Do not let her attend the party or write a story — This option fails to inform the public and to tell the truth. It also does not serve the public interest.

Option 3: Have the reporter write an article on the topic without attending the party — This option is similar to the first, in that it is supported by most of the principles. While it may be less sensationalistic, it also may lack the kind of information that captures readers' attention and alerts them to the problem.

Based on This Analysis, What Is the Best Solution to This Situation?   You are now ready to make a decision that is based on careful reasoning rather than on gut feeling.

In our example, a case could be made for options 1 and 3. Option 1 is more likely to draw readers' attention to the problem because it will include a first-person account of what goes on at these parties. And indeed, it was that option that was picked at the newspaper that faced this situation (The Washington Post).

How Would You Defend Your Decision to Your Most Adamant Detractor?   You should be able to write an article that will enable even someone who disagrees with your decision to understand why you believe that your decision is the best one. While the article does not necessarily have to be published, the act of writing it provides one final check that you did the right thing.

In the example we've been using, the Post's ombudsman, Richard Harwood, addressed the topic in his column. Harwood noted that Post editors felt that sending the reporter to the party was the right thing to do:

You should be able to write an article that will enable even someone who disagrees with your decision to understand why you believe that your decision is the best one.

The story, they say, shed light on a neglected problem and woke up people "who had their heads in the sand." One of the school officials quoted in the story ... has said, "There's no LSD use by any kids in any school."

Another presumed "good" is the central message of the piece: LSD can mess you up real bad. And most significantly, perhaps, parents of some of "The Acid Kids" now know their children were involved and are taking steps to deal with the problem.

Addressing the concerns of those who felt it was improper to have a reporter watching teens who might have bad reactions, Harwood added that the reporter had decided before the party that if things had turned bad, "She would have given aid and called for help."[11] In that sense, her presence at the party made the teens safer than if she hadn't been there.

While taking the time to answer the questions in this model might seem unrealistic, some editors use just this sort of process regularly. As one example, another former Washington Post ombudsman, Joann Byrd, has addressed these questions in a series of worksheets she has designed for specific ethical issues. A copy of Byrd's worksheet for privacy issues is on Pages 184 and 185 (Figure 6.2). In discussing her worksheets, Byrd has written:

> These questions aim to bring order to a tangle of opinion and gut reaction and not leave out anything that should be considered. [The process] wants us to sleep well at night, and to explain clearly to people outside the newsroom, confidently to people who don't agree.[12]

If you approach ethical problems in such a thoughtful manner, you'll be able to come up with good answers to even the most difficult questions you'll face.

Ethical Principles

Many of those who teach media ethics argue that a grounding in general ethical theory is necessary to produce reasoned decisions. As Edmund B. Lambeth has written in "Committed Journalism: An Ethic for the Profession,"

> It is past time for journalists and owners of newspapers and radio and television stations to articulate principles of performance that are publicly visible, ethically defensible, and rooted clearly in a philosophic tradition that continues to justify a free press.[13]

Commonly cited ethical principles[14] include:

Aristotle's Golden Mean: Decisions should reflect moderation, avoiding both the tendency to do nothing and the tendency to go to excess.

Immanuel Kant's Categorical Imperative: Decisions should be made on principles that apply universally. For example, telling the truth is always right; telling a lie is always wrong.

continued

Deadline Ethics: Privacy

What do you need to decide and when do you need to decide it? _____

> **You may be about to rewrite it or write an exception, but is there a policy on this?**

1 What are the **facts**, from all perspectives?

> **Do you have enough information to decide?**

2 What is the story your readers need?

Could you tell that story in a way that honors the person's privacy?

3 On a scale of 1 to 10, how important to your readers is each detail that might violate privacy?

4 Which **two** ethical principles* collide most here?
__keep promises
__respect privacy
__serve the public interest
__do not cause avoidable harm
__inform the public
__act justly

5 Which principle would a disinterested observer have you rank more important?

6 Who is affected the most here?

__subject & family   __other news
__all journalists   organizations
__the news   __competitors
  organization   __readers/viewers

To which of those constituents are you most obligated? _____

7 What are your options? (Think of at least three.)

1.
2.
3.
4.
5.

8 Which option best supports the principle ranked most important in Question 5?

_____

Which option would be the likely favorite of your first-priority constituent (from Question 6)?

_____

Does any option offer an acceptable compromise?

_____

> **9** Which option seems most right?
> _____

Figure 6.2
Ethical issues worksheet.
Copyright Joann Byrd.

10 How can you reduce the cost of this decision to the principle that's been outweighed?

11 Does this change a policy or write a new one?

What will the policy say now?

And to those affected?

What will trigger exceptions?

For the ultimate double-check of your decision, write a story explaining your reasoning. Among those who will read it: the people hurt by your choice, journalists at the competing shop and your teen-age children. Publish it or don't; the writing should help clarify your thinking and reveal any holes. Here's a pointy-headed start:

(Name/the news organization) has decided_____.

The decision was reached after weighing _____ and concluding
                                          (principles and consequences considered)

that _____ is most likely to uphold the principle of _____ and
         (the option chosen)

serve _____ while minimizing damage to _____.
      (constituent)   (principles/constituents)

(I/We) believe the obligation to _____ outweighs in this case because _____
                                  (principle/constituent)

_____. (I/the news organization) chose not to

_____ because _____. (I/We) decided
(option rejected)

against _____ because _____.
        (another rejected option)

To reduce the damage to _____, (I/we) (will/have) _____
                          (constituent/principle)

_____. To help avoid _____, (I/we)

(will/have)_____.

With this decision, (name/the news organization) adopts a policy saying _____
_____.

John Stuart Mill's Principle of Utility: The best decision is that which produces the greatest good.

John Rawls' Veil of Ignorance: Decisions should protect the weakest parties. This can occur only if all parties step behind a "veil of ignorance," where roles and social differences vanish.

Judeo-Christian Tradition: The command to "love your neighbor as yourself" runs through most of the world's religions. As an ethical principle, it directs decision makers to act in ways that promote the well being of others.

No short discussion can adequately cover all the ethical theories an editor should consider in reaching a conclusion; that's the job of a media ethics course, which every communications student should take.

Notes

1. Marie Dunne White, "Plagiarism and the News Media," Journal of Mass Media Ethics, 4, no. 2 (1989): p. 278.

2. Mike Hughes, "Deja Vu All Over Again?" ASNE Bulletin, January/February 1992, p. 17.

3. Howard Kurtz, "On PBS, Negative Nabobs of Positivity," The Washington Post, 23 October 2000, sec. C, pp. 1, 7.

4. Jay Black, Bob Steele and Ralph Barney, "Doing Ethics in Journalism" (Greencastle, Ind.: The Sigma Delta Chi Foundation and the Society for Professional Journalists, 1993), pp. 163 – 164.

5. Ronald K.L. Collins, "Dictating Content: How Advertising Pressure Corrupts a Free Press" (Washington, D.C.: The Center for the Study of Commercialism, 1992).

6. Lawrence C. Soley and Robert L. Craig, "Advertising Pressures on Newspapers: A survey," Journal of Advertising, XXI, no. 4 (Dec. 1992): pp. 1–10.

7. William A. Henry III, "When Reporters Break the Rules," Time, 15 March 1993, p. 54.

8. Howard Kurtz, "Time to Newsweek: What's Wrong With This Picture?" The Washington Post, 24 June 1994, sec. B, p. 1.

9. Associated Press Managing Editors' Code of Ethics, *www.apme.com/about/code_ ethics.shtml.*

10. Thomas H. Bivins, "A Worksheet for Ethics Instruction and Exercises in Reason," Journalism Educator, 48, no. 2 (Summer 1993): pp. 4–16.

11. Richard Harwood, "The Acid Kids," The Washington Post, 25 August 1991, sec. C, p. 6.

12. Byrd, worksheets cover page.

13. Edmund B. Lambeth, "Committed Journalism: An Ethic for the Profession" (Bloomington, Ind.: Indiana University Press, 1992), p. 1.

14. Summarized here from Clifford Christians, Kim B. Rotzoll and Mark Fackler, "Media Ethics: Cases and Moral Reasoning" (New York: Longman, 1987), pp. 9–17.

Exercise

Use the 9-step model discussed in this chapter to justify how you would act in each of the following cases.

1. The police reporter of your daily newspaper has found out that the 15-year-old daughter of the county sheriff has been arrested for possessing a small amount of marijuana. While the newspaper typically would not report on such a minor arrest, the reporter argues that this case is different: The girl's father is the embodiment of law and order, and here she is breaking one of the laws that her father has repeatedly vowed to enforce. Do you publish it?

2. You are planning to run an article in your newsletter that will have a tremendous effect on your audience. Just before deadline, the person who wrote the article comes to you and says, "There's something I'd better tell you." She proceeds to explain that she got her juiciest information by looking in a confidential file while conducting an interview for the article. She defends her snooping by noting that the person she interviewed left the file on his desk while he was out of the room for several minutes. "I'm sure he expected me to read it," your writer says. Do you publish the article?

3. As editor of a magazine that deals with the future, you appreciate high technology. So when the publisher tells you that he has arranged to have a hologram printed on the cover of the next issue, you like the idea. But as the issue date nears, you realize that the hologram is actually part of an advertisement on Page One of the magazine; the cover will be cut out to let it show through. In essence, your cover will be an ad. What do you do?

4. One of your student reporters at the campus newspaper tells you that she has taken a part-time job at a local balloon-delivery shop. When she applied, she was astonished to find that she was expected to deliver balloons topless, but she agreed because the pay was good. Now she says she's being pressured to perform sex with her deliveries, and she believes the delivery company is a major prostitution ring using local college women. She wants to write an article for the paper. To finish her research and "nail the sucker," as she puts it, she has agreed to work with local police and wear a wire to record incriminating statements by her boss. As her editor, will you allow her to wear the wire?

5. A man recently broke into a home during daylight hours and raped a woman at crossbow point. Your newspaper has reported the case, but now you find that there have been four such rapes in the past month. Police have tried to

suppress the information so they can pursue the rapist quietly; now that you know, they're asking you to keep quiet until they can complete a sting. In the meantime, though, more women may be raped who could have avoided the tragedy if they had known about the series of attacks. Do you print or withhold the information?

6. A long-time source has given one of the reporters at your newsletter juicy information. But later in the day, the source calls back and asks that the material not be run. Do you run an article on the information and risk losing the source? Or do you kill the article to please the source, in the process denying your readers information they could use?

7. A freelance writer you have never worked with has submitted an article proposal that looks interesting. She has enclosed clips, and she seems to be a good writer. But you're sure one of the writers you have worked with before could do a much better job with the proposed topic. Is there any problem with sending a rejection letter to the writer who proposed the article, then assigning it to the proven writer?

EDITING FOR THE WEB

Ethics in Cyberspace

If making sound ethical decisions can be difficult in traditional journalism, doing so can be totally bewildering in the online world. Online workers have to face the same problems as their print counterparts do, as well as a host of new ones.

Unfortunately, online media workers are often less prepared for ethical decision making than their print counterparts. Many online editors do not have a background in journalism — and many online "news" sites are really commerce sites that offer news to try to draw customers. As Bruce Koon of Knight Ridder has noted, "Many dot-coms and new media players have moved into the business of providing news and 'content,' and they don't necessarily have any journalism legacy or traditional structure that safeguards editorial independence."[1]

Even online workers with a background in journalism often face a unique challenge online. "You are expected not just to gather and report and edit the news like in the safe old days," Fred Mann of Philadelphia Online notes. "You are expected to do all that and turn a profit ... soon."[2]

Adding to the problem is the fact that online media are moving targets. Several years after the Web rose to prominence, it's still undergoing a constant process of change. Each change brings potential new ethical problems.

Content vs. Commerce

Perhaps the most fundamental difference to emerge so far between online publishing and traditional print publishing is that while content remains king in the new medium, commerce has become an equally powerful queen. Discussing Time Warner's overhaul of the Pathfinder Web site, Lisa Allen of Forrester Research noted that the Web audience "has a different set of expectations: They look for utility and convenience and savings, as well as content." She added: "Online publishing blends content and commerce increasingly, as if the old lines between editorial and advertising are disappearing."[3]

One common example of this merging of content and commerce comes in book reviews. Read a review in The New York Times or Salon magazine, for instance, and if you'd like to purchase a copy, it's just a click away at Barnes & Noble. Such transactions — as well as links from reviews to buy CDs, purchase tickets to cultural and sporting events, make reservations or purchase other products or services — are undoubtedly convenient for the reader. Direct online transactions also benefit Web publishers, offering the opportunity to generate additional income. Many media analysts see these transactions as the "advertisements of the future."[4]

But with them comes one of the biggest ethical debates of the present. Such arrangements have the potential to influence content producers. New Media analyst Steve Outing notes:

Salon.com book review readers can easily click to Barnes & Noble to buy the book.

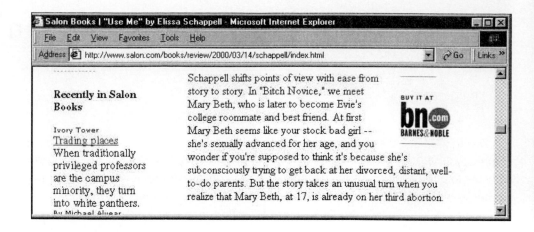

Positive reviews are of course more likely to generate more sales of a book. The danger inherent in schemes like this is that it could influence book editors to publish mostly positive reviews, because of the financial interest at stake. (Imagine if the bookseller offered a higher commission on certain books that it wanted to promote. The temptation might exist to write a positive review to take advantage of the financial bonus.)[5]

Online news publisher, analyst and academic Eric Meyer adds: "It's not so much a question of whether a sales link tempts your critics to write favorable reviews (although it might). It's more a question of how a sales link influences which performances critics will review."[6]

In order to avoid these problems, online sites should take several steps. First, publishers should formulate clear guidelines on handling direct online transactions. All employees should sign off on the guidelines, which should be available for public inspection on the publisher's Web site. For an example, look at the San Antonio Express-News, which has developed and published a new ethics code (*www.mysa.com/mysanantonio/aboutus/expressnews/ethics.shtml*).

Second, paid links should be labeled clearly as such. "Clarity sets appropriate expectations and establishes a context that the user needs in order to interpret the information," notes Steve Yelvington, editor of Star Tribune Online, the Web service of the Star Tribune in Minneapolis, Minn.[7]

Steve Outing suggests labeling direct transaction links as "Paid advertisements" and including a "disclaimer" link nearby to explain the site's policies about contextual advertising.[8]

Conflicts in Coverage

The conflict between content and commerce is not the only obvious conflict online publishers face. Because the Web is still developing, new laws are constantly being proposed to regulate one aspect or another of it. In many cases, online media have taken strong stands for and against proposals — in many cases signing on as plaintiffs. Readers are well-justified in asking how such positions affect coverage of the proposals. Once again, the best course is to divulge such potential conflicts, in every article if need be. Some critics further suggest that employees of editorial content sites should not own stock in companies that make, market or sell products covered by the site or engage in secondary employment or serve in organizations that involve topics covered by the site.

Privacy

To many people, the most troubling ethical issue of all is that of privacy. In order to access many Web sites — including some prominent news sites such as that of The New York Times (*www.nytimes.com*) — visitors have to register. In the process, they are asked for personal information, or they may find that the site has placed cookies on their computers to track their movements.

News of major Web firms tracking visitors' actions without warning them and selling personal information after promising not to has left the public jaded. News organizations cannot afford to lose credibility over this issue. Not surprisingly, once again the best policy is disclosure. The Times, for example, prominently posts a privacy policy on its site. The policy lists all the data that the Times collects as well as what's done with it. For instance, in a section on Statistical Analysis and Banner Advertising, the policy notes:

> The New York Times on the Web may perform statistical analyses of user behavior in order to measure interest in the various areas of our site (for product development purposes) and to inform advertisers as to how many consumers have seen or "clicked" their advertising banners. The Times also uses demographic and preference information to allow advertising banners on our Web site to be targeted, in aggregate, to the readers for whom they are most pertinent. This means that readers see advertising that is most likely to interest them, and advertisers send their messages to people who are most likely to be receptive, improving both the viewer's experience and the effectiveness of the ads. In this statistical analyses and banner advertisement targeting, we will disclose information to third parties only in aggregate form. Personal information about you as an individual subscriber will not be provided to any third party without your consent.[9]

Posting the policy is only the first step. Unless you follow the policy, you'll deservedly lose your visitors' trust — and the visitors themselves.

Linking

In Chapter 4, we learned that many Web editors are responsible for tracking down links to complement articles. That raises yet another question: Is a Web site ethically responsible for the content of sites it links to? For example, if a news site runs an article on online hate sites, is it unethical to link to some of those sites to show visitors what they're like? What happens, for instance, if a young Web surfer visits the linked sites without understanding the context in which they're offered?

This question has troubled online editors for almost as long as there have been online editors. Generally, their solutions involve one or two steps. The first is developing a clear policy about what type of sites should not be linked to. The New York

Times, for example, has guidelines that prohibit linking to sites that celebrate violence or present sexual content, as well as to sites that promote bigotry and racism.[10] The second step is notifying the visitor when he or she is about to leave the news site. Some sites do this by having a disclaimer page appear when a visitor clicks an off-site link. Others clearly indicate where related links are hosted (for example, a news story on Ford Motor Co. included a link to an article on the history of Ford, clearly marked as "From Brittanica"). Other sites avoid the problem by never including external links — which shows they don't understand one of the most useful features of the Web. Only the last approach satisfies some critics, though. Bob Steele of the Poynter Institute, for instance, stresses that a simple disclaimer is not enough. He notes: "We cannot just say 'Buyer beware.' That alone does not mitigate against the harm that can come from tainted information." Steele suggests instead actively warning visitors "when we are leading them to something that might alarm them."[11]

Even when the credibility of material on a linked site is not an issue, other potential problems lurk. One of the greatest benefits of the Web is the unlimited newshole that allows reporters and editors to post voluminous background material and primary documents. But doing so poses two risks. First, adding such material seems to indicate that readers are being given all the information available on a topic. That can never be the case; editors and writers are more likely to link only to material that supports the perspective of the story. Second, some primary material begs for elaboration. On its own, raw data can be confusing or misleading rather than enlightening.[12]

Notes

1. Bruce Koon, "Journalistic Credibility Online vs. E-Commerce?" Online News Association, 15 May 2000, *www.onlinenewsassociation.org/koon.html*.

2. Anne Stuart, "The New Right," Webmaster, June 1997, p. 56–58.

3. Alex Kuczynski, "Time Warner Closing Pathfinder Site," The New York Times, 27 April 1999, *www.nytimes.com*.

4. Steve Outing, "A Debate: Contextual Transactions on News Sites," Editor & Publisher Interactive, 6 January 1999, *www.mediainfo.com/ephome/news/newshtm/stop/st010699.htm*.

5. Steve Outing, "Read the Review, Buy the Book: How Ethical?" Editor & Publisher Interactive, 10 October 1997, *www.mediainfo.com/ephome/news/newshtm/stop/st101097.htm*.

6. Outing, "A Debate."

7. Outing, "Read the Review."

8. Outing, "A Debate."

9. The New York Times on the Web Privacy Information, *www.nytimes.com/info/help/privacy.html*.

10. Dianne Lynch, "Without a Rulebook," American Journalism Review, January/February 1998, p. 43.

11. Lynch, pp. 43–44.

12. Fred Mann, "What a Difference a Year Makes: New Media and Newer Challenges," Poynter Report, Spring 1998, p. 10.

Editor's Corner

Looking in on Tonya Harding

Computers make many things easier for journalists, but don't put ethics on the list.

By making so much information so much more accessible, computers plug today's journalist into a cybernet of opportunities, temptations and tests.

Consider the 1994 Winter Olympics in Lillehammer, Norway.

Athletes, officials and journalists from around the world came together in the Olympic Village, where they were linked electronically by Info '94, a computer that provided results, biographies and key historical information at the touch of a few keys. Info '94 also provided private electronic mailboxes for the athletes, journalists and others. When they arrived in Lillehammer, people with mailboxes could open them with their accreditation numbers and birth dates. Those numbers were not secret. Accreditation numbers were on credentials and entry lists; birth dates were in the media guide and bios. People were encouraged to change their pass codes to protect their privacy.

Some reporters wondered how easy it would be to get into an athlete's mailbox. Could they open the e-mail of, say, Tonya Harding? The American figure skater was a controversial figure at the games because of allegations about her involvement in an attack on her chief competitor.

Sitting down at a keyboard after a late-night dinner with other reporters, Detroit Free Press sports writer Michelle Kaufman tried. With an accreditation number taken from a photograph, she typed in the code.

The mailbox opened, and the screen showed Kaufman and the watching reporters that Harding had 68 unread messages. Kaufman closed the mailbox without reading anything. Case closed. Or was it?

A reporter who had heard about the snooping told the U.S. Olympic Committee. The committee's director of public relations called it a non-issue because nothing had been read and said, "I think it's an issue in terms of ethics that belongs in the court of journalism itself."

Journalists and ethicists showed no reluctance to get involved.

Howard Kurtz, media reporter for The Washington Post, said: "This is not a close call. For reporters to be snooping in other people's messages is troubling."

Dave Barry, humor columnist for The Miami Herald, said he had opened the mailbox himself. "This is being held up as some kind of a criminal thing," he said, "when in fact it's no different than a reporter reading someone's mail upside-down on a desk."

Back in Detroit, Michelle Kaufman's boss, Detroit Free Press Executive Editor Heath Meriwether, said the e-mail incident "underscores our obligation to follow the same rules we apply to any form of private communications." Meriwether added, "We have no right to look into a person's electronic mailbox or mail without

**Joe Grimm,
recruiting and
development editor,
Detroit Free Press**

their permission. Michelle is a fine journalist of great integrity, but she made a mistake she regrets, a mistake that reflects badly on her and the newspaper. Even though Michelle did not read anything, the mistake was to use the password at all and enter the mailbox. She and the Free Press have apologized to Tonya Harding for this breach."

Three blocks down the street, the arch-rival Detroit News published a front-page story under the headline "Free Press reporter busts into Harding's e-mail." In it, an associate professor of journalism called the snooping "reprehensible." A Colorado columnist called it "a monumentally stupid act."

A color photograph of the Free Press sports writer ran on the front page. How did the News get a color photo of a writer from the rival paper?

The photo was taken out of Free Press files — computer files.

Detroit's dailies have a joint production department with shared equipment, including computers. Each newspaper's files are proprietary, however. A Detroit News editor persuaded a production worker to take a copy of the photo out of Free Press files and drop it into News files. Not only did they open the mailbox, they stole the mail and used it to flog the competition.

As people read his newspaper's criticism of the rival reporter's computer snooping, Detroit News Editor and Publisher Bob Giles was writing memos that called the appropriation a "breach of security" and violation of professional courtesy.

Yes, computers make a lot of things simpler for journalists. But they might make ethics more difficult.

Making Words Match

Just like people, some words get along fine with others, but others cannot coexist harmoniously. Six of the most common problem areas are subject-verb agreement, pronoun-antecedent agreement, tense, parallelism, point of view and case.

Subject-Verb Agreement

Most writers and editors know the basics of **subject-verb agreement:** Every subject must match its verb. So it's clearly wrong to write a sentence like the following:

All subjects has to agree with their verbs.

Unfortunately, sometimes several words come between the subject and the verb, tricking the writer into making the verb agree with something other than the subject, such as in this sentence:

A youth group composed of rehabilitated juvenile offenders are taking the message "Just say no to guns" to high schools across the country.

The subject is *group,* which should get the singular verb *is taking,* but the writer incorrectly used *are taking* to make it agree with *offenders.*

The following hints will help you track down subjects and make sure they agree with their verbs.

Multiple Subjects.   When two or more words are joined by *and,* they take a plural verb:

The principal and the teacher freely praise the program.

But when multiple subjects are joined by *or* or *nor,* the verb must agree with the final noun:

The cat or the dog is scratching at the door.

Either the students or the teacher is responsible.

Neither the manager nor the workers like the contract.

Collective Nouns.   These words, such as *group, committee, company* and *staff,* can take either a singular or a plural verb, depending on whether the collective unit is acting in unison or separately:

The committee was unanimous in its decision. (acting together)

The committee were divided in their votes. (acting separately)

Some nouns that end in *s* cannot be counted (*mumps, measles, news,* etc.). Some take a singular verb, others take a plural, and still others can take either. When in doubt, check your stylebook or dictionary.

Indefinite pronouns also follow no universal rule. Use a plural verb with *both;* a singular verb with *everyone;* and either a singular or plural verb with *most,* depending on circumstances. Again, it's always best to check.

Prepositional Phrases.   One of the most common mistakes in subject-verb agreement is confusing the subject with another noun in a prepositional phrase that follows the subject. The easiest way to check is to mentally remove any prepositional phrases from the sentence. For example,

The director of a local school for gifted students has resigned.

becomes

The director ... has resigned.

Inverted Subjects.   Most sentences beginning with the words *here* and *there* can be improved by rewriting. If, however, that construction remains intact, the editor needs to remember that the first word is a false subject, and the verb should agree with the noun that follows it:

Here are *the* people *who get the job done right.*

There is *little* chance *of rain for the day of the company picnic.*

Phrases Set Off by Commas.   When a subject is followed by a phrase set off by commas, the verb agrees with the subject alone:

The colonel, along with six sergeants, was court-martialed.

None as the Subject.   If you follow The Associated Press Stylebook, you usually will treat *none* as a singular word meaning "not one." But it should be treated as a plural when it is used to mean "no two or more":

None of the packages has arrived.

None of the students coincide in their opinions.

Pronoun-Antecedent Agreement

Editors also need to watch the agreement between pronouns and the words to which they refer (their antecedents). The pronouns and antecedents must agree in gender and person as well as in number:

The 6-year-old ballerina looks cute in her tutu.

The young ballerinas look cute in their tutus.

Sometimes a problem develops in antecedent agreement as the result of a writer attempting to avoid sexism. An example:

Every student said they failed the exam.

Every student is singular, so its antecedent should be singular. Using *he* instead of *they,* however, excludes all the female students. One way around the problem:

All the students said they failed the exam.

(See Chapter 7 for more on sexism.)

Perhaps the most common antecedent problem is the lack of a true antecedent for the word which, as in this example:

They could see no ducks, which upset the hunters.

The antecedent for *which* is *ducks,* so the sentence says *Ducks upset the hunters.* Instead, try

The lack of ducks upset the hunters.

or

The hunters were upset because there were no ducks.

Also be careful when antecedents are collective nouns. Recall two examples used earlier:

The committee was unanimous in its decision. (acting together)

The committee were divided in their votes. (acting separately)

Problems also arise when antecedents are unclear, particularly when there is more than one possible antecedent for a word:

She told her that her best days were behind her.

There is no way for an editor to untangle this without turning to the writer for help.

Finally, be careful when dealing with agreement after *either/or* or *neither/nor.* The true antecedent in these cases is the word after the *or* or *nor,* so the pronoun must agree with the gender and number of that word:

Either the police or the 16-year-old girl they arrested lied in her account of the incident.

Neither the camera operators nor the star was happy with his contract.

To avoid such strange sentences, you might want to rewrite them:

Someone lied in recounting the incident: either the police or the 16-year-old girl they arrested.

The camera operators were not happy with their contract, and the star was not happy with his, either.

Tense

Media writers generally use one of two tenses, depending on the type of copy they're working on. **Past tense** is used for most news and feature articles; **present tense** is used in headlines, ad copy and text accompanying photos and graphics. There are exceptions, though. Some feature articles, for instance, are written in present tense, and news stories use future tense when discussing matters that haven't yet occurred, or past perfect tense for actions that occurred before those being covered. Generally speaking, however, a piece of writing should stick to one tense throughout. Once again, the editor is the enforcer.

The most common problem is a change in tense while describing actions that take place at the same time. An example:

In an interview with Allure magazine, Raquel Welch said she felt Madonna was being miscast in movies by people who didn't have her best interests at heart. "Don't you think that's just envy?" Welch asks.

Said is past tense, while *asks* is present. Both should be the same tense.

Past tense is usually the best base from which to start. Using past tense makes it easier to indicate actions that occurred earlier than the main action in the copy as well as ones that will occur in the future. Here's how to handle those variations:

- When an event has not yet occurred, future tense is appropriate.

  She said she will retire next year.

- When an action began before the main action of an article but is not finished, **present perfect tense** is used.

  The team members have taken ballet lessons for several years.

- When an action was completed before the main action of the article, **past perfect tense** should be used.

> The most common problem is a change in tense while describing actions that take place at the same time.

Before he arrived in America, he had lived in Germany for four years.

- When a belief or condition is ongoing, **present tense** is used.

  She believes that women should control their own destinies.

  They live in a cabin in a remote region of Wisconsin.

Parallelism

All items in a series should be alike (**parallel**). Mixing nouns with verbals or any other unlike elements can muddy meaning and confuse the reader. An editor can verify parallelism only by checking every item individually. One good way to do this is by stacking up the items in a row (at least mentally) to see if they are comparable:

The party promised		*a tax cut for the middle class,*
		more money for health care
	and	*to clean up air quality.*

If any items are not parallel with the others — for instance, the last item in this example — a change is in order:

The party promised		*to cut taxes for the middle class,*
		to allot more money for health care
	and	*to clean up air quality.*

Among the most common types of errors in parallelism are the following:

Mixing Verbals.   As we saw when discussing phrases, verbals are forms of verbs. The most common parallelism problem with verbals comes from mixing gerunds (*-ing* form of the verb) and infinitives (*to* form of the verb):

The fax modem allows sending faxes directly from the word-processing program or to receive faxes that view on screen or print out.

To correct this sentence, an editor either can change the first part to *allows you to send* or can change *to receive* to *receiving* in the second part.

Mixing Elements in a Series or a Phrase.   While verbals can function as nouns, they should not be mixed with regular nouns in a series:

It is no longer enough for schools to teach students reading, writing and to do math.

This sentence can be corrected by making all elements verbals (using the infinitives *to read* and *to write*) or changing the infinitive *to do math* to the noun *arithmetic*.

Adjectives and nouns should not be mixed, either:

The proposed auto emissions standards are stringent and of great complexity.

This problem is corrected simply by changing the last phrase to *complex,* which, like *stringent,* is an adjective.

Also watch that items following the words *either* and *both* are parallel. This one isn't:

*He said he would both **improve quality control** and **morale.***

If you can imagine the word *and* acting as the pivot of a seesaw, you'll see this is out of balance:

*He said he would both **improve quality control** and **morale.***

The left side of the seesaw includes a verb, while the right does not. The problem is easily remedied, by moving *both:*

*He said he would improve both **quality control** and **morale.***

Unnecessarily Changing Voice.   Most media writers use active voice, which makes their writing move along. Passive voice is avoided whenever possible. (Notice the difference between the last two sentences: The first uses active voice and flows; the second uses passive and just sits there.) While voice can change from sentence to sentence, for the sake of clarity voice should remain consistent within a sentence. In this sentence, voice changes from active to passive:

The company promised jobs to all employees with more than five years service, but workers with fewer years of employment were laid off.

To keep it active, the second clause has to be modified:

The company promised jobs to all employees with more than five years service, but it laid off those with fewer years of employment.

Inappropriate Use of a Clause.   Clauses should not be mixed with ordinary nouns in a series, as happens in this sentence:

The state inspectors promised time, funds and that the investigation would continue until all guilty parties were found.

Two options exist for fixing this sentence: Either make all the elements of the series nouns, or use two clauses:

The state inspectors promised time, funds and a commitment to continue the investigation until all guilty parties were found.

or

The state inspectors promised that time and funds would be committed and that the investigation would continue until all guilty parties were found.

In addition to these parallelism problems, watch out for **false series,** such as this one:

She planted tomatoes, spinach and sat back to await her harvest.

The verb *planted* obviously does not govern the last part of the sentence, so the sentence must be rewritten:

She planted tomatoes and spinach and sat back to await her harvest.

Point of View

Copy can be written from three different points of view: first person (I, we); second person (you); or third person (he, she, they).

First person is best used for copy in which the writer has played a key role:

I learned an important lesson about car maintenance when my long-neglected econobox died in the middle of the desert.

Second person speaks directly to the reader and is good for providing advice or instruction:

If you want to guarantee high returns on your investments, you need to follow three rules.

Third person is best for most other writing.

They were identified as members of a terrorist group.

Whichever point of view a writer chooses, it should be maintained throughout the copy. This lead shows what happens when a writer is careless with point of view:

Buying a new car is an unpleasant experience for most people [third person]. You [second person] have to put up with sneaky salespeople who will do anything to make a buck. That was always my [first person] experience, until I found a new way of buying cars that does away with most of the headaches.

Whichever point of view a writer chooses, it should be maintained throughout the copy.

Case

Pronouns can be used in three different cases: nominative, objective and possessive. While it seems obvious that the words can't be used interchangeably, sometimes it takes a little thinking to make sure a writer has used the correct case.

Nominative case is used when the pronoun is the subject or part of the subject:

She has earned the respect of the public in less than a year.

He and I cannot attend the reception.

She, as well as they, supports the measure.

Nominative case also is used when a pronoun follows *than* or *as* at the end of the sentence. Those words act as conjunctions, and the pronoun following them is the subject of a clause (the verb of that clause may be implied).

No other group of students were as good as they (were).

She sings as well as he (sings).

Nominative case also is used when the pronoun follows any form of the verb *be:*

Look over there — it is she.

It may have been they at the door.

Objective case is used when the pronoun acts as an object. There are several types of objects.

*   A **direct object** follows a verb (other than a form of *be*):

    The president will meet them at noon.

*   An **indirect object** follows a verb and an implied *to* or *for:*

    The accountant brought (to) us all the records.

*   An **object of preposition** follows a preposition (*to, from, for, with,* etc.):

    Send the letter directly to her.

*   **Objects of participles** and **gerunds** follow *-ing* forms of verbs:

    Finding her, the group went home.

    Liking them is not easy.

- An **object of an infinitive** follows the words *to be:*

  It was not likely to be them.

  Objective case also is used when a pronoun is the subject of an infinitive:

They wanted her to be healthy.

When dealing with *who* and *whoever,* it is sometimes difficult to determine whether the word acts as a subject or an object. One easy way to get an answer is to try substituting *he/she/they* or *him/her/them* to see which makes the most sense:

The company will award the prize to whoever/whomever sells the most magazines.

Him sells the most magazines doesn't make sense; *he sells the most magazines* does. So nominative case — whoever — is correct.

Why won't you tell me who/whom you were talking to?

You were talking to he doesn't make sense; *you were talking to him* does. So objective case — whom — is correct.

  Possessive case is used when a pronoun is possessive:

Your money is no good here.

Possessive case also is used when a pronoun is followed by a gerund:

She could no longer tolerate your scolding her.

Exercise

Correct all spelling, punctuation and style errors in the following article. Also correct any comma splices, fragments, incorrect clauses, misplaced modifiers and errors in agreement, tense, parallelism, point of view and case.

By Holly Fenton

When graduating from high school, you are full of emotions about the future. Thoughts of college, jobs and taking on new responsibilities were thrusted upon you. But when the graduate steps off the stage with their diploma in hand, their first thought is, "Let's celebrate!"

My thoughts weren't much different when I graduated. Four friends and me packed our clothes, radio, junk, and lots of beer. Once we arrived in Ocean City, it was a constant party with continuous drinking.

The party finally ended a week later. My group had to return home to nromal activities. We drank all our alcohol, had taken lots of asprin, and lost our sun tan lotion. So we ventured back home, still care-free, but now tired and hungover as well.

When I arrived home, my mother met me at the door. She told me I received three phone calls from girls I graduated with and it sounded important. Before I could reach the phone it rang again. This time it was my good friend, Karen.

"Holly," she said, "I have bad news. Micky is dead." At first I thought my week long hang over was effecting my hearing. After Karen calmed me, she told me that our friend Micky and another person died in a drinking and driving accident. I realized that one of my closet friends who I shared so much with was dead. How could this have happened.

The call was devastating, my first reunion with my classmates was in a funderal home just ten days after crying with joy about graduating. They all looked so different. There was no smiles, no joy, we all left our happiness behind.

That reunion after the tradgedy was a tear stained and sobering realization that one of us from the class of 00 were gone forever. As we looked around the room the unspoken thought was that it could have been anyone of us. We had to except the truth that the alcohol, which killed our good friend, Micky, could have killed us just as easily.

CHAPTER 7

Sensitivity and Taste

One of the ethical concerns discussed in Chapter 6 was avoiding offense to readers. This chapter takes an in-depth look at the two key aspects of the concern. First, we'll look at the issue of sensitivity to diverse members of the population. Second, we'll explore the question of taste.

Sensitivity

One of the most significant changes in the United States in recent years has been the growth of traditional minority groups. In many areas throughout the country, blacks and Hispanics are now in the majority; in other areas, these groups soon will compose more than half of the population.

This change in the composition of the population has been accompanied by demands for recognition and equality by these and other traditionally disenfranchised groups: women, gay men and lesbians, people with disabilities, old people and many others. While some in government and the media refer to these groups as "special interest groups," members of these groups constitute a significant majority of the population of the United States.

Every communicator needs to remember that fact. As our country increasingly moves from being a melting pot to being a mosaic, it is vital for writers and editors to treat every citizen as they would like to be treated. At its simplest, that means treating every person *as a person,* and not as the person's race, gender, religion, sexual orientation or any other characteristic.

In the minds of some journalists, such treatment is an ethical imperative. Aly Colón, a member of the Ethics faculty at The Poynter Institute, has written:

> Being ethical means you need to take into account all the different types of people in your coverage area. Being ethical means being accurate and fair in the best sense of those words: getting the details that make a story right and seeking out different perspectives that offer a more complete understanding of the people and issues you're covering.[1]

It is vital for writers and editors to treat every citizen as they would like to be treated.

More and more, groups are speaking out or taking action when they feel they have been ignored or portrayed poorly by a media outlet. A protest in the mid-1980s over coverage of blacks in The Washington Post Magazine ended with Editor Ben Bradlee publicly apologizing for the paper's treatment and promising that the paper would do better. During the 1990s, students at colleges across the United States stole tens of thousands of copies of campus newspapers to protest stereotyping and exclusion. In 1993, complaints led long-distance giant AT&T to apologize for a racist illustration in an employee magazine.

You might think that treating all people as equals would strike virtually everyone as a reasonable goal; it is, after all, one of the guiding principles of most of the world's religions. However, many of those who have long enjoyed privileged treatment — and are afraid of losing it — disparage open-mindedness in the media as being "politically correct." As far as those critics are concerned, the media would be better off if they just ignored the disenfranchised. But that's a dangerous attitude. As researchers at the University of Missouri put it:

> Mainstream journalists still do little to help create understanding between the races. And some of what they do still does harm.[2]

Editors can help make the world better — or they can help make it worse.

Unfortunately, equal treatment is not found consistently within the media. As former Washington Post Ombudsman Joann Byrd has written:

> When journalists either aren't like, or don't know, the people they are writing about, they can operate with no ill will whatsoever and still not recognize that a statement does not ring true. It may be even harder to see how deeply offensive a common perception is ...
>
> One reason for the invention of editors is that someone else can see presumption and implication that is invisible to the author. So editors need to have particularly sensitive antennae.[3]

Editors need to have their antennae especially attuned to problems in two main areas:

Invisibility. Look through any newspaper or magazine and count the number of articles about members of traditionally disenfranchised groups. Chances are you won't find many articles. While women, minorities and people with disabilities are showing up more often, they still are underrepresented.

Stereotyping. Disenfranchised groups argue that when they do receive coverage, it tends to fall into one of three types:

a. "Problem stories" — News or feature articles often focus on the problems caused by the disenfranchised: crime, costs to society and so forth.

b. "The exception to the rule" — News or feature articles sometimes highlight a successful individual as though he or she is an exception to the rule.

c. Athletes and entertainers — A handful of celebrities generate a tremendous amount of coverage, at the expense of coverage that deals with most members of their groups.

> While women, minorities and people with disabilities are showing up more often, they are still underrepresented.

One of the reasons that some people resist increased sensitivity is that there is a fine line between being sensitive and being rabidly politically correct. Asking writers and editors to be sensitive does *not* mean that they have to — or even should — resort to phrases like *follically challenged* for someone who is going bald or *vertically challenged* for someone under 5 feet tall. What it does mean is that writers and editors make sure that descriptions of hairlessness and height are necessary to an article, and, when they are, show the reader through good description rather than by merely sticking in an adjective. For example, in a profile of a chef in Smithsonian magazine, the writer noted that "half his hair has deserted him," a much more engaging manner of saying the chef is going bald.

Being Sensitive vs. PC Mania

What one publisher told University of Missouri researchers about minority coverage could easily be extended to any disenfranchised group:

> News coverage of minorities does not show minorities in context. The news coverage focuses on aberrant behavior, both good and bad. News coverage focuses on entertainment figures; it focuses on minorities who are particular "firsts" in their disciplines. And, of course, the criminal element. What news coverage doesn't do is show minority people participating in the day-to-day life of their communities.[4]

Disenfranchised groups argue that because media portrayals help the public form their opinions, only when the media break out of these habits and fairly and accurately portray all people will the public begin to accept all people as equals. As diversity scholars Clint C. Wilson II and Felix Gutierrez have written, media portrayals "can become reality in our minds, especially if we have no personal experiences to balance against them."[5]

Editors need to stay alert to omissions and stereotyping if their publications and organizations are to win the support of a wide spectrum of society. The following sections discuss the most common trouble spots and suggest ways for editors to avoid such problems.

Sexism

More than half the people who live in the United States are women, and in recent years women have made great gains in every area of society. Yet sexism continues to thrive throughout the media.

Despite the number of women in the country, the most common problem in media coverage is their *invisibility.* News and feature articles are far more likely to include interviews with and comments from men than from women — even when the issue might be of far greater concern to women. An article on the invention of a new birth control method for women, for instance, might not include a single quote from a woman. It's not easy to spot this type of insensitivity, because an editor has to look for something that is not in the copy. When editors find such a case, though, they should ask the writers if there weren't qualified female sources. If time permits, they should be sought out and their comments added to the copy.

Another problem is the *assumption that all people are men.* This manifests itself in a few different ways. First is the use of male terms to represent all people. A typical case is the use of *he* to represent all people:

When the average student graduates from college today, he'll be looking at 10 years of loan repayments.

Such cases can be easily repaired:

When students graduate from college today, on average they'll be looking at 10 years of loan repayments.

A word of warning: Be careful that in weeding out such sexism you don't cause problems in agreement. If you change only *he'll* to *they'll* in the first sentence, for example, the sentence will be grammatically incorrect.

Not all cases of this problem involve the use of *he* or other masculine pronouns. For example, an ad that describes a stereo speaker as having "superb sound as well as looks that your wife will love" assumes that all readers are male — which may be one reason more women aren't audiophiles. In those few words, the ad copywriter further assumes that (1) all readers are heterosexual, (2) all readers are married and (3) men have no appreciation of aesthetics. Simply changing the line to read "superb sound as well as a beautiful finish" eliminates all these assumptions.

Other problems in this area include the use of words that end in *-man* and seem to exclude women — *fireman, chairman, freshman* — and the use of words like *poetess, actress* and *coed,* which indicate a secondary status for women. The solutions to these problems should be obvious: Use *firefighter, chairperson, first-year student; poet, actor* and *student.* Most stylebooks offer guidance in choosing such gender-neutral alternatives.

A final manifestation of the assumption that all people are men is found in phrases such as *female police officer* and *woman conductor.* The inclusion of *female* and *woman* reinforces the stereotype that only men do these things. Solution: Cut the offending words.

A third problem area is the *treatment of women as though they are the property of men.* A common example of this is demonstrated in the following sentence taken from a news article:

The allegations involved questions about whether Mr. Sessions tried to evade paying local taxes and whether he and his wife improperly spent FBI funds for personal use.

It is only six paragraphs later that *his wife* is named and given an identity of her own. That identification should take place the first time the woman is mentioned. In another article, a sentence reads:

> The inclusion of *female* and *woman* reinforces the stereotype that only men do these things.

As soon as he noticed the fire, Stoner ran next door and asked his neighbor's wife to call for help.

The woman isn't a neighbor? That's what this says. The fix: Change it to "asked his neighbor."

This tendency is also seen in stories about women that mention, for example, "She is the wife of Jake Smith, a local accountant." Because stories about men do not routinely divulge the names and occupations of their spouses, neither should stories about women.

Many media organizations have taken an additional step to move away from the treatment of women as men's property: dropping courtesy titles for women. While some organizations still require courtesy titles for men and women after first reference (Ronald Decker, Mary Hollings; Mr. Decker, Ms./Miss/Mrs. Hollings), most have decided to end the inequality of signaling women's marital status with courtesy titles. In such organizations, courtesy titles are used only to distinguish between husband and wife in the same story.

Another way that writers treat women as second-class citizens is by *commenting on appearance*, as if women existed largely for men to ogle. Shortly after Bill Clinton became president, two stories in the same issue of The Washington Post about Bill and Hillary Rodham Clinton attending governmental meetings showed a distinct contrast. In the story about Mrs. Clinton, she was referred to as "sporting the patterned fuchsia suit recycled from the inauguration, sans the much buzzed-about blue hat." The story on Mr. Clinton included no details on what he wore in his meetings that day. This practice infers that it's not important what a woman does or says — simply how she looks. Unless you're handling copy for a fashion magazine, you should cut such description.

At the end of Clinton's stay in office, some media outlets drew criticism over their commentary on the appearance of another woman, Florida Secretary of State Katherine Harris. A key player in the 2000 post-election drama in Florida, Harris found her appearance the subject of scrutiny by many in the media — and of a lengthy attack in The Washington Post. Fashion Writer Robin Givhan's column included this passage:

> Her lips were overdrawn with berry-red lipstick — the creamy sort that smears all over a coffee cup and leaves smudges on shirt collars. Her skin had been plastered and powdered to the texture of pre-war walls in need of a skim coat. And her eyes, rimmed in liner and frosted with blue eye shadow, bore the telltale homogenous spikes of false eyelashes. Caterpillars seemed to rise and fall with every bat of her eyelid ...

Later in her column, Givhan mused that Harris seemed to have copied her makeup from ads instead of thinking for herself. "Why should anyone trust her?" Givhan asked.[6]

The Post was flooded with critical phone calls and e-mails, one of which noted, "The implication that there is a serious connection between makeup and seriousness ... is one that women have been struggling against for decades."[7]

Finally, women often are *stereotyped as incompetent and unintelligent*. For example, an ad to promote auto-care classes for women featured a caricature of a baffled woman asking, "Carburetor? Fuel pump? Transmission fluid? Alternator? Where can I go to learn about all this stuff?" In reality, plenty of women know how to repair cars — and plenty of men don't. Such copy itself is in need of major repair, as are the many advertisements that continue to depict women as sex objects or as people who live for the joys of housekeeping.

A less conspicuous example of this problem occurs when writers seem to "ooh" and "ahh" about women achieving things that men never would receive accolades for. In a profile of Emmy-winning television newscaster Marjorie Mezvinsky, for example, a list of her accomplishments includes this:

And over the summer, she threw a huge wedding with 14 bridesmaids for daughter Lee Heh Margolies, 28.

Can you imagine that being written about Dan Rather? The best rule of thumb in this and all other aspects of sexism is simple:

If you wouldn't treat a man a certain way, don't treat a woman that way, either.

One final point: Objects have no sex. To call a car or a boat *she* is simply wrong. Even a hurricane, with its male or female name, is sexless. In all cases, it's an *it*.

Words to Watch for:

- Avoid all slang words for women, including *airhead, babe, bimbo, broad, chick, dumb blonde, gal, girl* (if 18 or over), *skirt* and *sweet young thing*. In addition, avoid *lady; woman* is preferred.

- Avoid words that refer to appearance: *buxom, foxy, gorgeous, striking* and other adjectives. Many women consider *perky* a reference to their breasts, not their personality.

- Avoid words and phrases that include stereotypical references to women such as *housewife* (use *homemaker*) and *old wives' tale* (use *superstition*).

- Avoid *coed;* it dates from a time when women entering college were not thought to be serious.

- Avoid *catfight* in references to disputes among women. The word implies that women are petty, trivial or animal-like.[8]

Bias Based on Race, Ethnicity and Nationality

Elizabeth Wissner-Gross, author of "Unbiased: Editing in a Diverse Society," offers several principles for eliminating racial bias from copy. At the top of her list are these two:

1. Avoid categorizing people by race.

2. Only mention a person's race if you have determined that race is necessary to the story.[9]

The same guidelines should also apply to ethnicity and nationality. When are these attributes vital to include? Consider these examples:

- A news article reveals that members of minority groups are being told that apartments are taken when the apartments are still available for rent to whites.

- A feature article focuses on a new line of cosmetics for black women.

- A news release announces a conference on problems faced by Asian American women in the U.S. work force.

When references to race are gratuitous, writers and editors must weed them out, as in this sentence from a news article:

The victim could describe the robber only as black.

That description is hardly enough to help a reader spot the robbery suspect; for that, the reader would need many more details on the person's appearance. So the reference to the suspect's race is gratuitous and does little more than reinforce prejudices.

Editors also need to be sensitive to negative stereotyping, both in words and in graphics. Such stereotyping often occurs when foreigners are perceived as any sort of enemy. For instance, during the Persian Gulf War in the early 1990s, Saddam Hussein often was portrayed on news magazine covers with the features of Adolf Hitler.

When Chinese officials initially refused to release the crew of a U.S. Navy spy plane that landed in Chinese territory in April 2001, another wave of stereotyping swept through the media. From columnist David Broder's comment that "The Chinese are not nice people" to a racist cartoon by Pulitzer Prize-winning editorial cartoonist Pat Oliphant, the media were filled with offensive remarks and images.

It's not hard to imagine such depictions fueling resentment of and hatred for Americans of Arab and Asian descent. Any media outlet that wants to maintain credibility with the public should avoid resorting to images that demean a large part of the world's population.

Even members of groups that hardly can be seen as threatening do not always escape media stereotyping. An article on a U.S. congressman described him this way:

True to his Norwegian heritage, he is a man of few words and ranks among the least quotable members of Congress.

That sentence not only stereotypes an entire nationality, but it insults its members. Native Americans, Latinos, Italians and countless other groups have been targets of similar bias in the media.

An additional form of bias is **ethnocentrism,** the belief that our culture and habits are correct, and everyone else's are wrong. For example, an article on how an outsider politician must adjust to Washington tried to make the point with this analogy:

Think of it this way: Your plane has crash-landed in the middle of Brazil and you find yourself surrounded by a curious and possibly hostile tribe. Instead of giving them beads and eating the monkey tongues they offer you, you decide you don't need their help. Fine, but don't be surprised if you end up with poison darts in your backside.[10]

A reader — an anthropologist who is a native of Brazil — responded in a letter:

More likely, you would be offered rice with pequi, a warm cup of coffee and delicious fruits. But if you decided not to accept the hypothetical "monkey tongues," surely you wouldn't end up with poison darts in your backside.

Let's imagine a more real scenario. Your plane crashes somewhere in Washington. You find yourself surrounded by curious and possible hostile neighborhood members. Instead of giving them your business card and taking the crack they offer you, you decide you don't need their help. Fine, but don't be surprised if you end up with bullets and stabbings in your backside.

Ethnocentrism can pop up anywhere. A magazine cover headline for an article on Caribbean food, for instance, read, "It's Hot, It's Weird, It's Here." An editor should have wondered whether it was fair to call something "weird" just because it is unfamiliar.

Words to Watch for:

- Avoid any derogatory references to race or ethnicity: *brave* (as a noun), *colored, dragon lady, gook, Indian, Jap, nigger, Chinaman, Paki, gook, spic, kike, Oriental* (all right when applied to objects, such as Oriental rugs), *redskin, wetback* and the like.

- Also watch words like *ghetto, gyp* (from gypsy) and *Indian giver,* which carry negative connotations.

- When race or ethnicity is essential in a description of a person or group of people, it's always best to make sure any references are acceptable to and appropriate for those being labeled. For example, *Native American* is preferred by some, while others prefer to be referred to by their particular tribe's name. And *Latino* refers to a person of Latin-American ancestry but not Spanish or other heritage.

- Also avoid derogatory terms applied to whites, such as *cracker, gringo* and *paleface.*

- Avoid metaphors that help perpetuate the myth of Native Americans as savages (e.g., *circle the wagons, on the warpath*). Also watch for similar usages in sports headlines (e.g., *Braves get a new chief*).[11]

- Avoid using *alien, illegal* and *illegal alien* for Latinos and others. Such usages are dehumanizing.[12]

Religious Stereotypes

Certain religious groups often have been stereotyped by mass media. Jewish people, for example, have long complained of offensive depictions. One classic method of defaming Jewish people, Arnold Forster and Benjamin R. Epstein have written, "is to generalize about all Jews from the alleged specific characteristics or acts of some Jews that may or may not have anything to do with their Jewishness."[13]

Fundamentalist Christians have also found themselves the victims of hostile treatment. In one example, a series of editors at The Washington Post let slip into print a passage that described followers of television evangelists as "largely poor, uneducated and easy to command" — although, the editors later admitted, there was no factual basis for that statement. Any statement that attempts to summarize the characteristics of an entire religious group deserves serious scrutiny.

Words to Watch for:

- *Jewish person* is generally preferable to *Jew.* Avoid terms such as *Jew down* (use bargaining).

- Avoid *Bible-thumper, Holy Rollers.* Use the term preferred by the person being referred to: *evangelical, fundamentalist* or *born-again Christian,* for example.

- Be alert for references to religious extremists. As Elizabeth Wissner-Gross notes, "The implied message is that religion is good to a certain point, but if one becomes too religious or extremely committed to one's own beliefs, terrorism is the automatic outcome."[14]

Stereotypes of Lesbians and Gay Men

As lesbians and gay men have pressed for equal rights and recognition, they have found themselves appearing more regularly in the media. Unfortunately, as with other groups, the images that appear often are not flattering. Gay men routinely are stereotyped by accounts and pictures of flamboyant and outrageous behavior, or as victims of the AIDS virus. Lesbians still suffer from media invisibility.

Words to Watch for:

- Avoid *dyke, faggot, fairy, fruit, limp-wristed* and *queer.* Use *person with AIDS* rather than *AIDS victim.* With research supporting the idea that sexuality is genetically determined rather than chosen, *sexual orientation* is preferred to *sexual preference.*

Ageism

It is not hard to find stereotypes of old people. Portrayals of those over 60 or 70 years old as frail and feeble-minded still seem widespread in our culture, despite the fact that today many people are leading active and productive lives into their

> Any statement that attempts to summarize the characteristics of an entire religious group deserves serious scrutiny.

80s and 90s. As one report noted: "America's image of the aged has changed for the worst during recent decades. ... old people are viewed as weak, depressed, querulous, and forgetful — even incapable or foolish. ... it is clear that the media today help reinforce and perpetuate myths and stereotypes about aging and the aged."[15]

Insensitivity toward older people often shows up as backhanded compliments. For instance, a sentence that describes a 72-year-old as "still spry and alert" perpetuates the stereotype that most older people *are not* spry or alert.

Words to Watch for:

- Avoid *codger, coot, dirty old man, geezer, granny, senile* and *senior citizen.* If it is relevant, the preferred terms are *the aged, older people, the retired.*

Class Bias

The salaries of many top media workers have increased over the years, placing many writers and editors firmly in the upper middle class or the upper class — and sometimes out of touch with most of the population. For example, a columnist writing about Bill Clinton's election as president joked about how pathetic it was that before becoming president, Clinton was making $35,000 a year as governor of Arkansas. "That's embarrassing, isn't it?" the columnist wrote. For the columnist, who makes several times that amount, apparently it is. But in a country in which the average salary was far less than that amount, it was the columnist's snobbery that was embarrassing.

Words to Watch for:

- Catching this type of bias is generally more than a matter of watching for a certain word. Editors need to watch for demeaning references to blue-collar workers, low- and medium-income workers, and others. Phrases like *white trash* and *trailer trash* are particularly offensive.

Physical Disabilities

People with physical disabilities often are portrayed stereotypically in the media, too. Depictions of those with physical disabilities typically include one of two problems:

1. Word choice often focuses more on the disability than the person, more on what the person cannot do than on what the person can. So editors need to watch for words such as *crippled* (*disabled* is preferred) and *confined to a wheelchair* (*uses a wheelchair* is better).

2. People with physical disabilities often appear as one of two extremes: either as a super-person who despite a disability has managed to reach the heights of success, or as a down-and-out person who has lost everything. Neither of these stereotypes does justice to most people who have disabilities.

Insensitivity toward older people often shows up as backhanded compliments.

Words to Watch for:

- Avoid *crippled, handicapped* (as an adjective) and *disabled* (as a noun); instead use *disabled* (as an adjective) or *person/people with disabilities.* Instead of *dumb* or *mute,* use *speech impaired.* Avoid *invalid.*

- *Down syndrome* is the preferred phrase for that condition.

Mental Illness

One of the last areas of enlightenment for those in the media has been the portrayal of the mentally ill. Terms related to mental illness are used offhandedly and incorrectly throughout the media, often in a light manner. An advertisement to promote tourism in Pennsylvania, for instance, touted the multifaceted commonwealth as a great place for "multiple personalities." For a person with a mental illness, such insensitivity can be harder to live with than the illness itself.

An additional area of concern is the portrayal of the mentally ill as violent. For example, articles on horrendous crimes often cite a suspect's previous treatment for mental illness. In reality, the mentally ill are no more violent than the general public; most people with mental illness are, in fact, introverted.[16]

Quotas for Quotes

When Mark Willes was named publisher of the Los Angeles Times in 1997, he decided that the paper needed to do more to reflect the diversity of its community.

"When our readers read the paper, they don't see themselves in the paper," Willes said "People want to feel like the paper's theirs. They can't do that if it's a fundamentally white-male newspaper."

To accomplish that, Willes set specific goals for increasing the number of women and minorities quoted in stories. Editors' pay was based partly on how well their reporters met those goals.

Not everyone applauded the move. David Mazzarella, editor of USA Today, told The Wall Street Journal that having a specific tally "is difficult if not dangerous because it just subverts news value." And the plan raised many questions. Among them:

Which stories count toward the minority criteria? Would a story on getting out the black vote count, since it would unavoidably quote black people? If an article or photo is negative — say a picture of a Latino murderer — would that count? How does a reporter politely ask sources on the phone if they are minorities? Will there be goals for each minority group or just minorities as a whole?[17]

Nevertheless, Willes' plan highlighted an ongoing problem in journalism, one that every editor needs to be aware of.

Words to Watch for:

• Avoid *basket case, crazy, nuts, insane* and *vegetable*. Use of *psychotic* and *schizophrenic* should be confined to persons clinically diagnosed with those conditions.

Bias Against White Men

White men can be stereotyped as easily as any other group. In fact, as sensitivity toward traditionally disenfranchised groups has increased, the stereotyping and bashing of white men has seemed to rise. One example was the stereotyping of members of the Men's Movement as people who were primarily concerned with gathering in the woods to bang on drums. Just as with any other group, generalizations should be avoided and labels should be scrutinized.

Words to Watch for:

• Avoid *hillbilly, redneck* and *white trash. WASP* is considered stereotypical and is possibly offensive.

Taste

The matter of taste is also largely an issue of sensitivity. Editors must balance the amount of information and how it is presented against reader sensitivities. The question of taste usually arises in matters concerning sex or violence, although it is not limited to those matters. Some general rules:

Graphic Depictions — in Either Words or Pictures — Should Be Used Only When a Compelling Reason Exists for Using Them.   Consider the following passage from an article handed in by a newspaper reporter:

The boy accused his foster mother of performing fellatio on him, masturbating him, as well as forcing herself on top of him several times and placing his penis in her vagina numerous times throughout his stay with her, court documents show.

And now consider this passage:

The boy accused his foster mother of engaging in sexual relations with him numerous times throughout his stay with her, court documents show.

It would be hard to argue that the second paragraph lacks substantial information. It merely lacks sensationalism — and the ability to upset many readers.

Photos can pose particularly tough decisions. Editors need to consider carefully whether graphic depictions are necessary to make their points, and sometimes those decisions are close calls. For instance, one classic photo showed a grieving family standing over a body bag. Inside the bag was a young boy who had drowned after swimming in an unsafe area. Some editors defended the use of the

The question of taste usually arises in matters concerning sex or violence, although it is not limited to those matters.

picture, saying that it would make people pay attention to the dangers of swimming in such areas. Others said the photo was sensationalistic and added nothing to the accompanying article.

A more recent example of a photograph that split editors was the shot of a dead U.S. soldier being dragged through the streets of Mogadishu. Former Washington Post Ombudsman Joann Byrd reported that the use of that photo — as well as television footage of the incident — was highly debated throughout the media. She wrote:

> There were good reasons not to run it. If they could recognize the body, it would add to the pain of the slain pilot's family. It could exacerbate the fears of others whose spouses, siblings and children are in Somalia. Publishing the picture might further objectify the soldier's body.
>
> The picture's force made it a political propaganda tool, and printing it could look like trying to sway public opinion. Readers might turn against the Somali people. There was no picture of any of the 200 Somalis reportedly killed in the same fighting. The photo might be read as racist.
>
> Weighing against all that was, predictably, the media's obligation to keep people informed. ... The picture was painful to see but filled with information — information that would be hard to see with words that are not interpretations. Readers and viewers who studied it could come to very different opinions.[18]

Confronted with a graphic photograph, some editors will compromise by placing the photo inside the newspaper and running a warning on the front page, thereby giving readers the option of looking at the photo.

Follow the Golden Rule.   An article quoted comedian Denis Leary as saying: "I feel bad for poor Lou Gehrig. He died from Lou Gehrig's disease. You'd think he would have seen it coming." An editor should have asked, "If I had Lou Gehrig's disease, would I find this comment funny?"

Think About People Eating Breakfast.   When I worked as a newspaper editor, one of our guiding rules was that we never should run a picture that would turn the stomach of someone reading the paper while eating breakfast. As the news media publish ever-more-graphic photographs of dead bodies, it seems that editors might do well to keep this rule in mind.

Obscenities, Vulgar Language and Racial Slurs Present Special Concerns.   While journalists should not use such language in their writing, sometimes the use of off-color or insensitive remarks by a source is newsworthy, particularly if that source is a government official or a public figure. That was the case during the 2000 presidential election, when George W. Bush called a New York Times reporter "a major league asshole" — a remark that was accidentally picked up by microphones. Everyone agreed the event was newsworthy, but media outlets differed widely in how they reported the word itself. Some used the full word, some used dashes, some substituted "expletive" — and one reported that Bush had called the reporter a "rectal aperture."[19] The use of such language presents editors with two concerns:

First, *is it accurate?* Before attributing offensive remarks to a person, you need to be certain that the person made those remarks. If the person is being misquoted, you run the risk not only of unfairly harming the person's reputation but also of unnecessarily offending readers (and possibly losing a libel suit). Not surprisingly, people sometimes deny making offensive remarks. One way to get them to own up was suggested in Quill magazine by Richard P. Cunningham, former reader's representative for the Minneapolis Tribune. Cunningham suggested that rather than calling the source to ask if he or she made the statement, "What about calling him or her to say we consider it newsworthy that someone in his position should say what he or she has said and asking for his or her comments as part of the story?" Doing that, Cunningham suggests, will reduce the chances of the source trying to "wriggle off the hook."[20]

Second, *is it necessary?* While foul language is no stranger to routine conversation, many people object to seeing it in print. In most cases, removing spoken obscenities will not affect a speaker's meaning. The best rule of thumb is this: If the use of vulgar language is essential to conveying information or attitudes, use it. Otherwise, delete it. When an athlete uses obscenities to discuss how he's going to beat an opponent, the obscenities add nothing. If a business owner uses obscenities to refer to people suing his company because its products had injured them, the obscenities provide a reader with insight. Even then, however, his other words and actions might get the point across without the obscenities.

Editors need to watch for foul language and rude gestures in photographs as well as in words. A newspaper editor in Texas was fired for running a photograph of the band the Deftones in which singer Chino Moreno wore a sweatshirt with the logo of Los Angeles clothing company "fuct." Features Editor Nora Garza said she didn't notice the logo in choosing the photograph. "I don't use that language, and that's why I never interpreted it as an obscene word," she said.[21]

The Medium Determines Acceptability.   Most newspapers think of themselves as "family" publications, and indeed many include sections aimed toward children. Therefore, readers are likely to have a low tolerance for profanity and sexual details. Online publishers do not feel the same restrictions. For example, both Salon.com and Slate.com used George W. Bush's "major league" comment in full. Scott Rosenberg, vice president of site development and managing editor for Salon.com, defended that choice by noting that his publication is "aimed at adult readers." He continued:

> Our current policy is that where possible we try to avoid "gratuitous" use of profanity, and as a rule we try to avoid using it on our homepage. But if it's relevant to a story we publish it.[22]

What's Funny to One Person Is Often Offensive to Another.   Writers and editors are often tempted to use sexual puns and innuendoes. While they might find their handiwork amusing, readers might find it disgusting. For example, ad copy for a bicycle pump included this line: "Anything else just blows." Sure it's catchy — but is it worth using if it turns off potential customers?

While foul language is no stranger to routine conversation, many people object to seeing it in print.

Notes

1. Aly Colón, "Making Connections Within Diverse Communities," Quill, July 2000, p. 70.

2. "Guide to Research on Race and the News" (Columbia, Mo.: Missouri School of Journalism, 2000), p. 9.

3. Joann Byrd, "Blind Spots," The Washington Post, 7 February 1993, sec. C, p. 6.

4. "Guide to Research," p. 10.

5. Clint C. Wilson II and Felix Gutierrez, "Minorities and Media: Diversity and the End of Mass Communication" (Beverly Hills: Sage, 1985), p. 32.

6. Robin Givhan, "The Eyelashes Have It," The Washington Post, 18 November 2000, sec. C, pp. 1, 7.

7. Michael Getler, "Mascara Smear," The Washington Post, 22 November 2000, sec. A, p. 26.

8. Elizabeth Wissner-Gross, "Unibiased Editing in a Diverse Society" (Ames, Iowa: Iowa State University Press, 2000), p. 101.

9. Wissner-Gross, "Unbiased Editing," p. 23.

10. Sally Quinn, "Making Capital Gains," The Washington Post, 15 November 1992, sec. C, p. 1.

11. "News Watch" (San Francisco: Center for Integration and Improvement of Journalism, 1995), p. 12.

12. "News Watch," p. 44.

13. Arnold Forster and Benjamin R. Epstein, "The New Anti-Semitism" (New York: McGraw-Hill, 1974), p. 106.

14. Wissner-Gross, "Unbiased Editing," p. 152.

15. American Jewish Committee, "Conference on Images of Old Age in American Media," a report of a conference in cooperation with the Columbia University Graduate School of Journalism and the ACLU (New York: The American Jewish Committee, 1978), p. 3.

16. James Willwerth, "It Hurts Like Crazy," Time, 15 February 1993, p. 53.

17. Lisa Bannon, "The Publisher Plans New-Type Faces for the L.A. Times," The Wall Street Journal, 15 May 1998, sec. A, p. 1.

18. Joann Byrd, "Picture from Somalia," The Washington Post, 17 October 1993, sec. C, p. 7.

19. Lori Robertson, "Language Barriers," American Journalism Review, November 2000, pp. 38–41.

20. Richard P. Cunningham, "A Suggestion for Handling Offensive Quotes," Quill, June 1990, p. 4.

21. Teri vanHorn, "Newspaper Editor Fired Over Deftones Photo," Sonicnet.com, 1 November 2000, *www.sonicnet.com*.

22. Robertson, "Language Barriers," p. 41.

Exercise

Edit the following article, removing any offensive material that cannot be defended.

Howard Hunter isn't the kind of guy most woman would bring home to meet the family. In fact, he isn't the kind of of guy that many women would want to bring home at all — or even talk to.

The shock comedien doesn't mince words when it comes to women, or anyone else.

"Women are good for one thing," Hunter says, "and that's carrying men's babys. Men are smarter, stronger and more rational."

Nevertheless, Hunter's shows draw more than a few women?and lots of men, of course. He's been packing clubs across the nation in a 3-month tour of insults and invectives. He'll be spewing his special brand of venom at the local Comedy Center this Friday and Saturday.

"A lot of people think that I'm just acting," Hunter said. "Some other comedians like me, they say, 'Oh, that's not really what I think — this is just an act.' Well, it's no act with me. I say exactly what I think. And I think we've got a lot of problems in this country caused by women who think they're as good or useful as men. Hey ladies: You're not and you never will be."

Of course, Hunter doesn't play favorites: He blasts any group that he doesn't agree with. Take homosexals, for instance.

"Yeah," Hunter says, "take them and lock them up in solitry confinement. These people aren't natural. The bible says that a men and a woman make a family — not two of a kind. All they're doing is spreading disease and lowering morales in this country. If it was up to me, I'd take them all out and shoot them. Well, I might let some of the dikes put on a little show for me before I shot them. These people shouldn't get equal rights — they should get last rights."

There isn't a minority group that escapes Hunter's attacks. But, suprisingly, his performances only rarely draw protestors. Mary Lettis of the local chapter of the National Organization for Women says that most of Hunter's targets feel the best thing to do is to ignore him.

"It's hard to turn away from the ugly face of misogyny and racism," Lettis says. "But we feel that anything we do will just feul the fire — Just add to his media hype. So we're content to let him run his course. People won't think his shtick is funny for long."

Hunter's reply? "She can bite my shtick. I'm going to be perfroming long after her and her queer friends are dead of A.I.D.S."

EDITING FOR THE WEB

Building Community

One of the things that the Web does well is to cater to diverse audiences. Well-known sites provide news, entertainment and commentary targeted to readers based on race, ethnicity and gender. As a Washington Post article reported:

> The sites often feature news about minorities that have been underplayed by the mainstream media. Many include historical information about immigration patterns and feature chat rooms where users can make friends with people of similar backgrounds.[1]

Among the best known:

- StarMedia (*www.br.starmedia.com*) serves Spanish and Portuguese speakers worldwide with news and services;

- AsianAvenue.com features news and chat about Asians in the United States and Asia and serves as a hotbed of Asian American activism;

- BlackPlanet.com hosts chat rooms in which users discuss everything from love to politics;

- PlanetOut (*www.planetout.com/pno*) offers news, politics and entertainment information to the gay and lesbian community; and

- iVillage.com provides a portal to a vast range of material of interest to women.

In addition, the Web offers two powerful tools for connecting writers and editors of traditional publications with their audiences: **direct communication** and **community building.**

Direct Communication

Most online publications offer readers direct access to writers and editors via e-mail. That connection drastically changes the traditional model of writing-editing-delivery, allowing readers to interact with the publication. As columnist Jon Katz wrote of his work for the online site HotWired:

> Response to columns is diverse, fast and furious. The line between friend and foe is fuzzy, with critics becoming close friends and admirers turning ugly at the drop of a column. Still, we are a community of sorts, bound by the experience of communicating with one another in this way.[2]

Any attempt at interactivity spells more work for editors and writers. As Web scholar Mindy McAdams notes in a column for the online American Journalism Review, good two-way communication requires allowing staff members time to do the job.

PlanetOut provides a unique perspective to gay and lesbian readers.

"Don't assume that a busy staff will be able to squeeze in a few minutes for e-mail," she writes. "You [the management] need to emphasize its importance and promote its use."[3]

Such direct communication breaks down barriers between readers and editorial staffers. While it might not lead to unanimous agreement, it at least gives all parties the sense that they are being heard.

For example, in late 2000, Dean Smith, the arts editor of the Charlotte Observer, found himself in the midst of an unexpected controversy. The controversy revolved around a proposed photo illustration for the cover of the paper's Sunday Arts section. The photo, used with an article about a new cable TV show, "Queer as Folk," showed two young men leaning toward each other about to kiss.

Just as the presses were about to roll, some of the press workers objected to the photo and asked the newsroom to reconsider using it. After discussion, Managing Editor Frank Barrows decided to replace it, noting that "I thought it was too erotically charged for a general-readership newspaper."[4] Dean Smith recounts what happened next:

> Once word of the incident spread outside Charlotte, it was vetted from every perspective, on journalism Web sites like poynter.org and gay-themed ones like gay.com. ... The hate e-mail rolled in from Charlotte to Berkeley, Calif. ... I was called, alternately, a traitor to gay people or an agent of the homosexual agenda.[5]

While there was obviously no unanimity on whether the photo should have been run, the feedback from readers — and other Web sites — allowed Smith and his colleagues to put the matter in perspective. As Smith summarizes the issue:

Too much for some. Not enough for others. What we printed, finally, stands in between. Because that's still where gay people stand here. Wish it or not, things are as they are.[6]

Building Community

The second powerful tool that the Web offers for bridging the gap between writers and editors and their audiences is the creation of online communities. One news site that has excelled in that is MaineToday.com, a division of Blethen Maine Newspapers in Portland, Maine.

MaineToday.com President Joe Michaud explained the concept of community publishing as "providing powerful online publishing tools to official community groups so they can easily post information within their designated area of our branded sites." But he noted that MaineToday.com goes beyond that to "bionic content":

> The concept represents an overall drive to draw in the experience and expertise that's in our communities. This effort includes community publishing but also some individual outreach to community contributors and finding ways to connect relevant information from the community with the journalism from our newsrooms. Our community organizer, Jessica Tomlinson, says: "Bionic content is when people and machines join forces to create powerful information."

The goal, Michaud explains, is for "people to interact with the news instead of react to it."[7] As of 2001, MaineToday.com had more than 1,400 groups in the communities section of MaineToday.com, as well as a wide variety of nonjournalistic content from the community scattered throughout other sections of the site. Michaud saw that effort as a hint of what lies ahead for online news sites. "I believe there's a great future in bringing community experience, information and voices to our products," he predicted.[8]

In other cases, community can be established on a temporary basis. In conjunction with its widely praised six-week series "How Race Is Lived in America," The New York Times set up discussion areas on its Web site. Forums were tied to specific stories, and each began with specific questions for visitors to ponder. In addition, the site included a questionnaire that asked readers about personal experiences with racism. Discussions continued long after the series ended. Sig Gissler, a Columbia University professor who runs workshops on journalism, race and ethnicity, praised the forums as a good starting point. "The Internet can facilitate some candor," he told Columbia Journalism Review. "It opens up a valuable vein of conversation and new chambers of possibility."[9]

New Reason for Concern

While the Web in some ways helps to shrink the gulf between writers and editors and their audiences, it also poses new challenges. Chief among them is the challenge of making sure that all audience members can access all content.

Internet Resources for Newsroom Diversity

- The Caldwell Journals, by Earl Caldwell, *www.maynardije.org*
- National Association of Black Journalists, *www.nabj.org*
- National Association of Hispanic Journalists, *www.nahj.org*
- Asian American Journalists Association, *www.aaja.org*
- Native American Journalists Association, *www.naja.com*
- The Freedom Forum, *www.freedomforum.org*

(*Resources provided by Wanda Lloyd, The Greenville News*)

The U.S. Census Bureau reports that more than 54 million Americans have a disability. In many cases, those disabilities do not interfere with use of the Internet. But people with visual, hearing, speech and motor disabilities often face challenges in accessing online information.

That becomes even more important when you realize that disabled Web surfers spend twice as much time online as their able-bodied counterparts — 20 hours a week, not counting sending and receiving e-mail — and in many cases they rely much more heavily on the Internet for research and shopping.[10]

Add to that the aging population — with its decreasing visual, hearing and motor skills — and you have a compelling argument to pay careful attention to providing universally accessible Web content.

Accessibility to Web content is already codified in the law. The federal government issued rules on Dec. 21, 2000, that mandate virtually all government Web sites be fully accessible to people with disabilities. Randall Adams, an attorney who specializes in Internet law, warns that "the time is fast approaching when businesses will have to include accessibility into their Web site design, or face the threat of legal action. The federal guidelines ... will reinforce the fact that no one is exempt from fully conforming to the Americans with Disabilities Act."[11]

The threat of legal action has already materialized. Lawsuits have been filed against several public agencies and America Online for failure to provide information in an accessible manner. Michael Paciello, one of the leading experts on the topic, adds, "I believe private publishers have plenty to be concerned with."[12]

Creating accessible Web content is not hard, but it does require a good bit of knowledge — and additional time. The best place to start your education in creating accessible content is the World Wide Web Consortium's Web Content Accessibility Guidelines (*www.w3.org/TR/WAI-WEBCONTENT*). Offline, Michael Paciello's "Web Accessibility for People with Disabilities" (Lawrence, Kansas: CMP Books, 2000) is must reading for anyone involved in Web publishing at the dawn of the 21st century.

Notes

1. Ariana Eunjung Cha, "Ethnic Sites Grow in Popularity," The Washington Post, 28 December 2000, sec. E, p. 6.
2. Jon Katz, "Mixed Media," Netizen, 14 November 1996.

3. Mindy McAdams, "Lesson 1: Make Sure Your Electronic Newspaper Is Plugged In," AJR Newslink, *www.newslink.org/mmcol.html*.

4. Dean Smith, "Flap Over 'Gay Kiss' Proves Instructive," The Charlotte Observer, 19 December 2000, *www.charlotte.com*.

5. Smith, "Flap."

6. Smith, "Flap."

7. Mark DeCotis, "The Force Behind Bionic Content," Poynter.org, 19 December 2000, *www.poynter.org/centerpiece/121900.htm*.

8. DeCotis, "The Force."

9. Lauren Janis, "On Race, Online: The Digital Afterlife of a Powerful Series," Columbia Journalism Review, March/April 2000, p. 37.

10. Denise Dubie, "Going Global," Publish, August 2000, p. 66.

11. Michelle Delio, "Fed Opens Web to Disabled," WiredNews, 21 December 2000, *www.wirenednews.com/news/print/0,1294,40790,00.html*.

12. Michael G. Paciello, "Re: Information Request," 26 October 2000, personal e-mail.

Editor's Corner

The Color of Media Diversity: Not Just Black and White

Wanda Lloyd, executive director, The Freedom Forum Institute for Newsroom Diversity at Vanderbilt University

When I got my first newspaper job in 1970, what we now know as diversity hardly existed. Looking across the newsrooms of America, the view was mostly white and male. The buzzword then was "integration," and if there was concern about staff makeup, the trend was to encourage hiring more women as reporters and copy editors. At the time, few women were moving up the ranks as directing editors.

This era was a few years after the civil rights movement of the late 1960s, after the death of Dr. Martin Luther King Jr. and the urban riots that followed, and the 1969 Kerner Commission report that warned: America is "moving toward two societies, one black, one white — separate and unequal."

During the riots, newspapers found themselves in the uncomfortable position of trying to cover urban unrest with white reporters who were scared, intimidated and unprepared for the hostile media. That's when the newsroom integration movement really began.

In the early 1970s newsrooms began to hire more and more black reporters, copy editors and photographers. It was a trickle at best. But the key word here is "black." That's how diversity was defined in that era — in black and white.

In Louisville, Mervin Aubespin, an artist in the advertising department at the Courier Journal, cried "send me" when he learned that his colleagues in the newsroom were struggling to accurately (and safely) cover local racial unrest.

Aubespin's cry was echoed across newsrooms and in cities across the nation. African Americans stepped up to challenge the newspaper industry to let them help increase the accuracy and tone of coverage that, until that time, had largely been the professional role of the black press.

The major stumbling block in those days — and to some extent today — was to find and train enough people of color, to build the ranks of qualified journalists who would make a difference.

Now comes diversity of the 21st century. America and newsrooms are changing. We no longer define needs for staffing in black and white. As gatherers and disseminators of news we must reflect the populations of the news consumers we serve.

Diversity today goes beyond black and white, beyond race and color — even beyond gender. In the year 2000, just under 12 percent of newsroom professionals were people of color (far below the goal of parity with the U.S. population). We are black or African American, Hispanic or Latino, Asian American, Native American and Caucasian. We are women and men.

But America is more and so are we. We define diversity in news pages and broadcasts in terms of who we hope will buy and use our products. Journalism is, after all, a business.

Diversity differences are economic, religious, geographic, educational, socio-economic. We define ourselves in terms of what kinds of things we do in our leisure time, whether we are married or single, whether we are parents, empty nesters or without children, whether we are straight or gay, whether we have lots of time on our hands or we have no time for leisure activities.

Imagine, if you will, going to another country and trying to read the newspapers or watch television in a language you don't understand. That's what many people will face in the United States (even without the language barrier) if we don't continue to address the issue of diversity. We must stretch our range of coverage to the furthest degrees, inclusive of every segment of society.

We must merge sources and ideas in this melting-pot media, a concept called mainstreaming — the inclusion of people of color in stories not necessarily about their race or ethnicity. For example, a story about the collapse of a local bank would include reactions not just from, say, white male banking officials, but banking experts who also happen to be African American or Hispanic. Likewise, the same diversity concept should be used when interviewing bank customers. After all, people of all colors and races use bank services. Why shouldn't they see themselves in stories about the things that drive their lives? After years of ignoring this concept, why would they want to use a publication that continues to segregate by omission? What would that do to the business of journalism?

If all business stories quote or profile only balding white guys in boring suits, where will we get our women readers, our young readers, our African American and Hispanic readers?

If all crime stories are only about young black men from single-parent homes, where will white America get its positive images of African Americans?

If all book reviews are of books by and of interest to white Americans, why would blacks and other people of color care to check the weekly best-seller list? When we don't see ourselves in a segment of society, we often assume that segment doesn't speak to our needs, and we move on.

Here are some of the diversity challenges for the future:

- In order to meet the goal of parity in newsrooms, the industry must increase the number of young people in the pipeline. That means more journalism programs in middle schools and high schools.

- Retention is a key factor in diversity. Editors and human resources leaders must make newsrooms comfortable working environments for the increasing cross-cultural work force.

- More people of color must be identified and trained for newsroom leadership roles.

Newsroom staffs must be prepared to cover the total community. Our business is inclusion, not exclusion. That should be the business of all news media.

Using Quotes

Quotations are an essential element of good writing. At their best, quotes enliven writing that otherwise would just sit on the page; they give a sense of a source's personality; and they add important or interesting information.

Not every quote is worth using, however, and not every good quote is used correctly. Following are guidelines for handling quotes.

First, Kill All the Useless Ones.   An editor was obviously on autopilot when this lead got into print:

A jet from the U.S. Navy's "Blue Angels" precision flying team crashed in a wooded area in southern Georgia Thursday, killing both pilots on board, a Navy spokesman said.

"One of our Blue Angels jets went down," U.S. Navy Cmdr. Jack Papp said. "It landed in a wooded area. Both pilots were killed."

Obviously, the quote adds nothing to the opening paragraph — it merely repeats it, almost word for word. Examine every quote carefully. When you find one that merely echoes the accompanying copy, delete it. Even when a quote is not an exact repeat, kill it if it says nothing. Quotes like "That's interesting" are not interesting.

Don't Change Words in Direct Quotations.   Because editors are never present when speakers are talking, editors never should change quotes without checking with the writers. There are only two exceptions:

Exception No. 1: Correcting minor grammatical errors. Most publications let editors fix grammatical mistakes in quotes. Everyone makes them in speaking, but printing a quote with such mistakes makes the speaker look like a fool — and in many cases, it's impossible to determine whether the error was the speaker's or the writer's.

Some writers and editors do not extend this policy to major political figures — a practice that became a subject of reflection after George W. Bush was elected president. During his campaign, Bush regularly mangled sentences (e.g., "Will the highways of the Internet become more few?"). Few journalists were willing to help Bush with his grammar.

"I can't imagine quoting the president-elect, or indeed the president, in any fashion other than directly, word-for-word, wart-for-wart, wisdom or not," Miami Herald political writer Mark Silva told The Baltimore Sun. Richmond Times-Dispatch Managing Editor Louise Seals agreed. "In a day when folks see so much live, especially with someone as visible as the president, I would be very hesitant to clean up quotes," she said.[1]

Exception No. 2: Revising phonetic spellings (*gotta* and *gonna,* for instance) and deleting fillers such as *uh, like* and *you know:*

Original: *"Uh, I, I, my message is for the voters of the country. Uh, I ask for their support. I'm not taking a single vote for, for granted."*

Revised: *"My message is for the voters of the country. I ask for their support. I'm not taking a single vote for granted."*

If you **must** insert or change material into a quote to make it make sense, enclose it in parentheses to indicate it wasn't the speaker's words:

"You may be kind to clean up (a politician's) quotes, but you're not being fair, (because) then the reader is not going to realize what a boob he is," Carr says.

Unquote Messy Quotes.   Sometimes a writer has done so much work to construct a quote that it ends up almost unreadable, full of ellipses and parentheses. In those cases, it's better to simply paraphrase the quote:

Direct quote: *Martin said he "intend(s) to (resign) ... after the (current) season (ends)."*

Paraphrase: *Martin said he intends to resign after the current season ends.*

Watch Out for Impossible Quotes.   While it is fine for writers to quote partial sentences, editors must make sure that partial quotes could have been spoken. The most common problem is the use of the incorrect personal pronoun:

She said the project "has given her great satisfaction."

While assuming that *her* should be changed to *me* seems reasonable, remember that good editors never change quotes without checking with the writers.

Look Carefully at Where Attribution Is Placed.   For most short quotes, attribution is best placed after the quote:

"I never thought the pain would end," she said.

With longer quotes, though, a reader shouldn't have to wait until the end to find out who's speaking. Put the attribution either at the beginning of the quote or in the middle. When placing attribution in the middle of a line, look for a natural break:

Wrong: *"The thing," he said, "I enjoyed most about the job was the continuous learning."*

Correct: *"The thing I enjoyed most about the job," he said, "was the continuous learning."*

Make It Clear When the Speaker Is Changing.   Always put attribution at the beginning of a new quote that follows a quote from a different speaker. Otherwise, the reader assumes that the same person is still talking. Example:

"The cutback in work force will hurt virtually no one. Most cuts will be made through attrition," the mayor said.

"Plenty of people will suffer under this plan. The mayor's just dead wrong," Councilman Michael McBride said.

Placing the attribution at the start of the second paragraph would eliminate reader confusion. In this and all other matters, keep one point in mind: If a reader has to read a passage again, an editor should have done so first.

***Said* Is Usually the Best Word for the Job.**   While the word *said* has many relatives, most synonyms have unwelcome connotations. Consider:

"I am the father of two children," he said.
"I am the father of two children," he admitted.
"I am the father of two children," he blurted.
"I am the father of two children," he confessed.

A reader hardly notices *said,* but other words may stop the reader *and* may change the meaning of the quote or paraphrase. Look carefully at any quote that uses a word other than *said* for attribution and make sure that the word is appropriate.

   According to can be particularly troubling, because it suggests to some readers that doubt is being cast on a speaker's words. While the phrase is fine when referring to a nonhuman source (report, record, etc.), it should be avoided when quoting people.

Note

1.   Gary Dorsey, "Caught in the Muddle," The Baltimore Sun, 29 December 2000, sec. E, p. 1.

Exercise

Correct all spelling, punctuation and style errors in the following article. Also correct any comma splices, fragments, incorrect clauses, misplaced modifiers, errors in agreement and errors in handling quotes.

A professional association for psycotherapists has changed its ethics code to allow memners to attend the assisted suicide of a client. So long as they do not provide the poison or devise used as a means of death.

The new policy, adopted by the National Association of Social Workers also advices its 145,000 members to be "open to full discussion" of suicide with clients considering it.

"We didn't take a stance on whether this is morale or immorale" said Vicki Peay who chaired the panel that developed the new policy on assisted suicide.

The policy adopted last month by the groups delegate assembly, does not require a social worker to comply with a clients request to attend the suicide. It also forbids social workers from actively assiting in the suicide or providing the means to carry it out.

"Social workers should not promote any particular means to end one's life, but should be open to full discussion of the issue" the policy says.

The American Psuchiatric Association does not have a policy on whetehre it's members can attend the sudicide of a patioent. But Jeremey Lazarus, former chairman of APA's ethics Committee, said it probably would be unethical to do so.

Lazarus said that psychiatrists, who are also physicians, are "ethically bound not to participate (in a suicide) in any way. It most likely would be considered unethical by our association," he said.

CHAPTER 8

Getting the Best Out of Writers

If I were looking for a catchy title for this chapter, it might be "Everything I Know About Editing I Learned from Writing." While that's not totally true, writing and reporting experience is valuable for every editor. If nothing else, you'll learn how to avoid making the mistakes your editors made.

For example: I had been writing about bicycling and other outdoor activities for years when I got an offer to write an article for a new sports and fitness magazine. The pay was good, the magazine was backed by a leading publisher, and the editor was someone I had worked with before. In short, it seemed like a perfect opportunity.

And initially, it was. The editor liked my first piece, ran it in the premiere issue with barely any revisions, then asked me to write an article for the second issue. Again, everything went swimmingly, and I got an assignment for the third issue. That's when all hell broke loose.

Between the second and third issues, I was assigned to work with a new editor. On the surface, everything still seemed to be going smoothly. We had a clear discussion about what she wanted; when I delivered the piece, she assured me it was just what she had in mind.

But when the issue hit the newsstands, the article had been edited so drastically — no, make that *rewritten* so drastically — that if my name had not been on it, I would not have recognized it. To make matters worse, it was written in the style of a high school cheerleader who had had one too many Big Gulps: all fizzy! and peppy! and embarrassing.

I was mortified and felt totally violated. As a freelance writer, I was used to my work being modified. Not long before that incident, I had seen a carefully constructed 4,000-word article morph into a half dozen short "nuggets" — but in that case, my editor had guided me through the revision process, and I got to make most of the major changes. We *collaborated,* and when we finished, we both had something we were proud of (although I would have liked to have had my name spelled correctly in the Table of Contents).

But in the latter case, the editor had taken my article and proceeded to rewrite it as though it were hers. There was no respect for my voice or intention. And as soon as I saw it in print, I knew I would never write for the magazine again. (Did I smile when the magazine folded a few issues later? You bet.)

Collaboration Is Key

"At its worst," Providence (R.I.) Journal writer Gerald M. Carbone has commented,

> editing is a form of dictation, where either a writer dictates to a deadline-harried editor or an editor dictates to a writer, thus taking over a story. Most often, editing is a series of compromises made by both the editor and writer. At its best, editing is a collaboration, where writer and editor act on each other's suggestions, trying them out to see if they'll work, scrapping the ones that don't, incorporating those that do.[1]

More than anything else, such collaboration is the key to good writing — and the key to an editor's sanity. By regarding writers as partners, editors can help them reach their fullest potential. Along the way, writers will take more pride in their work and avoid the kinds of mistakes that drive editors crazy at deadline.

"Editing copy is a craft," says Beryl Adcock, assistant news editor, Knight Ridder Washington Bureau, "but it is also an art — the art of diplomacy and collaboration. Editors must be good at both."[2]

In order for such collaboration to work, you might have to revise your conception of what editing is. If you think of editing as what you do when copy shows up in your inbox or on your computer screen, you're in for a miserable life. Instead, you need to think of editing as an ongoing process that begins when a writer develops an idea — a process of exploration and nurturing.

This chapter offers several suggestions for making that shift in perspective and for getting a writer to produce the highest level of work. To some extent, the tips in this chapter are advanced. The editors who have the greatest responsibility and opportunity to collaborate with writers are those who work with writers from the inception of an idea (called **assigning editors** at newspapers). Typically, that's a position that requires several years of experience in reporting or editing. But even if you find yourself initially employed as a lowly copy editor, the suggestions in this chapter can help make your life easier. And when the day comes that you move up the ladder, you'll be prepared to work even more closely with writers.

It's the Story, Stupid.   When Bill Clinton ran for president in 1992, aides used the slogan "It's the economy, stupid" to keep him focused on the primary issue on voters' minds. Similarly, editors — and writers — need to keep this lesson in mind: The final product is always more important than any writer or editor. Both should share the same goal: delivering information to readers in a clear, compelling manner that makes the importance of the material obvious. Egos need to be checked at the door.

While the goal of collaborative editing is to build an atmosphere of cooperation between writers and editors, editors need to remember that their ultimate responsibility is to the readers. If editors cannot convince the writers to make needed changes, editors should not hesitate to make them themselves.

"It's amazing to me the number of times badly done, confusing, boring or overly long articles get into print simply because the writers wrote them that way," says Tony Barbieri, managing editor of The Baltimore Sun. "Too often editors are reluctant to order stories cut, restructured or redone because they wish to avoid an unpleasant confrontation or hurt a writer's feelings. So the reader loses."

Karanja Ajanaku, deputy metro editor of The Commercial Appeal in Memphis, Tenn., agrees: "As a reader advocate, I let go of my editorial mantle. I read as a reader. That's my responsibility: How is this affecting a person, checking the flow, the missing pieces."[3]

Get Personal.   Striving to remain objective is no excuse for not taking time to get to know the writers you work with. For many editors, this can be a challenge: days fill up quickly with meetings and deadlines, and it's easy to become isolated. Even if you can spare only a few minutes now and then for small talk, making the effort will pay off handsomely. First, you'll begin to recognize your writers' personalities, thereby providing insight into their working habits. If you're an assigning editor, this will help you determine who is best for various assignments (series, investigative pieces, etc.).

Second, you'll come to recognize writers' individual needs. Some writers need more coaching than others, and some need coaching more at certain stages than at others. Mimi Burkhardt, training editor for the two-year reporter program for The Providence Journal, points out that writers vary greatly:

> Some want to discuss the reporting in detail as it progresses, and talk out the whole approach before they write a word; others need to sort it out more or less on their own, with an editor as a sounding board.[4]

Finally, your writers will get used to seeing or talking with you; in turn, they won't automatically recoil in horror every time you call or show up.

It's important for you to take the initiative in getting to know your writers and letting them know you want to collaborate. If you don't, many writers will assume you're not interested in working with them.

In some newsrooms, the process of acquainting writers and editors is formalized. For example, Sue Burzynski of The Detroit News devised a training session to bridge the gap between copy editors and reporters:

> Called "Reporters Are from Mars, Copy Editors Are from Venus," the session began with a question: What one thing would you like the others in the room to know about your job? It led to a thoughtful discussion about what it's like in the other person's shoes. The upshot: Some myths were destroyed. And the reporters and copy editors talked about common concerns and looked for solutions to problems together.[5]

Be Involved From the Get-go.   Coaching should take place at all stages. To gain the most from coaching, assigning editors must be involved in the entire writing process. From idea through final draft, editors should take time to check in with writers.

"Editors need to be aware of their role before the story is written," Baltimore Sun Deputy Managing Editor Steve Proctor says. "Everyone needs to agree on what information needs to be gathered before the writing begins. There is an intimate relationship between good writing and good editing."

Leonard Witt, editor of Minnesota Monthly magazine, notes:

> You, as an editor, can make stories great — or at least you can help writers make them great. But to do so, you must be proactive from the moment a story idea is conceived. To wait until stories arrive on your desk means you will most often be talking about damage control — not greatness.[6]

The Baltimore Sun's Tony Barbieri adds: "The worst problems in editing are almost always the result of surprises. When an editor stays with a story step by step, the misunderstandings get ironed out early and the holes get filled quickly." Talking with the writer for even a minute at each stage can lead to a better final product.

Read First, Talk Second.   Take the time to read through copy completely before discussing it with the writer. A section that might seem fuzzy or incomplete may be clarified or filled in by information that comes later. If you begin talking with the writer before you finish reading the copy, you might end up making a big deal out of something that can be repaired with little effort.

"Don't type in any notes on the first read," advises Sebby Wilson Jacobsen of the Rochester Democrat and Chronicle. "Even correcting a typo can interrupt the flow and insert your voice into the story."[7]

Think Positive.   I'll never forget one editor I worked with in my early days on the copy desk. It seemed that every time he received an article to edit, he ranted and raved. He'd scream rude comments about the quality of the writing and reporting and cuss out the writer (all in a voice loud enough for everyone else to hear). Finally, he'd spring from his chair and track down the writer, inquiring how such a bonehead ever could have gotten hired by a major newspaper. Perhaps it wasn't surprising that this editor did not get good results from writers.

A far better tactic is to be gentle and positive. Editors often find it easier to point out what's wrong with a piece of writing than what's right with it. As partners in the creative process, editors need to let writers know when they are doing good work as well as when their work could be improved.

Start by looking for the best aspects of the copy. No matter how weak the writing, you can always find something on which you can compliment the writer. Madeleine Blais, a Pulitzer Prize-winning reporter and currently a journalism teacher, says she often tells students, "There's a lot to work with here" — a comment that encourages them without making them think their work is done.[8]

Make the compliment meaningful. Don't say, "You have a great lead, but the rest of this story stinks up the place." That negates your compliment, and the next time you offer a compliment, the writer will be waiting for the other shoe to drop.

You also need to beware of giving false praise; most writers have good B.S. detectors and can tell when you don't mean what you say.

Sebby Wilson Jacobsen of the Rochester Democrat and Chronicle offers this Golden Rule of Editing: "Do unto reporters as you wish editors had done unto you. (Don't belittle, scoff, ignore, humiliate or give false deadlines. Do treat them with honesty, respect and good humor.)"[9]

Critique the Copy, Not the Writer.   Anyone who's ever written, even just for a class, knows how vulnerable a writer can feel. A good editor helps a writer feel at ease by focusing on the copy, not the writer. Instead of saying, "You totally lost me in this part," try "I'm not sure I understand the point of this passage. Could you tell me what you were trying to say?"

Good editors also never play off one writer against another. While it's good practice to publicly praise excellent writing, it's bad form to tell a writer she's not as good as another writer — and just as bad to tell her she's better than someone else.

If Time Permits, Let the Writer Take the Lead.   You've surely heard the adage, "If you give a man a fish, he'll eat for a day. But if you teach him how to fish, he'll eat for a lifetime." The same approach applies to writers. Writers won't learn from changes you make to their copy — in fact, they're more likely to become frustrated and stop reading the published versions. As a result, they'll keep repeating the same mistakes.

Communicate.   For people in the communication business, editors don't always do a great job of communicating. In dealing with writers, editors need to focus on four main areas of communication:

- **Ask, don't tell:** Paula LaRocque of The Dallas Morning News suggests starting your discussion of a writer's work by asking the writer if he or she is satisfied with his or her story or approach. The answers can be revealing.[10]

- **Listen:** While your writers are talking, you need to stop talking and listen. As silly as it sounds, active listening is a skill that takes effort.

- **Be direct:** Again, Paula LaRocque offers good advice: "Launch into the critical portion of the session quickly and courageously, with candor and directness. Constantly gauge the writer's reaction to your words to avoid plunging heedlessly past a rough moment."[11]

- **Be clear:** You need to be as clear as possible as to what you expect from the writer so he or she can deliver it to the reader.

Be Available.   This is particularly important for assigning editors. The only way to keep the lines of communication open is by being available to writers throughout the writing process. "Nobody is too important," notes Ralph Williams Jr. of the Manchester, Conn., Journal Inquirer. "I'm a busy fellow, but if I'm not prepared to hear my reporters out, I'm derelict in my duties."[12]

When You Do Need to Rewrite, Honor the Writer's Voice.   Sometimes, because of time constraints or other factors, a writer will not be able to deliver what you need. In those cases, an editor has to finish the work. Unfortunately, many editors are frustrated writers and like nothing more than getting their hands on copy so they can rewrite it "the way it should be done." That's the attitude I encountered in the experience I talked about at the start of this chapter. As was the case then, you'll find that such action is a fast way to lose a writer's respect. A top-notch editor will make only the necessary changes and will pay attention to the writer's style and rhythm in making them. A good rule of thumb is that a writer should not notice changes made by an editor.

"You have to write in the style of the reporter," says Elizabeth Runefein of The San Jose Mercury News. "I find I actually can write in a lot of different styles. I can feel myself almost climb into his skin and I can feel phrases come into my head that would never be there if I were writing my own story."[13]

Choose Your Battles Carefully.   Intelligent, well-meaning people sometimes can do no more than agree to disagree. When you find yourself in this situation with a writer, you need to ask how important it is to your readers — not to your **ego** — to win the battle. Conceding a small fight every now and then will help you win the big wars.

Admit Your Mistakes.   A primary criticism of coaching is that it can lead those involved to shirk responsibility, blaming others for errors and holes in the finished product. Such buck-passing works to everyone's detriment. You and your writers must each take responsibility for what you produce. If you screw up, admit it, apologize, and get on with your life. Next time, you'll be a little smarter.

Be Flexible.   Good assigning editors rarely approach a project with fixed ideas about its deadline, length and structure. Only by working with writers can editors determine what is best for any given piece of writing. Similarly, editors need to be open to new ideas. The lack of such flexibility has driven many great writers — especially minority writers — out of the business. Angelo Henderson almost quit after his article ideas about dealing with the African-American community were regularly dismissed. Instead, he persevered and was hired by The Wall Street Journal — where he won the 1999 Pulitzer Prize for feature writing.

"You have to value my difference," Henderson told those attending a journalism conference. "You can't make me what everyone is."[14]

When You Get Work, Write.   Even if you moved into editing from a writing or reporting position, it's a good idea to write occasionally. Writers respect editors who know how to write, and the experience will help remind you of how vulnerable writers feel.

Above All, Do No Harm.   At the end of your editing, there's one final thing to keep in mind: The writer's name — not yours — is on the piece. Therefore, it's critical that you make sure you have not hurt the copy in any way. Change copy only when doing so will make it more complete, accurate or understandable.

Share the Goods.   Editors should be teachers. One of the most important rules of writing is "Show, don't tell." Good editors provide writers with examples of good writing from newspapers, magazines, books and newsletters. Other techniques also can be used to inspire writers to new heights. One of the simplest is public compliments: When a writer produces good work, let him or her know within earshot of other staffers. Also helpful are informal critique sessions with writers in which they're asked how the editing process could have been more helpful.

Dick Weiss of the St. Louis Post-Dispatch explains one of the teaching tools his paper employs:

> We don't just celebrate our best work, we take it apart. Each week, we take a story and highlight what makes it sing. It flatters the writer and helps the staff see the thinking that goes into great pieces. Rather than write an essay, I annotate the story and make it available through our Web site. A computer program can make it easy to highlight material in the story.[15]

Alice Klement of the Associated Press offers another tactic:

> Re-create a successful profile to encourage inexperienced writers to move beyond the basics and be bolder. Start with a good profile that can serve as a model. Debrief the reporter who wrote it and assemble the material used to write the story. That would include the reporter's notes, audio tapes, photographs, anything that the reporter used to develop the story. Gather your staff — including the writer — and discuss how the story came together.[16]

And Rene Kaluza of the St. Cloud Times recounts her paper's unique teaching method:

> We created a "Potty Training" course that produced weekly fliers on troublesome style issues. The fliers were posted in the bathrooms because we found that is the one place where everyone sees and reads notices. The messages were short and relatively clever.[17]

For more ideas, see James C. Clark, "Newspaper Training Editors Guide," published by The Freedom Forum (*www.freedomforum.org/newsstand/reports/trainingeditors/trainingeditorsguide.pdf*).

Making It Formal.   Many newspapers, magazines and newsletters have established formal programs for collaboration. Perhaps the most ambitious is the **Maestro Concept,** which was developed by Buck Ryan of Northwestern University and has been adopted by many newspapers. On every major project, one person acts as a maestro coordinating the work of all those involved: not just the writer and the copy editor, but the assigning editor, graphic artists, photographers and others who will be involved with the project. Rather than merely turning over copy at some point, the writer also is involved in generating headlines and cutlines, coming up with ideas for graphics and undertaking other aspects of producing the final package. Editors who have worked with the Maestro Concept say that the plan works well — and that it reduces the amount of work that editors are required to do.

But even when collaboration is informal, it can have a powerful effect on improving writers' work. In the end, that's the only thing that matters.

Notes

1. Gerald M. Carbone, "The Power of Words: 'Pain Without End,'" Providence Journal (online only), 26 April 2000, *www. projo.com/words/tip0426.htm.*

2. Beryl Adcock, speech to News Editing class, Towson University, 4 December 2000.

3. APME Reporting Writing and Editing Committee, "Line Editors Speak Out (Associated Press Managing Editors, 1997), p. 5.

4. APME, p. 9.

5. James C. Clark, "Route 66: Newsroom Training Editors Offer 66 Steps to Greatness" (Arlington, Va.: The Freedom Forum, 2000), p. 3, *www.freedomforum.org.*

6. Leonard Witt, "How Do You Make a Story Great?" Folio:, 15 September 1994, p. 41.

7. APME, p. 23.

8. "Madeleine Blais: Good Writers Need Good Editors," Providence Journal (online only), 3 June 1998, *www.projo.com/words/tip603.htm.*

9. APME, p. 24.

10. Clark, "Route 66," p. 27.

11. Clark, "Route 66," p. 27.

12. APME, p. 40.

13. APME, pp. 30–31.

14. Pamela T. Newkirk, "Guess Who's Leaving the Newsrooms," Columbia Journalism Review, September/October 2000, p. 36.

15. James C. Clark, "Top 40: Newspaper Training Editors Present Their Favorite Exercises and Ideas" (Arlington, Va.: The Freedom Forum, 1999), p. 17, *www.freedomforum.org.*

16. Clark, "Route 66," p. 3.

17. Clark, "Route 66," p. 8.

EDITING FOR THE WEB

Teamwork on the Web

Andre A. Jackson of The St. Louis Post-Dispatch and Stan Austin of KCStar.com (the online edition of the Kansas City Star) have seen the future of journalism, and it looks like teamwork:

> Journalists, especially those from the Old School, are notorious lone wolves. "Tell me what to do, then leave me alone to do it in my own way and style," is an attitude still prevalent in newsrooms. New Media is changing that. ...
>
> New Media staffs are also a lot more interactive (usually) than is found in the top-down, labyrinthine structure of traditional newsroom management. The job requires being able to work with others.[1]

Kathy McAdams came to the same conclusion after she took a year off from her position as a University of Maryland professor and worked as an editor at WashingtonPost.com:

> Editors must work with artists, computer folks and other editors to make connected digital pages come together. Many editorial changes need to be negotiated because of impacts on other parts of the product; some traditionally trained editors find this difficult, especially if they have worked in an "editor is god" setting. They must be ready to learn from anyone and everyone in the newsroom.

One of McAdams' predecessors at WashingtonPost.com, Mindy McAdams (no relation to Kathy), had a similar reaction:

> I have been stopped short more than once by one or another of the non-journalists among us and forced to reconsider something because he or she said, "Why do you do it that way?" and brought me to the realization that my idea was very newsroom-like and not likely to be intuitive to the non-journalists who will be our users.[2]

Jackson and Austin agree:

> You'll find yourself often bouncing ideas off people informally and playing off each other's strengths and weaknesses. It's all part of adapting to new issues and dealing with a growing workload.[3]

As in any new venture, things don't always go smoothly. In some cases, conflicts and culture clashes between journalists and "techies" can create standoffs. Shortly after WashingtonPost.com began publishing, the technical people said they could do a better job without editors. So all the editors were laid off. The editors were rehired after two weeks, by which time the techies had realized that it takes a team to create a good product.

Time for a W.E.D.ding

The idea of teamwork is nothing new in journalism. For years, some of the best print journalism has come from teams organized under the W.E.D. concept: Throughout the writing process, a **writer,** an **editor** and a **designer** work together to produce an integrated product.

Using the W.E.D. process is even more appropriate on the Web, with its rich palette of multimedia. Throw in a programmer to handle the HTML coding and maybe someone with television production experience to handle video, and a W.E.D. team can create a rich production carefully crafted for each piece of writing. Rather than demanding that editors and other Web producers be able to do everything on their own, this mode of working and thinking instead requires only that editors know what's needed to make a story its best and be able to help coordinate efforts to make that a reality.

Back to Jackson and Austin for the last word: "There's no getting around it, teams are the future. Those who know how to play well with others will have a definite advantage in the job market."[4]

Notes

1. Andre A. Jackson and Stan Austin, "How to Make It in New Media," speech at the ASNE job fair at the University of Missouri-Columbia, 30 October 1997, *www.freep.com/ jobspage/academy/weboptions.htm.*

2. Mindy McAdams, Inventing an Online Newspaper," Interpersonal Computing and Technology: An Electronic Journal for the 21st Century, 3, no. 3 (July 1995), pp. 64–90, *www.sentex.net/~mmcadams/invent.html.*

3. Jackson and Austin.

4. Jackson and Austin.

Exercises

1. Team up with another member of your class for a coaching session. First, choose a publication that the two of you work for. Next, have your partner come up with an idea for an article. Give your partner three minutes to present the idea, uninterrupted. Then you get three minutes to ask questions and suggest revisions. Once you're done, switch roles. Afterward, each of you should write a critique of the other's behavior while acting as editor.

2. Read through the following article written for a student publication. As you read it, make a list of questions you would ask the author to help improve the final version.

Imagine going from living a completely healthy and happy life one day to a state of silence the next. It sounds like a nightmare, and for Neil Shipinsky this nightmare lasted three months of his life. He was 22, a student ready to graduate from college, and his family was told that this dream would never happen.

He got into a tragic car accident and was left in a coma. He would never be the same person, he was told.

Shipinsky was a senior getting ready to graduate in May. He belonged to a fraternity and had many friends, both in and outside of it. "Neil sometimes kept to himself, but you knew deep down that he would always be there for you," said Mrs. Shipinsky. Neil's friends also knew this side of him and were there for Neil when he needed them most on that tragic night.

Last February 27, Neil and his friends decided to take a road trip for the weekend. They left late at night from campus. "We didn't want to deal with traffic on the roads, so we left around 10 or 11 at night," said Garrett Lancaster, a passenger in one of the cars. The group of friends decided to drive two cars because they did not want to be uncomfortable for the long trip ahead.

Shipinsky and his friends drove for two hours before taking a break at a rest stop. It was late at night and they wanted to get something to eat and drink to stay awake. The group of friends also decided to change their seats in the truck in order to be more comfortable. "I never thought that changing my seat at that moment would mean the difference of me living or almost dying," Shipinsky said.

Shipinsky moved his seat to the back of the truck behind the driver's seat. He thought he could sleep in the back seat without any interruptions for the rest of the trip.

The truck that Shipinsky was in left for the destination before the other car full of friends did. "We knew where we were going so we didn't bother waiting for the other car to leave," said Matt Roche, another passenger in the truck. "We thought we would just all meet up in the end."

However, the end of the trip came to an abrupt stop for the group of friends. Not long after leaving the rest stop, the truck came in contact with something in the middle of the road. "I didn't know what it was at the time. All I knew was that I had to move out of its way — and fast," said the driver of the truck. "I didn't find out until two days later because of all the confusion that it was a deer."

The driver of the truck swayed to the side of the road to get out of the deer's way. As he was doing this, the truck skidded on some rocks and proceeded to turn over. The truck flipped three times before finally stopping upside down. "I really don't remember much. It went too fast. It seemed like a dream, almost," said Garrett Shames. However, it was not a dream. The truck stopped and the reality began.

The second car of friends drove up shortly after the accident occurred. The car's lights shined on the road and fragments of broken glass were shimmering everywhere. "At first, we didn't recognize the car," said Eric Torres. "It was pretty bad looking. But we didn't hesitate. We ran out of the car quickly and went to go help them."

The truck was turned over and the driver and passenger in the front seat were strapped in by their seat belts. They were finally released with help from their friends in the second car. Garrett Shames and Matt Roche were sitting in the very back of the truck when it flipped over. They both flew out of the back window during this and suffered only minor cuts and bruises. The confusion and shock stopped and everyone was accounted for — except Shipinsky.

"I thought everybody was all right, but then I looked down and saw Neil underneath the truck," said Eric Torres. "All I saw was his legs, and they weren't moving." In a group effort, the friends lifted up the truck and pulled Shipinsky out. He was not moving, talking or breathing. "It was so scary to see him motionless, but I didn't think. I just started to do CPR," said Torres.

After a few seconds, Shipinsky started to breathe in small gasps, but he was still not conscious. The friends were getting worried and did not know what else to do for Shipinsky. "I felt like I wasn't doing enough for him. All I could do was stand there and talk to him," said Roche.

An ambulance finally arrived at the scene and took Shipinsky away in a stretcher. The group of friends left together for this trip, and they were determined to go home together. However, their dream did not come true this time.

Shipinsky was in a coma for a month before finally regaining full consciousness. He could not remember people's names, but he did recognize faces. "His face lit up when we walked in the room, but he could not remember all our names," said Shames. "It was hard to see him like that and not know if he was going to get better."

The doctors advised Shipinsky to go to physical therapy and mental therapy, and he agreed. He knew he had to get better and this was the only way. "I didn't want to go at first. They wanted me to learn the alphabet and what was one plus one," Shipinsky said. "But I knew I had to go back to the beginning before I could get ahead."

With the help of friends and family, Shipinsky did get better. After being in the hospital for three months, he was released to go home. He took it easy over the summer months. He continued his therapy and saw his friends frequently as well. "They stuck by me and helped me, when I didn't even want to help myself," Shipinsky said. "Without them, I wouldn't even be alive today. They saved my life that night."

Shipinsky went back to school this semester as a senior. He plans on fulfilling his parents' dream by graduating in December. "We're so proud of him. He's come so far in the past couple of months, and I know he'll only get better with time to come," Mrs. Shipinsky said.

Shipinsky has overcome a great disadvantage that came into his life. He feels he has awakened from the nightmare that entrapped him for three months and is living his dream of life now. Shipinsky ended by saying, "My friends were right. We were all going to go home together that night. It just took me longer to catch up with them."

Editor's Corner

An Editor and Writer at Work

I sat at my writing desk the other morning becalmed in a Sargasso Sea of false starts on a new book when Irene Sege, who has taken over as editor of my "Over 60" column in The Boston Globe, called. She had asked me to rewrite a column on how the new consultive medical care affects the elderly, and now she was suggesting a revision of the revision.

At the age of 75, I know I will never achieve security as a writer. A slight question about my writing can spark despair and an ex-paratrooper defensiveness. I am not used to being asked to rewrite a column, and now I was being asked to revise a revision. Yet when I hung up, I did not feel the writer's too often normal anger, resentment or inadequacy. Instead I felt an adrenaline surge of eagerness to return to the draft.

It helped, of course, to sense she was right. The first and second columns could have been published, and would have been with some other editors, but I was trying to do two things in the column. I tried to compare the old family doctor medicine with the new consultive medical culture, barely exploring how it affected me emotionally, and then I backed off to pay tribute to a book I had read on the topic. The result was an undeveloped personal essay combined with an undeveloped tribute to the book that had inspired the column.

Of course I didn't intend to write a bad column each time. I worked hard to do my best and, indeed, thought I had. My editor thought differently. It did help that she kept telling me how good she thought I could write in specific terms. She didn't offer me vague praise but specifically referred to a column on which we had worked when she had filled in as editor in the past. When she finally accepted the third version after she had suggested some more cuts and line changes and we had worked together on new versions of two paragraphs, I sat back to reconsider the experience.

The fact is that I don't get much editing, and when I taught journalism that was my beginning students' greatest complaint. What they wrote went in the paper, and they were not continuing to learn. Sixty years at our craft, I know I need editors and have had many good ones, but I wanted to figure out what made this experience with Irene so positive, and I realized the key was respect. She knows I respect her as a writer and an editor, and I know she respects me as a writer.

It goes beyond that. We both respected the topic: the fact that patients today — elderly and young — are forced to make life and death choices of medical treatments for which they are unprepared. If we respected the topic, we had to go below the surface and I had to discover and then share how I felt about it.

We both respected the reader. We had to be candid and clear, and we had to do it with a certain grace. And we both respected our craft. We are both compulsive, obsessive, concerned. Every small detail makes a significant difference.

Donald M. Murray, freelance writer and pioneer in the movement to study writing as a process

Each word, its denotation and its connotation, its context, the words before and after, the space between words, the comma or dash, the pace, the voice, all could.

I respect the care and the time Irene gave to my column, and I appreciate our collaboration as we go over the column line by line, each trying to make it as good as we can. I treasure the lonely hours at my writing desk, but I celebrate the joy of working with an editor who cares as much as I do that our words deliver meaning and feeling to each reader.

Misused Words Part 1

Clear communication depends in large part on using the right words for the job. Unfortunately, writers often don't examine their word choices carefully, and what they write is not what they mean. This and the next two installments of Grammar School catalog some of the most commonly misused words an editor is likely to encounter.

One warning: Many of the entries in this list have other legitimate uses beyond those discussed here. In order to keep things manageable, though, only the pertinent usages are included in this list.

ACCEPT To receive.

EXCEPT To exclude.

ADAPT To change or adjust something to make it suitable for a task, role, etc.

ADOPT To take up and use an idea, etc., to vote to accept, or to select.

The organization adapted the old computers to keep track of their contributors.

The committee adopted the interest group's plan.

ADVERSE Poor or bad.

AVERSE Opposed to.

Schools were closed for a week because of the adverse weather.

Corporate executives are averse to the plan to limit salaries of top officials.

ADVICE An opinion given.

ADVISE To give advice.

ADVISER Preferred over *advisor* by the AP Stylebook and many other sources.

AFFECT (verb) To have an effect on.

EFFECT (noun) Consequence. (verb) To bring about.

It was too early to tell how the budget cuts would affect them.

The effects of the tornado were obvious to those passing through the area.

The regulations should effect a reduction in traffic.

Sentences in which *effect* appears as a verb usually can be rewritten to sound better and be less verbose:

The regulations should reduce traffic.

AGGRAVATE To make a condition worse.

IRRITATE To incite or provoke.

_____ 11 The artist *a) canvased b) canvassed* the art stores looking for a

new brush.

_____ 12. The surrogate mother *a) breeched b) breached* her contract with the

couple who had paid for her services.

_____ 13. The chain looked expensive, but it was only *a) 10-carat b) 10-caret*

c) 10-karat gold.

CHAPTER 9

Handling Headlines

No matter how much work writers and editors put into crafting brilliant copy, the copy will be read only if it first catches the eye of potential readers. This chapter and the next one look at the tools editors use to make copy visually appealing: headlines, graphics and creative page design. While those elements often are intertwined in creating attractive packages, we start with headlines because even the simplest printed materials typically include them.

Two Types of Headlines

Headlines appear in every form of print communication: newspapers, magazines, brochures, news releases, pamphlets and advertisements. At the most basic level, all headlines try to accomplish two missions: catch the reader's attention (sometimes with the help of graphic design) and let the reader know the subject of the accompanying material. Every headline is primarily either **informative** or **attention-getting.** Informative headlines quickly alert the reader to important information. Attention-getting headlines use word play to capture a reader's attention when the copy is more interesting than important. In the rest of this chapter, we'll look at:

1. the process of writing informative headlines;
2. the process of writing attention-getting headlines;
3. ways of combining headlines for more impact; and
4. common problems in headline writing.

Informative Headlines

Informative headlines are best for copy containing urgent news; the headline summarizes the news for readers. Informative headlines let readers quickly digest major points and decide whether the accompanying article is worth reading. Most headlines in the news section of a newspaper are informative headlines, as are headlines in journalistic newsletters and in some news-oriented magazines.

An informative headline quickly should answer the reader's question, "Why is this being published?"

Informative headlines should present information as completely and specifically as possible. Some beginning headline writers believe that informative headlines that tell the whole story are failures because they might not lead readers to read all of the accompanying copy. So the novices write a headline that doesn't clearly state the major point of the copy, believing that doing so will force the reader to read all of the copy. The reality, however, is that people have varying levels of interest in different topics, and they do not have the time to read everything that interests them. An informative headline quickly should answer the reader's question, "Why is this being published?" The best bet is to tell the reader as much as possible in the headline, not to hold back information or try to be mysterious.

Some examples of informative headlines:

President pushes health-care plan

Mideast leader stable after shooting

Notice that this type of headline includes a verb; in the second example, the verb *is* is understood.

Whenever informative headlines include information that cannot be verified by an outside observer, that information must be credited to a source. The best bet is to provide full **attribution** in the headline:

Hostages are in good health, captors say

Notice that the news comes first. The news always should be more prominent than the attribution.

In some cases you might not have enough room in a headline for full attribution. In those situations, you can compromise by using **qualification,** which lets readers see that the information has not been verified:

Auto-focus cameras called best bet for novices

While readers do not know who's calling the cameras a best bet, they at least should realize that the information in the headline is not to be regarded as indisputable fact.

Writing a good informative headline presents a challenge to editors: Tell a story in as few as four or five words. In most cases, writers prepare copy, and editors write headlines. Writers do not write their own headlines because they do not know how much space will be available. (One exception is newsletters, which typically use headlines of uniform size throughout, written by the writers. In some cases, the headlines are written before the articles to help writers focus on the most important aspects of their articles.[1]

Because editors usually write headlines for articles written by others, the first step in writing a headline is to **read the article thoroughly.** If the article is well-written, the most important information will be in the lead. But as Chapter 3 pointed out, writers often bury the most important information. Further, many articles concern complex topics, from arms agreements to zoning regulations to federal budgets and beyond. A quick glance at the lead of such an article cannot give an editor the understanding needed to write a good headline.

It's often painfully obvious when editors have not read articles carefully before writing headlines for them. Editors at one newspaper I worked for recalled a colleague who in the 1970s was given an article reporting recently discovered information about Abraham Lincoln. The writer had used a delayed lead, with the first paragraph beginning, "In 1863, when Abraham Lincoln issued the Emancipation Proclamation ... " The editor apparently was asleep at the wheel, because his headline read:

Lincoln signs Emancipation Proclamation

More recently, I came across a headline on a news story that read:

Viruses: An overblown epidemic?

The first eight paragraphs of the story focused exclusively on a lawsuit against a company that made software designed to track down computer viruses. The suit alleged that the program made consumers think another firm's software contained viruses; the second firm claimed it was losing business. Only in the ninth paragraph — on a jump page — did the article raise the question of whether the problem of viruses had been overblown. I suspect I wasn't the only reader who wondered what that headline was doing on that article.

After reading an article, an editor tries to summarize it in a short sentence. While the sentence should summarize the main point, it shouldn't be taken verbatim from the lead. Many headline writers find it helps to isolate a subject, verb and object that make up the essential message and present them in that order. While that may sound easy, it takes keen attentiveness to isolate those elements quickly — and a few years of practice doesn't hurt, either. In the next section, we'll look at how the process works.

First Steps

With the 2000 presidential election results still too close to call as newspapers went to press the day after the election, headline writers faced a unique challenge. Typically, the winner is known by deadline, but in this case it was unclear whether George W. Bush or Al Gore would take the election. While some newspapers jumped the gun and pronounced one or the other the winner long before the results were final, most papers elected to act more moderately.

Let's say you were writing the headline for the Page One story about the election results. We'll start by picking a subject. While the obvious one is "election," there is a problem with that one. In any given city, there were several other elections of interest to the readers: House, Senate, gubernatorial, etc. We can avoid confusion by making the subject "presidential election," but that takes a lot of space. Fortunately, the presidential candidates had nice, short names, so we can try "Bush, Gore."

Now for the verb. This is a little tricky because the candidates really weren't actively involved at this point. One temptation, therefore, is to use a word like "wait," but it's better to use a stronger verb. We'll try "battle."

When we come to the object, it's important to realize that we're not necessarily talking about a traditional direct object (such as "I dropped *the dish*"). Instead, we're looking for the idea that completes the headline. It could be a single word, but it is more often a phrase, sometimes preceded by a preposition (*by, for, from, to, with,* etc.). So if we start with "Bush, Gore battle," we might want to use the phrase "down to the wire" as our object. The final headline reads

Bush, Gore battle down to the wire

That headline quickly and clearly conveys the most important point of the story.

While the subject-verb-object model we used here is preferred most of the time, it's good to vary the style occasionally to keep things interesting. Sometimes, an introductory phrase or clause is used for variety:

As the floods recede, the cleanup begins

In other cases, a phrase or clause nestles between the subject and the verb:

Some toy guns,
dead ringers
for real thing,
trigger concerns

Any word order is fine as long as it meets the basic criterion: It must be clear.

Having a Fit

If you're lucky, your first headline will drop snugly into the space allotted for it. But life usually isn't that simple. In many cases, an informative headline has to fill a specific amount of space, and you will have to revise the headline until it fits.

Most headline writers today have the luxury of using computers that let them know whether headlines fit. In noncomputerized offices, headline writers have to check headline size manually. This can be a simple or slightly more complex process:

1. At some publications, editors are given a direct headline count, for example, "Write two lines counting between 13 and 15 each."

2. At other publications, editors are given **headline orders,** which relate basic information about how the headline will look. A headline order is a series of three numbers such as 4 – 48 – 1:

- The first number (4) indicates how many **columns** wide the headline will run.

- The second number (48) indicates the **point size** of the headline. The larger the number, the larger the type used and the fewer characters that fit on one line. The smallest headlines are 18 point; the largest can reach 96 points or more.

- The third number (1) indicates the **number of lines** in the headline.

To determine the actual count for a headline order, editors must consult a **headline schedule,** which lists the maximum number of characters of a given type style that will fit in a line for various headline orders. Typically, headlines must fit within one or two counts of the maximum. A headline schedule is included in Appendix B.

Once the maximum headline count is determined, there is one more factor to consider: Like people, letters and numbers differ in size. If you're on a hotel elevator with a posted limit of 12 passengers, and the doors open to a waiting group of sumo wrestlers, you'll probably pray that 11 of them don't try to squeeze in. The elevator probably could hold more than 12 marathon runners, though. That's why elevators also have a posted weight limit, and that's why it is important for headline writers to consider the relative weight of characters, such as these:

i x W 3 ;

To accurately determine the size of a headline, then, headline writers have to assign different weights to different letters, something computers are programmed to do automatically. While this requires extra work, for all practical purposes characters can be assigned to one of four weight groups, as shown in the table below.

Count (weight)																				
1/2	f	l	i	t	j	1	I	()	.	,	:	;	'	–	!					
1*	a	b	c	d	e	g	h	k	n	o	p	q	r	s	u	v	x	y	z	
1 1/2	A	B	C	D	E	F	G	H	J	K	L	N	O	P	Q	R	S	T	U	V	X	Y	Z
1 1/2	2	3	4	5	6	7	8	9	0	?	$	&	—	%	m	w				
2	M	W																		

(* The space between words in a headline also counts as one character. Do not count a space after the last word in a line.)

If you have to count a headline manually, the best way to do so is to print the headline and make a mark above each character that gets a whole count and a mark below each character that gets a half count. Then you simply add the marks. Here's how the process works on the headline we wrote earlier:

  ⸍ ⸍ ⸍ ⸍ ⸍⸍ ⸍⸍⸍⸍ ⸍ ⸍ ⸍⸍⸍ ⸍ ⸍⸍⸍⸍⸍ ⸍⸍ ⸍⸍   (27)

Bush, Gore battle down to the wire

  ⸍   ⸍ ⸍⸍   ⸍⸍⸍ ⸍ ⸍ ⸍ ⸍ ⸍   (5.5)

There are 27 marks for whole counts and 11 marks for half counts. Add 27 and 5.5 (11 times one-half) for a head count of 32.5.

Suppose the maximum count for this headline is 25; serious trimming is needed. Having to shorten headlines is the most common problem headline writers face. Often, the task can be accomplished by substituting words in the headline. In the headline we just wrote, for example, instead of "battle down to the wire," we can use "fight to the finish." In other cases, moving words also can cut a headline.

Such weight-reduction plans don't always work, though. Sometimes all the effort in the world won't get your headline to fit. When that happens, the only solution is to take an entirely different approach.

Headlinese

As deadline nears, frustrated headline writers often reach not only for the antacid tablets but also for their lists of special headline words. Over the years, desperate editors have refined a language consisting of words almost never used by normal people: verbs like "eyed" and "mulled," phrases like "set to act" and "said to." Such language has earned the epithet **headlinese,** and it is best avoided. As veteran headline writer Vince Rinehart of The Washington Post notes: "This unique language developed by generations of headline writers can get in the way of good heads. Especially if you're trying to reach a younger audience not raised on newspapers, you're more likely to attract them with headlines that reflect how people really talk and write."

Headlines With Style

Headlines follow most of the same rules of style as body copy does, but certain rules differ, and others apply only to headlines. The following list is an overview of the most common headline style rules.

Typically, headlines are written in what is known as **downstyle.**

Capitalization.   Typically, headlines are written in what is known as **downstyle.** This style calls for capital letters only on the first word of a headline and on proper nouns in the headline; in other words, it follows the same rules that apply to copy. In multiple-line headlines, only the first word of the first line is capitalized unless other lines begin with proper nouns:

New cars
to cost more,
Japan warns

Downstyle has two advantages over other styles. First, because headlines written in downstyle follow the same capitalization rules as body copy, the style is familiar to readers. Second, because few capital letters are used in downstyle, headlines can contain more information than heads written in other styles. For example:

Mayor to speak at local college
Mayor to Speak at Local College
MAYOR TO SPEAK AT LOCAL COLLEGE

The second headline is written in **upstyle,** which requires that every word is capitalized except short prepositions (*in, of, for*) and articles (*the, an, a*). The third example, using all capital letters, needs more space to present information than the other two styles. It's also harder to read.

While downstyle dominates, upstyle often is used across the media, perhaps more for the sake of tradition than for any logical reason. And some magazine and advertising headlines are written in all capital letters. If your organization uses one of these styles, you'll have to follow it, but if you're elected to help set a style, carefully consider downstyle before picking one of its competitors.

Articles.   Like telegrams, headlines typically do not include the words *a, an* and *the.* But if an article is necessary to make a headline easy to follow, it should be used, such as in this example:

Disney's 'Imagineers' Craft a Past

Punctuation.   While headlines follow some of the standard rules of punctuation, there are several differences.

1. Headlines on news and feature articles do not end with a period:

Population boom forecast for India

Article headlines typically use periods only in abbreviations:

L.A. motorists warned on carjackers

2. When quotation marks are needed in article headlines, a single mark is used:

President pledges 'full support' to allies

3. Commas perform much the same function in headlines as they do in copy, with one important difference. In an informative headline, a comma can take the place of the word *and,* as in these examples:

Mayor, governor discuss plan
Residents push, pull for extra funds

Do include the word *and,* though, when it is necessary for clarity. This headline begs for an *and:*

Women find jobs, families do mix

4. Semicolons are used to separate two independent clauses (usually appearing on two or more separate lines):

Temperatures soar into 60s; snow forecast for weekend

5. Colons serve two main purposes in headlines. They can be used to name a topic and make a statement about it:

Bed & breakfasts: the inn places to stay

Colons can also be used to set off attribution:

Surgeon general: Cancer deaths falling

6. Dashes also are used with attribution, but in this case the attribution follows the statement:

Cancer deaths falling — surgeon general

Dashes also can be used to capture the element of the unexpected:

Woman hit by bus — in her living room

Numbers.   For consistency, it is best to follow the same rules for use of numbers in headlines as in copy. But in an effort to fit the most information into the smallest amount of space, some publications (including many newspapers) use numerals exclusively in headlines. So you run into strange situations such as a headline that says "7 killed in fire" over a lead that says "A fire in a boarding house killed seven people today." Even worse is such inconsistency within a headline: "Two men killed in 3-car crash." While you don't have much choice but to go along with your organization's policy, this is another point to consider when the policy comes up for review.

Verbs.   Rules about the use of verbs vary across the print media. Here are the basics.

Don't use a verb without a subject. While a few tabloid newspapers specialize in headlines such as "SLAY 6 AT CHOIR PRACTICE!" most publications insist that a subject be included in every headline that has a verb.

Informative headlines almost always are written in **present tense,** to lend them freshness and spontaneity. Because the words *is* and *are* are understood, at first glance some headlines appear to be written in the past tense:

Ohio town razed by twister

Home offices threatened by tax changes

Notice that time elements generally are not included in headlines that refer to events that have already occurred.

If an event has not yet happened, **future tense** is used. Future tense can be conveyed in three ways:

Simple future:

Photographers will find innovative gear at show

Infinitive:

Country's top drag racers to meet at local speedway

Present tense with time element:

Green Grocer's new store opens Friday

If an event has happened and it is important to include the time element, **past tense** is used. For instance, the following headline, which was published in July, reported on an event that had happened in May. The headline writer felt that it was important to make it clear when the event had taken place:

New home completions jumped
by a hefty 12.8 percent in May

Using "jump" would have been clumsy.

Some publications and organizations require past tense in any headline referring to a long-past event, even when the time element is not stated:

Meteors killed the dinosaurs

Abbreviations.   Abbreviations often act as roadblocks to conveying information. Readers have to stop and try to remember what an abbreviation stands for before they can make sense of the headline. When readers come across a headline like "PUC OKs TMI pact," they just might turn the page. Therefore, few abbreviations are acceptable in headlines for general-interest publications. Among them are FBI and CIA; states that have two words in their names (N.Y., S.D.); and a handful of cities (NYC and L.A.).

Specialized publications often use abbreviations more frequently. Readers are expected to know the lingo of their field and shouldn't be intimidated by a headline like "FRA takes action to assure compliance with RSPA." But remember: Every reader is initially a new reader who won't necessarily know all the abbreviations yet, so it's always a good idea to keep abbreviations to a minimum.

Repetition of Words.   Editors take pains to avoid repeating words in the small space of a headline. Even if the headline consists of several elements, editors try to use synonyms to avoid repetition:

Firm says
less oil
recovered
*Colonial lowers
amount cleaned up*

FCC sets
cable TV
rate cuts
*Rules will lower
monthly bills 15%,
agency sources say*

But there's nothing wrong with repeating words in a headline for special effect. My favorite repetitive headline was written for a story about a stack of used tires that caught fire at a dump. For three days, fire companies tried to extinguish the fire, but it kept smoldering. Finally acknowledging that the fire posed little hazard to anyone, the firefighters gave up and left the fire to burn itself out. The headline read:

Firefighters tire of fighting tire fire

If you can write a headline that good by using repetition, feel free to break the rule.

Every reader is initially a new reader who won't necessarily know all the abbreviations yet, so it's always a good idea to keep abbreviations to a minimum.

Attention-Getting Headlines

Like a hammer, a good informative headline is a powerful tool — but neither is practical for every job. When the purpose of a headline is to convey something interesting rather than earth-shaking, an attention-getting headline is a better choice.

Attention-getting headlines usually are found in magazines and newspaper feature sections, often over articles that exist for the sheer pleasure of reading. Attention-getting headlines rely on stylistic devices to capture readers' attention. Betsy Graham, author of "Magazine Article Writing,"[2] has compiled a list of nine such devices; each is presented below with a recent example.

Rhythm: You'll be pleased to be seated

Rhyme: Shirt alert

Alliteration: Winter warnings

Parallelism: No scandal, no story

Balance/contrast: Low-fat, low-calorie foods: Key to health or green light for gluttony?

Word play/humor: A free ride for mini-vans?

Allusions: Weird science

Curiosity: Buildings that work for a living

Irony: Is being positive a negative on the AIDS beat?

Notice that several of these headlines use more than one device; the last one, for example, has rhythm as well as irony. Also notice that unlike informative headlines, attention-getting headlines often do not contain verbs.

Attention-getting headlines are used not only when the accompanying copy is light or unimportant. Weekly news magazines, for instance, use attention-getting headlines on important stories that readers likely will have heard about already. For instance, when the stock market crashed in 2001, it was fine for newspapers to use informative headlines such as this one:

Dow drops to lowest level in two years; Nasdaq falls 1.5% as uncertainty mounts

By the time the news magazines could cover the story several days later, however, everyone knew about the crash, so their headline writers had to write attention-getting headlines to rekindle reader interest. Here is how Time and Newsweek headlined that story:

Looking Beyond the Bear

A Bad Case of 'Mad Dow'

While aspiring advertising copywriters relish the challenge of writing memorable attention-getting headlines, they are not always the best choice. Philip Ward Burton advises in "Advertising Copywriting" (Business Books, 1990) that attention-getting headlines — especially clever ones — may be difficult for readers to interpret, may have no sell and may not indicate a direct benefit to the reader. "If in doubt," Burton suggests, "use a strong news [informative] headline with an appealing benefit. Look for the news value in your product and find its most important benefit. ... News and benefits [are] always good and always in style."

Many publications and organizations have a policy on the use of informative and attention-getting headlines. Newspapers, for example, typically require informative headlines on the news pages but use attention-getting headlines on the feature pages.

Writing a good attention-getting headline begins the same way that writing a good informative headline begins: with a careful reading of the article. In fact, a thorough reading might be even more important in writing attention-getting headlines because the theme or most interesting point of a feature article can be more difficult to find than the major point of a news article.

The next step is brainstorming words, phrases and ideas that convey the point you want to make. Often, attention-getting headlines play on well-known slogans, themes and sayings, giving them a twist; sometimes well-known expressions are used intact, but in an unexpected context. The ideal attention-getting headline not only makes its point, but leaves the reader with a smile, too. Your imagination is the only limit to creating successful attention-getting headlines.

Here's how four publications headlined their reports that Mexican food, long believed to be healthful, is loaded with fat:

Taco Shocko

Mexican food tips fat scale to 'mucho'

The Whole Enchilada:
It's Too Fat for You, Study Says

The Taco Belly!

Some other good examples:

An article about the purchase of The Boston Globe by The New York Times played on the Times' slogan, "All the News That's Fit to Print":

A deal that's fit to print

A headline on a news release announcing a bicycling shoe with a sole that is stiff while cycling but flexes while walking read:

Cannondale flexible with
its new cycling shoe

An article about a clinic to be held to tattoo pets for easy identification was headlined:

Mark your calendar to mark your pet

A piece on a bungled burglary was headlined:

There oughta be a law against burglars like this one

The headline on an article about talk show host Jerry Springer resigning after two disastrous nights as a TV news commentator read:

On the Next Jerry Springer: 'TV Fiascos!'

An article about how two merged companies were combining into a firm called PriceWaterhouseCoopers was headlined:

What's in a Name?
Funnyyoushouldask

And the headline over a column about the word "whom" falling out of fashion read:

The bell tolls for 'whom'

Let's try an example. Your assignment: Write an attention-getting headline for an article about the 10 best places to get pizza in your area. Start by listing all the words and phrases you can think of that relate to "pizza" in the first column below, then all the words and phrases that relate to "the best" in the other column:

PIZZA	THE BEST

Now combine your ideas to create attention-getting headlines. Don't worry about counts right now. Attention-getting headlines usually get more latitude when it comes to fitting into a given space. Write your ideas here:

Here are some possibilities for this exercise. Yours might be even better:

There's no topping these pizzas

The best pizza for the dough

The slice is nice

A cut above

Truly clever attention-getting headlines are a treat for the reader, but not every attempt at cleverness is worthy of publication. Notice that the examples cited above do not sacrifice the goal of informing the reader; the cleverness is a bonus, not a substitute for information.

Headline writers also should make sure that their headlines seem clever to others. I once worked with an editor who wrote terrible pun headlines that caused him to roar and everyone else to wince. One example:

Search for pygmies yields tall clue

The other editors — and I'm sure most of the public — would have preferred a straightforward headline, without the forced attempt to be clever.

Finally, be on the lookout for overused phrases. For example, the TV show "Who Wants to Be a Millionaire" spawned countless parody headlines. Initially, some of the variations worked well, but after a while, the headlines lost all freshness and impact.

Sometimes headline writers use typographic puns. These are two of my favorites:

The 🪲 🪲 are nearly gone, but battle is only beginning.

MaybeEditorsShouldAskAuthors ToTightenUpTheirWritingaBit

An attention-getting headline always must be appropriate for use with the information being presented. If in doubt, use an informative headline. In the same media packet in which the Cannondale Corp. announced its flexible cycling shoes was a news release headlined:

Cannondale announces production increase, cutback of mail-order business, more service personnel

(sidebar)

Truly clever attention-getting headlines are a treat for the reader, but not every attempt at cleverness is worthy of publication.

These were serious matters, and announcing them with a pun would not have been appropriate. Furthermore, the headline on this release has a lot of work to do, announcing three major developments. Using an attention-getting headline undoubtedly would have meant losing some of the information.

To a great extent, determining the appropriateness of a clever headline requires being sensitive to the concerns of others. In an article in the Bulletin of the American Society of News Editors, retired editor Clarke Stallworth confessed to writing a headline for an obituary that read:

Dentist fills last cavity

It was written as a joke — but it almost was published. Had it been, neither the dentist's family nor Stallworth would have had much to laugh about. Other headline writers have not been so lucky. One classic case occurred when Jimmy Carter was president. An editor's joke headline on an editorial about Carter made it all the way into print:

Mush from the wimp

There's a moral here: Editors *never* should commit to paper or computer anything that they don't want to see published.

Headline Helpers

Whether it's designed to inform or get attention, a headline usually can benefit from having a "helper" headline (Figure 9.1). While these helpers go by a wide variety of names, for the rest of this chapter we'll use a standard vocabulary to refer to headline elements. The words we'll use are the **main headline,** the **underline** and the **overline.** The example below shows how the three elements work together:

Overline:	<u>**Swift and Simple**</u>
Main headline:	**MORNING LIGHT**
Underline:	*Brighten your breakfast by trimming traditional fare*

The primary line in a headline is the main headline. An overline is an additional headline element above the main headline; an underline, an additional element below the main headline.

The chart on Page 278 shows how these terms correspond with the terminology used across the media.

Figure 9.1

Where headlines and headline helpers fit in.

Used with permission Miami Herald.

Teaser

Illustration

Main Headline

Underline

Subhead

Caption (at start of cutline)

Information Graphic (Text Box)

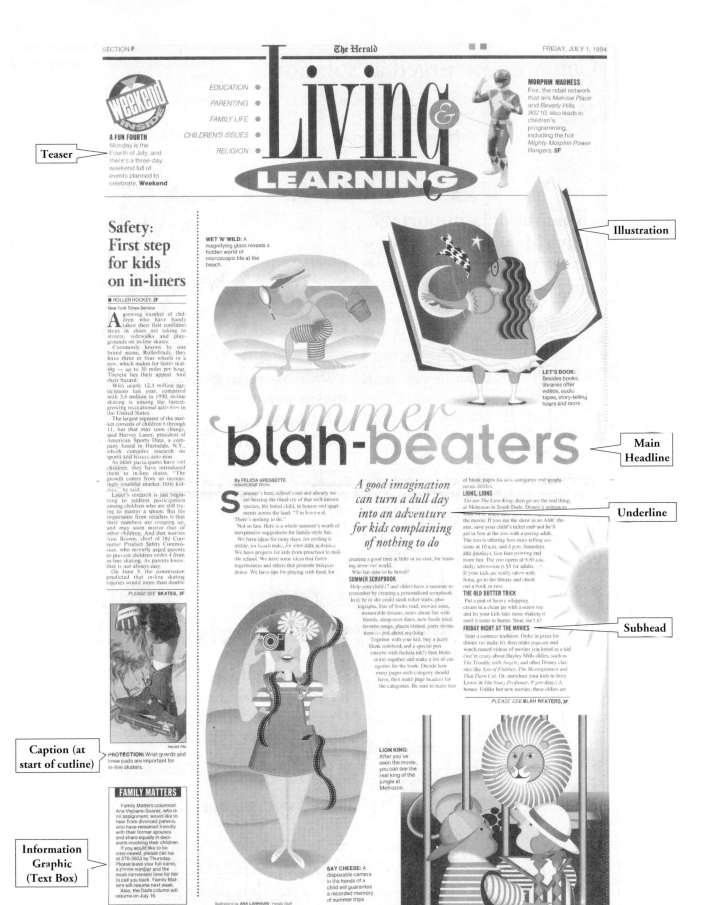

SECTION F   The Herald   FRIDAY, JULY 1, 1994

Living & LEARNING

EDUCATION •
PARENTING •
FAMILY LIFE •
CHILDREN'S ISSUES •
RELIGION •

A FUN FOURTH
Monday is the Fourth of July, and there's a three-day weekend full of events planned to celebrate, **Weekend**

MORPHIN MADNESS
Fox, the rebel network that airs *Melrose Place* and *Beverly Hills, 902 10*, also leads in children's programming, including the hot *Mighty Morphin Power Rangers*, **5F**

Safety: First step for kids on in-liners

■ ROLLER HOCKEY, **2F**

New York Times Service

A growing number of children who have barely taken their first confident steps in shoes are taking to streets, sidewalks and playgrounds on in-line skates.

Commonly known by one brand name, Rollerblade, they have three or four wheels in a row, which makes for faster skating — up to 30 miles per hour. Therein lies their appeal. And their hazard.

With nearly 12.4 million participants last year, compared with 3.6 million in 1990, in-line skating is among the fastest-growing recreational activities in the United States.

The largest segment of the market consists of children 6 through 11, but that may soon change, said Harvey Lauer, president of American Sports Data, a company based in Hartsdale, N.Y., which compiles research on sports and leisure activities.

As older participants have had children, they have introduced them to in-line skates. "The growth comes from an increasingly youthful market: little kiddies," he said.

Lauer's research is just beginning to address participation among children who are still trying to master a spoon. But his impression from retailers is that their numbers are creeping up, and may soon mirror that of other children. And that worries Ann Brown, chief of the Consumer Product Safety Commission, who recently urged parents to prevent children under 4 from in-line skating. As parents know, that is not always easy.

On June 9, the commission predicted that in-line skating injuries would more than double

PLEASE SEE **SKATES, 2F**

PROTECTION: Wrist guards and knee pads are important for in-line skaters.

Herald File

FAMILY MATTERS

Family Matters columnist Ana Veciana-Suarez, who is on assignment, would like to hear from divorced parents who have remained friendly with their former spouses and share equally in decisions involving their children. If you would like to be interviewed, please call her at 376-3633 by Thursday. Please leave your full name, a phone number and the most convenient time for her to call you back. Family Matters will resume next week. Also, the Dads column will resume on July 16.

WET 'N' WILD: A magnifying glass reveals a hidden world of microscopic life at the beach.

LET'S BOOK: Besides books, libraries offer videos, audio tapes, story-telling hours and more.

Summer blah-beaters

By FELICIA GRESSETTE
Herald Staff Writer

Summer's here, school's out and already we are hearing the ritual cry of that well-known species, the bored child, in houses and apartments across the land. "I'm b-o-r-e-d. There's nothing to do."

Not so fast. Here is a whole summer's worth of inexpensive suggestions for family-style fun.

We have ideas for rainy days, for cooling it inside, for beach trips, for after-dark activities. We have projects for kids from preschool to middle school. We have some ideas that foster togetherness and others that promote independence. We have tips for playing with food, for

A good imagination can turn a dull day into an adventure for kids complaining of nothing to do

creating a good time at little or no cost, for learning about our world.

Who has time to be bored?

SUMMER SCRAPBOOK
Help your child (7 and older) have a summer to remember by creating a personalized scrapbook. In it, he or she could stash ticket stubs, photographs, lists of books read, movies seen, memorable dreams, notes about fun with friends, sleep-over dates, new foods tried, favorite songs, places visited, party invitations — just about anything.

Together with your kid, buy a jazzy blank notebook and a special pen (maybe with fuchsia ink!) then brainstorm together and make a list of categories for the book. Decide how many pages each category should have, then make page headers for the categories. Be sure to leave lots

of blank pages for new categories and spontaneous entries.

LIONS, LIONS
Go see *The Lion King*, then go see the real thing, at Metrozoo in South Dade. Disney's animators went there when they were creating the movie. If you see the show in an AMC theater, save your child's ticket stub and he'll get in free at the zoo with a paying adult. The zoo is offering lion story-telling sessions at 10 a.m. and 4 p.m. Saturdays and Sundays, lion face painting and more fun. The zoo opens at 9:30 a.m. daily; admission is $5 for adults. If your kids are really taken with lions, go to the library and check out a book or two.

THE OLD BUTTER TRICK
Put a pint of heavy whipping cream in a clean jar with a screw top and let your kids take turns shaking it until it turns to butter. Neat, isn't it?

FRIDAY NIGHT AT THE MOVIES
Start a summer tradition: Order in pizza for dinner (or make it), then make popcorn and watch rented videos of movies you loved as a kid (we're crazy about Hayley Mills oldies, such as *The Trouble with Angels*, and other Disney classics like *Son of Flubber*, *The Moonspinners* and *That Darn Cat*. Or, introduce your kids to Jerry Lewis in *The Nutty Professor*, if you dare.) A bonus: Unlike hot new movies, these oldies are

PLEASE SEE **BLAH BEATERS, 3F**

SAY CHEESE: A disposable camera in the hands of a child will guarantee a recorded memory of summer trips.

LION KING: After you've seen the movie, you can see the real king of the jungle at Metrozoo.

Illustrations by ANA LARRAURI / *Herald Staff*

	Newspaper term	Magazine term	Brochure, Newsletter term	Advertising term
Main Headline	Headline, Top	Title, Headline	Headline	Headline
Underline	Underline, Deck (Bank), Readout (Dropout)	Subtitle (following title)	Subhead, Lead-in, Kicker	Subhead
Overline	Kicker (Eyebrow), Hammer (Reverse Kicker, Barker)	Subtitle (preceding title)	Kicker	—

The Underline

When the main headline is informative, the underline can go deeper, adding important background information or explaining what the news means. When the main headline is an attention-getting headline, an underline tells the reader the news: what has happened, what will happen. Each element should answer a different question that readers might ask. Newspaper editors refer to this as **layering:** Every part of a headline adds another layer to the reader's understanding.

While the underline should be tied clearly to the main headline, each line also must stand on its own, with the underline playing a secondary role and being set in smaller and/or lighter type. The underline typically has its own subject and verb, as in this example:

Cabinet members will help sell economic proposals to public
Appointees to visit home states to make direct appeals

Magazines and newspaper feature sections often add an informative underline to an attention-getting main headline. Some examples:

Rebels with a cause
An anti-establishment trend sweeps Europe

There's no specialization like home
Making a career out of the place you live

Fairfax buckles down on heavy metal belts

Schools ban accessory, fear use as weapon

My brilliant career & his

Couples on a roll confide how they keep their relationships from going into a tailspin

Less common is a combination of an attention-getting main headline and an attention-getting underline, but it can be effective:

A clear view of heaven

The sky-lit sanctuary of Metropolitan Community Church

Another combination often is found in magazine articles and advertisements. The main headline asks a question and the underline answers:

Should rapists ever be set free?

Prison doctors said the man who raped me was no longer a sexual sadist. I knew he might rape again — and I had to keep him in jail

In newspaper work, some technical considerations govern whether an underline is called a deck, an underline or a readout. A **deck** typically consists of two or more lines under a one-column headline:

2 teen-agers arrested in fatal fire

Police say firebomb was an attempt to silence witness

An **underline** is a single line usually centered under a main headline that stretches across several columns:

L.A. beating trial jury chosen
Judge refuses request to bar resident of riot area

A **readout** is one or two columns wide and is usually two lines deep. It sits below a main headline that covers several columns (such main headlines are called **banners**):

High school girls wrestle for acceptance
*In a "guy's sport,"
numerous obstacles*

The latest variation on the underline has been popping up in newspapers around the country. Sometimes called a **blurb,** this underline is set one column wide in type slightly larger than the body copy and summarizes the article:

Supreme Court nominee faces quick approval
*In a conciliatory mood,
Senate is likely to take it
easy on Ramirez*

The Overline

Overlines, too, can be primarily informative or primarily attention-getting. On a news story, for instance, an overline can add even more information to an informative main headline:

Slick roads turn traffic into game of bumper cars
Sleet storm arrives unannounced

Notice that like underlines, overlines also stand on their own and play a secondary role to main headlines.

An overline also can be used to introduce a main headline. This style often is used in magazines:

*At this bookstore, the customers —
not to mention the sales clerks, cashiers,
advertisers, publicists and security guards —
are children*
These kids make books their business

In some cases, the overline flows into the headline:

As a civil rights worker, then an advocate for children, Marian Wright Edelman has spent a lifetime putting into practice what her parents taught her:

Make things better for somebody

Overlines also can be used to package two or more stories (Figure 9.2).

As steel staggers, a new punch comes

Mini-mill: Latest threat

USS dumps 5 officials in reshuffle

Big Steel as big victim: PR ploy?

Figure 9.2
The overline can serve to package two or more related articles.

Copyright Pittsburgh Post-Gazette. Reprinted with permission.

Two special types of overlines are found in newspapers: the kicker and the hammer. The **kicker** is set in smaller type than the main headline and is usually no more than half its width. As a result, the kicker contains almost as many characters as the main headline, and it may be a complete headline in itself. It usually is set flush left and often is underlined. The kicker must complement the main headline rather than compete with it. It usually does this by adding important but less essential information to the headline:

Hopes for pennant spot dwindle

Tigers' losing streak hits 10 games

Sometimes the kicker does not contain its own subject, relying instead on the subject of the main headline:

Calls for return to moral values

Pope condemns sex education in schools

Many newspapers have dropped kickers, preferring instead underlines or hammers. If kickers are used at all, they serve as **standing headlines,** short titles above features that appear daily or weekly. Typical standing heads include "Around the Town," "Update on the News" or "From the Chairperson." In other cases, the kicker carries the name of a writer whose work appears regularly, replacing the byline. A headline may or may not follow:

Many newspapers have dropped kickers, preferring instead underlines or hammers.

Backstage

At Shakespeare,
A Shrewd Divorce

A **hammer,** also known as a reverse kicker, is set in larger type than the main headline. A hammer is not as wide as the headline under it; instead, it includes white space to open the page. As a result of their large point size and narrow width, hammers can't say much. They often run just two or three words and rarely exceed five words. Hammers present the one case in which the dominant visual element in the headline package is *not* the main headline. Their lack of words makes it clear that the hammers are not expected to do most of the work.

Hammers often add impact or a clever touch to a headline. For example:

Class Wear
Pride, prejudice and the not-so-subtle
politics of the working-class uniform

NOW hear this
Epithets greet council plan to welcome feminist group

Hammers also can be used to package related pieces of writing. Editors are always on the lookout for ways to make information more accessible to readers. One means of easing access is by placing related articles near one another. The articles can be boxed together, and a hammer can be used to let readers quickly see what the articles are about (Figure 9.3).

One other specialized headline, which doesn't fit into any of the main categories, is important in most publications: the **jump head.** Jump heads are used to let the reader know where a continuing article picks up when it doesn't continue on an adjacent page. For instance, a newspaper article that begins on Page One may be continued on Page 12; a jump head is placed at the top of the continuation (known as the "jump").

Several different approaches are used in writing jump heads. The first uses some or all of the same words in the jump head as in the original headline, to make it easy for the reader to find the jump. For example, the jump head on an article headlined "30 powerful natural remedies" might be condensed to "Powerful remedies."

A second approach is a one-word jump head; the continued line at the end of the last page before the jump instructs readers to look for that one-word headline on the jump page. For example, the first part of a story headlined "Tax increases called likely" ends with a line that reads "See Taxes, page 19." The jump head simply reads "Taxes."

China Connection

People's Republic engineers here

By Tom Barnes
Post-Gazette Staff Writer

Two officials from China's Institute of Atomic Energy are in Pittsburgh this week to learn about how water is used to cool nuclear power plants.

The representatives from the People's Republic of China are two of the 1,300 engineers, chemists and scientists from 120 counties attending the three-day International Water Conference at the William Penn Hotel. The conference, which began yesterday, is sponsored by the Engineers' Society of Western Pennsylvania.

"This conference is useful for us, especially the water chemis-try of a nuclear power station," said Lin Fang-Liang. "We have been doing research into that."

"This is my first time in the United States," said Lu Jingju. "I am glad to get a chance to visit America."

Michael C. Skriba, an environmental engineer from Westinghouse Electric Corp. and one of the program organizers, said the conference gives scientists from around the world a chance to exchange information about uses of water.

Later this week, the two Chinese officials will meet with Westinghouse officials, Skriba said. Westinghouse is competing with other countries, such as France and Germany, to sell Chi-na 10 nuclear power plants, he said.

The conference is important to the city for both economic and prestige reasons, Skriba said. He estimated it will pump about $500,000 into the local economy, in spending on hotels, meals and shopping during the three days.

"This has a beneficial impact on the local economy and gives Pittsburgh visibility around the world," he said. "We have an international reputation."

He said the conference has been held annually in Pittsburgh for the last 45 years. It was begun by some Pittsburgh manufacturers because of the importance of clean water to local industry.

Pitt, Chinese pharmacy college to share

By Carl Remensky
Post-Gazette Staff Writer

The pharmacy schools of the University of Pittsburgh and a college in China have agreed to exchange information and faculty.

Pitt President Wesley Posvar and representatives of the Nanjing College of Pharmacy will sign a formal exchange agreement Thursday. A five-member delegation from Nanjing arrived here last night.

"The Chinese are interested in upgrading their curriculum and research capabilities, while we are interested in examining different types of traditional Chinese medicines," said Dr. Randy Juhl, a professor in Pitt's school of pharmacy.

Juhl was one of four Pitt pharmacy professors who traveled to Nanjing, a city in southern China, last June and laid the groundwork for the exchange. He said Lan Wong, a Pitt pharmacy professor and a native of Hong Kong, initiated the contact which resulted in the agreement.

The exchange will begin next spring when Pitt faculty members go to Nanjing to teach. Chinese faculty will come to Pitt in fall, 1985.

In the United States, pharmacists are trained to dispense drugs — most of them prepared by large manufacturers — and information about their effects to customers, Juhl said. The training of Chinese pharmacists focuses on preparation of medicines, something which pharmacists in the West are no longer concerned with, he added.

"I would compare pharmacy in China to pharmacy in the United States in the 1930s or 40s," Juhl said. "The Chinese want us to help bring them into the information and research era of pharma-cy, but they are adamant about maintaining their tradition of preparation. They want to add to what they do by combining preparation and information techniques."

Juhl said Pitt professors will have a chance to examine ancient Chinese medicines — such as various types of herb teas used to treat everything from pain to kidney stones — to try to determine what makes them effective.

"The Chinese know certain plant material preparations are effective in certain medical applications, but they don't know why they work," he said. "Some of them have been used for centuries but never subjected to Western-style scientific scrutiny. That's what we want to do."

The exchange agreement also should help to open each country's pharmeceutical market to the other, he added.

Figure 9.3
A hammer can be used to point out the common elements in two articles.

Some newspaper editors like to take an entirely different approach to writing the jump head than they took in the main head. They believe that an interesting jump head might snare readers who passed by the beginning of the article.

Common Headline Problems

There's no more embarrassing place for a mistake than at the top of a page in large type. We'll finish this chapter by looking at some of the most common headline problems.

Generic Headlines

Every headline should be as specific as possible. One rule of thumb is that a headline that can be used on more than one piece of copy is *not* a good headline. Some examples of headlines that do not pass this test:

Lecture scheduled
Meeting to be held

Merely being specific is not enough, though. For example, a newsletter from a medical center contained this headline:

Public grand opening
for Pathways on Oct. 31

True, the headline is specific. But equally true, it is dull and uninviting. Unless readers know what "Pathways" is, they probably won't read the accompanying article. That would be a shame, because as the article makes clear, "Pathways" is the first program in the area to offer treatment for chemical dependency, an epidemic problem among teen-agers. Far better would be a headline such as this one:

Pathways is first local program
for chemically dependent teens

While the second headline is slightly longer, it would have fit into the available space.

Spelling and Grammar Errors

As obvious as headline errors might appear to readers, far too many get by editors. The most common headline problem of this type is misspelling, as this headline about a missing doctor illustrates:

Doctor found after four years on lamb

No, the doctor hadn't developed a fondness for livestock; the headline writer just didn't know how to spell.

It wasn't a misspelling but the omission of space between two words that resulted in this headline:

Governor's penis busy

Grammatical problems also often turn up in headlines. Consider this headline and underline:

Safes can be cracked easier than oysters
But it's worth all the trouble

Is the article about cracking safes — or cracking oysters?

Dangling modifiers also can create confusion:

Another casualty of hurricane, judge terminates adoption

Foster parents had given back two adopted children after a hurricane devastated the parents' home and business, so the judge terminated the adoption. But *the judge* wasn't a casualty of the hurricane, as the headline says.

Another common problem is using words that can serve as various parts of speech, as in these examples:

Consumer calls down to a trickle

Taxpayers not alone in filing traumas

Friendly Left Bank
For S&L Fugitive?

In the first example, a reader initially might see the noun "calls" as a verb. In the second example, a similar problem lurks in the word "filing." It initially might look like a verb (controlling the direct object "traumas"), but it is actually an adjective. The third example is perhaps the most confusing; question headlines usually aren't clear. It is unclear whether the word "Left" is a verb or another part of speech. Rewriting would have eliminated the confusion in all of these headlines.

Senseless Headlines

Pressed as they are for time, newspaper editors are more likely than editors in other media to create headlines that leave readers more confused than informed. Here's an example:

N.Y. man enters Alford plea in killing

The lead said the man "conceded that prosecutors had enough evidence to convict him," and the second paragraph said that he "entered an Alford plea." But nowhere does the article, let alone the headline, connect these two points so that the bewildered reader understands that an Alford plea *is* the concession that prosecutors have enough evidence to convict a suspect.

More confusing headlines:

Pension funds shortfall up sharply

How does something fall "up"?

Mother who tried suicide will be aided

To make sure she succeeds next time?

Campus Drive construction scheduled to be finished in approximately weeks

Was the number dropped — or is this another grammar problem?

Pressed as they are for time, newspaper editors are more likely than editors in other media to create headlines that leave readers more confused than informed.

Sometimes a headline looks fine on its own, but it doesn't line up with the story. One example:

Gunman slays 2
at Gettysburg farm

The lead says: "A man broke into a farmhouse early Saturday, killed three people, wounded four and apparently shot himself before holding police at bay for two hours, authorities said." Here's another example:

Man gets life sentence
for murdering wife

The article says that a local man "is being held without bail ... charged with murder." If he's only been charged, he surely hasn't been sentenced to life in prison.

Poor phrasing of the headline can also lead to similar confusion:

Two charged in theft
of meat face trial

Keeping the phrase "theft of meat" together on one line would have made this headline much easier to follow.

Letting Sex Crawl Innuendo

While sex is a common selling tool, it's important to make sure that a headline doesn't carry unintended sexual connotations. If a headline can be read two ways, some readers will read it the wrong way.

For Ronald Reagan's inauguration in 1981, several inaugural balls were held throughout Washington. An editor I worked with wrote this headline without realizing how someone with a dirty mind would read it:

Washington turns out
for Reagan's balls

On another occasion, a co-worker wrote this headline for a story about an outstanding athlete at Gateway High School; the athlete's last name was Gay:

Gateway's Gay
athlete of the week

Here's a headline that apparently relates an unusual social movement:

Virgins against apartheid

Some readers who were presumably intrigued by the political display of a group of virgins were surely disappointed to find out the headline referred to the Virgin *Islands.*

A headline over a community events listing read:

Free women
& sexuality
program offered

The jump head on an article about appearances of the Virgin Mary read:

Sightings of Virgin
No Blessing for Towns

And a headline about romantic floral dresses said:

Time again for something soft and long

Other headlines that editors should have halted:

You can put pickles up yourself

Sawyer excited by head job

And one that's destined to be a classic:

Unusual wedding
Preacher comes on Shetland pony

The moral: Always scrutinize every headline you write. Better yet, have someone else scrutinize it, too.

Notes

1. Mark Beach, "Editing Your Newsletter: How to Produce an Effective Publication Using Traditional Tools and Computers" (Portland, Ore.: Coast to Coast Books, 1988), p. 33.

2. Betsy P. Graham, "Magazine Article Writing" (New York: Holt, Rinehart & Winston, 1980).

Exercises

Count each line in the following headlines.

_____   Earthquake

_____   kills 370

_____   in Egypt

_____   O'Leary Tightens

_____   Radiation Policy

_____   Nebraska ranks first

_____   in jobs participation

_____   GM directors

_____   warn chairman

_____   about UAW

_____   Situation at

_____   Zaporozhe

_____   nuclear site

_____   deteriorates

_____   Exemption

_____   is probable

_____   for Pistons

_____ Many states

_____ considering

_____ charter schools

_____ U.S. tank

_____ is chosen

_____ by Kuwait

_____ Tokyo political kingpin

_____ reportedly is resigning

Edit the following article and write a headline for it. Your instructor will specify the head order or count for the headline.

Late-night comedians can still get a laugh with jokes about cheep jewelry, available on cable television's shopping channels, but a new study says retail marketers need to come to terms with video merchandizing before they find their businesses at risk.

Television Shopping: The New Retailing is the title of a report on the study, conducted by WSL Marketing, a NYC consulting firm. WSL president Wendy Liebmann, says the results of the national servey show that shopping channels "are proving themselves to be a legitimate and dangerous competitor.

Acording to the report people who purchase goods through TV shopping chanels are a retualers dream.

"They have money, education, high level jobs and they shop at a wide variety of retail and nonretail outlets, said Liebmann.

"These people are not T.V. junkies or hermits" Liebmann declaires. "They are regular, traditional shoppers virtually all of whom have a high school degree and 25 per cent earn over $55000 annually."

WSL discovered that TV shopping has evolved to the point at which costumers now buy a wide range of merhandise.

"IT begins with the purchase of jewelry," Liebmann says, and the more often they shop they more they buy. As they become comfortable with tv shopping, she adds, they buy: clothing, collectables, consumer electronics, home appliances, beauty products, and housewares. Those sales come at the expense of traditional retail store sales, the report notes.

Grabbing Online Readers' Attention

If good headlines are a priority on the printed page, they're essential on the Web. Take a look at the opening page of any online news site, and there's a good chance you'll be confronted with dozens of headlines and story summaries. If an article is to have any chance of getting a reader's attention, it must have a compelling headline. In fact, many online readers tend to look at only the headlines — and not article summaries — before deciding whether to read an article.

Web usability expert Jakob Nielsen points out that online headlines have a harder job than their print counterparts for two reasons:

- In print, a headline is tightly associated with photos, decks, subheads and the full body of the article, all of which can be interpreted in a single glance. Online, a much smaller amount of information will be visible in the window, and even that information is harder and more unpleasant to read.

- Online headlines are often displayed out of context: as part of a list of articles, in an e-mail program's list of incoming messages, in a search engine hitlist, or in a browser's bookmark menu or other navigation aid. Some of these situations are very out of context: search engine hits can relate to any random topic, so users don't get the benefit of applying background understanding to the interpretation of the headline.[1]

With those problems in mind, Web headlines must meet a different set of criteria from those written for print. For one thing, there's no place on the Web for attention-getting headlines. Visitors want to know immediately whether they should bother clicking through to an article. There's no place for headlines that tease the visitor or use puns. As Nielsen notes, "Users have been burned too often on the Web to have time to wait for a page to download unless they have clear expectations for what they will get. In print, curiosity can get people to turn the page or start reading an article. Online, it's simply too painful for people to do so."[2]

Because many readers will first encounter a headline out of context, Web head writers should be sure that every headline begins with a key word or name from the article. That helps readers grasp the concept quickly.

Subheads

Just grabbing online readers' attention with a headline isn't enough. On the Web, subheads are also important. Because reading on a computer screen is more difficult than reading on paper, people tend to scan rather than read online content. Subheads — again written to be informative rather than cute — help them move through a story quickly and find the parts that are most relevant to them.

Editor's Corner

**Maria Stuart,
managing editor,
The Livingston
County (Michigan)
Daily Press & Argus**

Dress Your Headlines for Success

During 2000, I was involved in two important journalistic events.

The first was the move to daily publication for my newspaper. After more than 50 years of weekly — and more recently, twice-weekly — publishing, The Livingston County Daily Press & Argus made journalism history and bucked trends by becoming a daily newspaper in September 2000.

At a time when large metropolitan newspapers have been losing both circulation and advertising dollars, we've thrived. Part of our success is that we practice what we call "community journalism," which is a way of saying we provide the most complete, in-depth, local news coverage and opinions available; another is our attitude, shown in part through our frequent use of clever headlines.

We love clever headlines; in fact, we encourage them. At our weekly staff meetings we give awards for the photo, story and headline of the week, and the competition is intense.

Headlines are the front door to stories. They beckon busy readers in, whetting their appetites for the interesting work that follows. Good headlines must be complete, succinct and — above all — easy to understand. Great headlines also include some bit of humor or attitude or emotion.

I had noted a few of best headlines in my newspaper recently: "Barn to be wild" for a piece on barn murals in the county; "District's top dogs get meaty bones" for a story on administrative raises reaching 14 percent in one of our local school districts; and (one of my favorites) "In Livingston County, the cider house rules" for our annual listing of cider mills and U-pick apple orchards.

All of which leads me to the other big journalistic event I was involved in during 2000: I made American Journalism Review — and later a Dave Barry column.

You can tear American Journalism Review apart, but you won't find my name in there anywhere. But if you are a fan of the Take 2 blooper section, in which readers can send in really, really dumb mistakes and headlines they come across, you'll see my creation under the heading "Shouldn't be too hard to spot":

Search for woman in fertilized egg suit goes nationwide

That's my headline. You need to know that I worked and worked and worked on it. I needed three lines over two columns for an interesting story we've been covering off and on for several years. In 1997, a local woman filed suit against her ex-husband for control of five fertilized human eggs. Her eggs had been fertilized by sperm from her ex-husband while they were married, and the eggs had been kept frozen at a fertility clinic.

Before divorcing, the couple had a child from one of the fertilized eggs that had been implanted; the rest of the eggs were frozen. After the divorce, the woman wanted the remaining eggs implanted so she could have another child. Her ex-husband fought the release of the eggs. The judge in the case ruled the eggs had to stay at the fertility clinic until the divorced couple came to an agreement.

It is an interesting story on many fronts. The court battle over the frozen eggs made national news and brought up all sorts of legal and ethical issues that experts hadn't thought about before.

Then, in 1999, the woman fled the state with her child after her ex-husband had been granted unlimited, unsupervised visits. An alert reporter saw a photo of the woman and the child in a "Have You Seen Us" advertisement, and we did an update on the story and the nationwide search.

To me, it was important that the headline explain exactly who this woman was. Never mind that the information about the past legal battle was in the story. Never mind that the same information easily could have been conveyed in a subhead. And never mind that we would have done this story whether or not the woman had been embroiled in a lawsuit over her fertilized eggs.

For some reason, I was hung up on that distinction. And that's what caught me.

We were on a tight deadline and I was on front page duty. I feverishly wrote and rewrote and began all over again in my search for the perfect headline for the story. I just couldn't get it right. And as the minutes and then seconds to deadline ticked away, leaving me no more time to write or have a fresh eyes look over my work, I ended up with the headline featured in American Journalism Review.

So caught up in cramming so much information into one headline, I didn't even realize the humor in it until I saw it splashed on the front page. That's the moment of truth when you realize that despite the best of intentions and greatest of embarrassment, you have to live with what you wrote.

However, no experience is a bad one if you learn something, and from this I took a couple lessons I'd like to pass along.

- If it's too difficult to write the headline you want, write another. Don't get too attached to ideas and bursts of creativity that don't seem to be working out; there's a reason you're frustrated.

- If you're having difficulty with a particular headline (or lead or subhead or story), ask someone who knows nothing about what you're working on to give you an objective eye.

- Don't work so long on one particular piece that you leave yourself with no time to step away and consider the package as a whole.

- You have only so much space for headlines. Don't try to cram in more than what will fit. If you're confused writing the headline, imagine how the reader will feel when reading it.

- It is not the responsibility of one headline to tell the entire story — that's the reporter's job. A good headline must set the stage for the story that follows.

- Headlines don't have to be clever, though it's wonderful when they are. All headlines have to be is clear, concise and instantly understandable.

Just ask the woman in the fertilized egg suit.

Misused Words Part 2

COLLISION A violent contact between *moving* bodies. A car cannot collide with a tree, a lamppost or any other stationary body.

CLOTHES What you wear on your body.

CLOTHS Pieces of fabric.

COMPARED TO Used when looking at items in the same class or category without examining closely, as in an analogy.

COMPARED WITH Used when more carefully examining similarities and differences between items.

With its friendly disposition, a llama can be compared to a cat with long legs.

Our kitten, Samson, is hyperactive compared with our older cat, Caboodle.

COMPLIMENT (noun) Praise. (verb) Giving praise.

COMPLEMENT (noun) Something that adds to another thing to make it complete. (verb) To add to, accent or complete.

We complimented him on the way he had arranged the furnishings to complement the room.

COMPOSE To make up.

COMPRISE To include. *Comprised of* is always wrong.

Fifty states compose the United States.

The United States comprises 50 states.

CONFIDANT A close, trusted friend of either gender in whom one can confide.

CONFIDANTE The same, but exclusively female.

CONFIDENT Sure of oneself.

CONSCIENCE That little voice that tells you when you're being bad.

CONSCIOUS Awake or aware.

Not everyone's conscience is as strong as hers.

She did not become conscious again until hours after the accident.

CONTACT As a verb, the physical touching of things. It should not be used as a synonym for *call* or *write*.

The kicker's toe contacted the football.

CONTINUAL Repeated over time or intermittent.

CONTINUOUS Without stop.

Even her continual education had not prepared her for the continuous demands of her first graduate class.

CORD A string or an anatomical structure such as a spinal or vocal cord. It is also a unit of wood.

CHORD A string of a musical instrument or a combination of tones.

COUNCIL (noun) An assembly, usually a legislative body.

COUNSEL (noun) Advice or a lawyer. (verb) To advise.

CONSOLE (noun) A cabinet. (verb) To comfort.

CONSUL A person appointed by his or her government to serve a country's interests abroad.

The City Council voted to retain counsel in the matter.

His friends consoled him when he was not picked as the consul to Denmark.

COUPLE OF It's not correct to write *He tried on a pair pants,* nor *He bought a couple shirts.* Always include the *of.*

DAMAGE (noun) Loss or harm.

DAMAGES (noun) Legal term for money paid or ordered to be paid as compensation for loss or injury.

After the accident caused extensive damage to the property, Burton was ordered to pay $325,000 in damages.

DATA Like *media, phenomena* and *criteria, data* is plural. (*Datum* is the singular.) But it can take either singular or plural verbs. When *data* refers to a quantity as one unit, it takes a singular verb:

The data is overwhelming.

When *data* refers to individual items, use a plural verb:

The data were gathered in 10 cities across the nation.

DEDUCTIVE A type of reasoning that proceeds from general principles and applies them to specific instances.

INDUCTIVE Reasoning that seeks to make generalizations from specific cases.

Once you know the principles of intercultural communication, it is easy to use deductive reasoning to apply them to a specific country.

Using inductive reasoning, the researchers were able to draw conclusions about the tribe after studying 12 members of it.

DESERT (noun) A dry land. (verb) To leave.

DESSERT (noun) What you eat after a meal.

After a year in the desert, I wanted ice cream for dessert every night.

DIAGNOSIS An evaluation of a patient's condition.

PROGNOSIS An outlook.

Despite the earlier upbeat diagnosis, his prognosis was not good.

DIFFERENT FROM Preferred over *different than.*

Our values are different from our parents' values.

DILEMMA A choice between two equally unfavorable or disagreeable alternatives.

Her dilemma was choosing whether to quit her job or lose her student aid.

DISBURSE To pay out.

DISPERSE To spread out.

Security guards were called in to watch as officials disbursed money to the lottery winners.

After the event, the crowd dispersed quickly.

DISCREET Prudent.

DISCRETE Detached or separate.

They tried to be discreet about their affair.

A computer typically includes four discrete parts: a central processing unit, a keyboard, a mouse and a monitor.

DISINTERESTED Impartial.

UNINTERESTED Lacking interest.

He was uninterested in the search for a disinterested referee.

DISORGANIZE (verb) To disrupt the organization of.

UNORGANIZED (adj.) Lacking order, system or unity.

The intern disorganized the office.

Her successor found the place thoroughly unorganized.

DOMINATING Exercising authority by reason of superior power or influence.

DOMINEERING Exercising authority in a tyrannizing, bullying or arrogant way.

On the playing field, he was a dominating figure, but at home he was a domineering father.

DROWNED It is proper to say someone *was drowned* only when another person held his or her head under water.

The boy drowned after he was caught in a whirlpool.

The puppy was drowned by a mean neighbor.

DUE TO Should be used only when you can substitute *caused by.* It is not a synonym for *because of.*

The drop in earnings was due to an accounting change.

The change was made because of the new regulations.

ECOLOGY The study of the environment. Not a synonym for *environment.*

INCORRECT: Auto emissions have a major effect on the ecology.

CORRECT: Auto emissions have a major effect on the environment.

EITHER One or the other, not both.

INCORRECT: The teams lined up on either end of the field.

CORRECT: The teams lined up on both ends of the field.

EMIGRATE To leave a country.

IMMIGRATE To enter a country.

EMINENT Prominent or conspicuous.

IMMINENT About to occur.

The arrival of the eminent guests was imminent.

ENORMITY Abnormal wickedness. Not a synonym for *enormousness,* which means huge.

ENRAGE (verb) To put into a rage.

OUTRAGE (noun) An act of extreme violence or viciousness.

The community was enraged by the series of outrages.

ENSURE To guarantee.

INSURE To provide insurance.

The president said he would do everything he could to ensure that all citizens would be insured in a health plan.

ENVELOP (verb) To wrap up, obscure or hide.

ENVELOPE (noun) What holds letters and bills.

While I was shopping for envelopes, I could see fog envelop the store.

EPITAPH An inscription on a tombstone.

EPITHET A descriptive adjective applied to someone. Epithets usually are negative comments.

As he tried to write the epitaph for the mayor, he remembered all the epithets people had called him.

EVERY DAY Daily.

EVERYDAY Common.

Almost every day, she tries to do something to break out of her everyday routine.

FAMOUS Widely known, usually in a positive light.

INFAMOUS To have a bad reputation.

While we were visiting the famous theme park, police caught an infamous criminal there.

FARTHER Use in references to physical distance.

FURTHER Use in references to degree, time or quantity.

Further into the night, they realized they couldn't drive much farther.

FAZE (verb) To embarrass or disturb.

PHASE (noun) An aspect or stage.

The fact that she was going through a phase did not seem to faze her parents.

FEEL When used as a synonym for thinking or believing, it should mean being convinced emotionally rather than intellectually.

Even though no one has ever made it to the top of the mountain, they feel sure that they will get there.

FEWER Use with plural nouns.

LESS Use with collective nouns or mass nouns.

The school found itself with fewer teachers and less equipment than in years past.

FIANCÉ A man.

FIANCÉE A woman.

FIRST Often unnecessary, such as in "When I first entered the room."

FLAIR (noun) A natural talent.

FLARE (noun) A flame or an emergency signaling device. (verb) To blaze with sudden light or to burst out in anger.

Her flair for writing was noticed quickly by her teachers.

Tempers flared after one of the motorists involved in the accident hit the other one with a lit flare.

FLAUNT To show off.

FLOUT To mock or scoff.

The rich flaunted their wealth in flouting the president's call for belt tightening.

FLIER Preferred by The Associated Press as the reference for aviator or handbill.

FLYER Used only as part of a proper name.

FLOUNDER (verb) To struggle or thrash about.

FOUNDER (verb) To sink.

Lying on his back, the turtle floundered.

As the ship foundered, the crew jumped overboard.

FORMALLY The adverbial form of the word *formal.*

FORMERLY In the past.

FORTUNATE Involving good luck.

FORTUITOUS Happening by chance.

It was fortuitous that he was walking under the open window at the moment the workers dropped the piano through it.

FOREWORD An introduction.

FORWARD A direction.

FOUL Foul can mean many things, but it is never a noun meaning a bird, which **FOWL** is.

FORTH Moving ahead in time or place.

FOURTH What comes after third.

GET To fetch. Not a synonym for become.

As it becomes colder, stores may find it hard to get enough firewood.

Another misuse occurs when *get* is used with a second word in place of a shorter, more precise verb. For example, *evade* is better than *get around; endorse* is better than *get behind.*

GIBE To taunt.

JIBE To be in harmony with one another.

When he couldn't do even one push-up, his classmates gibed him.

They're a wonderful couple who really jibe.

GORILLA An animal.

GUERRILLA A soldier or rebel.

GRAFFITI A plural noun, graffiti always takes a plural verb.

Graffiti were found on the subway car.

HEAL To make better.

HEEL A part of a foot.

HEALTHFUL Something that improves health.

HEALTHY In good health.

Studies have shown that most healthy people eat healthful diets.

HIKE Not a synonym for increase. Save it for what Scouts and football players do.

HISTORIC Famous in history.

HISTORICAL Related to history.

On our picnic at the historic battlefield, she read a historical novel.

HOARD (verb) To gather a supply. (noun) Such a supply.

HORDE (noun) A large crowd.

HOLD UP (verb), **HOLDUP** (noun and adjective).

HOLE UP To take refuge.

HOPEFULLY While this word has gained acceptance as a synonym for *I hope,* it actually started life as an adverb meaning *full of hope.* Purists insist it should be used only for that purpose.

The hungry child sat hopefully on the steps of the candy shop.

HUNG Past tense of *hang,* applied to objects.

HANGED Past tense of *hang,* used when a person has been put to death by hanging.

Exercise

Choose the correct word in each example. (15 points)

_____ 1. The *a) historic b) historical* battlefield is a favorite visit for

schoolchildren.

_____ 2. His *a) epitaph b) epithet* read, "I'd rather be in Philadelphia."

_____ 3. Compared *a) to b) with* seven years ago, the price of clothing has

gone up.

_____ 4. The yoga class was canceled *a) due to b) because of* poor

registration.

_____ 5. The founder of the Fresh Flounder Co. *a) foundered b) floundered*

to try to keep control when he found his fishing vessel slowly

_____ *c) foundering d) floundering* to the ocean floor.

_____ 6. Andre Previn's composition included a wide variety of *a) chords*

b) cords.

_____ 7. Diana is *a) uninterested b) disinterested* in visiting Charles.

_____ 8. The cadaver had been *a) hanged b) hung* near the door.

_____ 9. His *a) conscience b) conscious* would no longer let him keep the

dark secret.

_____ 10. The fans began to *a) gibe b) jibe* the losing team.

_____ 11. She was kept awake all night by the *a) continual b) continuous* ticking

of the clock.

_____ 12. He felt as if he was going to *a) get b) become* sick.

_____ 13. While she is now a bank executive, she was *a) formally b) formerly*

a teacher.

_____ 14. Parents were *a) outraged b) enraged* when they found out that the

teacher had been supplying students with beer.

10 Graphics and Media Design

As our society continues to grow more visually oriented, publications are paying more attention to design. Thanks to desktop publishing, much of the responsibility for designing publications has fallen into the hands of editors. Even editors who are minimally involved in design should understand its basics, so they can work intelligently with others who handle the process.

Think W.E.D.

A good starting point in any discussion of design is the **W.E.D.** concept developed by Mario Garcia, a design consultant for newspapers around the globe.[1] W.E.D. stands for Writing-Editing-Design. As the name implies, these elements must be thought of as interlinked rather than as isolated processes. Words and graphics should complement each other, with the graphics doing chores that are difficult to accomplish with words alone. (That idea is sometimes referred to as **layering.**) Using the W.E.D. concept, every element should add to the reader's understanding and provide another entry point to the page — that is, another opportunity to hook a potential reader.

Producing designs that accomplish those tasks requires planning. As the discussion of the Maestro Concept in Chapter 8 indicated, design considerations should not arise at the last minute but as early in the editing process as possible. Only then is there a good chance that the final design will be the best design for the job.

> Every element should add to the reader's understanding and provide another entry point to the page.

Three Parts of the Whole

Every design includes three basic elements:

1. **type;**

2. **graphics,** including photography, informational graphics and illustrations (these are often referred to collectively as **art**); and

3. **white space,** the background that is used to unify type and graphics and to provide relief for readers' eyes.

By combining these elements, editors and designers create attractive pages. But the combinations cannot be done haphazardly. The elements must be chosen intelligently, and they must be combined following basic rules of design.

Type

Publications communicate information primarily through type, so it's important to choose type carefully. Careful selection begins with understanding common type terminology.

The broadest classification of type is by **styles** (also called **groups** or **races**). Every type style includes several type **families,** which may include several variations. A **font** is a single variety of type at a specific size; the word is often used incorrectly as a synonym for family.

Publications communicate information primarily through type, so it's important to choose type carefully.

Type Styles

Old-style roman type is a mainstay of publishing. The highly readable type is distinguished by **serifs,** little finishing strokes added to most letters. Brackets connect the serifs to the main letter strokes, creating a smooth transition between strokes. The thickness of letter strokes varies slightly in old-style type, with the variations particularly visible on the curved sections of letters like *o* and *e*. Another distinguishing characteristic of old-style type is that the bowls of letters like *o* and *e* appear to tilt slightly to the left. **Garamond** and **Caslon** are two popular old-style type families.

Example of old-style roman type — Garamond

Example of old-style roman type — Caslon

Modern romans share more than a passing resemblance to the old-styles, but they also differ in important ways. Variations in letter strokes are much more pronounced in modern roman type than in old-style romans. That difference adds impact in large sizes but makes letters hard to read in smaller sizes. Therefore, modern romans work better for headlines than for body copy. Serifs connect directly to the main letter strokes without brackets, further increasing contrast. Bowls of letters run straight up and down. **Bodoni** is the best-known modern roman type family.

Example of modern roman type — Bodoni

Transitional romans combine characteristics of old-style and modern romans, producing type that is as useful for body copy as for headlines. Letters tend to be lighter overall than old-style type, with more contrast between thin and thick strokes. **Baskerville** is a popular transitional type family.

Example of transitional roman type — Baskerville

Sans serif type is also a versatile performer. The uniform letter strokes and lack of serifs produce good legibility in both body copy and headlines. The crisp type looks more modern than roman type and generally is easier to read in head-lines. Sans serif type also works well when type is **reversed,** that is, when white type is printed on a dark background. In contrast, the fine lines of serif type fade into the background and make reading difficult.

Example of reversed sans serif type — Helvetica

Despite the qualities of sans serif type, it's rarely seen in body copy in the United States. That's because some designers believe the monotony of the letters makes large expanses of sans serif hard to read. However, sans serif is commonly used in many European publications, as well as in daring U.S. publications. **Futura, Franklin Gothic** and **Helvetica** are popular sans serif families.

Example of sans serif type — Futura

Example of sans serif type — Franklin Gothic

Example of sans serif type — Helvetica

Four other type styles provide variety for special uses:

Square serifs (also called **Egyptians**) mutated from roman type, with nearly uniform letter strokes and with serifs as thick as the main letter strokes. While difficult to read in smaller sizes, square serifs are good for headlines. **City Light** is a common square serif family.

Example of square serif type — City Light

Script and **cursive** type look like handwriting. They add a touch of class, but at the expense of readability. In script type, letters flow together; cursive type leaves gaps between the letters. Like square serifs, these typefaces are best saved for headlines and other accents.

Example of script type — Berthold Script

Example of cursive type — Pepita

Black letter, also known as **textur,** is formal and difficult to read. Aside from newspaper nameplates and an occasional magazine or newspaper feature head-line, it's rarely seen in publications.

Example of black letter (textur) type — Goudy Text MT

Novelty type encompasses a wide variety of type styles designed for special purposes (Figure 10.1). Type may look like a computer generated it or it was painted through a stencil, it may be composed of animals or people, or it may be decorated with flowers. Many varieties are available, and computer programs allow anyone to create new type styles — but it's important to remember that novelty type is good for special purposes only.

EXAMPLE OF NOVELTY TYPE — COTTONWOOD

Figure 10.1
The creative use of type in this headline reflects the mood of the accompanying article.

Used with permission of the Miami Herald

SCIENCE, 6C
EDITORIALS, **2C**
PUBLIC AFFAIRS TV, **6C**

VIEWPOINT

The Herald

SECTION C
SUNDAY, APRIL 3, 1994

D BRO PB

RANDOM THOUGHTS

SPIRITUAL AMERICA

"As a people, we are uneasy with the perpetual tension between our religious impulses and our unwavering commitment to a secular society. We profess fidelity to traditional morality yet champion individual freedom and resist religious authoritarianism. We want our leaders to adhere to spiritual values yet are suspicious of politicians who seem too eager to appropriate the trappings and jargon of faith. We find comfort in the familiarity of religious traditions, but the ways in which we experience our own spirituality often seem to bear little resemblance to the faith of our fathers and mothers."

Jeffery L. Sheler
writer,
in U.S. News & World Report

HISTORY

"By and large we don't know history because we're indifferent to it, except on those rare occasions when it bumps up against our real or fancied self-interest. We're an impatient people, ever on the go, so the notion of taking the time to devote careful study to the past has never sat well with us. We tend to agree with Henry Ford that history is bunk and, being ignorant of history, we tend to misquote him, since what he actually said was 'History is more or less bunk.'"

Jonathan Yardley
book critic and columnist,
in The Washington Post

FOUR-BY-FOURS

On the popularity of sport-utility vehicles with four-wheel drive:

"The American automobile has long had significance beyond its usefulness. Still, there's something absurd about the increasingly common sight of stockbrokers driving down city streets perched five feet in the air with bull rhinoceros guards — a sort of chrome battering ram — welded to the front of their safari cars.

"Sure, it's a free country.

"But the idea that sport-utility vehicles demonstrate respect for the environment is positively Orwellian: a big green lie."

Jamie Lincoln Kitman
a lawyer and a columnist
for Automobile Magazine and Car Magazine,
in The New York Times

HEALTH CARE

"Reform, as we all know, has been stimulated primarily by the rising costs of medicine, perhaps most disturbingly, the rate of rise of these expenditures. My colleague at the University of Chicago, Mark Siegler, captures Americans' sense of the profligacy of their health care system by recalling Jack Kent Cooke's explanation of why he fired George Allen as coach of the Washington Redskins football team: 'I gave Allen an unlimited budget,' snorted Cook, 'and he exceeded it.'"

Samuel Hellman, M.D.
a professor of radiation and cellular oncology
at the University of Chicago,
in The Brookings Review

WHITEWATER

"If Special Counsel Robert Fiske Jr.'s investigation provides the basis for more serious charges against the Clintons, then they will be forced, as they should be, to face the consequences. But until and unless more serious charges are substantiated, Clinton ought to be free to pursue his substantive agenda. If the GOP and the news media, and White House aides who have created more damage than they have controlled, succeed in creating enough smoke to engulf the Clinton presidency, then all Americans will lose."

Susan Estrich
law professor, University of Southern California,
in The Los Angeles Times

EUPHEMISMS

"Winston Churchill became Britain's prime minister in 1940, after the Nazi armies had roared through Europe. His powerful use of the language became an inspiring weapon of war.

"He told Parliament: 'You ask, what is our policy? I say it is to wage war by land, sea and air. War with all our might and with all the strength God has given us, and to wage war against a monstrous tyranny never surpassed in the dark and lamentable catalogue of human crimes. That is our policy.'

"If Churchill were speaking today in Washington, his words might come out like this: 'Our objective is the employment of tactical weapons in all theaters of combat, backed by maximum effort supplemented by the impact of divine assistance, in order to achieve a successful outcome in suppressing completely the condign opposition.'"

Robert A. Rosenblatt
a Los Angeles Times writer based in Washington,
in The Los Angeles Times

Compiled by Viewpoint Editor Rich Bard

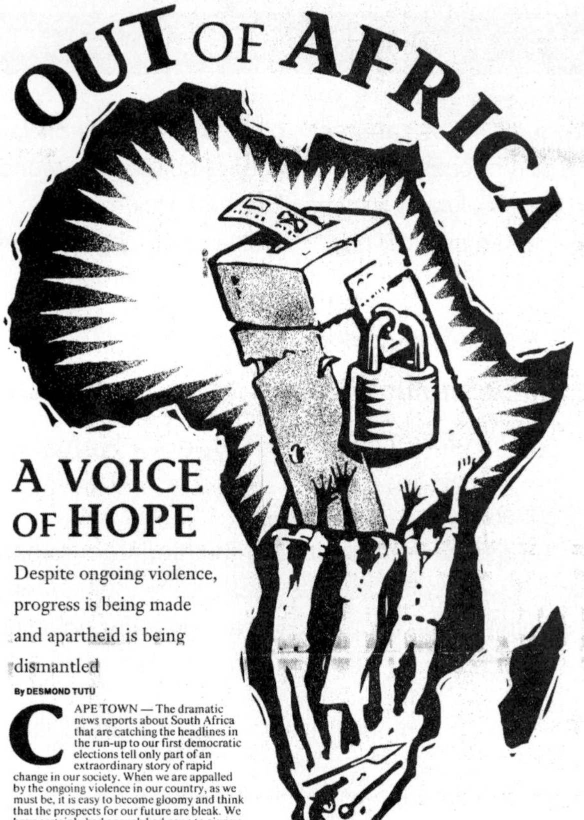

PATTERSON CLARK / Herald Staff

A VOICE OF HOPE

Despite ongoing violence, progress is being made and apartheid is being dismantled

By DESMOND TUTU

CAPE TOWN — The dramatic news reports about South Africa that are catching the headlines in the run-up to our first democratic elections tell only part of an extraordinary story of rapid change in our society. When we are appalled by the ongoing violence in our country, as we must be, it is easy to become gloomy and think that the prospects for our future are bleak. We have certainly had enough bad news to give us a sense of despondency recently:

■ The country's top investigative judge has uncovered evidence revealing, on the face of it, that top police generals, including the second-in-command of the South African Police, have been deliberately inciting violence between opposing political forces in the black community.

■ White right-wingers took to the streets in one of apartheid's discredited black homelands, Bophuthatswana, shooting and killing blacks at random, sparking the chillingly cold-blooded execution of three of them at the hands of homeland police whom they thought were their allies. As law and order broke down, there was widespread looting and destruction of shops.

■ Violence is on the increase in Natal province between supporters of the Inkatha Freedom Party (IFP), who are demanding more autonomy for their region — and a Zulu kingdom — and thus boycotting the election, and those of the African National Congress, who support a unitary state and want to vote.

■ We have seen unprecedented scenes of death and injury on the streets of Johannesburg as those pressing for a sovereign Zulu kingdom marched in support of their demands. The situation in Natal and KwaZulu is critical at present, with most people believing that troops will have to be called in if there is to be a chance of free and fair elections there.

But we have to keep things in a proper perspective. Nobody said it was going to be easy to bring about the massive transformation in our society that the abolition of apartheid entails. Eastern Europe has seen turmoil as well, and communist oppression there lasted only 40 years. In South Africa, the basis of apartheid oppression began more than 300 years ago, with the landing of the first white settlers.

When President F.W. de Klerk announced the unbanning of major political parties and the release of Nelson Mandela in 1990, we knew the transition to democracy would be rough. We did not know how rough, and we certainly underestimated the level of violence there would be. But we knew that apartheid had done enormous damage to our society, and that trying to avoid the disaster we were

PLEASE SEE **SOUTH AFRICA, 4C**

Tutu

Desmond Tutu is the Anglican archbishop of Cape Town. In 1984, he was awarded the Nobel Peace Prize for his activities opposing apartheid in South Africa. He wrote this article for Global Viewpoint.

Take me out to the ballgame – NOT

By MALLIE Z. DiBACCO

I have not been looking forward to the onset of another baseball season, which begins today. You see, in my professional opinion, baseball is not marriage friendly.

My first encounter with the sport was more than 30 years ago. It was Labor Day and I was to begin another first, labor pains at any moment. No reason to miss a doubleheader, my husband Tom reasoned.

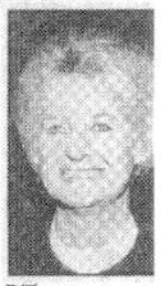

DiBacco

Mallie Z. DiBacco, Ph.D., who teaches at Palm Beach Community College, wrote this article for The Herald.

The Washington Senators were playing some really great ball, I was told. But what I remember most were my frequent trips to the ladies room, each escorted by Tom, of course.

During one such trip, a player on the opposing side (somebody by the name of Mantle) had a grand slam. I had difficulty understanding why so many runs gained by the other side should be considered a lost, memorable moment.

In the style of the college professor he was to become, Tom confided that he could easily have had a career in professional baseball, having been shortstop for the Shadyside Mudsocks. My pride knew no bounds. It was some time before I discovered that his stardom was with friends Stush and Bubba at age 12.

Over the years, I have become a fan in a desperate attempt to bridge the marital gap that looms each summer. Striving to belong to this universal fraternity of dreaming boys, I have learned to use my counseling skills. I ask open-ended questions to excite a two-way, thoughtful conversation — something that heretofore may have been one-dimensional and directed at the umpire, who always seems to be in need of ophthalmic care.

Here's the scenario

The scenario, either at the ballpark or watching the Marlins or Orioles on television, goes something like this:

"Dear, how long do major league games usually last?"

The double-take, in-depth reply is, "Hon, much shorter than ever before."

It's only the end of the fifth inning, and the game is more than 2½ hours old.

"Sweetheart," knowing that I am testing the moment with another interruption, "how would you suggest the game has been shortened from the early days at Griffith Stadium?," proud of remembering the place of my first game.

"Easy," comes the response, "the pitcher no longer has as much warm-up time."

Big deal.

There is another really insightful perspective on my part that I am dying to bring to the table, if you will. The inquiry into the lack of decoration that is terribly noticeable within the players' little huts. Understand, this is not a reflection or even a criticism toward one side or the other. This is just an area that I feel strongly that I have good instincts and a good eye — both of which I understand are important in baseball.

There is simply no attention to attractiveness or even comfort within these little houses, particularly when so much player time is spent there — and television cameras so interested in the player pleasantries occurring within.

I look toward Sweetie once more, trying to catch a possible wandering glassy eye that never seems to happen.

Toward the end of an everlasting evening, after trying hard to remain interested (to say nothing of awake), I contemplate one more baseball topic: spitting. I decide, however, that it is not the time to interject another of my well-planned aims toward baseball bonding. I've learned to save some things for another night.

It's going to be a long, hot summer. Again.

The unfairest tax of all

Donald L. Barlett and James B. Steele are investigative reporters for The Philadelphia Inquirer, a Knight-Ridder newspaper. They have written on taxation for more than 25 years and are authors of a new book, America: Who Really Pays the Taxes? *(Touchstone/Simon & Schuster). This is the second excerpt in a three-part Sunday Viewpoint series.*

By DONALD L. BARLETT
And JAMES B. STEELE

A BOOK EXCERPT

Almost anywhere in the United States, if you own a home you may fairly assume that someone who owns a home of equal value is paying much less in real-estate taxes than you are, and someone else is paying much more. In certain areas the disparities are lawful — indeed, they have been approved by the U.S. Supreme Court. In other areas, the disparities are illegal, but the politicians in charge choose not to correct the situation.

So that you may better appreciate the tax weight you are carrying in life's marathon, let's look at the real-estate taxes on two properties — one in California, the other in New Jersey. We'll begin in California, a state where disparities are perfectly legal. This house, located in the Holmby Hills section of Los Angeles, is owned by Charles Z. and Mary Jane Wick.

It's a nice neighborhood.

You may have heard of the Wicks: They are the closest of friends with Ronald and Nancy Reagan. According to Los Angeles County real-estate records, the house is 7,558 square feet in size, the equivalent of three to four typical suburban tract houses. It has six bedrooms and eight bathrooms. What's the Wick house worth? A conservative estimate — even in a declining real-estate market — would put the value at upward of $1 million. Possibly two or more times that amount.

And what is the real-estate tax bill for a $1 million house surrounded by houses worth $5 million or $10 million or $35 million?

In 1992, it was $5,756.

Percentage-wise, that's far less than the real-estate taxes paid by millions of middle-class individuals and families across the nation who own homes worth a fraction of that amount.

Like Bruce and Dawn Firus.

The Firuses and their four children live in Millville, a town of 25,000 in southern New Jersey. The family owns a five-bedroom, 2,800-square-foot, split-level house on two acres in a pleasant, well-kept neighborhood. The house had an estimated market value of $155,000 in 1993. The real-estate tax bill: $4,800.

If the Firuses were paying real-

PLEASE SEE **TAXES, 5C**

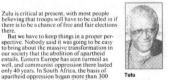

Family Values

Just as human families contain related but distinct members, so do type families. A family might include the following variations:

Variations on a type family — light condensed

Variations on a type family — medium condensed

Variations on a type family — bold condensed

Variations on a type family — ultra light

Variations on a type family — ultra light italic

Variations on a type family — light

Variations on a type family — medium

Variations on a type family — medium italic

Variations on a type family — bold

Variations on a type family — bold italic

Variations on a type family — bold extended

Variations on a type family — outline

Light, medium and **bold** refer to the weight of type and vary from one type designor to another. Generally, though, medium-weight type is the best choice for body copy, and bold type is best for headlines. Lighter type works well for headlines on pages that include several graphics.

Condensed type compresses type to make it seem more vertical. Condensed type is fine for special-effect headlines (such as one on overcrowding or sardines) but of little use for body copy.

Extended type stretches type out over a wider distance, creating an effect opposite that of condensed type. Extended type also is best saved for special uses, such as in a headline on an article about stretch limousines.

Italic type leans slightly to the right, providing a lighter and more elegant look than regular type. While italic type can be used for contrasts in headlines, it is best used sparingly because it is not as easy to read as regular type.

In the Mood

Through years of reading, people come to associate different type styles with different moods. Roman type suggests dignity and formality. Sans serif type appears to be informal and modern. Square serif type styles are powerful, while script and cursive type are delicate and graceful. Novelty type styles convey a wide range of moods.

Through years of reading, people come to associate different type styles with different moods.

Dignity

Power

Informality

Gracefulness

Type Size

Type is measured on a scale different from anything else in the world: the American Point System. There are 72 points to an inch. That wouldn't be so hard to deal with, except that you can't just measure a letter and convert its height to points. The point size of type is larger than any letter can be. To understand why, let's take a tour of type terminology.

A good starting point is the **baseline.** This is, not surprisingly, the line on which most characters rest. The **x-height** corresponds with the top of typical lowercase letters, such as the letter *x*. Letters that tower above the x-height (such as *f, k* and *l*) are known as **ascenders;** letters that drop below the baseline (such as *g, j* and *p*) are known as **descenders.** Type size is determined by measuring the distance from the top of ascenders to the bottom of descenders, then adding a small **shoulder** to keep descenders on one line from bumping ascenders on the line below. Because no letter has both an ascender and a descender — not to mention a shoulder — type size will always be larger than the height of any letter.

Two type styles of the same size can appear to differ in size. One reason is that different styles of type have different x-heights. Type with a taller x-height will appear to be larger than type with a shorter x-height.

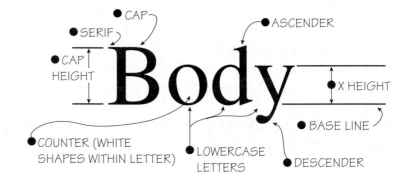

For most publications, body copy falls between 8 and 11 points. Anything smaller than 8 points is hard for most people to read; even 8- and 9-point type can be difficult for older readers. Type set in 5.6- or 6-point type should be saved for credits, box scores and classified ads.

Here's an example of 6-point type. Not too easy to read, is it?

Type set at 8 points isn't bad for body copy for younger readers.

But older readers appreciate this 11-point type.

Sometimes even larger type is used for body copy. When copy is set in wide lines, 12- or 14-point type may be more appropriate. A common rule of thumb is that the line length, measured in **picas** (a pica is a unit of measurement one-sixth of an inch wide) should be one-and-a-half to two times the point size of body copy.

Following that rule, a 3.5-inch-wide line (21 picas) could use either 11-point or 14-point body copy:

Here body copy is set at 11 points on a 21-pica line.

Here copy is set at 14 points on 21 picas.

Nine point type set on a 21-pica line is not as easy to read, is it?

Obviously, not as much copy will fit in a given amount of space when a larger size is used. Small blocks of larger type are sometimes used at the beginning of an article to add emphasis.

Type set 18 points or larger is referred to as **display type.** These larger point sizes are used for headlines and other small blocks of type intended to catch the reader's eye.

Traditionally, display type has been available in increments of 6 or 12 points:

18-point type

24-point type

36-point type

48-point type

60-point type

72-point type

While some publications also have used 30-, 42- and 54-point type, that was about the extent of the variety until recently. Computer typesetting has changed all that. Today editors can set headlines in 43.8-point type if they wish or go up to 1,000 points or more if the mood strikes.

Leading

Leading (rhymes with "sledding") refers to adding space between lines of type. It is named after the practice of slipping small slivers of lead between lines in the days when type was made of metal rather than of pixels on computer screens.

Between one-half and two extra points of leading are added to most body copy to make it easier to read. Both the x-height and the weight of type affect leading. Type with a short x-height has more apparent white space built in so it needs less leading than type with a tall x-height. Heavier type needs more leading than lighter type for the same reason.

Choosing proper leading for display type requires careful visual analysis. Enough leading should be used so that lines do not overlap, but at the same time lines shouldn't appear to be separate elements.

Leading is specified by listing it after the point size. For example, 10/12, called "10 on 12," means 10-point type set on 12 points of leading. Type with no extra leading is said to be **set solid. Reverse leading** removes spacing from the type. This practice, designated as 20/18 for example, works well only for display type set in all capital letters. In such usages, there is no risk that ascenders and descenders will collide.

This is an example of normal leading 10 on 12. This is an example of normal leading 10 on 12. This is an example of normal leading 10 on 12. This is an example of normal leading 10 on 12. This is an example of normal leading 10 on 12. This is an example of normal leading 10 on 12. This is an example of normal leading 10 on 12. This is an example of normal leading 10 on 12.

This is an example of no leading; 10-point type. This is an example of no leading; 10-point type. This is an example of no leading; 10-point type. This is an example of no leading; 10-point type. This is an example of no leading; 10-point type. This is an example of no leading; 10-point type.

A HEADLINE THAT USES REVERSE LEADING (24/20)

Mixing Type

Computers can put hundreds of typefaces at an editor's fingertips, but that can be as much of a curse as a blessing. A sense of coordination is as necessary when choosing type as it is when choosing clothing: Just because you have different colors of socks and shoes doesn't mean you should mix and match them. Many newspapers, newsletters and magazines use one standard body type and one headline type throughout.

The simplest method of mixing type is to combine members of a single family. Because members of a single family are closely related, they work well together. A medium transitional roman type might be used for body copy, the bold version of the same type used for main headlines, and the light italic version for underlines.

Alternatively, type with contrasting characteristics can be combined for a more casual look. For instance, a publication might use an old-style roman for body copy and a sans serif typeface for display type.

A sense of coordination is as necessary when choosing type as it is when choosing clothing.

Other combinations generally don't work as well. Combining two different romans, for example, doesn't provide much contrast yet doesn't look harmonious, either. Using type that "almost matches" is like wearing a blazer and slacks that are almost the same shade of gray: No one will be fooled into thinking that you're wearing a suit. You'd be much better off wearing a blue blazer with the gray slacks, just as you'd be much better off mixing a roman type and a sans serif type.

The most daring publications rely on a single type for body copy but adopt an "anything goes" attitude for headlines (Figure 10.2). This works particularly well in magazines, where the first page of one article is usually separated by several pages of type and ads from the first page of the next article. Therefore, an editor or designer can choose a headline typeface that best captures the mood of each article with little regard for how that headline will look next to a completely differ- ent one. Some newspapers also take this approach on the front pages of inside sections, especially in their feature sections.

Figure 10.2
Innovative use of type marks these two spreads from Texas Monthly.

Texas Monthly Magazine.

Alignment

One final important aspect of type is **alignment.** Alignment refers to the position of type within a given space. The elements on any page or in any package (e.g., headline, readout, article) should always be aligned the same way.

Generally, type is best set **flush left.** In a culture in which people read from left to right, a straight left margin makes it easy for readers to find the start of each line. When type is set even on the left side but not on the right, it is called **flush left, ragged right.**

This is an example of flush left type. The lines of type are aligned on the left side. This is an example of flush left type. The lines of type are aligned on the left side. This is an example of flush left type. The lines of type are aligned on the left side. This is an example of flush left type. The lines of type are aligned on the left side.

Type that is both flush left and flush right — also called **justified type** — provides a more formal appearance. However, justifying type creates uneven spaces between words and requires that many words are hyphenated to make them fit. Those compromises make reading justified type more difficult than reading type that's set flush left, ragged right.

This is an example of justified type. The lines of type are aligned on both sides. This is an example of justified type. The lines of type are aligned on both sides. This is an example of justified type. The lines of type are aligned on both sides. This is an example of justified type. The lines of type are aligned on both sides.

Type set **flush right, ragged left** requires the reader to work hard to find the start of each line and is best avoided.

This is an example of flush right type. The lines of type are aligned on the right side. This is an example of flush right type. The lines of type are aligned on the right side. This is an example of flush right type. The lines of type are aligned on the right side. This is an example of flush right type. The lines of type are aligned on the right side.

Small blocks of typography — such as headlines — can be **centered** and still easily read, but centering more than a few words is not a good idea.

The is an example of centered type. The lines of type are centered on the text measure with equal amounts of space on each side. The lines of type are centered on the text measure with equal amounts of space on each side.

Headlines and Beyond

Headlines, underlines and overlines can provide welcome contrast on a page filled with body copy. Other typographic devices further help spice up type-heavy pages.

Subheads are usually set in 12- to 18-point type and are used to break up long expanses of copy. At their simplest, subheads merely name the topic of the next section. For example, an article in an annual report from Polygram recordings uses subheads to separate copy dealing with each of the company's classical music labels. The subheads read "Decca/London," "Deutsche Grammophon" and "Phillips Classics."

In other publications, subheads summarize key points in upcoming sections, offering a lure to keep the reader reading. For example, an article on a replica of a rain forest at the National Zoo starts with a description of the entrance of the exhibit; after the first section, the subhead "Up the stairs to the rain forest" clearly indicates what comes next.

Breakout quotations (also called **lift quotes, pullout quotations, quote-outs** or **blurbs**) also help break up vast areas of type. These are passages from the main text that are pulled out and run in larger type. As the names suggest, a strong quotation typically is used for this purpose. For example, in a health newsletter article on a new dietary supplement, this breakout quote is used:

> ## "This is not a wonder drug," said the USDA's Anderson, "but it is certainly something that most everybody could benefit from having more of."

Breakout quotations provide another means of layering information and offer another opportunity to catch a reader's attention. In order for breakouts to work, they must add fresh material. The editor who wrote the following headline and breakout wasn't paying attention to that rule:

Storm warning a 'very scary feeling'

> ## "They just keep saying, 'Evacuate immediately. Evacuate immediately.' It's a scary feeling."

Breakouts usually are placed in the middle of body copy, but some publications place them on the side of a page, as they're used in this book. That placement adds white space to pages to make them look more inviting.

No matter where a breakout quote is placed, it never should reveal a surprise ending. For that reason, a breakout quote should not be taken from the last paragraph of an article; the idea is to entice the reader into the copy, not to give the story away.

When the words quoted in a breakout quote are those of the writer, no quotation marks need to be used around them; when the quote comes from a person interviewed for the article, attribution should be used. For example, a quote in which an economist predicts that a major worldwide depression will begin in a year shouldn't be run as a breakout without quotation marks:

> ## Within one year a full-scale depression is likely to sweep the globe.

Subheads are usually set in 12- to 18-point type and are used to break up long expanses of copy.

Quotation marks are mandatory here; attribution is even better.

Other typographic techniques used to break up vast expanses of text include:

- boldface **lead-ins,** in which the first few words of the copy are set in bold type:

    A **boldface lead-in** is when the first few words are bold and the following words are in normal type. A boldface lead-in is when the first few words are bold and the following words are in normal type.

    Lead-ins are usually the same size as body copy, but in some publications they are set in larger type:

    Larger type for this lead-in: Notice how the lead-in is set a few point larger than the copy that follows. Notice how the lead-in is set a few point larger than the copy that follows.

- large **initial letters,** which stand as tall as two to six lines of body copy:

    Sample text with initial cap that is 60-point type and the body text is 12-point. Sample text with initial cap that is 60-point type and the body text is 12-point. Sample text with initial cap that is 60-point type and the body text is 12-point. Sample text with initial cap that is 60-point type and the body text is 12-point.

- **dingbats,** which also sometimes signify the end of the copy:

    Notice how these paragraphs are separated by a dingbat character. Notice how these paragraphs are separated by a dingbat character.

    Notice how these paragraphs are separated by a dingbat character. Notice how these paragraphs are separated by a dingbat character.

- and **white space:**

    Notice how these paragraphs are separated by extra white space that gives the reader a break. Notice how these paragraphs are separated by extra white space that gives the reader a break.

    Notice how these paragraphs are separated by extra white space that gives the reader a break. Notice how these paragraphs are separated by extra white space that gives the reader a break.

Choosing Photographs

Used intelligently, type alone can make for an attractive page (Figure 10.3). But an entire publication that contained only words would be dull. Therefore, publications of all sorts also contain photographs and information graphics. Because photos are the most common graphic element, we'll start by discussing them.

At many publications, a picture editor, chief photographer or other person specializing in visual communication chooses photographs. That's not always

A Publication for Employees of William Rainey Harper College

Volume 8, Number 9   October, 1993

Development Office Announces Goals

The appointment of Felice Avila as Harper's Director of Development and External Affairs brings new energy to the office. Projects have been prioritized—both short and long term—and staff members are working closely with the Foundation Board to secure resources to support College projects.

Harper's Development Office has several short-term goals. During the next few months, members of the Educational Foundation will contact area corporations, businesses/industries and individuals for donations. In addition, Barb Knoff, who coordinated last month's golf outing, is now planning the Arts for Our Sake Ball slated for October 30. These events, says Avila, provide monies for projects that did not receive funding this year. Proceeds from the golf outing, for example, will provide grants for patients in the College's Northwest Cardiac Rehab Center. "We'll pay the tuition for patients who otherwise would not be able to use the Center," Avila explains.

Proceeds from the ball, on the other hand, are earmarked for the arts—specifically Harper's art, music, speech and theater areas. In addition, the Alumni Association is now working with its corps of 125 charter members to elect a board of directors, develop a mission statement, and define future activities and plans.

"We're also working with Pat Mulcrone of AED to improve our grants operation," Avila says. "We're setting up a system and putting together a manual to assist those who are seeking external resources." She adds that the office will also provide a library of resources, forms and grant writing procedures.

As the office's final short term project, Avila has assigned Cindy McShane the task of incorporating donor information into a software program.

In the long term, however, the College is set to embark on a major gifts campaign. The Board of Trustees recently appointed the consulting firm Clements and Associates to determine how to achieve the College's fundraising goals most effectively. Avila stresses, however, that she hopes that gift giving will come from all segments of the College community. "We hope to involve the entire community," she says. "This includes community leaders, alumni and residents as well as our staff. Even a donation of $1 shows a commitment to the College and its future."

Figure 10.3
Used with permission of The Insider.

the case, however, so "word" editors also should know how to select good photographs.

Just as with any piece of writing — and with any other graphic — a good photograph should make a clear point. This should be an editor's first criterion in selecting photos to use with a piece of copy. Photos that require the reader to work to make sense of them are worse than no photos at all.

Other criteria for selecting photographs include:

Impact.   A photograph typically is given the job of grabbing the attention of an inattentive reader. In order to accomplish that, a photo must have impact. Part of the impact comes from proper play on the page, which we'll talk about later. Even the largest display and most prominent play cannot make a weak photo grab readers, though.

Emotional Appeal.   The best photographs contain human interest, touching the reader emotionally. As hackneyed as it might seem, children and animals often provide strong emotional appeal.

When you have the choice between a shot that conveys emotion and another that doesn't, always choose the one that does. For example, a photo of a school supervisor presenting a teacher with a plaque naming her teacher of the year probably lacks emotional appeal. But a shot that shows delighted children listening to the teacher has plenty of emotion. If none of the shots available has strong emotional appeal, the best solution may be to run the copy without photos.

Presence of Action.   Stiff, posed shots are fine for the family album, but they have little place in the mass media. Photographs should show people doing something. Interesting composition and unusual perspective also help prevent mundane subjects from looking static.

Design Possibilities.   Photos and other visuals help to break the monotony of uniform lines of text. Two important considerations when choosing combinations of photos to package together are the shape of the photos and the perspective of the photos (Figure 10.4).

1. **Shapes:** Mixing horizontal and vertical photographs is the best way to create visual interest. Only when photos are closely related — such as before-and-after shots of a person or place — should they be exactly the same size and shape. In all other cases, variety should be emphasized.

2. **Perspectives:** Every photo package should include shots taken from a variety of perspectives. **Overview** shots are taken from a distance and set the scene, showing what a place looked like, how many people were there, the mood or ambience, and other details. **Medium** shots capture interaction among a few people. **Close-ups** are portrait shots of an individual person. Even a photo package that uses only two shots benefits from using different perspectives.

Artistic Quality.   While not easy to quantify, it is easy to *see* the difference between a snapshot and a carefully planned and shot photograph. Careful planning of lighting, mood, composition and depth of field elevate a photo from mundane to magnificent.

Style

WEDNESDAY
AUGUST 29, 1990

SECTION B

At Nunan's, in the Cape Porpoise area of Kennebunkport, the lobsters don't snap back.

Not far from the teeming carnival of summer people, worn-out tourists, and the president and his media entourage lies the calm, quaint and elegant village that first drew visitors to . . .

KENNEBUNKPORT

By J. BARRY MOTHES
Staff Writer

KENNEBUNKPORT – Standing at the edge of a garden in a Cape Porpoise backyard on a perfect summer night, a longtime resident says, "In a way, the war has really come to Kennebunkport."

She mentions hundreds of international media people crawling all over town and satellite-dish-topped mobile trucks and police checkpoints and who knows how many truly undercover types walking around in tourists' garb and King Hussein of Jordan dropping in for a couple hours to discuss the Iraqi situation with President Bush.

Just down the road, a vacationing family of four from New York sits down in a battleship-gray wooden booth at Nunan's Lobster Shack for a no-frills $50 or $60 feed on lobster and clams.

In Dock Square, the retail heart of Kennebunkport, summer people and worn-out tourists are looking for a place to park themselves for a cold drink after a day at Goose Rocks or Bush-watching. The traffic chugs by, as it has since early in the morning.

Such are the different sides of summer life these days in Kennebunkport and the surrounding towns and villages.

For decades a lush place of tree-lined streets, rambling turn-of-the-century summer inns, winding rivers and inlets and wide, firm beaches evoking a Jazz Age summer bliss, Kennebunkport has been drawn into the 1990s.

Kennebunkport (population 3,042; summertime population about 30,000) is easily the most-mentioned place in Maine these days. Maybe even the country.

With President Bush in the midst of an extended summer vacation at the family's coastal compound here, and events in the Persian Gulf gripping the world, it appears daily as a dateline in

Bush-watching along Ocean Avenue is big this summer.

STYLE ON THE ROAD

More from Style's trip to Kennebunkport:

Artist Mike Stiler is still at home in Kennebunkport, and if the town bears the signature of any one artist, Stiler's the one.

If you're walking the Kennebunkport streets and feel a sudden urge to get with the "kpm" style, check out this week's Temptations. . . .

Tips for finding good art, food and a haircut.
Pages 2-4B

newspapers and magazines around the world. Its craggy bluffs serve as a backdrop for nightly television reports.

But beyond officialdom and the non-stop scramble to find out when the president will be teeing it up over at Cape Arundel, there's

Please see PORT, Page 2B

There's much to see off the beaten path of Kennebunkport, postcard classics such as this vintage pick-up truck parked in a driveway in Cape Porpoise.

Most intricate house on the block: the Wedding Cake House along Route 35. Built in 1826, the house is closed to visitors but a gift studio is open.

Peter Spadone sands the edge of a hardwood table that he and partner Steve Rieger designed and made in a workshop.

Staff photos by Jack Milton

Figure 10.4
A mix of sizes, shapes and perspectives makes for an interesting photo page.

Used with permission of the Portland (Maine) Press Herald.

Technical Quality.   Editors working with students or other inexperienced photographers have to make sure photographs are technically acceptable. Even professional photographers can run into difficulties. Aspects that an editor must evaluate include:

1. **Contrast:** The printing process can turn a low-contrast photograph into undecipherable mud and a high-contrast photograph into a juxtaposition of dark and light spots with no range of tones in between. Fortunately, this problem usually can be anticipated and corrected through careful photographic printing.

   For most publications, a photographic print that looks great to the eye will also look great when reproduced. However, that's not as true for photos — especially black-and-white images — printed in newspapers. Newsprint absorbs ink and has a limited range of reproduction, so a slightly "soft" or "flat" print — one that has no real black or white — usually works best.

2. **Color:** Color photos and other color graphics also test many newspapers. Unlike magazines, most newspapers have problems reproducing strong colors such as bright red. What looks fine in a photo may well look washed out in print.

3. **Grain:** A print looks grainy when the photo has been shot with high-speed film (often used in low light) or, more commonly, when the print was made by over-enlarging a small section of a low-quality original. Digital retouching can soften the grain but not eliminate it.

4. **Focus:** Major details of photographs should be in sharp focus. Occasionally, however, a photographer will use selective focus to add emphasis to a shot, blurring everything but the focal point of the shot.

5. **Blemishes:** Dust specks, hairs and other blemishes are the bane of traditional photography. Most can be eliminated or touched up. Scratches are another matter. They usually are on the film, so touch-up work is the only solution and one that tends to be obvious to readers.

   Digital photography and retouching can help eliminate such problems in two ways. Photographers who use traditional cameras can clean up scratches and other problems with computer programs such as PhotoShop. Photographers working with digital cameras produce photos without using film, so dirt and scratches are not a problem to begin with.

Editors must be as careful in checking the accuracy of photographs as they are in checking the accuracy of words.

Photo Accuracy.   Editors must be as careful in checking the accuracy of photographs as they are in checking the accuracy of words. While it is possible to get inaccurate information from photographers, the bigger risk comes when editors use old photos from the files. At a minimum, editors should verify that (1) an image is of the correct person (photos sometimes are misfiled) and (2) the image is up-to-date. A good rule of thumb: Don't use file photos that were taken more than two years ago. Editors of the Business section at The Washington Post learned that lesson when they ran a file photo of a local executive who had lost 60 pounds since the photo was filed.[2]

Choosing the best photographs for publication can be a challenge for begin-
ners. David Griffin, former assistant director of layout and design for National
Geographic, suggests that a good first step is asking what you want the photos
to accomplish. In this sidebar, he explains his philosophy.

**Selecting
Photographs**

- **Do you want images that illustrate exactly what the text is claiming?**
  This can be as specific as wanting to see head shots of every person interviewed in the text, or as vague as choosing images that reinforce a sense
  of mood presented in the written part of the story. Using "content" as the
  only criteria can unfortunately push you into the corner of allowing inferior
  photographic quality to creep into the story.

- **Do you want images that will act as "eye candy" to attract a reader to
  the page?** Here may be the other extreme, where images need to be bold,
  colorful, pleasing or shocking. The down side of relying heavily on impact is
  that the images may end up telling a completely different story than the text
  does. While this may be the easiest way to create striking designs, they will
  be shallow of meaning, leaving readers possibly confused, or worse, no
  longer interested in your disjointed publication.

- **Do you want the photographs to tell their own story altogether?**
  Allowing the images to follow a narrative as seen from the photographer's
  point of view is most often done with the traditional photo story. You will
  need to consider how the story opens, create a sequence of information
  that fits the subject and then make a logical exit. The core responsibility as
  designer will be to find the correct balance of images that attract and
  images that tell a story.

At National Geographic, editors and photographers strive to mix these three
approaches but lean heavily toward the creation of photo stories. Contrary to
what many word editors claim, we understand that readers often look at the
photographs before deciding to read a published story. This means the photographs must be able to explain the subject matter fully, on their own. It also
means the photographs should resonate with the text.

Photography is too often a poorly handled afterthought at many publications. Many editors choose photographs based on the specifics of the text,
regardless of the image's ability to stand on its own. The choice is justified by
claiming, "It makes sense once you've read the text." Here's the problem
though: People don't read the text first — they look at the photos.

Careless use of a file photograph can mislead readers. Time magazine came
under fire when it ran a cover photo of an exasperated President Bill Clinton and
adviser George Stephanopoulos under a headline referring to the investigation of
Clinton's Whitewater affairs. In actuality, the photo had been taken weeks before
the issue of Whitewater had emerged. A Time spokesman defended the use of the
photo by noting, "I don't think the readers of Time expect the cover photo is going
to be a representation of that event."[3]

**Scanning
Photographs**

Increasingly, photographers are turning to digital cameras that let them download their work directly to an office computer. But in smaller publications, traditional photographs are still common. For editors working with desktop publishing software, that means taking an additional step: scanning them in.

A scanner is simply a device that translates a continuous tone photograph into a series of dots. Black-and-white photos are translated into black dots on a white background. Color photos are translated into three sets of dots using combinations of red, green and blue (called RGB). Because of that, the computer file created by scanning a color photo is three times as large as the file created by scanning a black-and-white photo.

When you're ready to scan a photo, you start by launching an image editing program such as PhotoShop. First select the software supplied with the scanner as your capture device (File>Import>Select TWAIN_32 Source or TWAIN Select), then run the program (File>Import>TWAIN_32 or TWAIN Acquire).

Once the scanning window opens, you have several options (Figure 10.5). First, you need to select the mode. Most scanning software lets you choose between line art, halftone, grayscale and color. Line art is the best choice for simple pen-and-ink illustrations, such as comic strips. Halftone is used to capture photos that have been printed in newspapers and books. Grayscale is the best choice for black-and-white photos, while color is the obvious choice for color photos. If prompted to choose RGB or CMYK (cyan, magenta, yellow and black), pick RGB.

Once you've chosen the proper mode, you should prescan the image. During this step, the scanner takes a quick picture of your source. Then, using a selection tool, you choose how much of the source you want to capture. For instance, you may want to just use one person's face from a group photo; scanning the whole image would waste time and possibly result in a lower quality image.

The next step is choosing size and resolution. These two are interrelated; scanning an image at 100 percent and 72 dpi (dots per inch) is the same as scanning at 50 percent and 144 dpi.

The space you're trying to fill in a page layout determines the size. The type of publication you're producing determines the resolution. A photo to be used in a newsletter is probably fine at 120 dpi; a photo for the front cover of a glossy magazine will more likely be scanned at 1,200 or 2,400 dpi. Keep in mind that doubling the resolution causes file size to quadruple — large photos can eat up lots of computer disk space.

The final step is saving your scanned image. The best format for photographs is TIFF (Tagged-Image File Format). To save in this format, choose File>Save As in your image editing program. (In PhotoShop, you first may have to choose Layer>Flatten Image.) Once you've chosen TIFF as your format, you'll have to specify the byte order (IBM or Macintosh). You're then ready to import the photograph into your desktop publishing program.

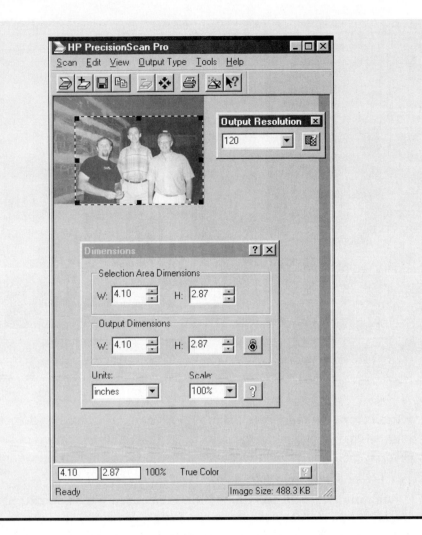

Figure 10.5
Scanning software allows the user to select a wide range of settings.

Cropping Photos

Once editors have selected photos, they have to crop and size them.

Cropping is the visual equivalent of editing a piece of copy. The idea remains the same: Cut away all unnecessary information to emphasize the essential information. Cropping has been called "looking for pictures within pictures," that is, cutting to the heart of the picture.

Good cropping starts with assessing the point of the photo. Properly cropped, that point will dominate a given space, rather than being hidden in a larger image crammed into the same space.

Photos can be cropped either manually or electronically. Working manually, an editor uses a grease pencil to put marks in each of the borders of a photograph to indicate what section should be used. Editors working with computers can crop photos with a few clicks of the mouse (Figure 10.6).

While the mechanical part of cropping takes little skill, the aesthetic part requires a good deal of it. Like photography itself, cropping is more of an art than a science, so there are no simple formulas to follow. While the basic rule is to eliminate everything except the heart of a photo, several other points are important to consider:

Figure 10.6
Cropping with a computer program is a simple matter. Just drag a "marquee" around the area you want.

Screen capture by Anne Martens and Steve Konick.

- **Good cropping preserves the mood:** An overview photo of a homeless person sleeping alone in a large cemetery carries a distinct mood of loneliness. Cropping out everything except the person destroys that mood — and probably loses the point of the picture.

- **Background should be retained if it is necessary for context:** Similarly, a medium shot that shows firefighters preventing a mother from entering a burning house loses much of its context if the house is cut out.

- **Leave room for movement:** When a photo shows movement — and remember, photos *should* — editors need to allow space for the subjects to move into. A baseball player charging into the edge of a photograph is a clumsy sight.

Sizing: Bigger Is Better

If you're going to use photos, use them BIG. Not surprisingly, the bigger the photograph, the more likely readers will notice it. With luck they'll go on to read nearby copy.

In the "Eyes on the News" study, Mario Garcia and Pegie Stark found while a little more than half of all readers looked at one-column newspaper photos, between 87 and 94 percent of readers took notice of photos covering three to five columns (Figure 10.7). So while any photo is better than no photo, larger photos are much more successful than smaller ones at catching readers' attention.

One warning about large photos: The larger a photo is made, the more obvious its technical flaws will become. Only the best photos can be played large on high-quality magazine pages and covers.

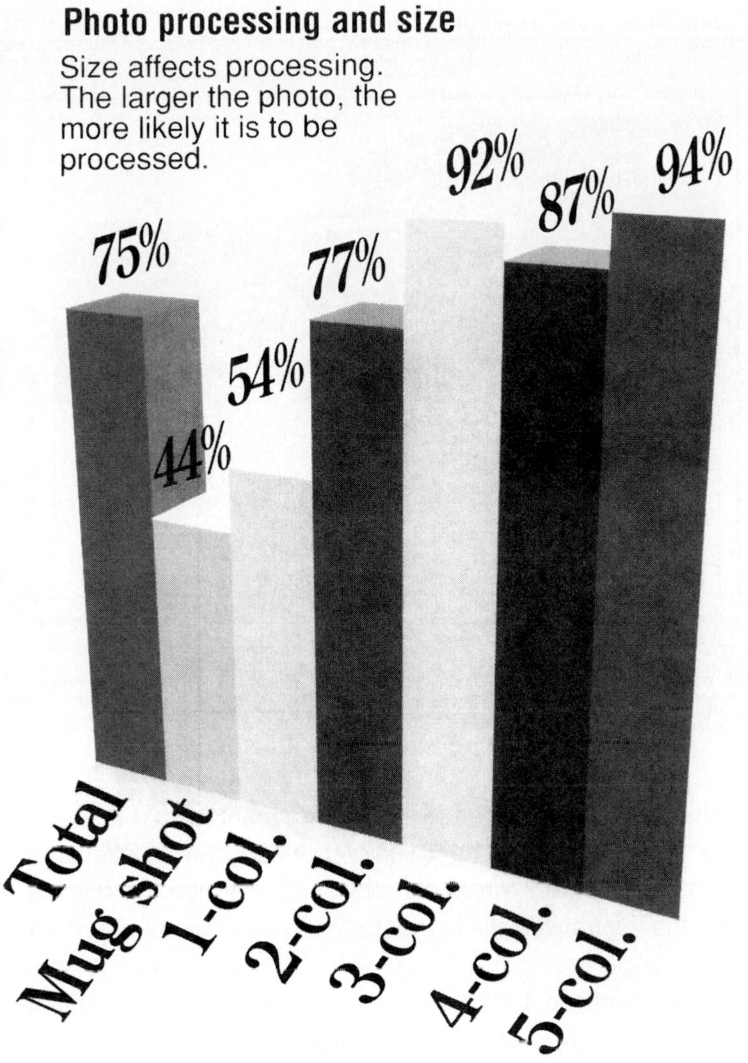

Photo processing and size

Size affects processing. The larger the photo, the more likely it is to be processed.

75%   **44%**   **54%**   **77%**   **92%**   **87%**   **94%**

Total   Mug shot   1-col.   2-col.   3-col.   4-col.   5-col.

Figure 10.7
Large photos generally attract attention better than small ones.

Reprinted from "Eyes on the News." Used with permission of Mario Garcia and Pegie Stark.

Rarely will a cropped photograph fit exactly into a space that an editor has available. A photo usually has to be **sized** to fit, that is, reduced or enlarged.

Not long ago, editors who needed to size photos hunkered over their sizing wheels to determine how big the photos would end up being. Fortunately, computers have laid the sizing wheel to rest. A few clicks of the mouse button let an editor quickly determine the final size of a photo.

One warning on sizing photographs: Editors can select *either* how wide or how deep a photo should be. The computer then determines the proportionate change in the other dimension. Typically, editors select a width, then use the computer to tell them how deep a photo will be at that width. What editors *cannot do* is change the width and depth independently; doing so would grotesquely distort the image (Figure 10.8).

Writing Cutlines

"Every picture tells a story," Rod Stewart once sang, and indeed every good photograph should convey a clear message. Unless a photo is used only as an

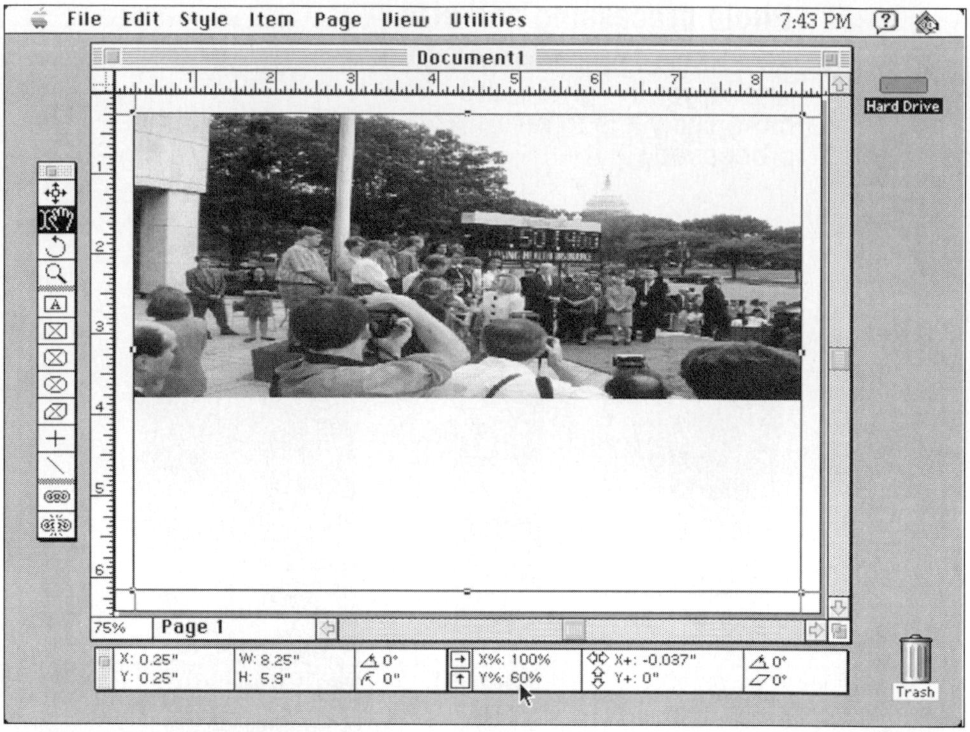

Figure 10.8
An editor can specify either the depth or the width for a photo to be cropped. Trying to manipulate both independently results in distortions like this one or loss of part of the image that was wanted.

Screen capture by Anne Martens and Steve Konick.

Cutlines provide yet another opportunity for layering, providing information to the reader that the headline and photo do not contain.

illustration that runs with a feature article, however, it should be accompanied by words in the form of **cutlines.** The "Eyes on the News" study offers support for the importance of cutlines: While readers looked at only about a third of all cutlines (29 percent), that figure was still higher than the percentage of text they looked at (25 percent).

Cutlines, like captions (the headlines that often run above or beside photos — we'll get to them next), provide yet another opportunity for layering, providing information to the reader that the headline and photo do not contain.

Cutlines run the gamut from concise to packed with information. The simplest cutlines run with **mug shots,** small portraits that accompany an article and add visual appeal to a dull page. Some publications permit only the most basic information to accompany a mug shot: the person's name. While such a **nameline** is better than no cutline, it's not *much* better. A key reason to run a mug shot is to try to catch readers' attention. Once readers take the bait, they'll most likely next move to the cutline to identify the person. If readers find that an unfamiliar face is accompanied only by an unfamiliar name, though, they'll likely move along.

Far better is a nameline that includes a second line of type that tells who the person is or what he or she has said or done (Figure 10.9). That additional information can make all the difference in keeping or losing a reader's attention.

Photos other than mug shots that run with an article use a type of cutline often referred to as **skeleton lines** (Figure 10.10). The name of this type of cutline is derived from the fact that the accompanying copy will provide most information the reader needs; therefore, the cutline needs only to identify people in a photo and tell what they are doing. Some publications limit skeleton lines to one line of type; other publications allow as many lines as needed.

Angus King

Says "We've come a long way"

Staff photo by Jack Milton

Pamela Perkins, the voice of USM's new
automated telephone system, wonders if a
student caller will recognize her voice in public.

Figure 10.9 (left)
A nameline.

Used with permission of the
Portland (Maine) Press Herald.

Figure 10.10 (right)
Skeleton lines. This photo ran
with an article.

Used with permission of the
Portland (Maine) Press Herald.

Wild lines (Figure 10.11) are the most heavy-duty of all cutlines. They are
used with stand-alone photos. Photos can stand alone when there is no accompanying article or when the article is located elsewhere in the publication. For
example, newspapers often run photos on the front page of a section to promote

Tractor-trailer overturns in Falmouth

Staff photo by David A. Rodger

A Falmouth firefighter pours foam on the diesel tanks of an overturned tractor-trailer on an entrance ramp to Interstate 95 Thursday, while
others work to move the trailer off the truck cab. Rescue personnel used a power rescue tool to free Jerry Howard, the driver. The accident
was one of four reported in Falmouth within an hour during afternoon rush-hour traffic. None resulted in life-threatening injuries. Story, 1B

Figure 10.11
Wild lines. The article
accompanying this photo
ran on a different page.
Notice also the caption
that runs above the
photograph.

Use with permission of the
Portland (Maine) Press Herald.

an article inside that section. Because they are not placed next to an article that will help inform readers, wild lines have to do more work than either other type of cutline. Consequently, they typically run at least two lines long, and three and four lines are not unusual.

When writing skeleton lines or wild lines, following these guidelines will help you produce effective results:

Don't Restate the Obvious.   Remember that a cutline should add to what the reader can see in the photo. Cutlines such as this one, which ran during the 1992 presidential election campaign, aren't helpful:

President Bush raises both hands, Bill Clinton raises one as Ross Perot watches.

If there was nothing else to say about the photo, why was it used?

Make Sure the Cutline and Photo Go Together.   At the same time, the cutline and photo should not be strangers. The two should seem to belong together. A large, full-color front-page newspaper photo of President Clinton delivering his State of the Union address was accompanied by a cutline reading

President Clinton works on a revision of his State of the Union address in the Oval Office.

Evidently, the photo was changed once the address began after the first edition deadline, but no one replaced the cutline.

Identify Every Visible Face.   People like to read about and see other people. When faces are visible in a photo, names should be given for their owners. When necessary, use locating words ("center," "to his or her right," etc.) for clarity. Better yet, identify people by a visual reference:

Author Charlotte Wynne presents a copy of her latest book to Randi Barrett, head of the county library association.

Make Sure Identities Are Correct.   This should be obvious, but many mistakes get through. Sometimes they result from careless editing, as in this example:

Among the artists were Amand Corn, 10, daughter of Bryan Tammy Cooper of Brooklyn Park; Lori Koch, 10, daughter of Conrad and Koch of Sunnyfield Estates; and Dwayne Campbell, 10, son of Dwayne Debbie Campbell of Brooklyn Park.

Another case of gender bending probably took place beyond the editor's grasp, most likely in the newspaper composing room, where a worker placed a cutline under the wrong picture. The picture, of two men, read:

Jennifer Neuse and her mother, Pat Dunton, of Corpus Christi, Texas, whose father's plane was shot down in the Korean War.

A photograph of two women on the jump page carried the same cutline. Presumably, it was correct in that placement.

Even nonhumans need to be identified carefully. In one publication, an article about the famous Chesapeake Bay crabs of Maryland was accompanied by a photo of a stone crab, found a few hundred miles to the south.

Please Explain.   Readers should be illuminated by cutlines, not bewildered. Such illumination requires answering all possible questions about the photo. One photo showed an 86-year-old woman, a handgun and a Chihuahua wearing a coat. The cutline explained that the woman had fired at an intruder (presumably with the gun), but offered no clue as to what the dog had to do with things.

Similarly, sometimes the significance of a photo is not clearly visible. A picture of the president signing a bill, for example, should tell the reader why the event is significant enough to merit a photograph:

POOR: *The president signs the jobs bill.*

BETTER: *The president signs the jobs bill. Supporters say the bill will create as many as 150,000 new jobs within the next year.*

Make Sure What You Write Is What We See.   No one should attempt to write a cutline without seeing how a photo will be cropped. Otherwise, the cutline might refer to people or other elements that were cut from the photo.

Try to Give Each Photo Its Own Cutline.   When two or more photos are used together, the tendency sometimes is to write a group cutline. Such a cutline works only when it physically touches all the photos being described. Even then, no cutline should try to describe more than three photographs. Cramming information for more than three photos into one cutline makes it hard for a reader to find information.

Don't Start With an Unfamiliar Name.   If a cutline is intended to attract attention, it should start with something catchy. These opening words aren't much of a draw:

Len Fu, 6, joined hundreds of others in protesting a new law that Asians say discriminates against them.

Far better would be:

Protesting a new law that Asians say discriminates against them, 6-year-old Len Fu joins hundreds of others at East Park.

Avoid Clichés, Puns and Mind-Reading.   At the same time, don't struggle to write a clever cutline. It's more likely the reader will notice the struggling than the cleverness. Clichés and puns are generally not good ideas. Just tell the reader what's happening, and don't go beyond that, as this example does:

Fido the dalmatian seems to be thinking that he'd like to join his master for a cold drink on a recent dog day afternoon.

Don't Try to Make a Cutline Do Too Much.   An artsy photograph of Chinese bicyclists framed within the front wheel of another cyclist carried this cutline:

Tens of thousands of people on Flying Pigeon bicycles pass the Forbidden City's Tiananmen Gate in Beijing every day. China is reported to have 400 million bicycles on its roads.

All well and good. But then this line was added:

The switch to a market economy has now forced state-owned Flying Pigeon to compete with privately run bicycle companies.

That may be true, but it (a) breaks the mood of the cutline and (b) introduces a second idea that begs for elaboration.

Use Present Tense to Describe the Action.   The action shown in a photo typically is described before any other information is given, and present tense is used in describing that action. If a time element is needed in the cutline, it is best to place it in a separate sentence:

POOR: *Mob kingpin Joseph Galliani heads into court for his trial on extortion charges yesterday.*

BETTER: *Mob kingpin Joseph Galliani heads into court. His trial on extortion charges began yesterday.*

Similarly, place references to events that have not yet occurred outside the first sentence:

Mob kingpin Joseph Galliani heads into court. His trial on extortion charges began yesterday. Three of Galliani's aides will go on trial next month.

Give Credit Where It's Due.   The photographer or organization that supplied a photo always should be credited. Credit style should be consistent throughout a publication. If photos are manipulated, that information should be stated clearly in the cutline. Merely labeling it a "photo illustration" or otherwise attempting to weasel out of telling the truth is shameful behavior.

Writing Captions

While almost every photo needs a cutline, not all photos get captions. Captions are headlines that summarize the photo in two to five words (Figure 10.12). They offer one more layer on the page, so they also should present a new piece of information to the reader.

NURI VALLBONA / Herald Staff

AT LAST, A SMOKE: Security guard Alberto Falcon smokes outside the Dade County Courthouse, where smoking is prohibited inside.

Figure 10.12
This caption, called a read-in, introduces the cutline.

Used with permission Miami Herald.

Captions should be informative above all else. The reader's main question upon seeing a photograph is, "What's happening here?" The caption should answer that question immediately. So, for example, the caption above a photo of a pile of decomposing bodies reads:

Massacre at Rwandan religious community

While it would be a rare editor who would try to be clever with a caption for that photo, misplaced cleverness is not hard to find. A photo of a man being searched by police ran with this caption:

Frisky business

And one obnoxious copy editor wrote this caption for a picture that showed a member of the Italian Parliament yanking on another member's ears:

Lend me your ears

(All right, I'll confess — I wrote it!)

As with cutlines, captions need to make sense to the reader. Remember the bicycle photograph? The caption read "Flying Pigeon." There wasn't a bird in sight in the shot, so it's hard to imagine a reader's reaction other than confusion.

Captions sometimes appear as the first few words of a cutline. When that style is used, the caption is called a **read-in.** Other than the name change, the same rules apply.

> The reader's main question upon seeing a photograph is, "What's happening here?" The caption should answer that question immediately.

Creating Information Graphics

As powerful as photographs may be, they can't do everything. If an editor handling an auto story wants to rank car manufacturers by sales, indicate what states

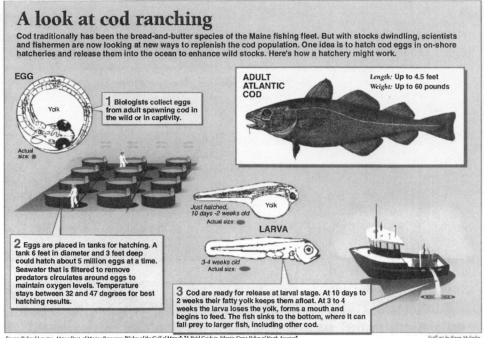

require auto emission tests or track changes in car sales during the last 10 years, photos can't do the job.

Enter information graphics, better known as **infographics.** Infographics include a wide range of devices — text boxes, charts, maps, illustrations and diagrams — used to present information outside the confines of an article (Figure 10.13). Placing information from an article into an infographic can make the article easier to read and the extracted information easier to understand. The graphic treatment also provides another entry point on the page for readers.

While complex infographics are left to artists, desktop computers have given editors the power to create simple infographics in minutes. The ability to create computer infographics is becoming a requirement for many editing jobs. In the next section, we'll look at the types of infographics editors might be expected to create.

When to Use Infographics

In "The Newspaper Designer's Handbook," Tim Harrower suggests the following questions to determine whether an infographic is appropriate. They apply to newsletters, magazines, corporate reports and other publications, as well as newspapers.

Ask yourself:

What's missing from this story? What would complete the picture for those who read it — or draw readers in who might otherwise turn the page?

Is the text bogged down by a series of numbers? Details? Dates? Definitions? Comparisons? Can something be pulled out and played up?

What data needs further clarification: Statistics? Geographical details? Trends? History? Does the story overestimate the readers' knowledge?

How much time and space do we have for a graphic or sidebar? Can we squeeze in a quick list? A small map? A huge clip-'n'-save poster page?

What's the point of this sidebar or graphic? Is there one clear idea we're trying to illustrate — or are we just compiling a lump of statistics?[4]

Working With Words

The most basic infographics are simply text in a box. These **text boxes** often are shaded to contrast with the articles they accompany, but they do not have to be.

Text boxes perform a variety of functions. Common uses include:

Lists.   In our information society, people never seem to tire of lists. Just ask David Letterman how popular lists can be; his nightly "Top 10" list has long been a popular feature of his program. A list of interesting tidbits or suggestions can complement virtually any article. For example, a feature article on an increase in vegetarianism might be accompanied by a list of vegetarian restaurants. An article on rising executive salaries might be accompanied by a list of the 10 highest-paid chief executive officers in the country.

Indexes.   Indexes are commonly associated with Harper's magazine, which has grouped together related items in its monthly index to provide insights into the modern world (Figure 10.14).

Fact Boxes.   A close cousin of lists, fact boxes (Figures 10.15 and 10.16) present vital statistics on people or, occasionally, things. Fact boxes often are used with articles on political candidates. They also can be used to give readers a quick overview of a plant or animal.

"What You Can Do" Boxes.   These text boxes offer readers information useful in following up on an article (Figure 10.17). For instance, the text box accompanying a magazine travel article might offer tips on how to get to the destination; when to go; where to stay; where to eat; and what to do. A text box that accompanies an article focusing on a problem can offer readers hints on combating the problem.

Summary Boxes.   Some newspapers use short summaries either just before the text begins or in a box placed in the text. This additional entry point into the story offers one more chance to hook the reader's attention.

Chronologies.   Long sequences can be presented at a glance in boxes that offer the reader quick insight into the background of an event.

Reader Participation Boxes.   Coupons to request more information, contest entries and polls are all examples of this type of text box.

Excerpts.   Articles on writers or poets often include one or more excerpts of their work to give readers a sense of the authors' styles.

Figure 10.14
An index.

Courtesy Glamour. © 1994 by
Conde Nast Publications Inc.

THE WEDDING INDEX

Median age at first marriage in 1992: Men, 26.5 years. Women, 24.4 years.

Median age at first marriage in 1955: Men, 22.6 years. Women, 20.2 years.

Median age at first marriage in 1890: Men, 26.1 years. Women, 22.0 years

Year in which the highest number of marriages was reported: 1984, with 2,477,192 marriages.

Year in which the highest number of divorces was reported: 1992, with 1,215,000.

Month with the most marriages in 1992: June.

Month with the most divorces in 1992: July.

Percent of couples to marry in a judge's chambers at city hall: 0.4.

Percent of couples marrying on a Saturday: 83.9.

According to wedding-day folklore, the unluckiest day of the week on which to be married: Saturday.

Percent of brides who will keep their own names: 29.

Percent of marriages in which the bride, groom or both have been married before: 40.

Cost to get married at City Hall in Manhattan: $30 for the license; $25 for the ceremony, payable in cash.

Average cost of a formal wedding: $17,470.

Average cost of an engagement ring: $2,917.

Average cost of a wedding gown (including headpiece): $869.

Average cost of a groom's formal wear (rented): $77.

Most-popular engagement ring sold at Tiffany & Co.: one-carat solitaire diamond in a six-prong platinum Tiffany setting.

Top-three most-popular bridal-registry items at Home Depot in Paramus, New Jersey: skittle saws, recessed lights, lawn mowers.

Number of wedding witnesses the ancient Romans thought were needed to ward off evil spirits: 10.

Average number of wedding guests: 188.

Number of marriages performed per month at the Graceland Wedding Chapel in Las Vegas: 200–250.

Percent of weddings at the Graceland Wedding Chapel at which an Elvis impersonator appears: 25–30.

The current most-popular first-dance tune: "A Whole New World" from *Aladdin*. Other popular ones: "Love Me Tender," sung by Elvis Presley and "Evergreen," sung by Barbra Streisand.

Most-popular honeymoon destination: Within the continental U.S.: Florida. Outside continental U.S.: Hawaii.

Projected percent of couples marrying today who will see their marriages end in divorce: 50.

Sources: National Center for Health Statistics; Bride's & Your New Home (February/March 1992); Bride's & Your New Home "1993 Reader Survey"; The Gallup Poll News Service; Modern Bride "Consumer Council Study" (October 1993); U.S. Bureau of the Census; Bride's & Your New Home "Marriage Now Facts & Figures"; Tiffany & Co.; Graceland Wedding Chapel; Nancy Cook (owner of Dial-A-Wedding Song)

Charts Add Charm

Charts present information in a more visually appealing manner than mere text in a box. Charts also can do a better job of presenting complicated information, especially numerical data. Charts come in four main varieties: tables, line charts, bar charts and pie charts.

Facts on a drink that goes down easy

► The USA is the only country in the world where freshly brewed tea over ice is preferred to hot tea.

► Americans drink nearly 95 million glasses of iced tea a day, according to the Thomas J. Lipton Co.

► Tea contains no calories, sodium, fat, carbonation or sugar, and has one-third to one-half the caffeine of coffee.

► A recent poll conducted by the University of North Carolina at Chapel Hill found that 61% of iced tea drinkers say they prefer unsweetened tea to sweetened.

► Among the beverage companies that have jumped on the bottled/canned tea bandwagon: Stroh Brewery Co. (with their Chaos line); Canfield Beverages; Perrier (partners with Celestial Seasonings); Pepsi (Thomas J. Lipton Co.) and Coca-Cola (Nestle).

► Food historians differ on iced tea's origins. Some say Southerners developed it in the 1800s as a summertime thirst quencher, while others say a vendor at the 1904 St. Louis World's Fair invented it when he couldn't sell hot tea at the summer event.

Figure 10.15
A fact box.

© 1993. USA Today. Reprinted with permission.

RAINBOW JELLYFISH

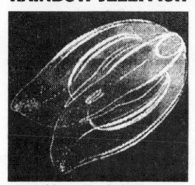

Mnemiopsis leidyi

NATURAL HABITAT: This white, opaque animal is very common along the North Atlantic coast of the United States down to South Carolina. It is pearlike in shape and the swimming lobes are two-fifths longer than the body.

FEEDING: Feeds mainly on copepods and mollusk larvae. When they appear in large swarms near oyster beds, the rainbow jellyfish devour thousands of oyster larvae.

ADAPTABILITY: The adaptability of this delicate creature to temperature and the salt content of the water is astounding. The animal was accidentally introduced to the Black Sea and first observed there in 1982.

SOURCE: Grzimek's Animal Life Encyclopedia

THE WASHINGTON POST

HOW TO JOIN

Today is the last day to sign up for a Reader Roundtable.

Joining is easy. Find a convenient site on the list of Roundtables on Page 3C. Then call 1-800-499-0043 and give your name, address, phone number and the Roundtable you are interested in. If you get the message machine, just leave the information. We will get back to you today or Monday to confirm your signup.

The first meetings are this week, led by facilitators who have been specially trained to lead the discussions. The last meetings are the week of Oct. 23. Participants should plan to attend all four of their Roundtables, to ensure a full airing of all perspectives.

Background materials will be published in the Maine Sunday Telegram on each of the four weeks of Roundtables.

Figure 10.16 (left)
A fact box that presents a "profile" — in this case, of a jellyfish.

© 1994 The Washington Post. Reprinted with permission. Source: Grzimeck's Animal Life Encyclopedia.

Figure 10.17 (right)
This text box gives readers information they can use to accomplish a task.

Used with permission of the Portland (Maine) Press Herald.

Figure 10.18
A table that shows rank order.

Used with permission Miami
Herald.

OUR FAVORITE CEREALS

According to Publix Super Markets,
the five top-selling cereals in Dade
County by units sold are:

1. Frosted Flakes (Kellogg)
2. Honey Nut Cheerios (General Mills)
3. Fruit Loops (Kellogg)
4. Corn Flakes (Kellogg)
5. Special K (Kellogg)

In Broward County, the top five are:

1. Honey Nut Cheerios (General Mills)
2. Raisin Bran (Kellogg)
3. Special K (Kellogg)
4. Total (General Mills)
5. Corn Flakes (Kellogg)

According to Nielsen Market
Research, the top five brands nationally
are:

1. Frosted Flakes (Kellogg)
2. Cheerios (General Mills)
3. Frosted Mini Wheats (Kellogg)
4. Honey Nut Cheerios (General Mills)
5. Corn Flakes (Kellogg)

Tables are the charts that most closely resemble text boxes. Tables are split into rows and columns, with each resulting "cell" carrying a piece of information (Figures 10.18–10.21). The information can be compared easily.

Tables often are used to:

1. show rankings, as in poll results or sports standings;

2. compare features and benefits, such as in a list of automobile safety devices;

3. build a fact box that relies solely on statistical information, such as in a company profile;

4. show changes over time, as in a table that compares how current federal nutrition guidelines differ from older standards; and

5. compare fees, attendance, property damage and other numerical data.

In long tables, alternating lines should be tinted for easy comparison, or white space should be inserted between every two or three lines.

Line charts (also called **fever charts**) show changes in numbers over time (Figures 10.22 and 10.23). A scale running along the bottom of the chart measures time; one running up the side measures quantity. Points are plotted along the scales and joined by a solid line. The line can be stylized to make it more interesting; for instance, it can be turned into a belt for a chart on Father's Day sales. However, a thick line can make it hard to distinguish which values on the chart should be read: the ones at the top of the line, the ones at the bottom of the line, or the ones in the midpoint of the line.

How the exercise guidelines have changed		
	1985 guidelines	**1994 guidelines**
Number of studies on which this was based	Eighteen	43
Heart rate	140 beats per minute maximum	No general restrictions*
Aerobics	Time limit of fifteen minutes	No set time limit*
Physical conditions that might preclude exercise	Nineteen listed	Six listed: 1. high blood pressure; 2. early rupture of amniotic sac; 3. too-early labor during prior or current pregnancy; 4. incompetent (weak) cervix or cervical cerclage (cervix stitched closed); 5. persistent second- or third-trimester bleeding; 6. slowed fetal growth
Safety	"Little research has been done on the effects of exercise during pregnancy ... and ethical considerations make it almost impossible to define the limits of safety."	"...there are no current data to confirm that, with the specific exceptions mentioned here, exercise during pregnancy has any deleterious effects on the fetus."

*To be determined on an individual basis, in consultation with a woman's doctor

Figure 10.19
This table compares information from two sets of guidelines.

Reprinted with permission of Jennifer Cadoff. Published in Glamour, June 1994.

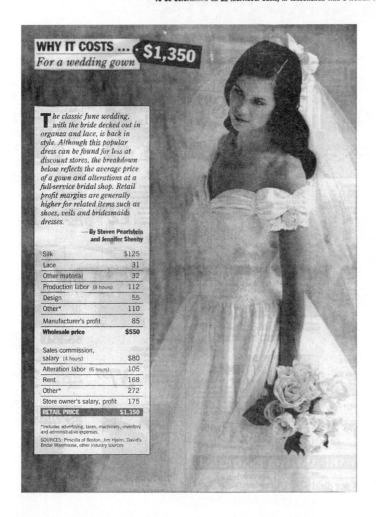

Figure 10.20
This table lets readers see at a glance why things cost what they do.

© 1994 The Washington Post. Reprinted with permission. Sources: Priscilla of Boston, Jim Hjelm, David's Bridal Warehouse, other industry sources.

HOSTING SOCCER

International soccer games played at RFK Stadium that the local World Cup Host Committee has played a major role in staging and promoting.

GAME	WHEN	ATTENDANCE
U.S. vs. Ireland	May 1992	35,696
Germany vs. Brazil	June 1993	34,737
Brazil vs. England	June 1993	54,118
A.C. Milan vs. Torino	August 1993	25,268
U.S. vs. Mexico	October 1993	23,927
Norway vs. Mexico	June 19, 1994	Sellout
Netherlands vs. Saudi Arabia	June 20, 1994	Sellout
Italy vs. Mexico	June 28, 1994	Sellout
Belgium vs. Saudi Arabia	June 29, 1994	Sellout
World Cup Group C runner-up vs. Group A runner-up	July 2, 1994	Sellout

SOURCE: World Cup Host Committee

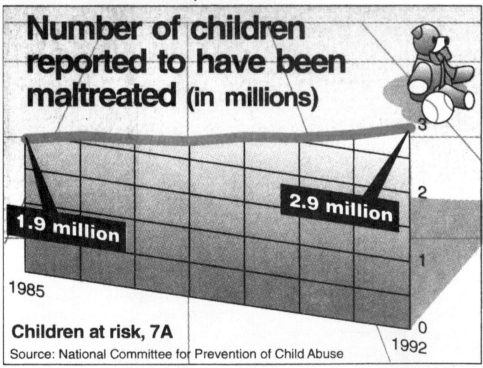

USA SNAPSHOTS®

A look at statistics that shape the nation

Number of children reported to have been maltreated (in millions)

1.9 million

2.9 million

1985

Children at risk, 7A

Source: National Committee for Prevention of Child Abuse

1992

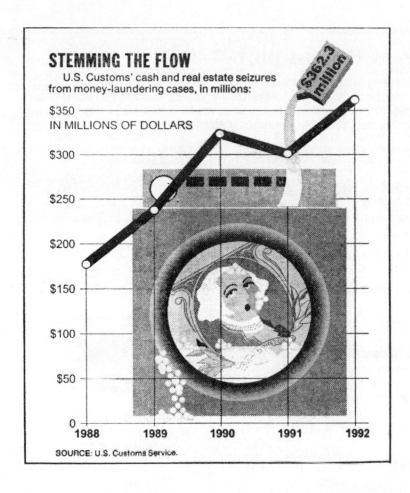

Figure 10.23
A line chart incorporating a graphic.

Used with permission Miami Herald.

Up to three lines can be used on a line chart to compare different items. For example, one line might show the rise in the cost of living over 10 years, another might track the rise in housing prices during the same time, and a third might show the rise in wages during the period. Multiple-line charts work only if all lines can be clearly distinguished.

While line charts are useful tools, they must be constructed carefully so they don't mislead readers. First, increments along both scales should remain constant. Changing the size of the increments can distort the message. For example, a chart that tracks average household income every decade from 1900 through 1990 should include the same amount of space between each decade. Compressing 1900 through 1940 into the amount of space used for each later decade misleads the reader.

Second, most line charts should have a zero point so that minor changes don't seem to be major ones. Only when a chart is based on a nonzero standard — such as the consumer price index, which uses 100 as the standard — should it start at a point other than zero. If the important values are clustered together far from the zero point, a broken line can be used between zero and an appropriate point on the scale.

Third, only significant changes are clearly visible on a line chart, so minor changes are better handled in a table or a bar chart.

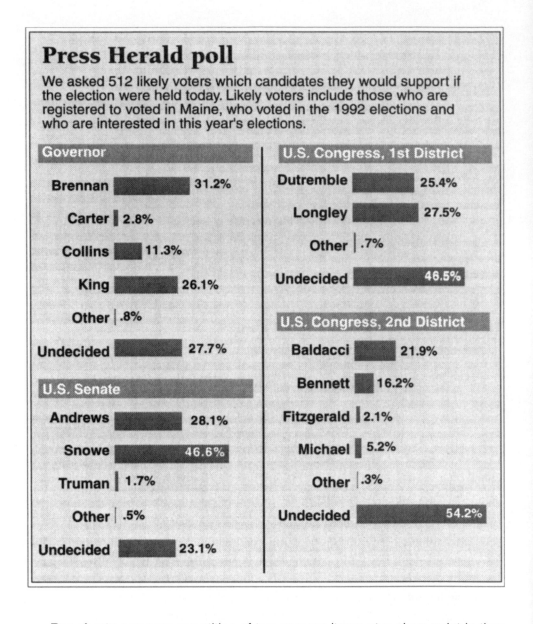

Figure 10.24
A simple bar chart.

Used with permission of the
Portland (Maine) Press Herald.

Bar charts compare quantities of two or more items at a given point in time
(Figure 10.24). **Grouped bar charts** (Figure 10.25) also can indicate how those
quantities have changed over time. Technically speaking, bar charts use horizontal bars; the more commonly seen charts that use vertical bars are appropriately
called **column charts.** In the publishing business, however, both are referred to as
bar charts.

Stacked bar charts can be used to provide even more information than a simple bar chart, but at a possible loss of clarity. For example, bars can be used to
represent total population in several towns. Each bar can then be divided, bottom
to top, by race, age or other characteristics of the population.

Like line charts, bar charts should have a zero point. Bar chart designers
should be careful to keep values consistent in charts that will run side by side.
Otherwise, a reader easily can get the wrong impression (Figure 10.26).

Simple bars generally work better than **pictographs,** which substitute symbols for the bars (Figure 10.27). Pictographs can be harder to compare because

Bar chart designers
should be careful
to keep values
consistent in charts
that will run side by
side. Otherwise, a
reader easily can get
the wrong impression.

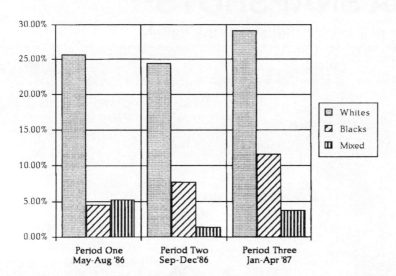

Coverage of Blacks and Whites: Percentage of News Hole
by Four-Month Period

Figure 10.25
A grouped bar chart.

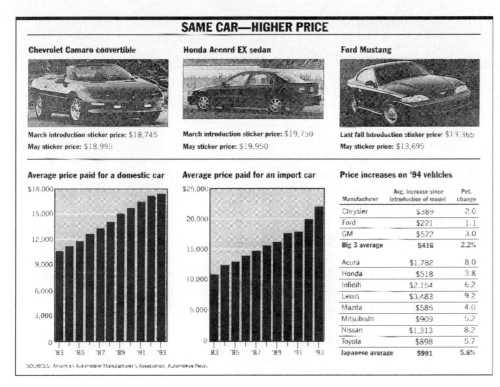

Figure 10.26
The different scales used in these bar charts make it look like the average domestic car costs more than the average import — when just the opposite is true.

© 1994 The Washington Post. Reprinted with permission. Source: American Automobile Manufacturer's Association, Automotive News.

the volume changes as the height changes. Bar charts done in 3-D also can cause confusion. Readers are apt to read values at the top of the shadows rather than at the top of the bars.

Pie charts show how the parts make up a whole. Because pie charts with many slices can make comparisons difficult, pie charts generally should include no more than eight slices. All slices should be substantial enough to be seen easily. Each slice should be labeled consistently either inside or outside the slice.

Only round shapes should be used for pie charts. While a designer may think that a state map, a house or some other symbol would add a touch of interest to

Figure 10.27
A pictograph, which uses
symbols instead of bars.

© 1993 USA Today. Reprinted
with permission.

Figure 10.27
A pictograph, which uses
symbols instead of bars.

© 1993 USA Today. Reprinted
with permission.

a pie chart, such odd shapes also make it harder for the reader to compare the slices. A good compromise is to place the pie chart within another symbol.

Infographic Guidelines

Just Like Copy, Every Infographic Should Be Accurate.   The information in an infographic not only should be checked on its own but also should be compared with information in any accompanying text (Figure 10.28).

Every Infographic Should Be Edited Tightly.   An infographic should contain just enough information to make its point, and no more.

Numbers Should Be Checked to Make Sure They Add Up and Make Sense.   While the pieces of a pie chart always should total 100 percent, it's not unusual to find overstuffed pies that contain 115, 120 or even 150 percent (Figure 10.29).

Data Shouldn't Be Fudged.   Missing data must be indicated clearly. If critical data cannot be obtained, a different type of graphic may be better. For instance, in some cases a bar chart works better than a line chart. When a great deal of data is missing, no infographic should be attempted.

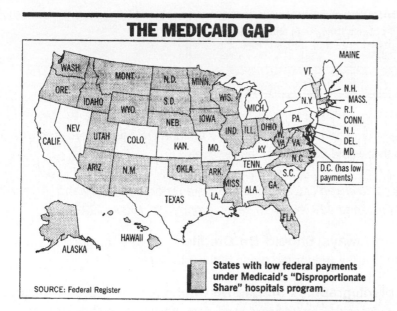

Figure 10.28
Those mischievous Midwest states of Illinois and Indiana switched places in this map.

© 1993 The Washington Post. Reprinted with permission. Source: Federal Register.

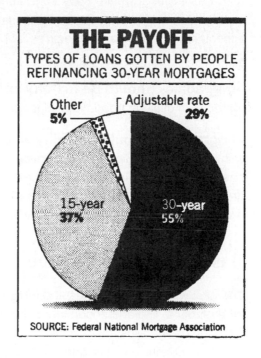

Figure 10.29
This overstuffed pie chart includes slices that add up to 126 percent, instead of the 100 percent it should show.

© 1993 The Washington Post. Reprinted with permission. Source: Federal National Mortgage Association.

Every Infographic Should Have a Headline. In just a few words, a headline should indicate why the reader is being shown an infographic. Examples are:

U.S. airways getting more crowded

Dimensions of a disaster

Make Sure an Infographic Is Worth the Effort. The following table took up space in which five lines of type could have fit:

Cases of Lyme Disease in Maryland		
1990	1991	1992
238	283	185

But the information in the table easily could have been expressed in a few sentences that would have taken less space:

In 1990, 238 cases of Lyme disease were reported in Maryland. A year later, the figure jumped to 283, but then cases dropped to 185 in 1992.

Sources Always Should Be Credited.   Every infographic should carry a line that tells the reader the origin of the information used in it.

Style of Infographics Should Be Consistent and Clear.   Just as editors use a stylebook to make copy consistent, so too do editors and designers use style guides for graphics. Such guides, which can run 30 pages or longer, specify acceptable typefaces and type sizes, abbreviations, color palettes and dozens of other guidelines.

Infographics Should Be Tasteful and Appropriate.   Using humorous pictographs to depict a tragedy obviously is not appropriate.

Infographics Should Simplify Information.   Maps often are combined with other infographics and illustrations to produce visual packages. Designers have to be careful in putting such packages together, though. The purpose of graphics should be to make things easier for readers; "mega graphics" can be as daunting for readers as the longest articles (Figure 10.30).

Basic Principles of Page Design

The best writing, photographs and infographics are of little use if they're not easy for a reader to find and understand. That brings us into the final topic of this chapter: page design. Most magazines and many newspapers have design editors who handle important projects and packages. For instance, typically a design editor handles the front page of a newspaper features section. But copy editors are responsible for designing other newspaper pages — often including Page One and all inside pages. The same holds true for many small magazines and for many in-house publications. Therefore, at a minimum, copy editors should understand design so they can work with design editors; in many cases, copy editors will be called upon to use that understanding to design pages on their own.

Design Goals

First, Make Sure the Design Delivers.   The most important task of any design is to communicate information to the audience. Good design, like good writing and editing, is based on a thorough understanding of the audience and the

Figure 10.30
"Mega-graphics" can be overwhelming to the reader, but this one strikes a good balance in presenting lots of information.

Used with permission Miami Herald.

role the publication plays for that audience. For example, the primary goal of a daily insiders' newsletter is to deliver information instantly to its readers. In this case, good design means a simple, easy-to-follow format: easy-to-find headlines, short paragraphs, lots of bullets and lists (Figure 10.31). Anything fancier can distract the reader. But an entertainment magazine will use lots of color and exciting graphics to help grab the attention of potential readers who don't *need* to read anything in it (Figure 10.32).

Design never should make a publication difficult to read. Designers occasionally get so carried away with putting together eye-catching pages that the pages end up being virtually unreadable.

Design never should make a publication difficult to read.

Every Page Should Have a Single Focal Point. Newspaper design expert Mario Garcia talks of the **center of visual impact,** also called the **CVI.**[5] This is the point on a page that is designed to grab the reader's initial attention. It can be a photograph, an infographic, a headline, a breakout quote or some other device. The location of the CVI is not critical; a good CVI will grab a reader's attention no matter where it is located (Figure 10.33).

Nevertheless, there are two caveats about placing the CVI:

First, since we read from left to right, most readers look to the left side of a page first so it's better to put the CVI there than on the right.

Second, designers working with broadsheet newspapers generally place the CVI on the top half of a page so readers can see it even when the paper is folded in half.

Every Page Should Have Movement. Just as every sentence should have action verbs, so should every page have movement that carries readers along after they notice the CVI. Garcia calls this movement the **progression** of the page. It can be accomplished by arranging elements in various shapes, such as T or L shapes; by including smaller visual elements opposite the CVI; or by structuring the page so that the elements on one part (top, bottom, left side) run vertically and the elements on the other part run horizontally.

The Hierarchy of Elements on a Page Should Be Apparent. When more than one article is run on the same page, a reader should be able to distinguish which item is the most important, which is next most important, and on down the line. This typically is accomplished through placement (most important at the top) and type size (larger headlines mean more importance).

Grids Can Help. Many publications use **grids** that map the page into multiple and often overlapping columns (Figure 10.34). These grids lend an order to the elements placed on a page. Grids help establish consistency while also leaving room for experimentation.

Until recently, laying out a page of any publication was a two-step process. First, the editor drew a model of the completed page on a **dummy sheet** that showed the publication's grid. That sheet would then go to the production department, where the typeset elements would be placed on a layout sheet according to the dummy (Figure 10.35 a, b).

THE KIPLINGER WASHINGTON LETTER

Circulated weekly to business clients since 1923—Vol. 71, No. 43

THE KIPLINGER WASHINGTON EDITORS
1729 H St., N.W., Washington, D.C. 20006-3938

Dear Client: Washington, Oct. 28, 1994

     Business groups and unions are now cooking up plans for '95...
what they hope to get through Congress and what they'll oppose.
We talked with them this week, and here's what we found out...
their priorities for next year and how we rate their prospects:

     <u>Getting a grip on gov't entitlement programs</u> will be a main goal
of the U.S. Chamber...restructuring Medicare, Medicaid, social security
and other obligations so deficits don't go haywire in the early 2000s.
Congress will hold hearings on this next year but won't take any action.
     <u>Passing GATT legislation</u> is tops at Nat'l Assn. of Manufacturers,
Business Roundtable, American Iron and Steel Institute and the Chamber.
The bill will probably be approved in the lame-duck session of Congress
right after the elections. If not, it'll sail through early next year.
     <u>Enacting a national highway system law</u> to upgrade 160,000 miles
of roads & bridges is the top priority of Associated General Contractors.
The bill barely missed this fall and will probably be approved next year.

     <u>Clarifying toxic-waste cleanup liability</u> is high on the lists
at American Petroleum Institute, Chemical Manufacturers Assn. and others.
It will be part of Superfund legislation that will be approved next year.
     <u>Easing restrictions on federal timber</u> will be one of the goals
of the Nat'l Assn. of Home Builders. But prospects for success are slim.
     <u>A merger of the bank and S&L insurance funds</u> will be opposed
by the American Bankers Assn. Congress will sidetrack the proposal.
     <u>Stopping state waivers from ERISA</u> is important to the Roundtable,
Nat'l Assn. of Wholesaler-Distributors and the Nat'l Retail Federation...
efforts by states enacting health reforms to add benefits or levy taxes
on firms that self-insure. Congress will be stingy about making changes.

     <u>Health care</u> will still be on the front burner at many groups,
even though it fizzled this year. Supporters are sure to try again...
smaller, more-piecemeal reforms. The big bugaboo is employer mandates,
fought by Nat'l Fed. of Independent Business, Nat'l Auto Dealers Assn.
and most other trade groups. Forget about substantial change next year.

     <u>A consumption tax</u> will be pushed by American Business Conference.
It favors an income tax that exempts savings and encourages investment.
Won't succeed in the next few years but might by the end of the decade.
     <u>Estate-tax changes</u> will be promoted by NFIB...a lower top rate
on family businesses if heirs are actively involved. Unlikely to pass.
     <u>A 25% deduction for self-employeds' health premiums</u> will be urged
by NFIB and others and will pass in early '95, retroactive to this year.
     <u>Tax breaks for marginal oil wells</u> and to encourage new drilling
will be promoted by the Independent Petroleum Assn. Hardly any chance.
     <u>Regulatory reforms</u> will be a goal for dozens of trade groups...
more focus on cost/benefits. An outside chance something will get done.

Figure 10.31

The model of the classic newsletter. The Kiplinger Washington letter uses a simple design that lets readers get the information they need with no distractions.

Reprinted with permission of Kiplinger Washington Editors.

Figure 10.32
The design of the St. Petersburg (Fla.) Times "kids page" is bright and hyperactive — just like its intended audience.

Reprinted by permission of the St. Petersburg Times.

monday, june 6, 1994

■ COMICS 8D
■ ANN&ABBY 2D
■ MOVIES 6D
■ X-PRESSIONS 3D

section [D] press

a floridian section of the St. Petersburg Times

INSIDE

School's out for SUMMER!

Our Newspaper in Education page is taking the summer off, but we are not going to leave you empty handed. We have a page full of summer fun! There are riddles, jokes and the all new, all X-citing, X-cellent Adventures. So take a look inside and let the fun begin.

See page 5D

X-PRESSLINE

True or False?

We are so over Beavis and Butt-head.

(Call the Timesline number for your county listed on page 2D and enter category 7600).

■ Push 1 for **TRUE** – Please remove them from my popular culture ASAP!

■ Push 2 for **Uh, FALSE** – Beavis and Butt-head rule!

Then, if you'd like to leave a comment, stay on the line.

It's An International Adult Conspiracy!!!

Whew! You really let us know what you had on your mind last week. We asked if you thought grown-ups should be allowed to call the X-press Hotline. Only **105** of you said **YES** — it's a free country. While **580** of you said **NO** — it's our phone line and all you adult better KEEP OUT! But that wasn't all of it, here's a little more:

Get those adults out of here

"You guys should change the number so adults can't call."

"What if parents are calling THIS time and not leaving messages?"

"If they're calling this number, they must be having a mid-life crisis!"

"They have their own numbers to call. They should go call a lawyer or something."

"X-press is for kids; it doesn't have boring adult stuff. They have the whole rest of the paper. We are lucky to have this. They shouldn't try to take it away."

"It's not fair; they get to do everything. They vote, go to their jobs, go to clubs. We don't get to do any of that stuff."

"This is mean, you should cut out all their votes, so they don't mess up our votes."

"Half of them are the ones who tell us to get off the phone when we try to vote."

"This is the only thing I can do without my mom knowing what I am voting for. It's like a secret ballot. And that's not always true with a lot of other things."

"If parents wanna call this number they should go to Never-Never land."

More conspiracy comments inside on page 2D

"That's weird that adults have been calling the line. It's weird that they've been reading the section. It's crazy. They definitely should not be able to call."

"Try to make it clear to them that they can't call this line. Can they follow directions or what?"

"I hope they see this article so they know we don't want them to call."

"They shouldn't get to vote. They get to drive and go on rides like the bumper cars at the fair because they're taller than us."

Hey, it's only fair

"It's not fair, *not* letting them call. It's kind of cute, you know, them calling the kids' line."

"Adults should be allowed because they may be a child at heart or they have kids or they may think it's fun. It would be cruel not to let them. It's a free country. Don't act like some dude that says blacks have to go in separate restrooms from whites. That's exactly what it's like."

"It's a free country. Why not have something fun for the parents, for the elderly ones, too."

And one more thing: Garbage?

Only three adults left comments this week. The most interesting was one woman who says she thinks X-press is ludicrous and a piece of garbage. She says she thinks a children's section has no place in a morning newspaper. What do you think? Call the X-press hotline above, vote on the Beavis and Butt-head question, stay on the line then tell us what is on your mind.

— FIRST PICKS

Forge ahead fashionably with NO FEAR

By HELEN A.S. POPKIN

The key words for dressing this summer are, "No Fear." Or maybe they're "Second Place is First Loser," or something like "He Who Dies With the Most Toys, Still Dies."

Hot weather calls for cool clothes. Ride the wardrobe wave in style.

At any rate, No Fear, the clothes line that specializes in T-shirts emblazoned with hard-line no-wimps-allowed phraseology, is setting the fashion standards for the hottest months of '94.

Mark Curinga, co-owner of the newly opened North Shore Surf Shop in Largo Mall, can't keep No Fear in stock. "We could bring in the ugliest No Fear shirt in the world and it would sell," says Curinga.

The surf shop is located

Mark Freifeld, 13, and Crystal Calhoun, 12, show No Fear.

Times photos — KATHLEEN CABBLE

smack dab between Largo High and Osceola Middle schools, and Curinga says the kids keep him up-to-date on what they want to wear. They like Da Hui environmental surf shirts, 26-inch baggy denim shorts, boxer shorts with obnoxious prints and anything Oakley. North Shore's got all that, and it has promised its loyal customers to get in Vans shoes and the Quik Silver clothes line ASAP.

We grabbed some kids from Tyrone Middle School to see how they would outfit themselves for summer if they could pick anything in North Shore.

Mark Freifeld, 13, of St. Petersburg, regularly outfits himself in Billabong and Stussi (which North Shore doesn't carry) and Yaga with Doc Martens to match.

For his first outfit, Mark went for stark Yaga in black and white — white Yaga T-shirt ($15.95) and Yaga black denim shorts ($44.95). For accessories, he chose a yin and yang rat tail necklace ($2.95) and a No Fear hat ($18.95).

"I figured it all matched," Mark says of his first outfit. "Black and white looks real-

— SECOND CHOICE

ly good together."

Crystal Calhoun, 12, of St. Petersburg, doesn't go for the baggy boxers popular with both guys and girls right now. They could be covered with globes, skulls, great big Dr. Seuss polka-dots or just plain blue. She doesn't care. "I think they're odd," Crystal says.

A two-piece claw-back romper by Panama Jack ($24.95) was Crystal's first choice, with a matching pink-stone choker ($2.95) and a peace sign bracelet ($4.95). "I like it because it's colorful and comfortable," says Crystal. "Also, it looks nice." Crystal compliments the casual look with her own Reebok Pumps.

Mark mixed it up with his second selection, topping off extra long and baggy green denim No Fear shorts ($44.95) and a mauve Redsand T-shirt ($15.95). "The two shades really stand out," Mark says. He accessorized with a retro-cool peace sign choker ($9.95).

Crystal is big on colors. For her second outfit, she chose a teal "Florida" cover-up ($11.95), something she could wear over her own one-piece bathing suit.

[COOLBEANS] HOTSTUFF

More beans, page 3D

Take a leap back 12,000 years!

Once upon a time, mastodons and saber-toothed tigers roamed the gulf coasts of Florida, and so did prehistoric people. Check out the lives of Florida's first people through five time periods at "Gulf Coast Prehistoric People: 10,000 B.C.-1,500 A.D.," now through Dec. 31 at the St. Petersburg Museum of History, 335 Second Ave. NE, St. Petersburg.

The exhibition, chock full of artifacts, many never before on public display, features hands-on exhibits in pottery design, ornamental "dress up" stations and way-cool mathematical mound construction puzzles. For information call 894-1052.

Figure 10.33
The large photo in the center of this page is a clear example of a CVI.

Used with permission of the Portland (Maine) Press Herald.

PORTLAND
Press Herald

FRIDAY
OCTOBER 7, 1994
CITY EDITION

Local & State

Billboard / 2B
Deaths / 13B
Weather / 14B

SECTION
B

BRIEFLY

Beacon Teen Center provides safe haven for homeless teens

The 2-month-old Beacon Teen Center got its official launch at a ceremony Thursday.

The center, designed with the help of the teens it is supposed to serve, provides a safe place for homeless and at-risk teen-agers from 6 to 9 p.m. two nights each week. Organizers hope it will fill the gap between closing time for soup kitchens and opening time for homeless shelters in the area.

The Junior League of Portland established the center in June at the Preble Street Chapel in conjunction with Youth and Family Outreach.

Katie Shisler, vice president of the league, said 15 to 20 teens have come to the center each night it has been open. She hopes the center will soon add a third night of operation.

Westbrook police charge local man with sex crimes

WESTBROOK — A 46-year-old local man was arrested Wednesday and charged with two counts of unlawful sexual contact with children, said Police Capt. Paul McCarthy.

McCarthy said children from the man's neighborhood were present when the alleged offenses occurred.

The man was arrested after he came to the police station Wednesday to be interviewed about the case. Police also searched the man's residence, but McCarthy would not say what kind of evidence was seized.

The man was released after posting bail. McCarthy said the investigation is continuing.

City plans roadblocks to catch drunken drivers

Portland police will set up a roadblock in the city tonight or Saturday night to catch drunken drivers, said Officer Bruce Coffin.

Police frequently set up roadblocks during holiday weekends, but don't let the public know the exact location.

Freeport Rescue benefit to fund thin-ice platform

FREEPORT — A fund-raising drive to buy a rescue platform has been started by the Freeport Rescue Company. Members will sell Sno-Pro automobile snow scrapers/brushes at $15 each.

A rescue platform is a two-pontoon device connected by guardrails that enables rescuers to make their way across thin ice. Rescuers currently use ropes, ladders, boats and cold-water suits to reach victims.

For information or to buy a scraper, call Edward Doughty at 865-9647.

Scarborough OKs means of requesting information

SCARBOROUGH — The Town Council has adopted a new process for handling requests from the public for municipal records.

From now on, information seekers will be required to fill out a one-page request form. The back of the form contains an explanation of the town's policy concerning Freedom of Access Law requests. Town workers will have five business days to respond.

William Stroud, one of the town's most aggressive information seekers, was thanked by the council for coming up with the idea. Councilors said the system will be more efficient and make it easier for them to monitor the municipal staff's effectiveness in responding to information requests.

South Portland already uses a system similar to the one Scarborough approved.

Municipal group awards town's report top honors

SCARBOROUGH — The town's annual report is a winner.

The Maine Municipal Association this week announced that Scarborough' 64-page annual report received the highest honor of supreme merit in the MMA's 1994 Annual Report Competition.

The award was to have been presented to Scarborough officials during the MMA convention in Bangor this week. A three-man panel of judges commended Scarborough officials "for providing this exemplary communication to your citizens."

— From staff reports

Drug, alcohol-use survey approved

● Scarborough students in grades 6-12 will be given the standardized questionnaire next month.

By DENNIS HOEY
Staff Writer

SCARBOROUGH — The Board of Education will follow Cape Elizabeth's lead and survey more than 1,000 middle and high school students to determine the extent of drug and alcohol use.

Board members, in another major decision Thursday, approved first reading of a policy governing the celebration of holidays. The policy, which is broad, leaves traditional school observances intact. A final vote will be taken at the board's Oct. 20 meeting.

A survey of substance abuse among 1,200 Scarborough students in grades 6-12 is set to begin next month. Students will have about three weeks to complete. Students will be asked to respond to the American Drug and Alcohol Survey, a standardized questionnaire developed by

> "We can't put our children in cages. We need to get parents involved and educated."
> **Jacquelyn Perry, board member**

the Rocky Mountain Behavioral Science Institute of Fort Collins, Colo. The survey is nearly identical to the one used in Cape Elizabeth.

Cape Elizabeth's survey showed widespread use of a variety of drugs, alcohol and tobacco in grades 6-12. After Cape Elizabeth's results became public, several students complained their school system had been unfairly singled out.

"We haven't made the headlines yet, but I think we have as serious a problem as any other community has," Jacquelyn Perry, a board member, said. "We can't put our children in cages. We need to get parents involved and educated."

After voting to spend $1,500 for

the survey, board members approved re-establishing the Community Health Task Force — once called the Substance Abuse Advisory Committee. The task force will be expanded to include parents, teachers, community leaders, social workers and students.

Scarborough's Task Force would be similar to the Cape Community Coalition, which shepherded the community through the survey's aftershock by bringing in experts to interpret survey results for

Please see SURVEY, Page 2B

The garbage keeps washing ashore

● Coastweek celebrates Maine's link to the sea, and the annual Coastal Cleanup reminds people to keep it clean.

By PETER POCHNA
Staff Writer

Mark Young has fished off of Maine for almost all his 28 years. Only recently has he come to realize that what he tosses off his boat is almost as important as what he hauls onto it.

"We make an effort to bring in all our garbage, and so do all the fishermen I know," says Young as he cleans his nets at the Portland Fish Pier. "That hasn't always been the case, but in the last few years people have become more aware of the problem. Everybody's trying to make the oceans cleaner."

One reason people are aware of the problem is Coastweek, an annual state-sponsored celebration of Maine's link to the ocean. This year's festivities begin Saturday with the celebration's main event — the 10th annual Coastal Cleanup.

But even as people increase their effort to keep the oceans clean, the flow of trash washing up on beaches remains steady. Dumping off Navy ships, problems with enforcing antidumping laws, and the fact that it's still easier to drop trash in the ocean then to haul it to shore all make garbage a continual threat to Maine's beaches and marine life.

During last year's Coastal Cleanup, 2,500 volunteers combed 132 miles of Maine's coast and removed 17,579 pounds of garbage. Included in the haul were a wooden Santa Claus, a hot-water heater and more than 13,000 cigarette butts.

Please see CLEANUP, Page 2B

Staff photo by John Ewing
Peter Woodruff on Thursday displays artifacts he has found along the beach at Reid State Park. He holds his favorite piece, a well-preserved stone knife blade that may be more than 1,000 years old.

COASTAL CLEANUP

Here is a schedule of some of the Coastweek '94 events in the Greater Portland area.

Cleanups

Cumberland: 9 a.m. Saturday at Cumberland Town Landing. Bring gloves and boots.

Falmouth: 9 a.m. Saturday, Mackworth Island. Wear sturdy shoes and work gloves.

Freeport: 9 a.m. Saturday, benches by the second parking lot in Wolfe Neck Woods State Park. Bring gloves and pencils.

Portland: 11 a.m. Saturday at Portland Head Light. Bring gloves, pencils and lunch.

Scarborough: 10 a.m. to noon Saturday at Kettle Cove parking lot, Ferry Beach.

Coastweek events

Portland Museum of Art: Admission is free Saturday from 10 a.m. to noon.

Bar Harbor – Acadia National Park: Daylong seminar Saturday on marine debris, concluding with afternoon cleanup at the seawall. Free. Advance registration required. Call Paul Super at 288-3893.

Augusta: Maine State Museum. Museum Gallery programs on lobstering and sardining. Admission is free Sunday. At the Capitol Complex at 1:30 p.m. Program continues through Friday.

Boothbay – Maine Department of Marine Resources: Friday — Open house of the Fisheries Laboratory. Admission free from 9 a.m. to 4 p.m.

Beachcomber scans sand for ancient artifacts, stories

● Peter Woodruff says interesting things often wash up on the beach, which he likens to 'the edge of a soup bowl.'

> "I feel as though I can just reach out and touch the past."
> Peter Woodruff

By PETER POCHNA
Staff Writer

GEORGETOWN — When most people look at beach trash, they see plastic cups, Styrofoam fragments and broken glass. When Peter Woodruff looks at beach trash, he sees a crystal ball.

Woodruff went to the beach at Reid State Park in Georgetown almost every day in 1992 to scavenge for garbage. He hasn't thrown any away. It's all in a weathered woodshed on Kennebec Point. Slowly, it is revealing to Woodruff

secrets from Maine's past.

Not everything Woodruff picked off the beach is standard. Dumpster-variety trash. There's the 6,000-year-old fishing weight, the fossilized shark teeth, a 17th century pipe, and his favorite piece of all, a remarkably well-preserved stone knife blade that may be more than 1,000 years old.

"It's as if the beach is at the edge of a soup bowl, and all the artifacts are washing to the edge of the plate," says the 46-year-old Woodruff, who works as a maintenance

mechanic at Bath Iron Works. "It's a large-time soup."

The beach at Reid State Park is a wispy 100-yard-long strip of sand and dune grass sheltered in a small cove. At first glance it looks perfectly clean, but as Woodruff walks near the lapping water, he can hardly take a step without investigating some object in the sand.

This beach is like hundreds of others along the Maine coast, Woodruff says. It's rich in treasures like the ones he's unearthed, available to anyone willing to hunt and to become slightly obsessed.

He began his inspection of the beach with the help of a $1,000 grant from the University of Rhode Island. His goal was to document the environmental damage caused by dumping trash in the ocean. His

Please see BEACH, Page 2B

Trucker extricated after crash

● Two accidents follow another in which a tractor trailer tips over into a ditch in Falmouth. In all, three people are hurt.

By DAVID CONNERTY-MARIN and ALAN CLENDENNING
Staff Writers

FALMOUTH — Three accidents within an hour and a mile of each other on Interstate 95 and Route 1 Thursday sent at least three people to local hospitals. None had life-threatening injuries.

A tractor-trailer carrying thousands of pounds of scrap paper tipped over into a ditch as it rounded a sharp corner at the end of the Exit 9 spur that connects the Maine Turnpike to Interstate 95 north at about 4:20 p.m., said state police Trooper Bernard Pender.

The driver, Jerry Howard, 23, address unknown, was trapped in the cab for about an hour as Falmouth firefighters worked to extract him from the truck's cab using the Jaws of Life extrication tool.

Pender said Howard was probably going too fast when the truck tipped over. The 18-wheeler was

Please see CRASHES, Page 2B

Bus driver faces more charges

● The Westbrook school bus driver enters innocent pleas to 21 counts of child endangerment and one count of OUI.

From staff reports

The district attorney's office has added 21 counts of endangering the welfare of a child to the OUI charge facing Cheryl M. Lowell, a Westbrook school bus driver.

Lowell pleaded innocent to all 22 felony charges during her arraignment in Cumberland County District Court Thursday. The plea was entered by her lawyer, Ricky Brunette. Trial was set for 1 p.m. Dec. 13.

Lowell, 41, has old convictions for OUI and failing to stop at red lights. But she had a clean four-year record of driving school buses before Aug. 30, opening day of school, when she wandered off her route after 3:30 p.m. with 45 first- and second-graders aboard the bus.

Alarmed parents and police found the bus in a business parking lot about 5 p.m. Twenty-one children had not been delivered home at that time — the reason for 21 counts of endangering.

Brunette has said a new medication prescribed only the day before school apparently reacted with another prescription Lowell was taking. He also said Lowell may have overdosed.

Originally, Lowell was arrested by Westbrook police only on the aggravated OUI charge. The district attorney's office added the 21 other felony counts.

Meanwhile, the state has suspended Lowell's driver's license.

Figure 10.34
Use of a flexible layout grid allows two spreads to look different yet still be unified.

Texas Monthly Magazine.

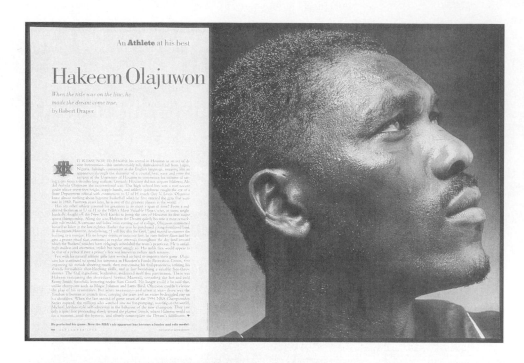

With more editors doing their own design on computers, many publications now use a one-step process referred to as **pagination.** In this process, editors pull all the elements of a page together on their computer screens. When they are finished, they send entire pages to the printer. No other makeup work is necessary.

Multipage Spreads Should Be Designed as One Unit.   When readers look at adjoining pages, they see one image. Therefore, pages that run side by side should complement one another rather than compete with one another. Designers often incorporate elements to tie facing pages together. Common elements include photos that cross the margins between pages, **bleeding** from one page to the next; and rules and headlines that run across the gutter between the pages (Figures 10.36 and 10.37).

When facing pages are not part of the same article, they still should work together. For instance, the last page of one article and the first of the next should be set up so that they do not contrast violently.

One of the designer's most helpful tools is the **rule.** A rule is nothing more than a line. It is specified in points, with 1-point to 4-point rules being the most common for publications. Hairline rules, smaller than 1-point rules, also are used in some publications.

Rules can be used by themselves or can be used to build **boxes** on a page. In either case, they can draw related elements together or keep unrelated elements apart.

Column rules run up and down the page between columns. They are used only rarely in modern publications because they reduce the white space on a page. Some publications still use them, however, to create a formal mood, and others use them when needed to help control confusing pages.

Rules and boxes also can be used for contrast on type-heavy pages. When no color or graphics are available, a box can go a long way toward spicing up a page full of text.

All Pages of an Article Should Share a Graphic Similarity to Each Other.   Even in magazines that permit a great deal of design freedom, the pages of each article must clearly be linked to each other. White space, rules, special typography and other graphic devices help establish such unity (Figure 10.38).

Every Page Should Include Contrasts.   Designers can create interest and movement by doing the following:

1. Using a variety of horizontal and vertical shapes on the page.

2. Using a variety of article and package sizes. For maximum excitement and minimum formality, the page should be broken down into odd proportions: thirds, fifths, etc. It's better to split a page so that one package takes up one-third of the page and another package takes up two-thirds than it is to devote one-half of the page to each package.

3. Making sure every page has dark and light elements.

4. Using different column widths on the same page. Many grids allow for different column sizes on the same page.

Every Page Should Be Balanced.   Formally balanced pages — the left and right sides perfectly symmetrical — are rare in publications. But informal balance is needed on every page. This type of balance results from distributing text, headlines, infographics, photos and white space on a page so that the heaviest elements do not cluster in the same spot or sit in a corner. When striving for balance, it helps to think of the various elements as shades of black and white: White space is the lightest, text and infographics are the grays, and photos and display headlines are the blacks.

Figure 10.35a
Before desktop
publishing became
so commonplace,
publication pages
were mocked up
on dummy pages
like this. After copy
was typeset, it was
pasted up into the
appropriate positions
on the page.

Used with permission
of the Portland (Maine)
Press Herald.

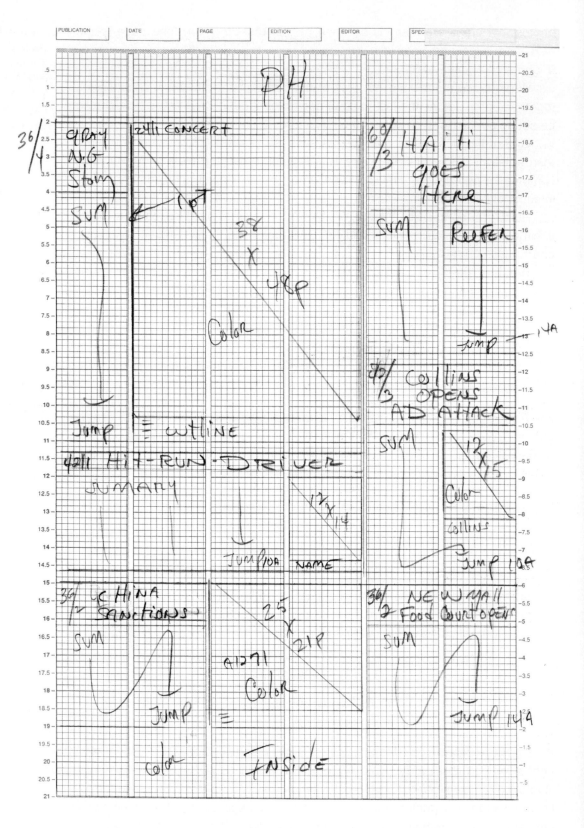

Figure 10.35b
This is the page that resulted from the dummy sheet shown in Figure 10.35a.

Used with permission of the Portland (Maine) Press Herald.

Figure 10.36
This two-page spread from Natural Health magazine appears to the reader as a unified image.

Reprinted with permission from Natural Health Magazine, September/October 1994. For a trial issue of Natural Health, call 1-800-937-4766.

Figure 10.37
A two-page spread is joined into one unit with a headline that bleeds, repeated pull quotes and a thin border.

Monsanto Company.

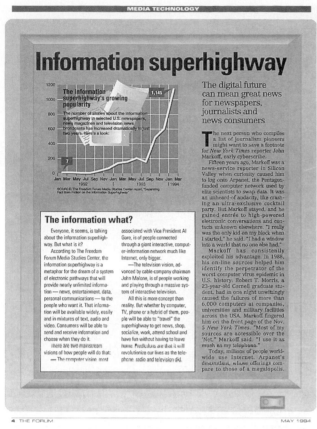

Figure 10.38
The different designs of the two pages in this spread make them look like they don't belong together.

The Freedom Forum

Working With White Space

Imagine walking into an art gallery where the walls are crammed full of paintings with no space between them. You'd find it hard to concentrate on any individual painting, and your eyes would have to work constantly. You probably wouldn't stay long.

That is the same effect that a page without white space has on a reader. White space is just as important as type and graphics in creating well-designed pages, and it should be engineered into every page (Figure 10.39). Pages with little white space tend to be perceived as darker and less inviting than pages with good amounts of white space.

Some editors have little regard for white space, believing that they should pack as much information into their publications as they can. To them, white space is wasted space. But if a reader is turned off by the heavy look of a page, then everything else on the page is wasted. White space:

- helps other elements on the page stand out;

- provides a rest for readers' eyes;

- ties together separate elements, while retaining an open quality to the page; and

- creates movement on a page.

Some white space is an integral part of every page. Margins are one example. Every publication frames its pages with margins. Large margins at the bottom and

Figure 10.39
White space is an important design element in this spread from Texas Monthly.

Texas Monthly Magazine.

on the outside edge of the page lend stability to the page and help the reader follow text. Smaller margins between columns and on the inside edge further lighten what otherwise might be a forbidding block of text.

Many publications use a system of **progressive margins.** What that means is that the sizes of the margins on each page are carefully orchestrated. The largest margin is the bottom margin. Second largest is the top margin. The margin on the outside of the page is third largest, followed by the margin on the inside of the page. The smallest margin on the page is the gutter between columns. Using progressive margins lends unity to the overall page while building in white space.

White space also is used between elements on the page, separating captions, photos, cutlines, headlines, bylines, breakout quotes, body copy and other elements. The amount of white space used in each of these situations should remain constant from one page to the next. White space also can be added by using hammers, ragged right type and extra leading.

When using white space to frame items that work together, it helps to follow two guidelines. First, in order to provide unity, the amount of white space between items must be narrower than the margins of the page — but at least as wide as the gutters between columns. Within those limits, the larger the items in the package, the more white space is needed.

Second, large amounts of white space generally work better on the outside of a page than on the inside. White space never should be **trapped:** locked between elements with no connection to other white space on a page. Trapping white space pushes related elements apart instead of drawing them together.

Using Color

Color is a powerful design tool that can help accomplish several of the goals discussed earlier, as well as offering other benefits. It can:

- attract readers' attention,

- add emphasis to a page,
- create a mood,
- unify a page through repetition, and
- create movement on a page.

Types of Color

Putting color on a page can be incredibly simple or extremely complex — or something in between.

The easiest way to create color on a page is to use colored paper. Simply printing with black ink on cream-colored or light gray paper can create an upscale image.

Color also can be added easily through the use of colored ink. Typically, colored ink is used in addition to black ink. Type is printed with black ink, and the colored ink is used for graphics, rules, illustrations, boxes, borders and other items on the page. Feature headlines and section titles sometimes are printed in color, too. Some newsletters print text in colored ink on white or colored paper for a distinctive look. Green ink on white paper, for example, can convey a message of environmental concern. Caution is always necessary when printing colored ink on colored paper. While white ink on blue paper might turn out well, red ink on yellow paper is an invitation to disaster.

A single colored ink used for emphasis is called **spot color.** To make sure they get exactly the color they want, editors and designers usually use the **Pantone Matching System,** which assigns codes to more than 1,000 colors. Each color has a specific mixing formula, so what editors or designers want is what they get.

Creative editors and designers working with spot colors can create a wide range of effects by using **tints.** Tints are variations of a color produced by letting only a fraction of the ink reach the page. For instance, a 10 percent tint of red will produce a pale pink. More tints can be produced by mixing a spot color and black ink. The resulting possibilities can help create a page that looks like more than two inks were used (Figure 10.40).

One common use of spot color is color **tint boxes.** These boxes often are used for short feature articles or sidebars. While they add pizazz, tint boxes can make text harder to read. For the best results, the tints should be light and the boxes should be small.

Black and colored inks also can be combined to print photos used for feature articles. Two negatives are printed, one in black and one in the spot color; either ink can dominate. These **duotones** exhibit a more limited range of hues than full-color photographs but are usually more interesting than black-and-white photos.

While spot color can enliven a page, it has clear limits. For one thing, using more than one spot color is expensive and impractical. For another, even a great page that uses spot color pales in comparison to pages using full-color printing.

Surprisingly, it takes only four colors to produce full-color printing: cyan (blue), magenta (red), yellow and black. These four **process** colors, mixed in various combinations, can produce any color imaginable. Printing plates are made by shooting the original images with a camera that uses special filters or by running the image through a laser scanner.

Figure 10.41
Anything goes in the
imaginative pages of
Wired magazine.

Top: Design by Thomas
Schneider.
Bottom: Design by John Plunkett.
Photography by Neil Selkirk.
© 1994 Wired Ventures Ltd.
All rights reserved.

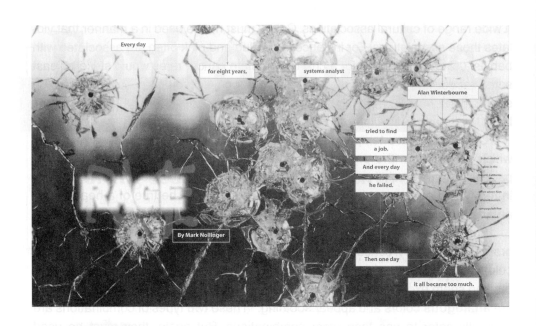

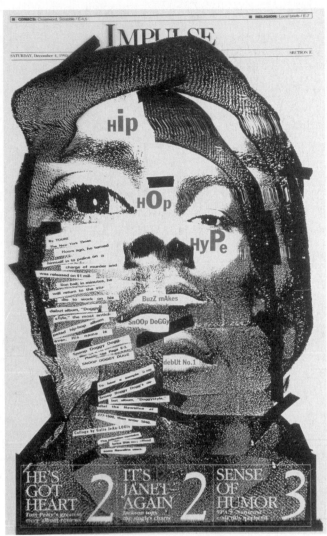

Figure 10.42
Gailie Jean-Louis'
cutting-edge design for
the Anchorage Daily News
won accolades and awards
from the newspaper and
magazine industry.

Galie Jean-Louis, design director.
Anchorage Daily News.

Exercises

Edit the article below. Using the type available on your computer or shown in a type book, choose complementary type for a main headline, an underline and a breakout quote. Write those items according to your instructor's guidelines. Also choose a technique for breaking up the copy.

By Larry Wolff

It was the Wednesady evening before homecoming weekend at Ryan State University. A night that was supposed to be filled with excitement and anticipation of a weekend of school spirit. Only hours earlier, groups across campus convened to kick-off homecoming with a spirited ear peircing "Yell Like Hell" competition.

But at eight o'clock that evening, the fun-filled festivities came to a screeching halt, when a somber crowd of nearly a thousand people assembled to join hands in a candlelight vigil honoring Joel Lee, a 21-year-old student who had been murdered in a hold up during the summer.

As I walked out the university union that evening, I glanced into the darkness and saw so many students that it looked like a demonstration broadcast on CNN. But this gaterhing didn't have any violence or chaos. Instead, it was a huddled mass of motionless stuednts.

As I joined the others, I immediately noticed the silence. No one was talking or even whispering. I never thought that silence could be that loud.

A rabbi led us in prayer and instructed us to light our candles. and for there first time there was movement and whispers as each student helped the student next to them light their candles.

As we began our procession, the glow of the candles highlighted the concern on the face of each stuednt. Any observer could easily see from their expressions that this was a solemn occasion.

The procession was so long and had so many lights that it resembled rush-hour traffic. A police car makred the spot where the procession was to turn.

The red and blue lights on top of the car flashed in the darkness, but the car sat as silent as the marchers passing it. The sound of our feet on the fallen leaves was the loudest noise we heard.

The procession touched even students who weren't in it. Normally raucous stuednts leaving their night clases fell silent as we passed by.

Finished with our march, we returned to the spot where the procession had originated. Tears rooled down the cheeks of Joel Lee's mother, Mary Lee, as she was embraced by his fraternity brothers. After remarks from her and some of Joel's friends, we silently went out way into the darkenss. Hoecoming was just two days away, but emotionally, it was much farther away than that.

Using the information below, come up with at least three ideas for graphics that could accompany an article based on this information. Consider photos, infographics and illustrations. Sketch out ideas for all graphics.

SOURCE: Annual Writing Report Card

PRODUCED BY: National Assessment of Educational Progress unit of the U.S. Department of Education

MAJOR CONCLUSIONS:

1. Students at all grade levels assessed — fourth, eighth and 12th — "have serious difficulty in producing effective informative, persuasive or narrative writing."

2. Eighth-graders spend two hours a week writing, at home and in school. They spend more than five hours a week on math and more than 14 hours a week watching television.

3. Eighty-three percent of fourth-graders, 88 percent of eighth-graders and 72 percent of 12th-graders reported watching more than one hour of television daily. But only 16 percent of fourth-graders, 27 percent of eighth-graders and 31 percent of 12th-graders spent more than an hour daily on homework.

4. Twenty-three percent of fourth-graders and 33 percent of students in grades eight and 12 read five or fewer pages per day, at home and in school.

5. Three types of writing were tested: persuasive, narrative and informative. Between 55 and 86 percent of students showed at least minimal competence in writing the narrative — but only 25 percent or fewer of all students produced competent persuasive writing.

6. White and Asian students performed better than black, Latino and Native American students at all grade levels.

7. Girls wrote better than boys at all grade levels.

8. Private school students did better than public school students.

9. Students in wealthier urban areas outperformed those in poorer areas.

Designing for the Web

When desktop publishing software became widely available, people everywhere thought they were designers. The fact that they were **not** became painfully obvious when they began producing hideous documents cluttered with dozens of typefaces.

To paraphrase Ronald Reagan, "Here we go again." The ability to concoct Web pages fairly easily has a lot of people with no sense of design thinking they are artists. So it's not uncommon to stumble across truly ugly Web sites, such as the Dip-a-Dee Donuts site (*www.dipadee.com*).

Fortunately, good Web design doesn't require the right set of genes or a degree from the Art Academy. Merely keeping the following principles in mind can help you produce a great-looking Web site (or at least speak intelligently with your designer).

Good Design Equals Credibility.   Just as errors in fact and style can undermine reader confidence, so too can poor design pull the rug out from under writers' and editors' best work. In an account of designing a Web site for Sun Microsystems, Web usability expert Jakob Nielsen wrote:

> People have very little patience for poorly designed WWW sites. As one user put it, "The more well organized a page is, the more faith I will have in the info."

Simpler Is Usually Better.   Because most Internet users still connect at relatively low speeds, designers need to keep sites simple to speed loading time. Some sites that debuted on the Web with splashy designs have since been redesigned, offering only a smattering of small graphics. One of the best-known examples of a redesigned site is CNET.com. (See Figure 10-43.)

Good Print Design Is Generally Good Web Design.   Mario Garcia, who made his reputation helping to redesign hundreds of newspapers around the world and now works on Web design, believes that the same basic design principles apply to both. "Eighty percent of print design transfers to the Web," Mario Garcia told a seminar at the Poynter Institute for Media Studies. Attention to typography, contrast and color are as important on the Web as on the printed page, he said. And the need for white space also transfers: Too many Web sites seem crammed to the max with words and graphics, with no area offering the visitor's eyes a chance to rest.

Design Should Reflect the Unique Personality of a Publication.   With an entirely new medium at their disposal, you might think that Web designers would come up with all manner of designs. The truth is far different, however, as

Figure 10.43
Text and a few small graphics combine to let the CNET.com home page load quickly.

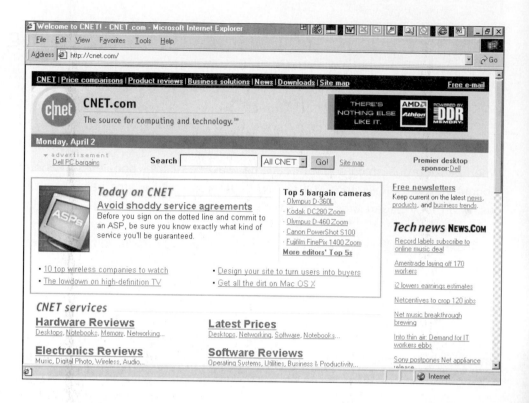

a visit to a number of online newspaper sites will show you. Far too often, designers model their sites on other sites they like or on print media on which they have worked, rather than starting with a blank slate. A few publications whose designers seem to get it include the International Herald Tribune (*www.iht.com*) (see Figure 10.44) and The London Times (*www.thetimes.co.uk*).

Designers Shouldn't Rest.   Even when Web site designers break new ground, they often seem content to sit on their laurels for long periods of time. Writing for the online edition of American Journalism Review, Mindy McAdams notes:

> In the rapidly changing environment of the World Wide Web, new functionality is introduced several times each year. Design options that were impossible 18 months ago are now passé. But newspapers seem to be stuck in their old print habits, looking on design as something that stays the same, something you finish and then don't think about for a few years.[1]

Too Much Choice Isn't a Good Thing.   Many site designers obviously believe that if a few choices are good, a tremendous number of choices is even better. So their pages are cluttered with dozens of buttons, pull-down menus and other devices, with no clear indication of what choices are the most important or useful. Take a look at the ZDNet home page (*www.zdnet.com*) if you want to be overwhelmed with choices.

Mario Garcia suggests that less is more when it comes to such choices. He recommends setting up a maximum of two "baskets of information" on any given page, each with no more than six choices. A good starting point for the primary

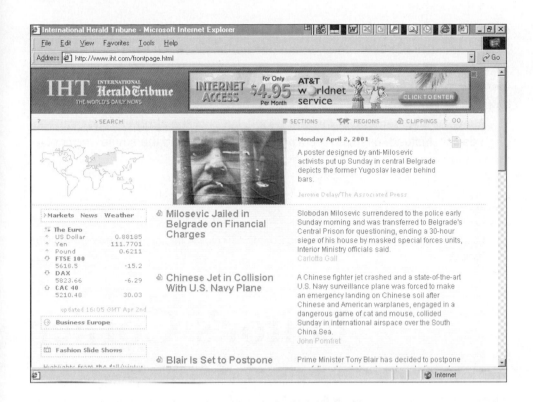

Figure 10.44
The International Herald
Tribune's Web site breaks
new ground in online news
design.

basket is the left side of the page, where readers look first for choices; the secondary basket can be placed at the top of the page. "Nothing beats get me in and get me out on the top and side of the page," Garcia says. But remember: These suggestions are only starting points — good site design is specific to the site.

Style Remains Important.   Every site should have a coherent, consistent style from page to page. While different parts of the site may cry out for different designs, some common elements are necessary for unity.

User Feedback Is Essential.   Web designers often forget that what pleases them may not please normal people. So users should be sought out to test navigation and features and make sure icons communicate what they are supposed to. (In one test by the designers of the Sun Microsystems site, users thought that an icon meant to represent technology — a man holding a lightning bolt — was simply a picture of a man being struck by lightning.)

Make Sure Users Know Where They Are — and How to Get Where They Want to Go.   Designers have developed a number of ways to let readers know where they are within a site. Perhaps the most elegant is a simple heading on the top of each page that indicates its location within the site:

Home-Sports-**Basketball**

It's also important that users be able to quickly find their way to whatever part of a Web site they want to visit. Indexes and tables of contents should appear in the same spot at all times, and users should never be more than three clicks away from any specific content.

Consider All Users. Some stunning Web site designs are useless for most people who connect to the Internet from home, because the sites take forever to download. And some sites are useless for users with visual or hearing impairments. Every site should be designed to be accessible to as many different users as possible.

Above all else, remember that few people log onto the Internet to admire Web page design. Instead, users are coming for information, and the sooner they get it, the happier they will be.

Note

1. Mindy McAdams, "Back to the Drawing Board," AJR NewsLink, *ajr.newslink.org/mmcol3. html.*

Editor's Corner

**Elliot King,
associate professor
of communication
at Loyola College in
Maryland, co-author
of "The Online
Journalist" and
editor of several
online and print
publications**

Working in a Multimedia Environment

The emergence of the World Wide Web as a publishing medium has had a dramatic impact on the graphical presentation of information. Editors can't just use graphics from a printed publication; instead, they must be edited specifically for this new medium.

This point was driven home to me when I served as editor of the eBusiness Transformation Report (EBT). EBT was a pioneering effort geared to reporting on the ways new technology such as the Internet was changing business practices. The target audience was high-level executives responsible for the technological development of their organizations. They needed timely research and information to guide their investment decisions.

Unlike traditional publications, EBT was designed to be delivered to readers in many different ways. The primary publication was on the Web. We designed a traditional Web site with a variety of interactive features, such as reader polls. The Web pages were just the beginning, however. On the Web site, we included a version of the publication in Acrobat format. Created by Adobe, Acrobat allows pages with fixed magazinelike layouts to be displayed on the Web. We also anticipated that some people would not want to click through a Web site to read stories. They would download and print the Acrobat file, converting much of the information on the Web site to print.

But that was not all. We also sent the publication in text-only form to subscribers via e-mail. The e-mail version contained summaries and longer versions of each article with links to the Web site. Because the e-mail was text-only, we could not include any graphics. Subscribers could download a text-only version from the Web site as well.

Finally, we also printed a version of the newsletter. While we used the Adobe Acrobat file as the basis of the printed version, the printed version of the newsletter was not identical to the version readers could download from the Web. The reason was this: We wanted our print version to fit precisely into eight pages. People do not expect half-filled columns in print publications. With the Acrobat version on the Web, we did not have the same space constraints. So the Acrobat version could include information that would not fit in the print publication.

When it came to including graphics, we had to assess the media we were using. For the Web, we clearly were not going to use photographs or other sophisticated graphics. The Web is not an effective medium for displaying high-resolution photographs, which considerably lengthen download times. While we didn't have that limitation with the Acrobat file, we did have to consider that it would be printed on a wide variety of printers, many of which would not be suitable for photographs.

At the same time, given the mandate of EBT, we knew that we had to include as many informational graphics, such as charts and tables, as we could. Our organization conducted proprietary research projects, and many of readers considered the numbers as important as the reporting and the analysis.

The complexity of managing information graphics for multiple publication channels was underscored after we completed a study about the adoption rate for the Windows 2000 operating system among Fortune 1000 companies. This had been a long project, and we co-published an eight-page white paper in an industry magazine. At the same time, smaller subsets of the study were published on our Web site, in the Web-based Acrobat version, in the e-mail version and the Acrobat-based print version.

In the co-published eight-page white paper, we included six relatively large graphs jammed with information that punctuated the text. On the Web, we cut the text by one-third and decided to run only four graphs. But the text was not continuous, as it was in the white paper. Instead, we rewrote the first paragraph to better summarize the study and added a snappy second paragraph. That material ran on the home page. Readers had to click on a link to get the entire story. The graphs were embedded into the body of the story.

For the online Acrobat versions of the material, once again we cut the story by one-third and cut two more graphs. For the Acrobat-based print version, we included only one graph. That graph was half the size of the graphs we included online. Finally, in the e-mail and text-only versions, we eliminated the graphs entirely.

Not only was the number of graphs used in each medium different, the nature of the graphics was different as well. You may suspect that as we winnowed the number of graphs, we would select only the most significant information to include. Unfortunately, the importance of the information contained in the graph was only one of the criteria we used to select graphics. Just as important were the production values of each medium. The white paper, for example, was printed on glossy stock paper, and each graph could fill a standard-sized magazine page. That allowed us to use complex graphs. In the printed Acrobat version, on the other hand, we were working with a 2-inch-by-2-inch space for each graphic. Therefore, the graph and legend had to be simple to be legible.

As we eliminated graphs, we had to rewrite the text to summarize the information that we were omitting. The balance between text and graphics shifted appreciably.

My experience with EBT proved that the emergence of the World Wide Web as a complement, supplement and alternative to print publishing has created a series of new challenges. Writers, editors and designers must enter projects with the idea that the same information will be used in a variety of formats. The final presentation of text and graphics will be determined by the strengths and constraints of each format.

IGNORANT Lacking knowledge.

STUPID Mentally unable to learn.

IMPACT A forceful striking together. It should not be substituted for *influence* or *effect*. Avoid constructions like "the impact of the report."

IMPLY What a speaker does.

INFER What a listener does.

The supervisor implied that all employees would receive raises.

The staff members inferred that the raises would be about 3 percent.

INTO To move *into* means from one place to another. A person who is on a boat and decides to go for a swim jumps into the water, not *in* the water.

INCREDIBLE Too wild to be believed. It can be used to describe people or statements.

INCREDULOUS Disbelieving or skeptical. It should be used only to describe people.

Stories about people sighting Elvis are incredible.

She was incredulous when the con man offered to double her money in a day.

IRONICALLY Saying something *ironically* is saying the contrary of what is expressed. Irony is a form of sarcasm. Ironically does not mean *by coincidence*.

"That's a nice Corvair you're driving," he said ironically.

IRREGARDLESS Not a word.

IRRELEVANT Not pertinent or relevant.

IRREVERENT Disrespectful.

ITS Possessive form of *it*.

IT'S Contraction for *it is*.

LABOR (verb) To make the same point repeatedly.

BELABOR (verb) To beat, hit or whip, primarily in the physical sense.

When he continued to labor the point, I wanted to belabor him to make him move on.

LAST The final one.

LATEST The most recent.

LAUNCH To send into space, not to begin.

LEAD (verb) The present tense of the verb.

LED (verb) The past tense.

He said he would lead the team, and he led them straight to victory.

LIABLE Exposed to an adverse action. It is not a synonym for **LIKELY,** unless the event designated is injurious or undesirable.

Children exposed to lead in household paint are liable to develop severe medical problems.

LIE To recline. Past tense is *lay.*

LAY To place. Past tense is *laid.*

She decided to lie out in the sun.

Let me lay my books down.

After she lay there an hour, she went to the library.

Do you remember where you laid your keys?

LIKE Joins noun and pronouns.

AS Joins clauses that include verbs.

She carries herself like a model.

The team played well, as defending champions should.

LITERALLY In a literal manner.

FIGURATIVELY Metaphorically.

INCORRECT: She was so angry she literally exploded.

CORRECT: She was so angry she figuratively exploded.

LOATH (adj.) Unwilling.

LOATHE (verb) To hate.

LOOSE (adj.) The opposite of tight.

LOSE (verb) To misplace.

LOSS (noun) The act of losing something.

MAD Insane, not angry.

MAJORITY More than half.

PLURALITY More than the next highest number.

In the three-way presidential race in 1992, Bill Clinton received a plurality of the votes, but no one got more than 45 percent.

MAN/WOMAN (nouns) Use *male* or *female* when an adjective is needed.

The female professor had problems with an insubordinate man in her class.

MANTEL A shelf above a fireplace.

MANTLE A loose garment.

MARSHAL (noun) A law officer; a person who directs the action at a ceremony. (verb) To bring together.

MARSHALL (noun) A proper name.

MARTIAL (adj.) Pertaining to military.

MEAN, AVERAGE The sum of the units divided by the number of units.

MEDIAN The number in the middle (such as the middle score or income): Half lie above, half below.

MODE The most commonly occurring number.

EXAMPLE: Nine students in a class got the following grades on a test: 64, 72, 72, 75, 76, 81, 86, 88, 92. The mean grade is 78.4; the median is 76; the mode is 72.

MEASLES, MUMPS Not *the measles* or *the mumps*. Both are singular.

She has measles, which is highly contagious.

MEDAL (noun) A small object given for achievement or worn as a symbol of religious belief.

MEDDLE (verb) To interfere.

METAL (noun) A material such as steel, aluminum or titanium.

METTLE (noun) Stamina, strength.

MELD A term used in playing cards, it often is used incorrectly as a verb meaning to blend or combine.

METICULOUS Overly concerned with trivial details. Calling someone *meticulous* is not a compliment.

MORAL The lesson of a story, or a principle to live by.

MORALE Mood or spirits.

MORE Used to compare two items.

MOST Used to compare more than two.

She is the more popular candidate in the two-person race.

The lions are the most popular animals at the zoo.

NAUSEATED Feeling or becoming sick.

NAUSEOUS Sickening or disgusting.

After we saw that nauseous sight, we all became nauseated.

380	Editing for Clear Communication

NAVAL Pertaining to the navy.

NAVEL A belly button or part of an orange.

NEGOTIATE Not a synonym for *climb* or *make one's way through.*

OFF OF No need for the *of.*

ONLY This word modifies the word directly after it, so careful placement is necessary in order to avoid confusion. Notice how placing *only* before each word in the sentence below changes the meaning:

Jose ate breakfast Friday.

VERBAL Using words.

ORAL Using the mouth.

She was always shy when it came to getting up in front of a room and giving an oral report.

PAROLE Release of a person who is serving a sentence that is still in effect. If he violates parole, he will return to jail or prison.

PROBATION A suspended sentence.

Many criminals go back to their old habits when released on parole.

Because she has no record and the offense was minor, she received probation.

PASSED Past tense of the verb *pass.*

PAST A noun or adjective referring to a bygone time; a preposition meaning *beyond.*

PEAK (noun) A projecting point or the top. (verb) To reach full capability.

PEEK (verb) To look secretly.

PIQUE (verb) To irritate or to excite by a challenge.

The challenge to climb to the peak piqued their curiosity.

PEDAL (noun) A small platform on which the foot rests. (verb) To turn the pedals of a bicycle or other object.

PEDDLE To sell from door to door.

PENULTIMATE The second to last, not a synonym for *ultimate.*

PERCENTAGE A figure derived by dividing one number by another (see Chapter 4).

PERCENTAGE POINT A figure derived by subtracting one number from another.

The dip of two percentage points in the unemployment rate — from 10 to 8 percent — was a difference of 20 percent.

PERSECUTE To harass or attack.

PROSECUTE To take legal action against a person.

PERSONAL Pertaining to a person.

PERSONNEL Those employed by an organization.

PERSPECTIVE (noun) A viewpoint, or looking at things in proper relationship to each other.

PROSPECTIVE (adj.) Relating to the future, expected.

From her perspective, none of the prospective candidates was worth hiring.

PERSUADE To plead with or urge a person so he or she will do or believe something.

CONVINCE To satisfy someone by proof.

She tried to persuade her captors to release her unharmed.

Eventually, they were convinced that they would fare better if they did so.

PLAGUE (noun) An epidemic disease. (verb) To burden.

PLAQUE (noun) A commemorative piece of wood or metal, or the gunk that the dentist scrapes off your teeth.

PODIUM A raised platform on which a speaker or conductor stands.

LECTERN A slanted table (either floor-standing or desktop) on which speakers place their notes.

DAIS A platform that can hold several people.

He walked onto the dais, stepped onto the podium and placed his notes on the lectern.

POPULOUS (adj.) Crowded or heavily populated.

POPULATED (adj.) Inhabited.

POPULACE (noun) The common people.

POUR To dispense fluid.

PORE OVER To study carefully.

PRECIPITATE (verb) To cause to happen earlier than anticipated; to throw violently.

PRECIPITOUS (adj.) Steep.

PRESENTLY Soon, not *now.*

PRETENSE A false show used to conceal feelings.

PRETEXT A motive put forward to conceal the real motive.

His praise of the book was all pretense.

She was dismissed on the pretext of irresponsibility, but everyone knew the real reason was theft.

PRINCIPAL (noun) The head of a school; money. (adj.) Main.

PRINCIPLE (noun) A rule or truth.

PRISON A maximum-security facility for persons convicted of felonies.

JAIL A facility normally used to confine persons awaiting trial or sentencing on misdemeanors or felonies, persons serving sentences for misdemeanors, and persons confined for civil matters, such as failure to pay alimony.

PROPHECY (noun) A forecast.

PROPHESY (verb) To predict, foretell or forecast.

PRONE Lying face down.

SUPINE Lying on the back.

PROSTATE A gland that causes problems for men late in life.

PROSTRATE Lying face down to show submission or adoration, or overcome by heat.

RACK (verb) To trouble, torment or afflict, or to oppress by unfair demands. You *rack your brains* and something exasperating is *nerve-racking*.

WRACK (noun) Ruin or destruction.

RAISE To bring an animal to maturity.

REAR To bring up a child.

RAZE To destroy.

RAVAGE To destroy or ruin.

RAVISH To fill with joy, carry away forcibly or rape.

RAVISHING Unusually striking.

RAVENOUS Extremely hungry.

RECORD To use the phrases *new record, all-time record* or *record first* is to be redundant.

REBUT To dispute a claim or charge.

REFUTE To disprove a claim or charge with evidence.

REGIME A political or ruling system. Usually has a negative connotation.

REGIMEN A system of diet, etc., for improving health.

REGIMENT A military unit consisting of two or more battalions.

REIGN (noun) Royal power or authority. (verb) To rule.

REIN (noun) Leather strap used to control a horse. (verb) To control as if using reins.

During the reign of King Olivar, the country's leaders tried to rein in runaway inflation.

RELUCTANT Unwilling to act.

RETICENT Unwilling to speak.

RESPECTIVELY In the given order.

RESPECTFULLY Showing respect.

Jim and Bob were respectively an actor and a professor.

The students respectfully heeded the professor's request to take off their caps.

ROLE The part played by an actor, or a job given to a person.

ROLL Many uses, but it's never a synonym for *role.*

SENSUAL Gratifying the senses or appetite, including sexual appetite.

SENSUOUS Pleasing the senses. When used to describe a person, *sensuous* means susceptible to the pleasures of sensation.

During college, his life was devoted to sensual excesses.

Silk is a sensuous fabric.

SET To place.

SIT What you do when you take a seat.

SHIP A large vessel.

BOAT A small vessel propelled by oars, sails or outboard motor.

SINCE From a time in the past. Not a synonym for **BECAUSE.**

STATIONARY (adj.) Fixed in place.

STATIONERY (noun) Materials used in writing.

SUIT A set of clothes; cards bearing the same symbol.

SUITE A group of furniture or rooms. Also a term used in music.

SUSTAINED Endured or withstood, not *suffered.* "He sustained injuries" should read "He suffered injuries" — or, better yet, "He was injured."

TALL Used to describe something attached to the ground.

HIGH Used to describe something not attached to the ground.

When she reached the top of the tall mountain, she marveled at the high clouds.

TEMPERATURE A measurement of how warm or cool it is, *temperature* can move only up or down. The **WEATHER** can become warmer or cooler.

THAN A conjunction of comparison.

THEN An adverb denoting time.

THEIR (adj.) Possessive form of *they.*

THERE (adv.) In that place.

THEY'RE Contraction for *they are.*

TROOP A group of persons or animals.

TROUPE An ensemble of actors, dancers, singers or the like.

UNIQUE One of a kind. The word never takes qualifiers. A good editor would cut the word *rather* from this sentence:

San Francisco is a rather unique city.

WERE This plural verb is used with a singular noun when expressing an idea contrary to fact.

If I were a rich man, I could retire now rather than in 25 years.

WHETHER OR NOT No need for the *or not.*

WOULD, COULD, SHOULD These three have very different meanings. If a judge says a man *could* receive life in prison, that is not the same as saying he *would* or he *should.*

YOLK The yellow part of an egg.

YOKE A frame that harnesses animals together.

Exercise

Choose the correct word in each example. (15 points)

_____ 1. We had discussed the issue many times before, so there was no

need to *a) labor b) belabor* it.

_____ 2. President Reagan underwent surgery on his *a) prostate b) prostrate.*

_____ 3. After drinking too much beer last night, Jane woke up feeling

a) nauseous b) nauseated.

_____ 4. The *a) temperature b) weather* should be warmer today.

_____ 5. The large insect's legs raced in the air after he fell into the *a) prone*

b) supine position.

_____ 6. There was only a *a) lectern b) podium* in the room, and no table to

put it on.

_____ 7. The Moral Majority *a) poured b) pored* over thousands of books

_____ before *c) poring d) pouring* gasoline over the offending volumes and

lighting them on fire.

_____ 8. I *a) loath b) loathe* going to my Spanish class; that's why I'm always

_____ *c) loath d) loathe* to go.

_____ 9. The coach tried to boost her *a) moral b) morale.*

_____ 10. Richard Nixon resigned and admitted his guilt to the entire

a) populace b) populous that summer.

_____ 11. The exact middle score of all exam grades is the a) mean b) median

c) average.

_____ 12. His parents a) raised b) reared him with strict rules.

_____ 13. How much are you going to a) peddle b) pedal your bicycle for?

APPENDIX A

Copy Editing Symbols

Even in this age of computers, some editing still is done manually. When using pencils or pens, you have to be certain your corrections will be interpreted correctly. The symbols in the following paragraphs are standard ones that are widely used and understood.

To insert a *word* or a ltter, place a caret at the desired spot below the line and write the material to be inserted above the line.

To insert a comma place the comma in the caret.

To insert a period, place either a period or an X inside a circle.

To insert quotation marks or an apostrophe (as in "Jills dog), place them in carets above the letters.

A hyphen is added by placing an equal sign above the spot where the hyphen should appear (for example, long term prospects). A dash — the mark used for a pause or to show contrast is indicated by the mark used in this sentence.

to indent a paragraph, use an "L"-type symbol, which also capitalizes the first word.

Use a curved line to join paragraphs when you do not want a new paragraph to begin.

To capitalize a letter elsewhere, such as in the word america, draw three lines under it. To lowercase an incorrectly capitalized word, draw a diagonal line through it. A diagonal line drawn through a punctuation mark deletes the mark.

To transpose letters words or use this symbol.

To delete all space be tween words, use a pair of curved lines above and below the letters. To tighten space but leave one space between words, use only the top line.

To delete a letter, use this symmbol.

The clearest way to delete a word or several words is to draw a line through the unwanted material and a curved line above it.

To insert space between words, use this symbol.

If a figure, such as 9 is used when a number should be spelled out, circle it. And vice versa: She owned more than seven hundred Barbie dolls. The circle is also used to spell out words that appear as abbrevs and to abbreviate words such as Federal Bureau of Investigation.

Headline Schedule

The chart below shows how many characters of a standard roman type face can fit into a given number of newspaper columns. If no count is listed, the given point size is not recommended for a headline spanning that number of columns.

Point Size	1 Column	2 Columns	3 Columns	4 Columns	5 Columns	6 Columns
24	13	27				
30	10.5	21.5				
36	9	18	27.5			
42	7.5	15.5	23.5	31		
48	6.5	13.5	21	27.5		
54	5.5	12	18	24	30	
60	5	11	15.5	22	26.5	33
72	4.5	9	14	18.5	23	27.5

Credits ⎯⎯⎯⎯⎯⎯⎯⎯⎯⎯⎯⎯⎯⎯⎯⎯⎯⎯⎯ ●

Index